EL INCA

The Texas Pan American Series

INCA GARCILASO DE LA VEGA 1539-1616

A modern concept of the Inca Garcilaso de la Vega painted by
Francisco González Gamarra. Courtesy of the artist and the
Casa-Museo del Inca at Montilla, Spain.

EL INCA

THE LIFE AND TIMES OF
GARCILASO DE LA VEGA

By John Grier Varner

UNIVERSITY OF TEXAS PRESS

AUSTIN AND LONDON

*The Texas Pan American Series is published with the
assistance of a revolving publication fund established
by the Pan American Sulphur Company and other
friends of Latin America in Texas.*

Standard Book Number 292–78375–2
Library of Congress Catalog Card No. 68–55059
Copyright © 1968 by John Grier Varner
Printed by the University of Texas Printing Division, Austin
Bound by Universal Bookbindery, Inc., San Antonio

To the memory of don José de la Torre y del Cerro, renowned archivist of Spain and much loved and respected hidalgo of Andalusia.

PREFACE

THERE HAVE BEEN differences of opinion as to the significance of the position which the Inca Garcilaso de la Vega holds in the scale of values as a chronicler of the Indies; but it is not to be denied that his position as one of the *great* chroniclers of the sixteenth century is secure. He did have the advantage, though not unique, of being on the scene during the Peruvian civil wars and of knowing personally and sometimes intimately the great conquerors and their rabble following who were responsible for those wars. And more important still, he knew intimately and was favored with the confidence and affection of many of the remnant Incas who had witnessed the devastation of their classic civilization and ancient realm. But Garcilaso is unique among early chroniclers in that he was born on American soil and in that, being born to the Quechuan tongue, he was able to obtain from native sources his information concerning the Incaic past as well as the present tribulations of his Indian relatives.

It appears unquestionable and inevitable that Garcilaso should reveal racial and patriotic bias in depicting both the Indian and the Spaniard, and historians have found it easy to condemn him for ennobling Indians, accepting with astonishing credulity both pagan and Christian traditions and superstitions, and in a number of other ways violating more recent codes of realism. This charge of bias and romanticism, however, can and has been made against most, if not all, of his contemporary chroniclers, who saw the whole episode of the Conquest from a different perspective and with different emotions. All made the claim that they had written the truth, a claim which appears to have become almost a literary device in an age which had long been absorbed in the books of chivalry and the lying histories; but one must not forget that it was the truth as they saw it, or, in far too many cases, the truth as they had heard it. Yet Garcilaso, perhaps in some instances at the expense of surface reality, has managed to attain an underlying verity not to be found in some of his contemporary chroniclers. He has given a graphically accurate picture of incurable romantics who, it cannot be denied, actually existed in an era of inflamed imagination, which already had been ignited by ancient poetic traditions. He has caught the mood and spirit of two civilizations, both to some extent in their death throes. He has enabled us to see the Incas, heirs to a proud and splendid tradition, weeping in desolation as they submit to old superstitions and new forces; and he has enabled us to see the Renaissance Spaniard, clinging to futile chivalric fantasies, as he encounters the trying realities of a previously unknown and scarcely believable world, and as he cautiously watches the slow but inevitable encroachments of a new democratic spirit upon a worn feudal civilization. He has caught the spirit of two merging worlds, both equally ancient, and he has foreshadowed the tragic aspects which were to haunt them down through the ages.

The Peru that Garcilaso knew was the fading Tahuantinsuyu of the Incas and the new Eldorado of the Pizarros; the Spain that he knew was the glittering age of Philip II and Philip III, known respectively as the Prudent King and the Picture King. It was the Spain of Lope de Vega and Cervantes. Among his friends and acquaintances in Spain were the decadent nobility, the multihued ecclesiastics, philosophers, and humanists, and the lowly and oftentimes desperate folk who worked the farmlands and vineyards of Andalusia to feed the social and political whims of the powerful. The story of Garcilaso's remote and noble Spanish progenitors is to be found in the enchantingly vintaged rhetoric of Washington Irving's *The Conquest of Granada* and *The Moorish Chronicles*; and the story of the Peruvian turmoils which were so closely interwoven into the tapestry of Garcilaso's boyhood and youth is revealed in the magnificent prose of William Hickling Prescott's *The Conquest of Peru*. Modern historians have relied extensively on Garcilaso's account of De Soto's exploration of the southern and southwestern regions of what is now the United States of America, and he has for several centuries been regarded as a primary source for information concerning the early Incas. Strangely and ironically some scholars, while condemning him for romanticism and debatable data, have persisted in using him, for his value as an authoritative source is undeniable.

In those areas of the Andean world which lie immediately north and south of the equator Garcilaso long has been regarded as a Messiah, and even today he is revered as a symbol by those who plead for the welfare of the Indians, mestizos, and creoles of America—not for the indigent, but for worthy men of all castes and races who seek human status and opportunity honestly. He believed in races and in the individual nobility of separate races, but he believed and vehemently proclaimed that there was but one world. He held to a democratic concept that all men should be provided equal opportunity but that their social and political status and power should be established and maintained by personal merit and not by arbitrary laws. Yet he appears never to have been able to deliver himself from the idea that such merit was most frequently to be encountered in men of noble blood. Such a concept was to him inevitable. He was a Renaissance man.

In my presentation of the life of the Inca Garcilaso and his historical background, it has never been my purpose to attempt to clarify or defend those of his statements which later historians have questioned. Instead, I have tried to present life as I believe he saw it. Much of it he saw through the eyes of the Spaniard; more of it he saw through the eyes of the Indian; and though he was in constant contact with painful reality, he, like the vast majority of the men of the Golden Age, did view it with the perspective of a romantic.

In a study of this scope my indebtedness is, of course, unlimited. My first and deepest obligation is to my wife, Dr. Jeannette Johnson Varner, scholar and trained linguist, whose name by all rights should occupy a place alongside my own on the title page of this book. She transcribed and translated scores of original sixteenth-century documents, translated a multitude of critical articles and books, listened patiently to and contributed valuable comments on my readings of passages of the original drafts, and tirelessly assisted with the multiple details involved in preparing a manuscript for publication. Together we personally followed the trail of the Inca Garcilaso from Cuzco and Lima to the Isthmus, and then on through the Azores to the archives of Seville, Madrid, Simancas, Badajoz, Córdoba and Montilla. I am next indebted to the Research Bureau of the University of Texas and to the Penrose Fund of the American Philosophical Society for financial grants which made possible our research in both the Americas and Spain, and to the Cultural Division of the United States Information Office, which by offering me employment for a number of years in Mexico and South America helped me to a more accurate understanding of and sympathy with the Latin psyche. There is not space here to list the names of individuals who came to our aid. Significant of course are the curators of archives in Spain and the Americas, and I wish especially to acknowledge the generosity of the following individuals: don José de la Torre y del Cerro who, after providing us office space, gave us severe and patriarchal advice tempered with good fellowship, revealed to us the unique charms of historic Córdoba, and bolstered our egos and courage by presenting our names for membership in the much respected Real Academia de Ciencias, Bellas Letras y Nobles Artes de Córdoba; don Rafael Aguilar Priego, archivist of the Sagrado of the great Cordovan Mosque-Cathedral; don Tomás Gómez Infante, who aided our research and enthusiastically entertained us at Badajoz; don Francisco Sánchez Rico, an official transcriber at the Archivo de Indias, who gave generously of his time and directed us through the nooks and corners of old Seville; don José Cobos, scholar and producer of famed vintage wines as well as the generally recognized custodian of Garcilaso memories at Montilla, who with his charming wife welcomed us to that fabled village and received us, not as aliens, but as one of their own; Padre Lorenzo Cirio Ruiz, who opened to us the records of the ancient Church of Santiago at Montilla, and when not dashing off for almost hourly requiem masses, fed us sweetmeats and entertained us with the chatter of a jolly friar; and to all the gracious people of Andalusia who taught us to regard that land with an affection approximating that of the Inca Garcilaso.

JOHN GRIER VARNER

CONTENTS

ILLUSTRATIONS

Frontispiece

A concept of the Inca Garcilaso by Francisco González Gamarra

Plates (following page 222)

EL INCA

PRELUDE

The Hispanic and Incaic ancestry

of the Inca Garcilaso de la Vega,

who was known in the Indies as the

mestizo Gómez Suárez de Figueroa.

THE CLASSIC RENAISSANCE CHRONICLER who wrote under the adopted name of the Inca Garcilaso de la Vega was a mestizo. Fused in his veins was the blood of both Spaniard and Indian, and woven into the fibers of his intellectual nature were the cultural threads of Catholic Spain and pagan Peru. Thus, to Andean Americans especially, he has come to symbolize the merging not only of two races but of two civilizations. For this reason his story should begin where he himself would have begun it, in remote times when, according to tradition, amalgamative forces were in the process of germination. He could never detach either his own fate or the fate of his people from the causative past, and in both pagan and Christian traditions, some of which went beyond the limits of recorded history and even of credulity, he found the seeds of his being and an explanation for the eccentricities of the world which molded him. The facts and legends of his Christian ancestors were easily accessible through written records and through the often repeated stories of both ecclesiastics and laymen; and those of his pagan forefathers had been preserved by the quipu-camayus and amautas, especially-appointed sages, who through oral transmission and by means of the quipu, an intricate mnemonic system of knotted cords, had in each generation recorded the history of the Incas.

Much of the story of both his remote and his immediate ancestors, Garcilaso wove into the prefaces and the contexts of his published works, and in telling that story he revealed, sometimes in tones of defense, a persistent conviction that the eventual merging of Incaic and Iberian races and civilizations was foredoomed by an ancient pagan superstition and by the traditional messianic zeal of early Catholic Spain. It was natural, therefore, that in searching for causes he would find significance in a familiar legend of an Inca prince who, at some time near the close of the thirteenth century, came face to face with an emissary of the Sun.[1] This prince, whom he identified as the son and heir of Yáhuar Huácac, seventh ruling Inca since the founding of the dynasty, had been banished to the green fields of Chita to dwell among lowly shepherds and tend the flocks of the Sun, not only because he had developed alien characteristics, but because his cruel and rebellious behavior appeared to strengthen a portent attached to his father, who from birth had shed great tears of blood. But new and more significant phenomena were now to occur; for, one auspicious day while the prince dozed in the shadow of a great white rock, there appeared before him an apparition, a robed and bearded figure who led a strange animal by a chain, and who identified himself as Viracocha, a son of the Sun and a brother of Manco Cápac, first Inca. The phantom Inca brought an ominous message of rebellion among vassal Indians who were moving on the Imperial City of Cuzco with an eye to its destruction; but before vanishing, this scion of the benevolent Sun deity made a promise of assistance so long as efforts were being made to perpetuate the glory and honor of the Inca realm.

Hastening to his father, the prince disclosed what he had seen and heard, only to be rebuffed and dispatched once more to his humble task at Chita. Yet when rebellious Chanca Indians did indeed appear and the blood-weeping emperor fled in terror to Muina, the prince, fully anticipating defeat but hoping to preserve the honor of the realm, met the insurgents at Sacsahuana. Here, on being unexpectedly joined by a contingent of friendly Quechuas, he recalled the promise made at Chita and assumed new courage; and though the battle was hard-fought, his enemies eventually succumbed, since they were bewildered by the increase in forces and were easily convinced by well-placed rumors that the Quechuas had emanated from the heavens and were sons of Viracocha. Such an intriguing concept found easy access to

[1] El Inca Garcilaso, *Los comentarios reales,* Pt. I, Bk. IV, Chaps. 16–24; Bk. V, Chaps. 17–28.

general credence, and soon the people of the great Inca realm known as Tahuantinsuyu began to regard this spirit Inca in somewhat the same manner as Europeans regarded their patron saints.

The victorious prince now returned in triumph to Cuzco and, seizing the throne, retired his cowardly father to a palace at Yúcay. Then as the years passed he began to assume more and more the role of the divinely appointed, accepting the name of Viracocha and emulating in every respect the appearance and mien of the apparition at Chita—a task facilitated by the fact that he, contrary to the general character of his race, was hirsute. Moreover, he caused to be erected at Cacha, sixteen leagues from his capital, a great image which revealed all aspects of the divine Viracocha—an image which down through the years was to keep before his people a vision of a strange, robed and bearded figure who led a most curious beast.

In time, the vassals of the Inca Viracocha came to confuse the man and the apparition and to regard with unusual respect the oracular communications of this ruler. It is of certain significance therefore that to him some attributed the origin of a divine message equally as portentous as the one he had received at Chita—so portentous indeed that through the years it remained the deeply guarded secret of those who wore the llatu or woolen headdress symbolizing authority. This was the ancient augury that when twelve Incas had ruled the empire it was destined to succumb to the power of a mysterious people who would absorb and submerge its culture as well as its sovereignty. Though the Inca Viracocha may have heard this warning from his predecessors, he was responsible for perpetuating it, and one may reasonably conjecture that he provided the somewhat optimistic note that the newcomers would be sons of the specter god Viracocha, and that their advent was to prove favorable to the honor and glory of the realm. Moreover, he also may have passed on some prophecy as to the color of the anticipated conquerors, since somewhere there crept into the Incaic legend the theory that the skin of the specter Viracocha as well as that of the first Inca was white.

Yet many more years of spectacular history were to unfold before the first tangible signs of this augury became manifest. In truth the realm was to reach its apex several generations later under the great emperor Túpac Yupanqui, eleventh Inca, who extended its limits from the frozen wastes of the Chilean pampas to the snowy peaks of Quito. But when the Inca Túpac Yupanqui in his dying hours placed the royal llatu upon the brow of his eighteen-year-old successor, he surely did so with apprehension since there already were prophetic signs, and the heir, Huayna Cápac, being twelfth in line of succession, was fore-ordained to be the ultimate sovereign to rule the unconquered Inca throne. And the apprehensions of the dying Inca emperor might very well have increased had he but heard certain messages in the wind; for, on the far side of the world, pale-skinned and bearded men who rode strange animals had only a short time previously wrought their vengeance upon two infidel races and already had initiated an exploration and a conquest which eventually was to penetrate into Tahuantinsuyu.

The year was 1493.[2]

The astounding potency of the Inca Túpac Yupanqui had made itself palpable upon his royal concubines as well as upon the battle plains, and his progeny numbered in the hundreds; yet there were but six males whom he had begotten upon his sister-consort, Mama Ocllo. Fourth among these legitimate heirs was Huallpa Túpac Inca Yupanqui, whose legitimate consort, Cusi Chimbo, bore him at least two offspring, the auqui Huallpa Túpac Inca Yupanqui and the palla Chimpu Ocllo, whose intimate contact with the quipucamayus and amautas and whose eyewitness experiences would qualify them to tell of the empire in both its glory and its decline.[3] And they indeed represent sources for much of the information known today about the Inca realm; for these two grandchildren of one of the greatest Incas to rule Tahuantinsuyu were to transmit much of their knoweldge to the palla's mestizo son, the Inca Garcilaso de la Vega.

The palla Chimpu Ocllo was born at some time after 1521 in the

---

[2] Historians vary on the dates of Inca emperors, but both the 1966 edition of the *Encyclopedia Britannica* and the *Handbook of South American Indians* give this date as 1493.

[3] Garcilaso, *Comentarios,* Pt. I, Bk. VIII, Chap. 8; Bk. IX, Chap. 38; also his *Descendencia de Garcí Pérez de Vargas;* and Aurelio Miró Quesada y Sosa, *El Inca Garcilaso,* p. 250. The term Inca applied to all members of the race but could be worn as a title only by the emperor or by the male descendants through masculine lineage.

Cuzco of her uncle, Huayna Cápac.[4] Thus for at least a decade she was
to witness the Incaic capital at the height of its splendor. And Cuzco in
those ancient times is said to have surpassed the dreams of men who
were searching the new world for Cairos and Cathays. Spread across an
emerald valley high against the heavens and nestled in frozen Andean
peaks, it had taken the shape of a great condor, the body moulded by
lowland contours and the vast outstretched wings by white and hovering mountains. Within, the radiance of its palaces and temples vied
with that of the Sun deity itself. For Cuzco was a city of untold gold—
gold whose sole value lay in ornamentation, gold that adorned roofs
and walls, interiors, and even gardens, one of which is said to have
been encrusted with golden clods from which sprang golden sheaves
with golden kernels of corn. As its great princes were borne through
the streets in litters of silver and gold, studded with precious gems,
theirs was a majesty which well might have been envied by the potentates of Christendom and Islam, or even by the great Khan of Cathay.
Moreover, to all Incas the Imperial City was a sacred city whose very
name, which means the umbilicus of the earth, signified its benevolent
and life-giving quality. It was a mother city linked to its children by a
nourishing cord, and when on approaching it men encountered travelers who but recently had passed through its great portals, they bowed
in deep reverence and respect.[5] Indeed the whole civilization of the
Incas had attained a standard of magnificence and sagacity which still
amazes students of ancient cultures.

This was the Cuzco and the empire that the palla Chimpu and her
brother Huallpa Túpac knew during the early and impressionable years
of their existence; and in attempting to penetrate their character and
personality, one must not ignore the richness and the pagan refinement
of their origin. They were not barbarians such as Europeans were to
encounter in some other regions of the Indies, but New World princes
who from infancy absorbed and assimilated many of the concepts and
traditions of a well developed culture. They were taught to place their

[4] Garcilaso, *Comentarios*, Pt. I, Bk. I, Chap. 15; Bk. IX, Chap. 38. The palla was
less than eleven years of age when she escaped the ravages of Atahualpa.

[5] *Ibid.*, Pt. I, Bk. II, Chap. 11; Bk. III, Chap. 20; José Gabriel Cosio, *El Cuzco,
histórico y monumental*, p. 7.

faith in an invisible deity, the all-sovereign Pachacámac, who ruled the heavens, the earth, and the seas through a visible god, the warm and generating Sun;[6] and they were told that they, like all royal Incas, were the descendents of the Moon and the Sun. Moreover, according to the palla's son they were taught that their gods were benevolent and that those who represented these deities among men were expected to do so according to the dictates of kindness and mercy.

Yet over the splendid world of these Andean children there hovered shadows; for with the swift runners who sped with news from the north and from the great sea to the west, there began to come warnings of the approach of pale, bearded and vested men, who rode strange beasts and bore before them a symbol much like the great cross of crimson and white jasper that adorned the Temple of the Sun. Soon the Inca world was to encounter the bold emissaries of Spain, and with them the phenomena of the matchlock, the swift sword, and, even more significant, the strange and terrifying beast known as the horse.

The first tidings of Europeans in the Indies had reached Huayna Cápac soon after Vasco Núñez de Balboa in 1513 had ascended the peaks of Darién and discovered a new ocean for the Spanish sovereign; and news of landings on the shores of Tahuantinsuyu followed shortly. Thus one may reasonably assume that the palla Chimpu in her earliest years encountered not only the legends of Viracocha but the prophecies which linked these legends with the approaching strangers. She may even have seen two ill-starred comrades who, left by Francisco Pizarro at the Río San Juan, eventually, so the story persists, came face to face with the Inca sovereign. And whatever credulity she already possessed would have been strengthened when news reached the Imperial City that Pedro de Candía, a giant among the newcomers whom the natives regarded as an apparition from the heavens, had landed at Túmbez and tempered the wrath of man-eating lions by simply holding before them a magic cross.[7] For afterwards, the first Spaniards to enter Cuzco

---

[6] Garcilaso, *Comentarios,* Pt. I, Bk. II, Chap. 2 *et al.*
[7] *Ibid.,* Pt. II, Bk. I, Chaps. 11, 32; William Hickling Prescott, *History of the Conquest of Peru,* Vol. I, pp. 276–278. A son of Pedro de Candía was one of Garcilaso's boyhood companions.

found the city replete with this symbol. Meanwhile, according to the sages, the elements had given notable warnings with flaming comets, blasts of thunder and flashes of lightning, tumultuous earthquakes and a tricolored nimbus which encircled the moon; and then one day when a host had assembled at Cuzco to adore the Sun, a giant eagle, pierced by the talons of invading hawks, plunged from the heavens and fell mortally wounded to the ground. The messages which diviners found in these signs foretold the death of Huayna Cápac and a war between his descendants which must terminate in the destruction of the royal family, the disappearance of their religion and polity, and the complete evanescence of the Inca realm.

Sensitive always to the language of the elements, Huayna Cápac summoned his sons, his captains, and his caciques, and disclosed to them the long-guarded prophecy concerning the termination of the realm;[8] and he added that since with him the specified number of twelve ruling Incas was completed, it was his suspicion that the fore-ordained conquerors were the men who now traveled along the shores of Tahuantinsuyu. Then warning of the imminent fulfillment of the ancient augury, he commanded his vassals to serve and obey their new masters as men who in all respects were their superiors. With these ominous words and this royal command, this last of the great ruling Incas pronounced the fate of Tahuantinsuyu, and then, yielding to the ravages of venal excesses and a vicious pestilence, which some proclaimed a curse from the newcomers, he left the four-cornered realm to its doom.

Huayna Cápac had hastened this doom not only by revealing an old secret but also by yielding to his affection for Atahualpa, a favorite but illegitimate son whose mother was a princess of Quito with no claim to a legitimate position among the royal concubines. To this ambitious youth the emperor had bequeathed, contrary to tradition, the northern corners of the kingdom, with the result that Huáscar, the weaker though legitimate heir, succeeded to but a portion of his rights as a direct descendant of the first Inca and of the Sun. Soon Atahualpa had

---

[8] Garcilaso, *Comentarios,* Pt. I, Bk. IX, Chap. 15. Garcilaso's sources for this prophecy were his mother, her brother, and her aged uncle.

seized the whole of the realm, and in the succeeding inglorious days he began a campaign to erase all Incas whose purity of blood made them a menace to his throne.

As the palla Chimpu and her brother Huallpa witnessed these terminal stages in the crumbling of an empire, they surely heard the prophecies of the great Huayna Cápac and the wailing and lamentations of his vassals as his embalmed remains were placed among the gold-encrusted mummies of his fathers in the Temple of the Sun. And afterwards, when multitudes of their kinsmen were driven by Atahualpa to the plains of Yáhuarpampa, about a league north of Cuzco, to be ruthlessly slain, these two Inca children formed a part of that condemned company which waited in horror as they watched men, women, and children fall victim to processes of extermination sufficiently varied to meet the tastes of any medieval or modern connoisseur of murder.[9] They later told of men beheaded as they knelt to pay homage to the humbled Huáscar, or tossed from lofty pinnacles or hurled into bottomless lakes and rivers, their necks weighted with stones. They told of women swinging high in trees or from lofty scaffolds, some suspended by the hair or by one or both arms or by thongs tied about the waist or by means too foul to be recorded—some clasping infants, aware that, when arms grew weak, their offspring would fall to the clubs of executioners waiting below. They told of starving children exterminated by degrees and with unspeakable cruelty. And they told of a great encircling chain of warriors ever on guard against escape until some of them, rendered compassionate by the swift ebbing of royal blood or by terror and despair in the faces of children, permitted certain ones, all under eleven years of age, to flee. History has recorded none of the names of those merciful sentinels and but few of the names of those spared, but among them were the palla Chimpu and her brother Huallpa. Neither is their place of concealment known. But from whatever refuge they found, they, during the next several years, would listen with bewilderment and hope to each new rumor of the slow approach of pale and bearded men who rode strange animals and wore the vestments of the divine and succoring Viracocha.

[9] *Ibid.*, Pt. I, Bk. IX, Chaps. 36–39.

It was the year 1532 when Atahualpa terminated his massacre, and the fresh blood scarcely had filtered into the soil of Yáhuarpampa when runners came with reports of new arrivals at Túmbez. By May Francisco Pizarro and a small band of Spaniards had landed and were moving slowly toward Cajamarca where the tyrant awaited them. Time and again Atahualpa could have erased these bold strangers from the earth, but he apparently was unable to overcome the superstition that they were sons of Viracocha and had come to fulfill the ancient prophecy disclosed by Huayna Cápac. Even as they proceeded they were met by messengers with placating gifts, and when on November 8, 1532, they appeared on the eastern horizon of Cajamarca, resplendently arrayed and moving to the blatant rhythm of trumpet and drum, the tyrant Inca retreated to his suburban baths and left a host of noblemen to render to the invaders those luxuries due men descended from the Sun. Shortly afterward, when visited by Hernando de Soto and Hernando Pizarro, he was impressed by the resemblance of these men to legendary descriptions of Viracocha as well as to the great carved image at Chita, and he entertained them lavishly. On the ensuing day he returned in dazzling splendor to Cajamarca to parley with the strangers and learn the details of their superiority. Here, in an encounter which represents a climax in the annals of Tahuantinsuyu as well as western Christendom, he met a black-robed friar and received an amazing lesson in the political and spiritual tenets of Spanish Catholicism.[10]

As the despot reclined on his litter, Friar Vicente de Valverde placed in his hand a small black volume, a sacred tome which could have meant little to a pagan confronted for the first time with the symbols of a written language. Then through the lips of an interpreter named Felipillo, a despicable coastal Indian who, even had he known the language of Cuzco, would have been hard pressed to find Quechuan words that could clarify Spanish ethics and mysticism, the devout religious attempted to explain his theology and to relate it to the

---

[10] *Ibid.,* Pt. II, Bk. I, Chaps. 19–36. Garcilaso heard the story of Cajamarca from a number of people who were present, and later confirmed his facts with the papers of Blas Valera, whose father was present, with some of the quipus woven at the scene, and with letters from schoolmates. Valverde's speech, after being put into Latin, fell into his hands and as a boy he memorized it so well that he never forgot it.

presence of these Spaniards in Tahuantinsuyu. He told of the Holy Trinity, of sin, depravity, resurrection, and salvation; he told of God's vicar at Rome, of the apostolic sovereign Charles V, and of the messianic crusaders of Francisco Pizarro; he told of a strange new division of the world which demanded Atahualpa's subservience to an alien master; and he tartly informed the pagan that willingly or otherwise, he must relinquish his religion, accept the Catholic faith, and pay whatever tributes were demanded of him.

Atahualpa was bewildered, not so much by Catholic theology, which he found not too different from his own, but by Catholic ethics. Historians are in disagreement as to the manner in which he responded, but the son of Chimpu Ocllo, who received his information from men who were present and from records woven into the quipus, maintained that, although Atahualpa expressed some suspicion that the Spaniards were tyrants bent on plundering the world, he ended by proclaiming his belief that they were divine emissaries and admonishing his vassals to receive them without resistance. But whether the reaction of the Inca was one of disgust or acquiescence, he made the fatal error of letting the sacred tome fall to the ground, thereby providing an excuse for carnage. Without warning, the Spaniards now gave the Inca and his host of warriors an awe-inspiring lesson in the uncanny efficiency of Christian arms, as well as additional encouragement in their superstition concerning the divinity of the bearded strangers and the hierarchy they represented. Atahualpa was seized and thousands of his vassals were either slaughtered or dispersed. The fate of the tyrant as well as that of the people he represented now lay in the hands of Francisco Pizarro, who, like his victim, bore the stigma of bastardy.

Some hope gleamed for the fallen emperor on his perceiving the yearning of his conquerors for silver and gold. A bargain was struck and soon the mountain passages to Cajamarca were clogged with Indians bearing precious ornaments to pay a king's ransom. Yet in the end the tyrant Inca was rewarded, not with freedom, but with an inquisition based entirely upon alien ethics and designed to confuse and condemn, a design which was furthered by the interpreter Felipillo, who now coveted one of the tyrant's concubines and thus had an additional impetus to betray him. The outcome of this farcical trial was that Atahualpa was condemned to burn. When on August 29, 1533, the flames mounted about his feet, the suffering pagan listened to the advice of Friar Vicente de Valverde and Friar Marcos de Niza, who stood piously by and told of a less agonizing way in which he might die if he would only accept the purifying waters of Catholic baptism. So here at Cajamarca, as so often had happened in Spain, flames won a victory for the Roman faith; the proud spirit of an infidel was reborn, and a vanquished Inca was given a Christian name. Francisco Pizarro, grateful for such an early evidence of triumph in his apostolic as well as his secular mission, thereupon agreed to give protection to the Inca's offspring, among whom were some winsome maidens, and sanctimoniously permitted the regenerated soul to take flight by means of the garrote. In this manner a pagan was spiritually bathed, the land of the Incas was purged of a tyrant, and the dissemination of Catholicism was begun in a rapidly disintegrating empire.

The incredible triumph at Cajamarca having been accomplished, the invaders now moved on to the Imperial City to pursue a ruthless campaign of rapine and conversion. Here, in 1534, they were joined by a host of Indians under the leadership of the Inca Manco, a legitimate son of Huayna Cápac and thus heir to the lost throne since the death of his brother Huáscar, whom Atahualpa had caused to be slain. When this new Inca sovereign had passed through the great portals of the sacred city and beheld the Pizarros, he too is said to have turned to his vassals and assured them that these men who so resembled the specter Viracocha were verily his sons and, as viracochas, should be served as the Inca Huayna Cápac had commanded.[11]

It often has been said, and with reason, that the true explanation of the success of the Spanish conquest is to be found in the word fear— fear inspired by pale-skinned men wielding swift swords and riding strange beasts, by the thunder of matchlocks which sent death from a distance, and by voracious dogs who charged from out the ensuing smoke and slew until their hides grew crimson. One cannot underestimate such human frailty or its exaggerated presence among either pagans or Christians when confronted with swift and inexplicable

[11] *Ibid.*, Pt. II, Bk. II, Chap. 11.

dangers. Some Spaniards even generously confessed afterward that during the uncertain interlude at Cajamarca, their fright was of such proportion that they were unable to control their urine. But in seeking an explanation for the facility with which a small band of Spaniards seized the vast empire of Tahuantinsuyu, one possibly should give some heed to the words of the traditional Inca sages. In the first place, they insisted, the realm had been weakened and torn asunder by a usurping tyrant. But the basic reason for this loss they found elsewhere. Even the tyrant had yielded, not through a lack of courage, but because of a divine semblance recognized in thost first intrepid horsemen at Cajamarca. Moreover, those Incas who had escaped the massacre at Yáhuarpampa to watch the approach of the Spaniards and the destruction of their oppressor, had interpreted the events at Cajamarca as the will of Pachacámac and had seen in these fair-skinned men a hope for the restoration of their ancient throne; and by the time they were able to dispel their illusions and perceive the real nature of the invaders, their empire was hopelessly lost. It was not fear, the sages insisted, but a blind faith in an old superstition and an old and sacred augury which had destroyed Tahuantinsuyu; and this explanation was heeded and respected always by the mestizo born afterward to the palla Chimpu Ocllo and destined to record the annals of his mother's people.

Somewhere, moving among that bewildered and deceived host of pagans, was the palla Chimpu Ocllo. One can only speculate on what had been her experiences since her flight from the wrath of Atahualpa. It is reasonable to suppose, however, that she, along with a number of her royal kinsmen, had remained with the Inca Manco, moving from one wilderness retreat to another, and that she formed a part of the Inca Manco's menage when he returned to her native city in 1534. If so, she would have heeded his demands for subservience to the new viracochas, and she would have known the hopes of all her people when shortly afterward her cousin Inca was permitted by the invaders to don the red llatu as a puppet sovereign of the ancient realm. And when during the ensuing celebrations the embalmed remains of former emperors were brought forth, as was customary at the feasts, adorned in their past splendor, she surely listened with renewed wonder and credence as the quipucamayus and amautas chanted the legend of the obstreperous prince once banished to the green fields of Chita.

Yet in the days and months and years which were to follow, the palla was to witness with some bewilderment the conversion of the Imperial City into an outpost of Seville: she saw the shadow of the cross and the gibbet fall across its pagan splendor, its women raped or pressed into concubinage, its nobility reduced to vassalage, its sovereign Inca cheapened and shamed, and its culture and civilization paralyzed with gradual injections of European and Catholic ideology. And when at length the disillusioned Inca Manco belatedly rejected a legend, rallied a host of enraged Indians and set forth to drive the false viracochas from his realm, she saw the everlasting fires of Tahuantinsuyu smolder into a darkness that resembled death. For the Inca was laboring against odds that were more than material; he was hopelessly hampered by the psychological force of merging cultures, a force which most surely found strength in the similarity of superstitions and legends.

Much of the achievement of the invaders lay in their talent for psychological conquest, in their sagacious willingness to delay their evangelism by submerging only gradually long-fixed pagan concepts. One may be sure that even at Cajamarca, when Atahualpa had found similarity between his deities and the Roman hierarchy, the sablerobed Valverde and the mendacious Friar Marcos, with the bumbling aid of the unreliable interpreter, Felipillo, had seen an opportunity to merge Incaic fables with some of the marvels of Catholicism. Thus when in 1536 the Inca Manco laid siege to Cuzco and made a last heroic attempt to redeem the realm, many of his followers were prepared psychically to see what they later claimed they did see.[12]

Eyewitnesses to that siege told of how the forces of Manco early became suspicious of divine odds when one of their most accomplished warriors fell victim in single combat to Francisco Chillchi, a baptized and despicable Cañari Indian whom the disdainful Spaniards had sent

[12] *Ibid.*, Pt. II, Bk. II, Chaps. 24–25; Bk. VIII, Chap. 1. Santiago is said to have lent his aid at Túmbez and Cajamarca, and afterward when the Inca Garcilaso's father was fighting Indians in the Charcas.

to answer a challenge. Herein lay mute evidence that they were strug-
gling against a hierarchy of gods more powerful than their own. Yet
more ominous warnings were to be made manifest in the chill blue
Andean skies. At one point, when during the night their flaming
arrows had succeeded in setting fire to a temple housing the enemy,
there suddenly swept over the heavens a most radiant light, and as they
looked aloft, they beheld not their moon goddess but a lady of ethereal
beauty, bathed in nacreous lustre and clasping to her bosom a most
gentle child. Then a fine dust, sifting like dew, blinded their eyes and
they fled. And again, at a time when the struggle was desperate and
both pagans and Christians were crying to the heavens for succor, the
hovering clouds parted to reveal a strange and magnificent warrior
charging through the empyrean on a milk-white steed. Yet this awesome apparition had come not to succor those who were searching the
skies for the divine Viracocha; for it was the militant Apostle Santiago,
or St. James, patron saint of Spain, whose revered bones lay at Compostela. Now that the followers of the Crescent had beeen harried from
Christian Castile, this traditional protector was directing his fury
against the Andean progeny of the Moon and the Sun. Since no earthly
force could withstand the withering strength of Santiago, the pagans
once more fled and for some time could not be persuaded to renew the
contest. Yet one must not leave this melancholy struggle with mere
visions of the backsides of Indians as they fled from sword, lance, mus-
ket-fire, and heavenly apparitions. History has shown that the struggle
of the pagans was heroic and more often than not the Christians were
hurled to the brink of destruction. Long after the Inca Manco, weakened by material deprivations, had withdrawn his warriors from the
Imperial City to brood sullenly in Villcapampa, men recalled a noble
Inca, armed with borrowed buckler and cuirass and wielding a formidable mace of copper, who calmly wrapped his mantle about him and
plunged headlong from the towering summit of the fortress of Sacsahuamán, thus striking a last blow for the freedom of his realm and
scorning to survive its dishonor.

The Imperial City of Cuzco now lay in desolation, its principal edifices, with the exception of walls, having succumbed to the devastating
fire of the Indians. Only four royal palaces had been spared, and only

two sacred buildings remained intact. But soon solid and imperishable Incaic foundations once more were made habitable with an ornate superstructure of Hispanic design, and most of the Indians who remained in the city concealed their basic paganism beneath a flimsy veneer of Christianity. Before long, baptized Indians had learned to pronounce the name of the Holy Virgin in Latin, Spanish, and Quechuan, and the Imperial City of the Incas was dedicated to Santiago. A likeness of the militant apostle, clasping dagger and serpentine sword and reviewing a host of dead and wounded pagans, now was painted on the wall of an ancient temple adjoining the plaza; and Indians who paused to gaze upon that image are said to have murmured that it was just such a viracocha as that one who had destroyed them in the dismal hours of the siege. Moreover, the great carved image which for years had remained only a few leagues away at Cacha, the new messiahs now declared to represent, not the specter Viracocha, but the blessed San Bartolomé, who, some Spaniards claimed, had trod that weary land.

These are some of the accounts left by the sages of the new Castile which sprang from the ruins of Tahuantinsuyu. Much that they recorded of both Indians and Spaniards represents unprovable tradition and must be taken on faith or regarded simply as poetry and superstition. But the effects of such traditions, whether pagan or Christian, are real and cannot be ignored in a study of the civilizations and cultures which molded the lives of the individuals involved in the present story. Out of the events which these sages recorded, events which enfolded a legend and a drama of glory and gold, of blood, conquest, false hopes, and despair, of shadows darkening over a dying empire and a new hope of salvation, the auqui Huallpa Túpac and the palla Chimpu Ocllo emerged, no longer royal pagans, but cleansed and reborn through the miraculous waters of baptism and accepted into the Holy Roman congregation, the one taking the name of Francisco, and the other, Isabel Suárez, a respected name from the lineage of the viracocha who became her master.[13] As the years moved on and the confusion of merging

[13] In one instance in his *Comentarios reales* Garcilaso refers to his uncle as Fernando Huallpa Túpac Yupanqui and in another as Francisco Huallpa Túpac Yupanqui. In his dedication to *Los diálogos de amor* he refers to his mother as "the Palla

faiths became more bewildering or slowly unraveled, and as bitterness
and disillusion made these two grandchildren of the Inca Túpac Yupanqui more conscious of deprivation and exploitation, they were to
lose some faith in the divine origin and mission of the men who, some
said, had come from out the froth of the sea. But in those dark moments when their people lay in desolation, both apparently did believe
that the Spaniards were sons of Viracocha and sent to succor the realm.
Thus they had not fled with the Inca Manco to fan the embers of
paganism at Vitcos but had remained in the Imperial City with a hope
of physical and spiritual well-being.

Supported as she was by this tenacious though confusing faith, and
by the example of many of her kinswomen, the palla Chimpu Ocllo,
during these turbulent years, submitted her body as well as her soul to
the pleasure and authority of Sebastián Garcilaso de la Vega, a handsome cavalier who rode into the Imperial City on a splendid horse, who
adorned himself with plumes, rich silks, velvets and taffetas, and whose
ancestors had written into the misty annals of Spain exploits equally as
valiant and poetic as those sung by the quipucamayus and amautas of
Tahuantinsuyu—a man who, though torn with the common lust for
flesh and gold, bore deeply embedded in his conscience a yearning to
assist in bringing the heathen of the world, by force or persuasion, into
the all-embracing fold of Christendom. It was a heritage from Catholic
ancestors of past centuries who had wielded their sword arms valiantly
to deliver Spain from the dark-blooded peoples of Islam.

Among the famed crusading forefathers of this cavalier who through
carnal relations with an Indian palla was to merge some of the noblest
blood in Spain with that of Inca kings, were Garcí Pérez de Vargas and
Garcí Lasso de la Vega, legendary knights of the thirteenth and four-
teenth centuries. These long-celebrated heroes had served to mold and
reinforce traditional concepts of chivalry, and in their prowess and accomplishments, perpetuated in both ballad and song and always in an
aura of romance, Sebastián Garcilaso, like many of his compatriots,
had discovered incentive for adventure. It follows naturally, therefore,

---

Doña Isabel," and in his *Descendencia de Garcí Pérez* he calls her "Doña Isabel
Palla Chimpu Ocllo." In her will the palla identifies herself as "isabel xuarez," and
in two documents relative to this will Garcilaso identifies her as "isabel suarez palla."

that his son, the Inca Garcilaso, would regard these two knights with exaggerated respect and turn to them as taproots of his Spanish lineage.

Garcí Pérez de Vargas was a son of Rodrigo de Vargas of Toledo, and through his veins flowed the rich blood of the ancient Goths. In many of his amazing performances, Spaniards perceived an irresistible mingling of drollery and derring-do, which while teasing and taunting Moorish adversaries left his comrades gasping with merriment; and they found in addition those qualities which chivalry demanded of an exemplary knight in both fact and fiction. And so it was that this man crept into their histories and folklore, and they came to believe that the crusades of the Holy King Ferdinand might have proven sadly ineffective but for the bolstering arm of the intrepid Garcí Pérez. Not only were they supported in their credulity by both chronicles and songs, but over the centuries there had remained upon one of the corroding portals of Seville, the fading eulogy of an anonymous rhymster which declared that Hercules had raised that ancient metropolis from out of the soil, that Julius Caesar had erected its lofty turrets and far-reaching walls, and that the Holy King had conquered it for Christendom—though with the effective sword arm of Garcí Pérez de Vargas.

It was in a clash between Christians and Moors at Jerez de la Frontera that Garcí Pérez de Vargas first received signal fame. Here in a battle whose outcome, according to tradition, was determined by the divine Santiago and his cavalcade of warriors, the stout-hearted cavalier displayed such amazing skill and courage that he was dubbed into the spacious honors of Spanish nobility, and thus it was as a knight of the Holy King Ferdinand that he acted out another role which was to enter his name in the annals of legendary heroes. The scene was Tablada, where the King had assembled an unparalleled war camp. Garcí Pérez, now famous among both Christians and Moors for his cool courage, was departing belatedly from camp with a cavalier companion and a lowly squire to overtake a company of foragers. Having proceeded but a short distance, they found their passage obstructed by seven Moorish horsemen, at which don Garcí's noble companion executed a hasty retreat, declaring that no code of honor obliged a man to make front against such odds. But not so the intrepid knight, who merely donned his arms and passed serenely on, accompanied now by no more than his squire, whose courage has never been adequately sung. Perceiving the identity of the man they would accost, the Moors contented themselves with accompanying him for a space while hurling taunts and threats, and then, realizing that he could not be ruffled, returned to their original station. At that Garcí Pérez disarmed, only to discover that he had lost his cap. Intent on retracing his steps and searching for the missing article, he once again requested his arms, to the utter dismay of his squire, who now pled with his master not to tempt fickle fortune again for the sake of a mere cap. But ordering the menial to hold his tongue, the cavalier explained that it was not a mere cap that he sought, but one which, having been embroidered for him by a fair damsel, he held at great price. Turning toward the Moors, who now fled in terror, he retrieved his headpiece from the dust and proceeded in all tranquility upon his mission.

The Holy Ferdinand, beholding from a distance such a display of courage, was restrained only by the advice of his counselors from sending succor. And when the bold cavalier returned to camp, he received lavish praise from His Majesty as well as a request for the name of the timid companion who had abandoned him at the offset. But a tenet of chivalry forbade the true knight to defame, and Garcí Pérez, generously lying, declared himself ignorant of the man's name, and, as a further precaution, charged his squire never by word or look to reveal it. Thus the people of old Spain came to recognize in Garcí Pérez all the qualities of an exemplary knight; and he, after forming an alliance close to the Crown, left a line of cavaliers who sought to emulate him in his chivalry.[14]

Equally revered in ancient Spain was Garcí Lasso de la Vega, who through an amazing display of courage had added the Vega to the Lasso name, won an *Ave Maria gratia plena* for the Lasso arms, and added one of the richest legends to the annals of Spanish chivalry. Down through the centuries Spaniards have dramatized and cherished

[14] Garcilaso, *Comentarios*, Pt. II, Bk. VIII, Chap. 12; *Descendencia de Garcí Pérez;* also Padre Juan de Mariana, *Historia general de España,* Vol. III, Bk. XIII, Chap. 7, pp. 270–271 *et passim*; Alonso Núñez de Castro, *Vida de S. Fernando el III,* Bk. II, Chap. 3, pp. 226–229 *et passim*; Washington Irving, *Moorish Chronicles,* Chap. 15, pp. 101–104.

this legend. It tells of the splendid forces of Christendom and Islam drawn up in the encircling vega, or plain, to vent their passions in the sacred cause of either the Cross or the Crescent. Suddenly, amid a burst of infidel laughter, a giant Moorish horseman emerged upon the field, fully armed and breathing defiance to Christians; and the fury of the latter broke all bounds when they perceived, dangling from the tail of the challenger's horse, a scroll bearing the name of the most Holy Virgin. The coveted privilege of avenging this sacrilege and insult was accorded one Garcí Lasso, a fair and beardless youth, who quickly mounted his steed, set his armor in order, breathed a devotion to the Mother of God, and defied the Moslem in the midst of his profane career. At that there ensued a breath-taking spectacle. Trial was made with both lance and sword, and at each attack it appeared that the Christian must succumb; but though inferior in strength, he was more agile. At length, when both warriors grappled, they fell to the ground, and then the giant, gaining the advantage, pressed a powerful knee upon the breast of his weakened foe and aimed a dagger at his exposed throat, while a unanimous cry of despair arose from the onlooking Christians. Yet once more Heaven intervened with attending marvels. In that desperate moment, when a heathen arm was lifted to strike, the fair Garcí Lasso shortened his sword and plunged it into a dark pagan heart. As a spiritual seed of the blossoming rod of Jesse, so it was said, he had been protected in his sacred mission, and the Holy Mother whom he adored and defended had provided him prowess and strength like another David to slay the giant champion of the infidels.[15]

Since this tale of youthful valor and devotion became a fiber of Spanish folklore, the deed has been suffered to shift in time and setting, falling frequently to the plains of Granada when, at the close of the fifteenth century, the Catholic Queen Isabel was administering the *coup de grâce* to an Hispanic-Moorish kingdom. Here the hero is Gar-

---

[15] Garcilaso referred to this ancestor in *Descendencia de Garcí Pérez* and in his "Dedicación" to the second part of *Los comentarios reales*; Lope de Vega used the story in three plays: "El cerco de Santa Fe," "Los hechos de Garcilaso de la Vega y Moro Tarfe," and "Los comendadores de Córdoba." For other sources, see Washington Irving, *Conquest of Granada*, Chap. 47, pp. 329–334; Howard Keniston, *Garcilaso de la Vega*, pp. 10–13; Miró Quesada y Sosa, *El Inca Garcilaso*, p. 8; Charlotte Yonge, *The Story of the Christians and the Moors of Spain*, pp. 286–289.

cilaso de la Vega, Lord of Los Arcos and father of one of the great lyric voices of sixteenth-century Spain. But by this date the Lassos long had worn the name of La Vega, and it appears more reasonable to accept the theory that the event occurred in 1340 on the vegas of Salado, and that the hero was a son of the first Garcí Lasso known to history, whose estate lay at Torrelavega in the kingdom of Asturias and who held high positions under Ferdinand IV and Alonso XI. The significant point, however, is that all who bore the Lasso blood in their veins could turn to this fabulous story as further proof of their nobility as well as evidence that they bore the special blessing of the Holy Virgin. It is small wonder, therefore, that among them were to be found some of the proudest houses in Spain, the ruling lords of Infantado, Feria, Los Arcos, Zafra, Belalcázar and Priego, men who bore such noble names as Mendoza, Lasso, Sotomayor, Suárez and Figueroa. At some time toward the close of the fifteenth century, the blood of the famed Garcí Lasso de la Vega was merged, though possibly not for the first time, with that of the equally famed Garcí Pérez de Vargas through the marriage of Blanca de Sotomayor Suárez de Figueroa, a great-niece of the first Conde de Feria, to Alonso de Hinestrosa de Vargas. These were the noble paternal grandparents of the mestizo who is the subject of the present biography.

As the eldest offspring of Gómez Suárez de Figueroa, "el Ronco," Lord of Torre del Águila, doña Blanca fell heir to the title and estates of her father; and her husband, as the second son of Alonso de Vargas, Lord of Sierrabrava, eventually became Lord of Valdesevilla and ruled a feudal domain in the borderlands of Estremadura.[16] In the turbulent days when the iron-willed Isabel was forging into solidarity a nobility of varied loyalties, don Alonso and his kinsmen may have shown some reluctant allegiance, but if so, they emerged eventually as faithful vassals of the Castilian queen, who in turn favored a number of them with appointments close to the Crown. Thus they were able to observe from a special point of vantage changes which were to affect their own destinies as well as those of Spain and the world. For as soon as the

---

[16] For the Vega-Vargas lineage, see Garcilaso, *Descendencia de Garcí Pérez;* Guillermo Lohmann Villena, "La ascendencia española del Inca Gracilaso de la Vega," *Hidalguía,* No. 29, Julio–Agosto, 1958, pp. 369–384, 681–699.

Catholic Queen had made manifest her triumph amid Islamic splendors at Granada, she granted to Cristóbal Colón the privilege of charting a route through unexplored western seas to Cathay. And even as the Moors of Castile were being baptized into New Christians or chastized from the land, this famed Genoese was sailing the Ocean Sea on a search that ended amid the green fringes of an unknown pagan world where it would become the apostolic duty of Spain to propagate Christian seed. Victory over the Moors of Granada had fixed even more forcefully in the minds of Hispanic people a vision of themselves as the true spiritual descendants of Aaron and Jesse and thus heirs of the far reaches of heathendom. And this vision became a conviction when on May 4, 1493, Pope Alexander VI issued a bull which gave proprietorship of the New World to Portugal and Spain.

To finance this crusade and the voyage which was to terminate in the Indies, the Catholic Kings, as they had done in suppressing the Moors, had utilized the gold of a race which traced its blood as well as its spiritual lineage back to the Kings of Judah; and two men whose resources were especially useful in this new enterprise were Abraham and Isaac, Sephardic Jews of the House of Abarbanal. After being driven from Portugal, where he had enjoyed the patronage of the House of Braganza, don Isaac by 1484 had become Minister of the Exchequer of Spain and was occupying this exalted position when in 1492 Torquemada and the Pope were urging the Crown to complete its crusade against infidels by purging the land of its Hebrews. The tragic sequence is common history. In the name of his oppressed people, Isaac Abarbanal attempted a bribe. In the name of a bartered Christ, Torquemada issued a veiled warning. Ferdinand and Isabel, torn between piety and much needed gold, yielded to spiritual persuasion, and on the second of August, 1492, there began the most frightful exodus in the history of Judaism. With that exodus went the Abarbanals, who terminated their flight in Italy, where, in 1502, Isaac's son Judah completed a philosophical treatise, later translated and published by the Inca Garcilaso, which ignored the false pride of nations and races, and which provided incentive for later humanistic questioning of the divine right of sovereigns. Calling it *Dialoghi Di Amore,* he acknowledged it under the pseudonym of Maestro Leone Hebreo Medico since he already was a renowned physician and as an Abarbanal bore in his veins the blood of the Shepherd King.

Thus the closing years of the waning century had witnessed the twilight of the forces of Judaism and Islam in Spain, and with it the dawn of a new world peopled with dark and pagan races. And as the initial years of the new century unfolded, somber shadows were moving across Spain. For the Queen was old, and sick, and saddened, and she was aware that her days were rapidly approaching an end. When on Holy Thursday of 1504 mysterious rumblings shook the heavens above Andalusia and Castile and the earth yawned, tearing many of the ancient walls of Christendom from their foundations, learned Catholics, like pagan Incas, read in such signs the doom of a sovereign. On November 12, the twelfth anniversary of the landing of her Genoese admiral at San Salvador, the Catholic Queen signed her last will and testament, and six weeks later, only a few days before her demise, she added a pious codicil enjoining her successors "to treat the Indians in the new possessions beyond the seas with the greatest kindness and gentleness, to redress any wrongs they might justly complain of, and to carry on the sacred work of civilizing and converting them to Christianity." And even while a lugubrious cortege of friars and grandees was bearing her remains to a sepulcher at Granada, Cristóbal Colón was at San Lúcar de Barrameda fretting for a third mission which would enable him to penetrate further into the limitless reaches of heathendom.

During these breath-taking years when an old order was dying and and the world of Spain was awakening to new physical and spiritual possibilities, doña Blanca de Sotomayor bore to her husband a son, Sebastián Garcilaso de la Vega, who was fated to join that vast crusade to bring light to an Indian realm. The birth records of Sebastián remain in oblivion; yet he is known to have been born at Badajoz in Estremadura, and paradoxical records in sundry documents suggest that he made his advent at some time during the first several years of the sixteenth century. He was the third male of nine children, four sons and five daughters.[17]

[17] Garcilaso, *Comentarios*, Pt. II, Bk. I, Chap. 6; Bk. VIII, Chap. 12; and his *Descendencia de Garcí Pérez;* also Lohmann Villena, "La ascendencia española del Inca Garcilaso de la Vega," *Hidalguía*, No. 29; *Cartas de Indias*, Vol. II, p. 784. The

The ancient border city of Badajoz offered rich nourishment for the dreams of a Renaissance boy. Rising above sturdy classical structures of the Caesars were architectural symbols of Saracenic dominion; and dominating all now were the ramparts and spires of Castilian Catholicism. The stones of its narrow streets bore ghostly shadows of both ancient and recent struggles; and situated as it was on direct routes to the western seaports, its air was redolent of travelers who already had savored adventure in mysterious new lands and haunted seas. From the initial stages of comprehension, the imagination of Sebastián was fed not only with the chivalric accomplishments of his cavalier ancestors but with the equally marvelous accomplishments of both Portuguese and Spaniards in the opening arenas of exploration, and all under the hypnotic and catalyzing spell of the "lying histories" and the "books of chivalry." As the boy increased in years and watched the men of Estremadura drifting off to the western sea-lanes, he too, surely, would travel the meandering routes to nearby Lisbon or Cádiz or Seville, where one saw mariners loading tall-masted galleons and caravels designed to seek out new Edens and convey back to Spain the marvels of the Indies.

Yet it is doubtful if any of the sons of the Lord of Valdesevilla, in either adolescence or youth, were encouraged to contemplate a career outside the limits of the old world. In general, it was the "sons of nobody" who in these years cast their fortunes where rewards were gained only with insuperable toil. The hidalgo could anticipate a more splendid and comfortable existence as a courtier in the political tournaments of Europe, and it was for this species of service that the offspring of nobility were commonly trained. The known facts concerning Sebastián's education indicate that it was in this direction his career was designed.[18] His training was in all respects that of a gentleman. He was taught the ennobling art of horsemanship, becoming a gifted

---

date of Sebastián's birth must be ascertained from statements as to his age when he left for the Indies and the number of years he spent there. His brothers were Gómez Suárez de Figueroa y Vargas, Alonso de Vargas, and Juan de Vargas; his sisters were Beatriz de Figueroa, Isabel de Vargas, Leonor de la Vega, Blanca de Sotomayor y Figueroa, and a fifth who, though mentioned in the records of the Inca Garcilaso, is not named.

[18] Garcilaso, *Comentarios*, Pt. II, Bk. VIII, Chap. 12.

equestrian with equal skill in either the Moorish or the Spanish saddle. Moreover, he was well instructed in the management of sword and lance. As a mere boy he amused himself with the colorful Moorish sport of jousting with canes, a sport in which his Vargas ancestors were renowned for their skill; and as a youth displaying his prowess in the pageants and tournaments of his homeland, he presented a memorable picture. Many years later, friends who knew him in those earlier years spoke of his "natural grace, his beauty of countenance, and his gallant and elegant appearance." Moreover, they attested to the acuteness of his wit and the facility with which he learned and retained what he received from his preceptors; and they spoke lavishly of his early wisdom, chivalry, prudence, and moderation, all of which, they said, entertained and gained the affection of his contemporaries as well as the wonder of his elders. These praises were eulogistic and came from men who were inclined to superimpose upon their hero most of the refinements of legendary chivalry. Yet in his ensuing career, Sebastián did reveal the virtues mentioned. He was always a courtier, refined, gay, handsome, and possessed of a certain immunity which frequently accompanies charm and noble blood. In addition he was endowed with an innate or acquired sense of cautious diplomacy which in general placed him on the safe side; and finally he had been inculcated from infancy with a devout and traditional sense of honor which demanded that he be forever conscious of his obligation to both Church and Crown.

Early in his life, Sebastián was afforded opportunities to witness some of the perils attending those who wavered in their loyalties. A close kinsman of his mother had suffered by casting his lot with Juana the Mad and Philip the Fair; and when death struck Ferdinand the Catholic, leaving the Spanish throne to the German Charles, both Figueroa and Vargas relatives had joined the "Comuneros" in a revolt against the fledgling king and then had paid painfully for their boldness.[19] Yet the sons of Alonso de Hinestrosa de Vargas undoubtedly remained loyal to the new sovereign in this internecine struggle.

---

[19] Sebastián's mother's first cousin, Pedro Laso de la Vega, a brother of the poet Garcilaso de la Vega, was a leader in the revolt of the Comuneros. Keniston, *Garcilaso de la Vega*, pp. 42–46.

Gómez Suárez de Figueroa y Vargas, the eldest, appears always to have been without martial ambitions; Juan de Vargas, the youngest, was scarcely of an age to participate; and Alonso de Vargas, second in line, as early as 1517 had enlisted in the service of Charles V under the alias of Francisco de Plasencia. Furthermore, the records of Sebastián indicate clearly that, though well trained in arms, he did not put them to use until some years after this revolt had terminated. Thus he remained free to seek royal patronage without apology.

Meanwhile, Spanish conquerors had continued to extend the western horizons of the realm, and each homecoming vessel brought stirring rumors. Already the islands and Tierra Firme had offered a wealth of marvelous stories and promises of treasure, and the vast kingdom of Montezuma had opened its golden coffers to bold men of Estremadura. Far north of the Mexican empire, Spanish explorers had sailed into a land of flowers and high potency waters, the unknown limits of which extended to the frozen regions of the Cod. Somewhere across the horizon of the Mar del Sur, the great sea known today as the Pacific, were said to lie islands of pungent spice; and stretching endlessly along its eastern fringes were unexplored regions which had whispered of treasure to the stranded heroes of Gallo. These were beckoning zones, and they offered more than mere treasure to men of inflamed piety and feverish blood. For here one found dazzling opportunities for knights-errant and knights-amorous; and here lay vast possibilities for those who, dreaming of extending the limits of the Holy Roman Church, felt that God had designated them specifically to do so.

Embedded in the youthful Sebastián's nature were most of the emotional urges of renascent Spain. Piously Catholic, he found it easy to correlate the idea of sowing Christian seed, if necessary with the mailed fist, while gathering material rewards in payment of the task. Nourished in the traditions of chivalric lore, he readily could visualize himself as an agent in the extension of an Amadisian mission. And adequately endowed with the amorous propensities of the Latin courtier, he no doubt quite early became adept in the rites of Venus. A firsthand knowledge of the pleasures of love was as essential to prove manhood as the growth of a beard, and it appears that there were few youths in Spain who had not tested their erudition with practical experience.

Years later Sebastián was to mention the presence in Spain of a natural daughter whom in all probability he engendered under Castilian skies.

All such urges, combined with the continuous arrival of fantastic rumors, served to quicken Sebastián's response to the call of the Indies; and strengthening this interest was the circumstance of his birth, which, by depriving him of primogeniture, undoubtedly had made essential a lucrative career—and this in an age when any effort at trade would have cast suspicion on the well-guarded purity of his blood and threatened his social status. Little choice was left him outside the court, the army, or ecclesiastical orders. Though three of his sisters did seclude themselves in convents, it is doubtful that Sebastián ever contemplated such vows; and his thorough training in arms indicates that he had dreamed of joining his brother Alonso in the service of Charles V. Certainly as the western world emerged more and more from the mists of the unknown, the prospects which it offered for the future were increasingly discussed among the nobles of Estremadura. They had seen a flow of relatives and associates departing for the Indies, and from them there had come stories of astounding adventure and sometimes of success. Then in 1527 and 1528, three significant conquerors, Francisco Pizarro, Hernán Cortés, and Pedro de Alvarado, all men of Estremadura, returned to Spain with glittering acounts of discoveries as well as enticing proposals for new and rewarding conquests.

The recruiting fifes and drums of Pizarro made enchanting music in Estremadura, and though this conqueror failed to acquire sufficient men to meet the King's demands, he did manage eventually to slip out of San Lúcar de Barrameda with adequate forces to initiate, along with Diego de Almagro, the conquest of Peru; and among his new recruits he numbered his three brothers, Juan, Gonzalo and Hernando, who became pivotal in the subjugation of the Inca realm. It was these fearless brothers who eventually wrought most in the destiny of Sebastián Garcilaso de la Vega, and their influence may already have touched him. But at the moment he possibly was attracted more by the noble and cavalier Pedro de Alvarado who held a special appeal for young courtiers. Though there are no specific records as to just when Sebastián Garcilaso initiated his western crusade, it is more than likely that he did so when in July of 1528 the gay vessels of Alvarado moved down the Guadalquivir and set sails for Vera Cruz.[20]

Documents concerning the movements of Sebastián Garcilaso during the next several years are scant. The indication is that he left Spain with the King's commission as a captain, that he was in possession of sufficient funds to finance a secondary conquest of his own, and that he may even have been accompanied by kinsmen and menials. He is seen at one point tilting canes in the plaza of the City of Mexico; and a legal receipt reveals him as a citizen of Santiago de los Caballeros, perhaps the Guatemalan city known today as Antigua. The chances are that he remained with Alvarado and followed him into Guatemala when the latter proceeded there to assume his government. Certainly in 1531 he was with Alvarado, and at some time during these years he was united with two cousins, Gómez de Luna and Gómez de Tordoya y Vargas, the latter of whom had been sentenced to death in Spain, undoubtedly because of acts committed in the revolt of the Comuneros.[21] For several years Sebastián was to be actively associated with this seditious cousin, whom he regarded with unusual affection.

News of the triumph at Cajamarca having sifted back to Darién, Alvarado was beginning to shift his sights to the rich and promising domains of Almagro and Francisco Pizarro. Yet when his new ambitions were made known by jealous associates to the King, they met with immediate disapproval. Nevertheless, Alvarado was able to produce an old capitulation that justified his exploration of southern territory outside the jurisdiction of Almagro and Pizarro, and with this he made haste to depart before a royal order could give him let. And Captain Garcilaso, gambling on his insight, boldly proceeded with this cavalier conquistador, launching upon a voyage which exposed him to the possible disfavor of his sovereign and to the furies of the southern continent.

[20] Garcilaso's statement in his *Descendencia de Garci Pérez* that at the time of his death (April, 1559) his father had served thirty years "in the conquest and settlement of the New World," makes this date appear likely.
[21] Garcilaso, *Comentarios,* Pt. II, Bk. II, Chap. 1; Bk. IV, Chap. 16; Bk. VIII, Chap. 12; and Prólogo (letter to the King, January 19, 1586); also Miró Quesada y Sosa, *El Inca Garcilaso,* pp. 7, 14, 15.

Avoiding Panama, the expedition of Pedro de Alvarado sailed out
of Nicaragua in December, 1533, five hundred Spaniards and several
hundred horses, and with them, cramped in the narrow confines of the
fragile vessels, hundreds of ill-fated Indians. Then after days of tossing through turbulent coastal waters, they arrived at San Miguel, sea-
sick and hungry and perishing of thirst, to begin a death march through
burning coastal sands and on toward the frigid and limitless stretches
of the Cordillera. The story of their progress toward Quito is one of
starvation and unendurable cold, of slow toil and painful struggle
over seemingly insuperable mountain passes, higher and higher into
the forbidding Andes, while behind them lay hundreds of miles of
wilderness trails strewn with the lifeless bodies of men and horses. At
length they were safe, they thought, when at nine thousand feet above
sea level they had reached the high tablelands in the region of Quito,
but here they encountered a new and different peril. For Francisco
Pizarro, alarmed by rumors of their arrival, had dispatched Diego de
Almagro to intercept them. There were brief skirmishes, secret confer-
ences, and eventually negotiations which led to a somewhat underhand
bargain wherein Pedro de Alvarado agreed to relinquish to Pizarro
both the invading men and the vessels which brought them and then to
retire from the field.

Sebastián Garcilaso somehow managed to survive that devastating
journey, and no records indicate that he resented Alvarado's settlement
with Pizarro or that he ever spoke of don Pedro except in praise. His
mature judgment undoubtedly assured him of ultimate advantages to
be gained in the bargain, and he indeed may have helped to maneuver
it. So one sees him next at Pachacámac amicably tilting canes with the
Pizarros and shortly after at Cuzco witnessing the rape of a realm. He
saw the puppet Inca Manco swaying on a worthless throne, and he
saw the beginning as well as the end of the struggle between Diego de
Almagro and Francisco Pizarro as each groped for possession of the
Imperial City. In 1535, when Almagro, holding tenaciously to his
rights, refused to relinquish Cuzco, Captain Garcilaso was among those
who pled with the old conquistador to abstain from hostilities until
some new and definite judgment could be obtained from the King;[22]

[22] Garcilaso, *Comentarios,* Pt. II, Bk. II, Chap. 19.

and he was at hand on June 12 when the two partners, after months of feigned friendship and armed vigilance, signed a new and solemn contract redolent of treachery.

Aware of the explosive nature of the men who now swarmed Cuzco, Francisco Pizarro wisely assigned new conquests. Many of those who had come into Peru with Alvarado soon joined Almagro in an expedition to Chile. But Captain Garcilaso, because of his high rank, his ostensible merits, or his financial ability to support an expedition, was granted permission to explore a region in the valley of San Mateo, near Puerto Viejo and the Bahía de Caráquez, which his companions optimistically had dubbed Buenaventura. Assembling two hundred and fifty men, he now set forth upon an expedition which was to bring little to compensate for the two years of misery it evoked. It led the adventurers into a maze of jungles through which in general they could advance only so far as they were able to hew their way with axes. It was a vast, green enmeshment of peril and destruction. Once, while crossing a treacherous river, Captain Garcilaso fell into the water and was saved only by the intervention of comrades who extended a lance for him to grasp while they tugged him ashore. As they moved tediously forward, he was torn by the sight of men dying or lingering on in slow starvation and torture; and gradually as burnished mail gave way to rotting fabrics and humiliating nakedness, there came anguished demands from the sufferers to retrace their steps and preserve what lives they could. At length Captain Garcilaso had determined upon such a debasing and costly course when he perceived birds flying low and dipping to the earth some five miles distant. So once more the desperate men, taking their cue from the flight of birds, set to work with axes and within a few days staggered naked and burned and starved into a small Indian village, where they were received hospitably.[23]

It was during Captain Garcilaso's exploration of Buenaventura that the Inca Manco had laid siege to Cuzco, which Francisco Pizarro, to whom the King had now granted the title of Marqués, had left under

---

[23] *Ibid.,* Pt. II, Bk. II, Chaps. 19, 32; Bk. VIII, Chap. 12. Garcilaso heard an account of this expedition from his father and from a man named Torralva, who still wept for the companions who had been left to die along the way.

the command of his brothers while he remained at the newly founded city of Los Reyes, known today as Lima. Answering a summons for assistance, Garcilaso hastened to the Marqués, and shrewdly insisting on being among the first to carry aid to the Pizarros at Cuzco, set out shortly after under the command of Marshal Alonso de Alvarado for the Imperial City. Along the route, messengers arrived with news that the Inca Manco had lifted his siege and withdrawn to Vitcos, but that Cuzco now lay in the hands of Diego de Almagro, who, fortified with a new cedula from the King, had returned to reassert his claims. Juan Pizarro had forfeited his life in the siege, and Gonzalo and Hernando languished as Almagro's prisoners in the fortress of Sacsahuamán. In the inevitable showdown between conquerors which ensued, Captain Garcilaso cast his lot with customary precaution and perception. When emissaries arrived at Amáncay to demand the withdrawal of Pizarrists to what Almagro termed their legal jurisdiction, Garcilaso pled in vain with his commander to grant the messengers diplomatic immunity; but when on June 12, 1537, an army arrived from Cuzco to enforce Almagro's demands and the majority of the Pizarrists shifted their allegiance, Captain Garcilaso and Gómez de Tordoya remained loyal to the Pizarros and in the end were borne off to Cuzco as captives.[24] In this condition they remained until April 6, 1538, when their freedom was bought by the blood of Pizarrists on the plains of Las Salinas.

The circumstances of Captain Garcilaso's strange captivity during this ten-month interval have never been made quite clear. One is led to believe that it was neither perilous nor painful nor even necessary, and that he may have regarded it as fortunate. He enjoyed the good faith of Almagro, and authentic records indicate that while others fretted in prison, he, sometimes if not always, was permitted the freedom of the city, bound with nothing more than the invisible chains of his cavalier honor. Escape surely would have been possible and perhaps facile, and his failure to achieve it must be attributed at least in part to ancient chivalric mores, though not to be ignored are his caution and political astuteness. He knew the wisdom of abiding with patience the outcome of delicate and debatable issues, and the pos-

[24] *Ibid.*, Pt. II, Bk. II, Chaps. 33–34; Bk. VIII, Chap. 12.

sible denouement of the present quarrel he had no means of fathom-
ing. Be that as it may, when shortly afterwards Almagro departed
Cuzco, taking with him Hernando Pizarro, to defy the Marqués by
establishing a settlement definitely within the latter's jurisdiction, Garcilaso apparently was left with no fetters other than a promise. For
when Gonzalo Pizarro and others, taking advantage of Almagro's absence, connived with guards and effected an escape, Garcilaso did not
join them. Cieza de León has recorded that while these men were
maneuvering their flight, Garcilaso and a companion were in the
countryside hawking and that when on returning the companion was
invited to join the fugitives, he refused to do so because of an oath
previously given Almagro. Surely Garcilaso also had taken that same
oath, and though his affection for the Pizarros was strong, it never did
and never would exceed his regard for honor. This was a point which
Gonzalo Pizarro could respect, though one which afterwards, to his
regret, he carelessly minimized.

Yet much of Almagro's faith vanished after he had generously and
injudiciously released Hernando Pizarro in an honorable compact which
Francisco Pizarro very promptly and dishonorably discarded. Aware
now of the danger of trusting men who had remained loyal to the
Pizarros, the old warrior, on learning that Hernando Pizarro was moving toward Cuzco with an army of vengeance, again apprehended
Garcilaso and some of his companions; and when on April 6, 1538,
the determining clash came at Las Salinas, these men were in Cuzco
behind prison walls.[25]

The contest at Las Salinas was bloody, and while it was in process
a host of Indian spectators, confused and amazed by Christian fratri-
cide, plundered the fallen and forewent an opportunity to annihilate
both armies because of the old admonition of Huayna Cápac. Almagro, too old and too ravaged with a venereal pox to remain astride his
horse, observed the scene from a litter, but when it became evident
that fate had ruled against him, he managed to mount a mule, a beast

[25] *Ibid.*, Pt. II, Bk. II, Chap. 35; Pedro de Cieza de León, *Guerras civiles del Perú*,
Bk. I, Chaps. 23, 60; Miró Quesada y Sosa, *El Inca Garcilaso*, p. 19. Seized with
Sebastián were three of his companions, Gómez de Tordoya, Diego Maldonado
and Pedro del Barco.

generally reserved for women and prelates, and soon the anxious inhabitants of Cuzco beheld him galloping furiously across the rim of the
city to seek haven in the interminable labyrinths of Sacsahuamán. In
swift and unrelenting pursuit came Gonzalo Pizarro, a horseman of
even darker destiny. The prisoners of Almagro were set free, and the
bonds, both visible and invisible, which had bound Captain Garcilaso
were shattered. Doubts were dispelled as to where he must place his
allegiance since Diego de Almagro, in the lottery of adventure, where
the prizes were splendid but few, had committed the blunder of losing.
Soon the previous deserters shuttled back into the confidence of the
victors, and the faithful were awarded new and alluring enterprises.
And coincidentally, on that auspicious day which had marked the termination of a compact that had lured Spaniards to the golden veins of
Tahuantinsuyu, a new and splendid armada hoisted sails and slipped
across the treacherous sandbars of San Lúcar de Barrameda into the
western sea lanes. It was the fleet of the Adelantado Hernando de Soto,
ertswhile companion of Almagro and the Pizarros in their plunder of
Peru. Envious of the fame and the apparent success of his comrades,
De Soto, bolstered by his share of the riches of Cajamarca, now was
launching the exploration and conquest of that vast region to the
north of Mexico which Juan Ponce de León had called La Florida.
With him were men whose lives later were to color the destiny of
Sebastián Garcilaso de la Vega, and who were to provide historical
details of that expedition for Sebastián's as yet unborn son.

    December of 1538 found Diego de Almagro, palsied with age and
infirmity, pleading with Hernando Pizarro for his obviously few remaining years. At length, however, on December 8, the old conqueror
was forced to yield to the death command of his wretchedly ungrateful
judge and submit his neck to the humiliation of the garrote. When his
last breath had been stifled, his body was carried into the market place
at Cuzco and deprived of its head as well as clothing, and in the evening a faithful Negro swathed the mutilated remains in a winding
sheet and bore them to the Church of La Merced. Among those left to
weep the loss of the fallen conqueror was his beloved son and heir,
Diego the Lad, a handsome mestizo in whose veins flowed the blood of
two ominously merging worlds. Soon Hernando Pizarro was sailing

back to Spain to explain recent developments to the Crown, and Captain Sebastián Garcilaso de la Vega had joined an expedition to the provinces of Collao and the Charcas under the command of Gonzalo Pizarro.

The destiny of Sebastián Garcilaso was to be interwoven darkly throughout the remainder of his life with that of Gonzalo Pizarro, and long after the threads of both lives had been severed, the shadow of the latter was to blight the future of Sebastián's offspring. Yet repeated pursuals of their relations lead to the conclusion that these two conquerors regarded each other with genuine admiration and affection, sentiments which found origin in common tastes and desires. Gonzalo, though illegitimate, could claim noble blood through his father, and he was sensitive ever to the respect due Sebastián's legitimacy and noble lineage. Moreover, both men loved fine horses and a colorful tournament in the plaza or a fair tilt with pagans in the field. Springing as they did from the same region, they surely must have known something of each other in Spain, but their ties now were to be drawn tauter by this expedition into the Charcas where they were to experience that strange comradeship which men share in the thrill of the hunt and that undefinable emotion which sweeps over them in the face of a common danger.

To Captain Garcilaso the undertaking was soul-satisfying—not a weary hacking of one's way through jungles where success depended largely upon the mattock and the axe, but a spirited and perilous crusade in which one could display chivalry and skill with both sword and lance. Adversaries were fierce and agile, and blood flowed freely on both sides. Spaniards afterward told of a struggle in which their entire number, only seventy in all, faced a force of thousands of Indians and still put them to rout; and they told of single combats more desperate than great battles. Indeed, at one point their plight became so critical that they were forced to send messengers to Francisco Pizarro for aid. Yet in the end it was the pagans who succumbed, for this was, after a fashion, a Christian crusade. In their moment of desperation, so they reported, there came a familiar rustling in the heavens as a band of angelic horsemen under the aegis of the militant Santiago descended and loosened its wrath upon screaming pagans. In all of these events

Captain Garcilaso took a significant part, and on his return to Cuzco he bore witness to the attending marvels. He also brought with him several captive Indians who lived in his house and served him faithfully for the remainder of his life.[26]

Captain Sebastián Garcilaso now was a seasoned conqueror with visible scars of exploration and conquest. Moreover, he had placed his allegiance cautiously and wisely, and he could anticipate reward from the man who was in a position to bestow it. And so it was that when Francisco Pizarro made his next distribution, Captain Garcilaso was favored with Tapacri, a rich repartimiento of from six to eight hundred Indians in the region of Cochapampa, the coveted lands surrounding the Imperial City having been assigned already to the earlier conquerors who had risked their lives and fortunes at Cajamarca.[27]

A significant element in the rewards of the conquest of all the Indies was the pleasure the conquerors took in the native women. Visible evidence of such adventures were rapidly accumulating from the northernmost points of exploration to the far reaches of Tahuantinsuyu, evidence made manifest in the race known as mestizos. This racial mixture in Peru undoubtedly began when the forces of Francisco Pizarro first touched those shores, and Pizarro himself made his contribution to its continuance, if not earlier, then most certainly by the time his ward, Angelina, daughter of Atahualpa, had attained a satisfactory age for carnal relations.[28] His distribution of Inca maidens, begun at Cajamarca, continued through those turbulent days when he was Hispanicizing the Imperial City; and since the men who joined him from the contingent of Pedro de Alvarado were feverish for such spoils, it can be assumed that he utilized this means to strengthen the ties of their loyalty.

---

[26] Garcilaso, *Comentarios*, Pt. II, Bk. II, Chap. 40; Bk. III, Chap. 1; Bk. VIII, Chap. 12; also Cieza de León, *Guerras civiles del Perú*, Bk. I, Chaps. 65, 86, 89.

[27] Garcilaso, *Comentarios*, Pt. I, Bk. III, Chap. 14; Pt. II, Bk. III, Chap. 2; Bk. VIII, Chap. 12; also Miró Quesada y Sosa, *El Inca Garcilaso*, p. 19.

[28] Garcilaso, *Comentarios*, Pt. I, Bk. IX, Chap. 38; Pt. II, Bk. III, Chap. 9. On Angelina, who later married Juan de Betanzos, Pizarro begot a son; on the ñusta Inés Huaillas, daughter of Huayna Cápac, he begot a daughter who afterward married her uncle, Hernando Pizarro.

Though praised posthumously for his continence, Sebastián Garcilaso obviously was not one to deny himself this species of reimbursement. The term was euphemistic and implied no more than relative
temperance or restraint. Yet the chastening veil of obscurity which
shrouds Sebastián's career while en route to Peru leaves uncertain the
date of his first contribution to the new race of mestizos. He may indeed have left significant traces of the Vega and Vargas blood in Mexico, Guatemala, or Tierra Firme. But at some time during his early
years in Peru, possibly soon after his arrival, he did beget a daughter
named Francisca de la Vega upon an Indian woman baptized as María
Pilcocissa.[29] Though almost nothing is known about this woman, the
few records which refer to her do mention Incaic origin, and in all
probability she was a lovely maiden named Pillcu Ciza who had regaled Hernando de Soto and Hernando Pizarro when they first encountered Atahualpa on the outskirts of Cajamarca. There are no
known records of any further relations Captain Garcilaso may have had
with her, though his solicitude for the welfare of his daughter suggests
that the mother was never abandoned and that she continued for some
time as an intimate member of his household. Be that as it may, by the
time Captain Garcilaso received his first repartimiento he had formed a
liaison with a second maiden, a royal granddaughter of the great Inca
Túpac Yupanqui, niece of the Inca Huayna Cápac, and first cousin to
the recently deposed Inca Manco.

She was the palla, Chimpu Ocllo.

The beginning of this liaison is as obscure as that of the Captain's
relations with María Pilcocissa, and it sometimes has been romanti-
cized to the point of sentimentality. The most plausible conception,
however, is that the palla was bestowed upon Captain Garcilaso as a
reward or a favor, and that through the ritual of baptism he converted
her into a new Christian and thus an acceptable concubine. For her
part, the palla, who still was no more than a child, simply would have
believed that she was carrying out the dictates of her ancestors and

<hr />

[29] Mexico, Archivo Nacional, Ramo Inquisición, Vol. 496, fols. 265–275v *passim*.
This collection of judicial papers henceforward will be listed as the Sarmiento Palacio
expediente.

would have accepted her new master with self-respect, pride, and loyalty; and to her the bewildering rite of baptism would have been as meaningful as a nuptial mass. There is no plausible evidence to indicate that she had ever cohabited with either Indian or Spaniard before coming into the possession of Captain Garcilaso, and her subsequent history suggests that she began her intimate relations with him at some time during the latter months of 1538.

PART ONE

THE MESTIZO

GÓMEZ SUÁREZ DE FIGUEROA

who was known in Spain as

El Inca Garcilaso de la Vega

CHAPTER ONE

O N APRIL 12, 1539, at Cuzco, Isabel Suárez Chimpu Ocllo, palla of Incaic lineage and concubine of the conquistador Captain Sebastián Garcilaso de la Vega, gave birth to a son.[1] This Peruvian boy, his copper skin paled with an alien pigment, was classified in the Spanish world as a mestizo. But it was as an Inca that he had entered the Indian world, an honor he could always claim, not because of his royal blood, since his descent was through a female of the line, but because of his having been sired by a fair-skinned conquistador whom the Indians superstitiously regarded as a viracocha and thus a legitimate descendant through male lineage of the Moon and the Sun.[2] According to his own later statement, he was born in the same dwelling as Diego de Alcobaza, another mestizo, whose father, Juan, is known to have served as the Captain's overseer. It is possible, therefore, that Captain Garcilaso at the time was tending his domain at Tapacri near La Plata, and had left his pregnant concubine in the care of the kindly Juan de Alcobaza, who held an estate just south of Cuzco called Surihualla. But whether at Cuzco or at Tapacri, Sebastián Garcilaso, as a pious Catholic, would have been as concerned with the welfare of his

---

[1] El Inca Garcilaso, *Los comentarios reales,* Pt. I, Bk. I, Chap. 1; Bk. III, Chap. 1; Bk. V, Chap. 10; also Pt. II, Bk. II, Chap. 25; Bk. IV, Chap. 42; Bk. VII, Chap. 1, See also title pages to Garcilaso's publications.

[2] Garcilaso, *Comentarios,* Pt. I, Bk. IX, Chap. 40.

son's soul as with his first breath, and he undoubtedly made arrangements promptly for Christian baptism. Thus while Francisco de Almendras, a first conqueror who had been at Cajamarca, stood by as spiritual godfather,[3] the mestizo was christened and given a name— not the customary saint's name so frequently and piously bestowed upon regenerated Indians, but a noble name long honored in Spain, a name borne by the Captain's eldest brother, by his maternal grandfather, and by many of his haughtiest kinsmen, among them the proud lords of Feria. Calling his mestizo Gómez Suárez de Figueroa, Captain Garcilaso tied him inexorably to Spain and bestowed upon him a fateful claim to a distinguished Hispanic lineage.[4]

The gift of an honored family name to a wilderness offspring, though not an unusual gesture among conquerors, is in itself an early evidence of a paternal solicitude which was to grow into an unusual tenderness and affection. Yet the birth of this infant so bound by blood to two ancient civilizations was to serve as something more than a means of arousing the Captain's paternal emotions. It was to bind him closer to the confused and defeated people of the Inca realm of Tahuantinsuyu; and it was to bring him the boon of a primitive allegiance that proved favorable to his fortune. For even though with a flexible conscience he could not have adjusted the event altogether to the discipline of his Catholic faith, the Incas found no such difficulty. To them this conqueror, by impregnating the palla, had bound himself with firmer ties than a Christian marriage vow, not only to the woman who bore his child, but to her royal kinsmen as well; and they in turn were willing to offer him both their fealty and their assistance in winning the land. The few existing records of Captain Garcilaso's experiences in the Indies indicate not only that he received this loyalty, but that he respected it and that he regarded the plight of the conquered with more sympathy and compassion than was usual among conquerors.

Since the infant Gómez' godfather had long been a resident of the Charcas, and since his own father was occupied during these times at Tapacri, he may have been taken in his earliest days, and even for bap-

---

[3] *Ibid.*, Pt. II, Bk. IV, Chap. 9.
[4] Garcilaso's baptismal name is to be found in many documents pertaining to his life, including the wills of both his father and his mother.

tism, to the chill regions of Alto Perú; yet the greater possibility is that he remained at Cuzco. Most certainly he was left in the custody of his mother, wherever she was, and it can be safely assumed that from the beginning he was subjected to the rigorous and traditional native customs which he afterward described with the clarity of experience. At birth and on each morning thereafter, Inca children were plunged into icy water before being wrapped in a comforting blanket, though in moments of tenderness a mother sometimes warmed the water in her mouth before applying it to indignant flesh. Babies who became ill were often bathed in their own urine or given thereof to drink, or, in rare cases, permitted to chew upon a detached remnant of their own umbilical cords. For three months their arms were swaddled in bands, and when they were old enough to leave the cradle, they daily were submerged to the chest in a cavity in the earth and left to amuse themselves with a few trifles.

But in no matters was their training more rigid than in those concerning food. For two years they were permitted no nourishment other than their mother's milk and that, regardless of hunger, only three times daily. Even when suckled, they were forced to rise on their knees and exhaust the supply of one breast before crawling to the other to repeat the performance. Never would an Inca mother take her child upon her lap lest he be weakened by coddling. The process of suckling a child entailed more than providing material nourishment, and the stoic lessons which the infant Gómez undoubtedly received while feeding at his mother's breasts will excuse his later overworking of the outworn Biblical metaphor of drinking in knowledge with his mother's milk. What is significant, however, is that the boy's earliest lessons and his earliest knowledge was Incaic. Even as he began to seek vocal symbols to utter his hungers and longings, a royal Inca mother placed upon his tongue the vocabulary of Tahuantinsuyu, and she instinctively filled his groping mind with the ideals, values, and concepts of her pagan people. The first words he uttered, it stands to reason, were Quechua, and the first knowledge he absorbed was the ancient wisdom of the Children of the Sun.

Because of his mystic origin, Gómez, like all mestizos, was set apart by his Indian relatives for special consideration, for they firmly believed that the blood of white conquerors or viracochas gave these boys superior claims. Yet before Gómez had scarcely reached the age of weaning, Peru was torn by new civil strife which anticipated the melancholy future of all mestizos in the Spanish colonies and at the same time established the fortunes of Garcilaso de la Vega. At Los Reyes, the mestizo Diego de Almagro the Lad, unable to forget what he had lost through the defeat and execution of his father, had yielded to the persuasions of a rash group known as the men of Chile and was contemplating extreme measures for defending his claims. Though warned several times of the plots of these men, Francisco Pizarro had underestimated their force and regarded their boldness with contempt. He was therefore unprepared and inadequately protected when on Sunday, June 26, 1541, Juan de Vargas, one of his pages, rushed to him with news that assassins were approaching. At the moment the Marqués was dining with his half brother Martín de Alcántara, Garcilaso's cousin Gómez de Luna, and other men of import who might have come to his assistance; but most of those present took immediate flight, and when one companion, sent to bolt the door, paused to attempt a parley, he was rewarded with a slash that left his head attached by no more than a mere skin. Lacking time to put on defensive arms, Pizarro and Alcántara, with the assistance of two pages, seized swords and struck out vainly at the foe. Soon Alcántara and both pages lay dead, and Pizarro, pierced through the neck and sprawling in his own blood, was pleading for a confessor. None being available, the mortally wounded man attempted his own absolution. Some say that he simply raised his hand and kissed it while feebly outlining a cross; others, that he dipped his fingers in his own blood and tracing the holy symbol on the floor, breathed a "Jesus" as assassins dashed out his brains with an earthen jar. In the waning hours of the afternoon, Negro menials dragged his body to the cathedral to give it hasty burial lest the head be severed and placed on exhibit by the men of Chile, who now were in command of the city and already had proclaimed Almagro the Lad sole Governor of Peru.

Temporarily a proud mestizo held the authority of the land. But the pretense of that mestizo was a vain yearning and a misguided dream, and his brief moment of command represents a tragic interlude. Even before the murder of the Marqués, the Emperor had ordered Cristóbal Vaca de Castro to Peru to cooperate with Pizarro in establishing peace and, in the event of the latter's death, to succeed to his government. Thus when Vaca de Castro arrived in his jurisdiction and learned of the death of the Marqués, he immediately began preparations to take up arms against Almagro and his rebellious comrades.

One of the pages who had perished while giving aid to the Marqués was Juan de Vargas, son of Captain Garcilaso's beloved cousin, Gómez de Tordoya , whom, because of his previous record of sedition in Spain, the King on February 13, 1541, had ordered banished from all realms under the jurisdiction of the Spanish Crown.[5] Yet when news of the upheaval at Los Reyes reached Cuzco, Gómez de Tordoya, who at the moment was in the adjacent countryside hawking, wrung the neck of his falcon, and crying that it now was time for a war with sword and flame, hastened back into the city and began organizing forces for the sovereign who had disclaimed him. Soon he was joined by Garcilaso, and together they led out a contingent of men to augment the gathering strength of Vaca de Castro. Subsequently there were negotiations for peace, but when Almagro discovered evidence of attempts to lure off some of his leaders, even in the midst of overtures for reconciliation, he flew into a justifiable rage, declaring among other things that he would never acknowledge or obey the new Governor so long as he consorted with such loyal Pizarrists as Garcilaso de la Vega and Gómez de Tordoya. Not only had he been provided occasion to observe the loyalty of Garcilaso in the previous struggle between the Marqués and the elder Almagro, but he regarded Gómez de Tordoya as one of the prime instigators of that struggle.[6] Eventually, on September 16, 1542, a dark and rainy day, the forces of the two leaders, both proclaiming loyalty to the King, met on the plains of Chupas to determine the course of Peru.

In the battle of Chupas, one of the bloodiest of the Peruvian civil

[5] Garcilaso, *Comentarios*, Pt. II, Bk. III, Chap. 7; Pedro Pizarro, *Relación del descubrimiento y conquista de los reinos del Perú*, p. 167; Sevilla, Archivo General de Indias, Audiencia de Lima, Legajo 566, Libro 4, folio 154.

[6] Garcilaso, *Comentarios*, Pt. II, Bk. III, Chaps. 11, 15; Bk. VIII, Chap. 12; letter dated November 8, 1541, in *Colección de domumentos inéditos del Archivo de Indias*, Vol. III, pp. 215–221.

wars, both Garcilaso and Gómez de Tordoya commanded contingents
for Vaca de Castro, though marshal of all the Governor's forces was
Francisco de Carvajal, who, but a few years later, was to seek Garcilaso's life. It was two hours before dusk when the armies met, and
there was reluctance on the part of certain royalists to enter the struggle, a reluctance intensified not only by gathering shadows but by the
fact that some had never ceased to feel that Almagro fought a justified cause. Nevertheless, hesitation was banished with promises of
repartimientos, and all scruples were dispersed by a sudden attack from
forces under the command of Paullu Inca, a son of Huayna Cápac, who
had remained loyal to the Almagros. Once begun, the desperate battle
continued into the night until the Almagrists either laid down their
arms or fled. As darkness enveloped the plains, cries were heard from
hundreds of wounded and dying who lay exposed to the fearful cold
and the ravages of plundering Indians, and when men sought out the
stricken to bring them aid, they found among them both Gómez de
Tordoya and Garcilaso de la Vega. The injuries of the latter apparently
were superficial, but those of Gómez de Tordoya were mortal, and
strangely he had to some extent evoked this fate. For, in order to display the magnitude of his deeds, he had vaingloriously worn over his
armor a conspicuous cloak of white velvet, studded with ornaments of
gold. The death several days later of this seditious but beloved Vargas-
Figueroa cousin, who had shared most of his early adventures in the
Indies, must have given some impetus to Captain Garcilaso in his next
mission, which was to hasten in pursuit of the Lad, who had slipped
away to join the Inca Manco Cápac at Villcapampa.[7]

In Cuzco the Indians had witnessed the progress of the quarrel with
a bewilderment and confusion of loyalties which the captain's concubine must have shared. As she watched her lord and master ride out in
pursuit of the mestizo pretender, she simultaneously had seen her
royal but pagan cousin, Paullu Inca, enter the city to gather recruits and
arms for the forces of that same pretender. And now as she awaited
the outcome of the battle of Chupas, she was to observe the defeated
Almagro speeding back into the city and tarrying beyond wisdom be-

    [7] Garcilaso, *Comentarios,* Pt. II, Bk. III, Chap. 18; Bk. VIII, Chap. 12; *Cartas
de Indias,* Vol. I, pp. 504–521.

fore hastening on toward the protection of the pagan Incas and the wilderness. Then in hot pursuit came her lord Garcilaso, too late to seize his prey, though the fugitives were not far distant and men capable of continuing the pursuit could be bought—Almagrists who were ready to barter their loyalties for the hope of pardon and reward. Even while these men of easy conscience were stalking the mestizo to whom they so recently had pledged allegiance, the bells of Cuzco were tolling the dead of Chupas, and in the church of San Cristóbal a pious friar was conducting a requiem for the departed soul of Gómez de Tordoya. The echoes of the bells had scarcely faded when the mestizo Lad was returned to Cuzco and placed in the custody of Captain Garcilaso de la Vega.[8] Meanwhile near the site of the recent battlefield, Francisco de Carvajal had apprehended and hanged Almagro's campmaster, Pedro de Oñate, whose death released a rich repartimiento as well as a manorial dwelling at Cuzco, both of which Captain Garcilaso perhaps already coveted and eventually was to receive.

Many were moved to compassion by the plight of the captive Lad, now but twenty years of age, who in reality had been but a tool in the hands of rash and ambitious comrades; and one would like to think that Captain Garcilaso, recalling the consideration he himself had received as a prisoner of the elder Almagro, was among those who pled for this handsome mestizo when Vaca de Castro arrived in the city to demand atonement. But soon the shadows of a new scaffold fell across the great market plaza, and shortly after, as Indians and Spaniards swarmed about the place of execution or peered from surrounding balconies, the ill-fated youth, accompanied by soldiers and consoling friars and protesting only when the town crier proclaimed him seditious, strode proudly to the block and knelt to receive the blow which removed his head. At length, when a merciful pall of darkness had settled over the city, friends bore his remains to the convent of La Merced and placed them alongside those of his father. The tapers which cast their dim lights in the Chapel of Mercy and the Latin

---

[8] Garcilaso, *Comentarios,* Pt. II, Bk. III, Chap. 17; Pedro de Cieza de León, *Guerras civiles del Perú,* Pt. II, Chap. 82; *Cartas de Indias,* Vol. I, pp. 504–521. In his flight, Almagro is said to have stopped in Cuzco long enough to permit a comrade to visit his concubine.

phrases which sped the soul on its journey through a Catholic purgatory were purchased with alms. The sole legacy of this tragic youth was an empty purse and a hopeless ambition. His unnamed heirs were the mestizos of Peru.

Such was the eventual reward which a bold half-caste received for holding too tenaciously to claims based on the services of one of the most significant of the first conquerors. And over many who witnessed the tragedy of this disillusioned youth there swept a foreboding sense of what eventually, in the tricky politics of the Spanish possessions, might await other offspring of Spaniards and Indians. Captain Garcilaso surely sensed it as his eyes fell upon his own son; and the little mestizo Gómez himself, scarcely three years of age at the time, may even have trembled with some innate premonition of his own destiny as he watched the dismal spectacle unroll. Decades later, when time had dimmed his infant memories and clarified the event, and when his own experiences had unfolded before him the obstacles awaiting mestizos who pretended, he declared with both compassion and praise that the younger Almagro would have been the greatest mestizo ever born had he but submitted to the authority of his sovereign.[9]

And yet in this somewhat ironical comment, he was but recording echoes of the sentiments of conquerors who had witnessed the whole somber tragedy of the Almagros—sentiments which, though mingled with compassion, were infused with thoughts of survival. For the doleful events of this drama had made men even more poignantly conscious of the capriciousness of professed loyalties and of the fact that throughout the limits of colonial Spain, both now and on down through the fickle years, their survival and their fortunes must rest not on justice but on a victory which eventually and inevitably fell to those who held the favor of their sovereign. To defy that sovereign was to gamble at great odds, and the loser must be prepared for violent atonement.

In the struggle with the elder Almagro, Captain Garcilaso, never certain of the King's pleasure in the matter, had gambled wisely. In the struggle with the Lad, there had been no question as to where he

---

[9] Garcilaso, *Comentarios,* Pt. II, Bk. III, Chap. 18.

should place his allegiance, and the element of chance was negligible. Now the reward was to be vastly more than mere survival. On October 3, 1542, scarcely a month after the battle at Chupas, the Cabildo named him Lieutenant and Captain General of Cuzco, Arequipa, and the Charcas; and on January 20 of the succeeding year, they informed the King of the meritorious role Captain Garcilaso had played in the apprehension of the Lad. But his material award was to come from an admiring and appreciative governor. On November 24, 1542, Vaca de Castro mentioned him favorably in a report to the King, and on February 12, 1543, he made his gratitude tangible with an award of some of the richest repartimientos in the coveted vicinity of Cuzco.[10] The decree of conferral not only reveals the magnitude of the gift but provides a record of Vaca de Castro's opinion of the loyalty of the man he was awarding. For herein he meticulously listed Garcilaso's services in the subjugation of the natives as well as in the ensuing struggles with the Almagros, and he added that the Captain had performed these services with his person and his arms and horse, and at his own expense and diminution.

Stated within the decree was a clause to the effect that Garcilaso had relinquished his claim on his repartimiento at Tapacri, and one is therewith led to believe that an agreement had been reached with Vaca de Castro before the bestowal of the gift and perhaps even when promises of reward were being made at the beginning of the battle of Chupas. Service to the Crown was a matter of honor and chivalry, but there was nothing dishonorable or unchivalric about driving a suitable bargain for recompense. The gold and silver of Potosí had not yet been uncovered, and Garcilaso like many others looked with yearning upon the estates near Cuzco which had fallen to the first conquerors. But the extent of his new fortune must have been even more than he had anticipated because he now was in possession of estates lying on three sides of the Imperial City, in the regions of Chinchasuyu, Cuntisuyu, and Collasuyu. Moreover, the significance of these estates can be

<hr>

[10] *Cartas de Indias,* Vol. I, pp. 473–494, 504–521, and Vol. II, p. 784; Garcilaso, *Comentarios,* Pt. I, Bk. III, Chap. 12; Pt. II, Bk. III, Chap. 19; Bk. VIII, Chap. 12. For a detailed description of the reward, see Archivo General de Indias, Justicia, Leg. 433, fols. 9v–10v. This collection of judicial papers henceforward will be referred to as the Martel-Cabrera expediente.

judged by the names of the men who formerly had held them: Hernán
and Pedro de Oñate, Bishop Friar Vicente de Valverde, and the Marqués Francisco Pizarro.

Possessed of new holdings, the Captain now was in need of an appropriate dwelling in Cuzco. Among the choice habitations available
was the manorial house which had belonged to the recently-hanged
Pedro de Oñate. Since records refer to this property as belonging to
Oñate as late as 1542, and since it passed about this time to Garcilaso,
it must have come simultaneously with the acquisition of the Oñate repartimiento.[11] It was located on the west side of the Cussipata, later
referred to as "the plaza of the races," since it served most frequently
for cane games and tournaments; and since this plaza was separated
from the Haucaipata or main plaza by no more than a small arroyo, the
two formed an immense public square. The house, like many in the
city, represented the typical Spanish construction superimposed as a
second and third floor on massive and indestructible Incaic walls.
Within were large and small rooms for eating and sleeping, and surrounding its several courtyards were numerous habitations which offered shelter to relatives, friends, retainers, and menials. In the rear
were stables with an outside entrance, though it was not unusual for
horsemen to ride in or out through a courtyard opening. Built across
the front of the house was a commodious gallery which not only commanded a superb view of the shimmering white peaks to the east, but,
opening directly on the two chief plazas, gave access to the very nerve
center of the city. Throughout his boyhood and youth, therefore,
Gómez was to witness from the portals of his father's mansion much of
the macabre panorama of life and death which moved fitfully across
the central stage of the ancient city.

With such a vast demesne, a manorial household and an enviable
fiefdom, Captain Garcilaso now could anticipate the enjoyment of his
New World possessions. Vaca de Castro had succeeded in establishing
a semblance of serenity in the whole of Peru, and though as Governor

---

[11] Garcilaso, *Comentarios*, Pt. I, Bk. VII, Chap. 11; Pt. II, Bk. V, Chap. 2. Gar-
cilaso mistakenly recorded that the house formerly had belonged to Francisco de
Oñate "who died in the battle of Chupas." It was Pedro de Oñate who died at
Chupas. See Aurelio Miró Quesada y Sosa, *El Inca Garcilaso*, pp. 42–49, 267–278.
The house still exists and can be seen in Cuzco today.

he sometimes was partial in his favors, Garcilaso was one of those who enjoyed that partiality. Also, the Indians seemed inclined more than ever to spiritual regeneration, and in their conversion the Captain, through his fortunate liaison with the Incaic family, exerted an unusual influence. In 1543, when Paullu Inca and his brother, Titu Auqui, sons of Huayna Cápac, were baptized, the one as Cristóbal and the other as Felipe, it was Captain Garcilaso who stood as their godfather.[12] Moreover, he apparently encouraged, and certainly did not discourage, the regular assemblies of the remnant Incas in his own dwelling, for his son has recorded that throughout his life in Cuzco, they came each week to the habitation of his mother to recount the glories of their vanished empire and to lament what they had lost.

Thus the Captain's mestizo, even in these early years, while still viewing the world through Indian eyes, was associated constantly with those who were most capable of relating the facts and fictions of Tahuantinsuyu. He was to know intimately not only Cristóbal Paullu, his brother Felipe Titu, and their mother Añas, but many of the other numerous offspring of the great emperor, Huayna Cápac, including Beatriz Coya and the ñustas Leonor and Inez, whose mestizo sons were his playmates. Furthermore, among those who came to visit with his mother were men and women whose experiences reached back to the time of his great-grandfather, the Inca Túpac Yupanqui. Profoundly honored by Isabel Suárez Chimpu Ocllo and always present at births and weanings and sickbeds was an aged sister of that great Inca; and possibly living in the vicinity was a daughter of the Inca Túpac Yupanqui, a woman who after marriage to the Indian Martín Huaman Mallqui became the mother of that curious and picturesque Quechuan historian, Felipe Huaman Poma de Ayala. But the most garrulous and consequently most informative of those who appear always to have been present were his mother's ancient uncle, Cusi Huallpa, and her brother, Francisco Huallpa Túpac. Gómez later declared that he had known more than two hundred Incas and pallas, and he would not have been able to estimate the number of Indians of lower status with whom he came in contact in Cuzco and in his wanderings through

[12] Garcilaso, *Comentarios,* Pt. I, Bk. VI, Chap. 2.

various parts of the realm. The significant fact is that all of these Indians were ever ready to pour into the mind of a beloved and eager mestizo the lore of Tahuantinsuyu.

Fortunately the boy's early years were passed soon after the conquest and before Hispanic ideas had robbed the natives of some of their more poetic Indian concepts. Living close to the earth and close to the heavens, they carried within them still a persistent sense of the oneness of the universe and a semi-pantheistic vision of all cosmic elements and forces. In their minds, all things formed one complete scheme, and in all things they looked for and found mysterious and personal signs and omens. And so it was that when the curious mind of the little mestizo first began to question the secrets of the enfolding world, his Indian kinsmen answered him with living and beautiful images which encompassed both meaning and purpose. They told of mysterious genii that dwelled in sticks and stones, in the birds and beasts, and in all visible forms. They told of an enchanting palla poised high in the heavens with a great urn from which she poured rain and hail and snow down upon a needy earth; and when the dread thunder and lightning pierced the Andean skies, they declared that an angry brother had struck that urn. They explained the milky galaxy and warned of the omens in comets, and they explained the splotches on the moon as the remains of a female fox who, enchanted by the beauty of the moon, had been mutilated when she sought to seize the chaste huntress. They pointed out to him the silent and inaccessible stars in the celestial realm and they said that stars, since they could be seen only at night, were the handmaidens of the Moon, the silvery queen of the heavens, who was sister-consort of the golden solar disk that rolled across the Andean skies, bringing life and warmth to the Children of the Sun. And they told of how the Sun, as he disappeared over the western horizon, dived like a valiant swimmer into the great Ocean Sea to dry up with his fires the waters on which floated the broad lands of Tahuantinsuyu. Then through the names of Manco Cápac and Mama Ocllo, first Incas, they linked his lineage with the Moon and the Sun and made him and all sentient and insentient things an integral part of a vast cosmos emanating from the great and invisible Pachacámac and bound by infinite ties of benevolence. To the little mestizo, shrouded in an Indian world, such concepts became realities, and each day as he set forth to regard the phenomena of that world, they became a permanent part of the structure of his eventually complex mind and nature.

These early concepts were to grow and modify as Gómez came in contact with Indians from other sections of the realm, and as he began to mingle with other mestizos whose mothers were not native to Cuzco; for these boys, like himself, had been indoctrinated in varied facets of Inca lore. Yet as the sons of Spanish fathers, they also had been subjected to the rudiments of Christianity, and over each there gradually was spreading a veneer of Hispanic mysticism which served to increase both their wonder and confusion as they observed the new intrigues soon to envelop the land. For many of the less hallowed forces of Christendom still reigned in Peru, and the tranquility that had marked the government of Vaca de Castro was not to continue. Carefully inseminated in the minds of these naive boys by Spanish mentors was the worn explanation that now as always the Devil was simply vexed by the progress of Christianity, but most of their sires professed to detect the Devil in this instance robed in the sable vestments of a Dominican friar, Bartolomé de las Casas, who, in his zeal to bring relief to the Indians, was sparking a flame which soon burst into a holocaust.

First priest to be ordained in the Americas, Las Casas for years had challenged the popular dogma that Spain's dominion in the Indies could be morally justified on the basis of the papal donation of 1493. Indeed he had succeeded in developing the idea that Spaniards in America were scarcely more than interlopers and as such should treat the natives with justice and mercy and under no circumstances hold them as slaves. In 1517, he won the approval of the Crown to a curious scheme designed to replace Indian slaves with Negroes, a scheme which not only failed but afterward humiliated him and tortured his conscience. Most of the next twenty-odd years Las Casas passed in the Indies; but in 1539 he had returned to Spain and exerted an unusual pressure on the conscience of the King with a series of frenzied tracts depicting Spanish cruelty in the Indies and laying the foundation for what is regarded today as the "black legend."

Many Peruvians who had known Las Casas in his secular days and later, distrusted his efforts, and when his activities threatened to deprive them of hard-earned fortunes and indeed to place them under economic duress, they declared that he was simply a misguided zealot who, under the guise of conscience and religion, had taken measures to deceive the Crown with proposals for the propagation of Catholicism and the increase of the royal revenue. But whatever the true purpose of Las Casas, the result of his latest efforts was the passage of forty decrees known as the New Laws, which, in addition to defining the powers and functions of the Council of the Indies and the audiencias being newly organized in America for the execution of those powers, demanded that these audiencias put an end to slavery as well as all other abuses of the Indians. And the definition of those who were to relinquish repartimientos of Indians was so all-inclusive as to leave few with any hope for exemption. Thus that nascent feudal aristocracy which in the past the Crown had set up to encourage conquest and subsequent exploitation was suddenly replaced by a system of royal absolutism which promised economic defeat and even ruin for the majority of those men who had been responsible for winning the New World and its riches for Spain.

The New Laws were ratified by Charles V on November 2, 1542, but they were not issued until April, 1543. Though met with bitterness in Mexico, serious trouble was averted there by the Viceroy Antonio de Mendoza and by Francisco Tello de Sandoval, the envoy charged with announcing them. The result, however, was to be different in Peru, where enforcement of the ordinances had been entrusted to a new Audiencia of quarreling justices, headed by Blasco Núñez Vela, a man of little patience and discernment, whom the King had named as his first Viceroy to that realm. Accompanying these men to Peru were the Viceroy's nephew, Juan Polo de Ondegardo, and his factor, Agustín de Zárate, both of whom eventually were to emerge as reliable chroniclers.

It was only after January 10, 1544, when the Viceroy arrived at Panama and began putting the new decrees into effect, that the men of Peru became seriously conscious of possible consequences. Núñez Vela was warned of the danger of seeking to enforce such statutes in a region where the survivors of the recent Almagro rebellion felt that they deserved further rewards rather than a diminution of the privileges and estates already enjoyed. But the pompous emissary, ignoring the advice of his Audiencia, merely replied with threats and proceeded to Túmbez, from whence he dispatched messengers to Los Reyes and Cuzco to announce his authority. Long before his arrival, the tenor of the new regulations had been published at Cuzco and the air was rife with blasphemy. On receipt of the news that he had been superseded in office, Vaca de Castro readily acquiesced and desisted from exercising his previous powers, but a short time before, he had taken the opportunity to bestow several plantations of Indians upon certain persons whom he felt to be deserving, among them Sebastián Garcilaso. And so it was that on March 18, 1544, the Captain came into possession of five more towns of Indians, formerly belonging to Francisco Pizarro, in the province of Havisca, which lay in the region of Cuntisuyu.[13] With this new reward added to his already vast estate, he therefore was eligible to become one of the principal losers under the threats of Blasco Núñez, and he of course shared the apprehension if not the bitterness of his companions. And this apprehension increased as the new Viceroy advanced south, since he continued to enforce the decrees to the letter and made no promises other than that he would bring complaints to the attention of the King. At length, when he arrived in Los Reyes and amid a display of crimson and silver was invested with his new authority, cabals were formed and warnings sent to other groups throughout the realm. The entire land was inflamed, but the turmoil at Cuzco exceeded that of any other city.

As a man of dignity and prudence, Captain Garcilaso surely confined most of his objections to the council chamber. Like a number of others, he nourished a hope that by sending a competent emissary to Los Reyes, holders of estates could persuade the Viceroy to delay enforcement of the New Laws until an appeal could be made before the King himself. Meanwhile, since Vaca de Castro had refused to take part in any opposition and instead had set out for Los Reyes to submit to the man who had succeeded him in authority, Captain Garcilaso did join with fellow citizens in a scheme to obtain someone else to represent them.[14] The most logical man, they concluded, and certainly the

13 Martel-Cabrera expediente, fols. 16–16v, *passim*.
14 Garcilaso, *Comentarios,* Pt. II, Bk. IV, Chaps. 7–8.

most capable, was Gonzalo Pizarro, who at the moment was enjoying a rich repartimiento at La Plata, where only a year or two previously Garcilaso had served as an alcalde. So to this man these anxious citizens now dispatched a plea for assistance.

Gonzalo Pizarro at first feigned reluctance and then accepted the invitation. In consequence, the fortunes of Peru soon came to rest perilously in the balance between two obstinate men: a half-mad and overzealous viceroy, and a proud, lovable, and ambitious procurator general who was unalterably convinced of his own right by both conquest and succession to the authority of the land. The petition rendered him had been made honestly and with no idea of sedition; yet, strangely, intimate associates like Captain Garcilaso apparently had misjudged Gonzalo Pizarro, since behind his veneer of reticence—his avowed hesitation to give the appearance of questioning royal dictates—there lurked a stubborn determination which could not be satisfied with subservience to a viceroy who threatened deserving conquerors with economic ruin.

Furthermore, Pizarro lacked the naive faith that a mere appeal bolstered with reason was sufficient to move the new Viceroy to mitigation. Like Francisco de Carvajal, whom he promptly drew to his assistance, he felt that smooth words would be far less effective than a show of arms. Thus when he arrived in Cuzco to make preparations for his mission, the city began to take on the semblance of an armed camp, and many were alarmed lest what purported to be a peaceful and justifiable plea should eventually come to be regarded as a manifestation of sedition. Captain Garcilaso, among others, remonstrated privately with Pizarro,[15] but the latter quickly excused the militant aspect of his preparations by referring to necessity for protection along the highroad against the guerillas of the Inca Manco and in Los Reyes against the Viceroy himself, who was known to have boasted of the power to deprive Pizarro of his head. Soon Blasco Núñez, on being advised of activities at Cuzco, sent messengers demanding that all citizens of that city repair at once to Los Reyes and submit to the authority of the King, and Garcilaso as well as his comrades was aware that to defy such a

15 *Ibid.*, Pt. II, Bk. IV, Chaps. 8–9.

summons was to subject himself to a suspicion of disloyalty. Nevertheless, when Pizarro threatened to return to the Charcas rather than
hurl himself unarmed into such a perilous situation, he won support;
and when eventually he departed for Los Reyes on a purportedly
peaceful mission, he was accompanied by a host of vassal Indians, a
glittering battery of artillery, an army of several hundred stalwart and
well-caparisoned Spaniards, and a plenitude of gold taken illegally
from the King's coffers. Furthermore, he had placed Francisco de
Almendras, godfather of the mestizo Gómez, along the direct route to
Los Reyes to intercept all travelers, and had left two vassals near Arequipa to provide whatever protection might be needed along the coast.

CHAPTER TWO

THOUGH PURPORTEDLY THE OBJECT of Gonzalo Pizarro's journey to Los Reyes was merely to represent the citizens of Cuzco in a plea that the enforcement of the New Laws be delayed, the military aspect of his entourage could have left little doubt as to his real design and the passions which drove him toward that design. His mission was not to be a supplication but a demand, which, if resisted, he would have the means of enforcing. And there now could have been but few who were unaware that he would not hesitate to utilize any favorable opportunity to assume the supreme authority of the land. Yet among those cavaliers who rode alongside Pizarro as he set out so militantly from Cuzco was Captain Garcilaso de la Vega. But Captain Garcilaso had begun that journey with much apprehension and surely under some duress; and even as he rode out of the city he was fomenting a conspiracy among friends to withdraw at the first opportunity from such a semblance of rebellion. Furthermore, by the time the contingent had reached the plains of Sacsahuana he and a number of his friends definitely had resolved to abandon the leadership of Pizarro and hasten in a separate group to submit to the summons of the Viceroy. Records vary as to how they managed to do so. Some say that they obtained permission from the Procurator to return to Cuzco for the purpose of putting their affairs in better order and obtaining more adequate supplies; others, that they merely fled under cover of darkness. Be that as it may, they were none the less gone, and Pizarro soon was aware of their desertion.

First, the fugitives did return to Cuzco, dashing back to their great houses to take on supplies for a long and circuitous journey to Los Reyes. Since they knew the route through the sierras and plains to be guarded, their only hope lay to the south by way of Arequipa and the coast, where they planned to seize Pizarro's vessels and proceed north across open and unobstructed seas. But horses must be shod and food provided for a number of days, and as servants and menials scurried back and forth, there were whispered confidences and cautions, and instructions for burying treasures and bolting doors, for always there were people eager to betray. At length, when everything was in readiness, forty fleeing horsemen vanished into the Andean night, speeding now toward Arequipa and the sea. And left in the Garcilaso mansion to meet whatever adversities might befall them were the Captain's concubine and two of his children, guarded solely by his majordomo, Juan de Alcobaza.[1]

Gómez was but five years of age when in 1544 he saw his father in this desperate flight from Gonzalo Pizarro; but he was old enough to experience some of the terror which accompanies the forces of vengeance. Huddled behind the doors of his father's house with his mother and sister, doubtlessly Francisca de la Vega,[2] he listened to the clattering hooves fading in the distance and anticipated the sound of avenging horsemen, who, all knew, soon would come. And come they did. For Gonzalo Pizarro, deserted by the very men who so earnestly had requested his aid, and so despondent that he was contemplating flight to the Charcas, had resolved first to focus his wrath upon those who had humbled him, chief among whom he regarded as Sebastián Garcilaso. And whatever his plans for vengeance, he without question was encouraged by Francisco de Carvajal, who notoriously held no

---

[1] El Inca Garcilaso, *Los comentarios reales*, Pt. II, Bk. IV, Chap. 10; Bk. VIII, Chap. 12; Agustín de Zárate, *Historia del descubrimiento y conquista del Perú*, Bk. V, Chap. 8, Diego Fernández, *Historia del Perú*, ed. Odriozola. Pt. I, Bk. I, Chap. 14.

[2] Garcilaso, *Comentarios*, Pt. II, Bk. IV, Chap. 10. "Quedaron ocho personas en ella desamparadas: mi madre fué la una, y una hermana mía, y una criada, etc." In speaking of his half sisters Garcilaso always used the word "hermana."

sympathy for men who under any circumstances shifted professed loyalties and who from that moment began to harbor an intense antipathy for Garcilaso de la Vega. Soon there came an ominous pounding on the Garcilaso doors, followed by an inrush of men with orders to raze the dwelling and punish the most intimate members of the Captain's establishment. At once plunderers seized everything they could lay hands on and would have left the house in flames but for several wise and persuasive tongues. But then all Indian servants were commanded to depart, and for a time the Captain's concubine and his children as well as his majordomo remained in imminent peril of death. Ultimately, however, Alcobaza was exonerated on the basis of his past selflessness, and Gómez, his mother, and his sister were saved when compassionate and reasonable men, friends of both Pizarro and Garcilaso, reminded avengers that simple women and children were not to be held responsible for the conduct of their masters.

But for many months these victims of a political quarrel which they scarcely could have comprehended lived in anguish and fear. Threats against them persisted, and they were constantly aware that vindictive soldiers might return at any moment to put them to death. Moreover, they shortly were to learn that at least one man had not relinquished his yearning to destroy the Captain's house. Trained ever on its entrance from directly across the market plaza was a menacing cannon, mounted before the house of Hernando Bachicao, Pizarro's master of ordnance. Once there were loud bursts of cannon fire as great iron balls thudded against the doors of Captain Garcilaso's house. But the massive portals held, the cannon was silenced, and the besieged were left to starve. This they indeed might have done but for faithful Indians who, until deterred by growing danger, managed to slip morsels of food into the house at all hours of the day and night. At length García Pauqui, loyal cacique of two of the Captain's towns of Indians, determined to risk his life in his master's interest and somehow managed to deliver a sufficient supply of grain to maintain the inmates for some months to come. Meanwhile, Gonzalo Pizarro, leaving a deputy at Cuzco, moved on to Huamanca. Here, from Pedro de Puelles, a renegade from the Viceroy, he received news that encouraged him to continue to Los Reyes, and, smarting still from his recent experience, he either now or shortly afterward promised the scurrilous Puelles the rich estates of Garcilaso de la Vega.

In abandoning Pizarro, Garcilaso had indeed deceived at a delicate moment a comrade to whom he owed much. But at the same time he had persisted in placing his allegiance where he always had intimated he would place it, and this in the face of possible ruin. Yet had Garcilaso and his companions been able to foresee the outcome of their flight, some of them at least might have altered their decisions. For on coming to Arequipa they learned that the ships they had hoped to utilize already had been seized and carried to Callao. In desperation they set about constructing a vessel, though none of them had knowledge of shipbuilding and all available timber was green. After forty days they had completed a ship which appeared seaworthy, but when laden it sank into the depths of the sea. Their only course now was to risk the perilous route along a hot, sandy coastline, and this they did, arriving by some miracle at their destination without interference or difficulty.[3] As the low mud roofs and green gardens of Los Reyes came into view, their spirits were lifted with the thought that at last they could unite with the forces of the King's Viceroy, and it was in this mood that they entered the city.

But they found no Viceroy.

What they found was a settlement teeming with fear and dissension. For during their flight, momentous changes had taken place in Los Reyes. Always at odds, Blasco Núñez and his Audiencia had permitted their rift to widen until it became a matter of public knowledge and interest. With the passing weeks the Justices had urged the rescinding of the New Laws, while the Viceroy merely grew more obstinate. Even Vaca de Castro, who had submitted without protest to the new government, the Viceroy had distrusted and kept in confinement. Then one evil night, in a moment of unjustified fear and resentment, he had murdered Yllén Suárez de Caravajal, an innocent and loyal adherent; and when he attempted to conceal his mad act, the citizens were thrown into terror. Many fled to Gonzalo Pizarro, while others turned to the Justices. At length, when Blasco Núñez, alarmed at the approaching

---

[3] *Ibid.*, Pt. II, Bk. IV, Chap. 10; Bk. VIII, Chap. 12.

cohorts of Pizarro, had spoken of razing the capital and shifting the seat of authority to Trujillo, the reaction of both Justices and citizens had grown violent. Seizing the Viceroy and placing him under custody in a vessel bound for Panama, the Justices had taken into their own hands the authority of Peru.

It is possible that had Blasco Núñez and his Audiencia but known that men of the caliber of Garcilaso de la Vega and his companions had abandoned Pizarro, they would have resisted the new threats with more courage, and the citizens of Los Reyes would have been less bold about shifting allegiance. But this was a condition contrary to fact and did not alter the dilemma in which the fugitives now found themselves. Again it was a dilemma which called for quick decisions. Some fled at once to the Indians, and some to the perilous wilderness of the Andes. Others chose to await the turn of events in Los Reyes, feeling some security in the fact that the city still remained in the hands of four Judge Advocates of the King, who, in an effort to restore order and rob Pizarro of all excuse for his march, had temporarily repealed the hated New Laws. Among the latter was Captain Garcilaso, who forthwith took lodging with Hernán Pérez Tablero, a soldier-servant of Estremadura, whose father and grandfather had served the Vargas household for many years in Spain. Here he awaited his destiny in accumulating consternation, for as the days fled, the strength of the Justices weakened and the increasing forces of the Procurator General moved menacingly closer toward Los Reyes.

Hoping somehow to stay the encroaching peril, the Justices dispatched messengers to inform Pizarro of the Viceroy's departure and the suspension of the hated ordinances, and to demand that he disband his militant entourage and retire to his estates. But the news borne by these messengers came late, since Pizarro, encouraged by defections, was prepared to reveal the real motive back of his mission, his ambition to become Governor and Captain General of the land. This post he now boldly demanded, and when the Justices sought to delay with excuses, he threatened Los Reyes with fire and sword. Then one somber night, while the city lay protected by no more than fifty men who could boast arms, Francisco de Carvajal crept in with a band of soldiers and, in his search for those who had abandoned his chieftain at Sacsahuana, came to the dwelling of Hernán Pérez Tablero and demanded entrance. But his voice was recognized and Captain Garcilaso, eluding an appointment with death, fled through the darkness to the Convent of the Dominicans, where he found security in the hollow vault of a grave.[4]

Twenty-eight cavaliers were seized by Carvajal on that night and thrust behind bars; and when the Justices continued to demur, the old lieutenant gave them impetus with a second visit. Seizing four men and placing them on the haunches of mules, he led them to a tall tree on the outskirts of the city and hanged them one by one. This miserable business completed, the heads of the dead were severed and placed on pikes alongside the roads leading from Los Reyes to Pizarro's camp. What persuasion had failed to accomplish, fear achieved. The apprehensive Justices hastened to bestow upon Gonzalo Pizarro the whole of the authority of Peru until such time as His Majesty should state his pleasure in the matter. Messengers were dispatched at once, and the upstart Procurator made preparations to bring his forces into the city.

October 28, 1544, was a dismal day for Captain Garcilaso de la Vega. From the Dominican cloisters he undoubtedly could hear the noises in the streets and catch occasional glimpses of festivities marking the triumphal entry into Los Reyes of an old comrade who now sought his life. Heading the procession were a vast number of Indians bearing twenty-five cannon, at least one of which had blasted the doors of the Captain's house at Cuzco. Then came the recalcitrant Spaniards, their ranks swollen with deserters, and in the midst of this gleaming mass of men and horses rode Gonzalo Pizarro, handsomely mounted and wearing a coat of burnished mail sheathed with a thin cloth of gold. Three companies of infantry served him as footmen, and behind them followed three choice contingents of horse, in the midst of whom rode three guidon bearers, one with the royal standard of Castile, another with the ensign of Cuzco, and the third with a great panoply on which were painted the arms of the Pizarros. Meanwhile, as cannons roared, trumpets blared, and drums rattled, massive iron bells rang out from all the churches, mingling their deep tones with the

---

[4] *Ibid.*, Pt. II, Bk. IV, Chaps. 18–22; Bk. VIII, Chap. 12. Pérez Tablero was an "hermano de leche" or foster brother of Sebastián's brother Alonso de Vargas.

merry sounds of oboes, lutes, and viols, of dancing and laughter—all
the unmistakable signs of gaiety and happiness. For the truth is that in
general the people of Peru loved Gonzalo Pizarro, and held great faith
in his willingness and ability to dispel the clouds of misery and danger
as well as to bring to an end the ugly threat of the hated New Laws.
Yet in the midst of this gaiety, somewhere among the dark recesses of
a convent, Garcilaso de la Vega lay hidden, grieving the loss of friends,
bewildered, condemned. He no doubt was aware by now that his vast
repartimiento had been promised to a renegade, that his house in Cuzco
had been sacked, and that the beloved members of his household
huddled perilously behind closed doors in hunger and terror. It was
the penalty exacted of a man for loyalty to the King's mad Viceroy.

Triumph had sweetened the bitterness of Sacsahuana, but Gonzalo
Pizarro neither forgot nor forgave the man who had brought him to
the brink of destruction. They had been comrades in conquest, had
eaten at the same table and slept in the same quarters; and of course
the riches of Tapacri had been bestowed on Captain Garcilaso by Gonzalo's brother. Their bond had been more than an impersonal association in a greedy conquest; yet the Captain not only had abandoned his
friend in a time of great uncertainty but, still worse, he had instigated
the flight of other fugitives. Thus when in the ensuing days the new
Governor seized upon the felicitous occasion to offer amnesty to all
who were willing to pledge their allegiance, he made two notable exceptions. One of them was Garcilaso de la Vega.

The next several months, therefore, found Garcilaso playing hide-
and-seek with the axe. Had Pizarro himself come upon his quarry, his
former admiration, respect, and affection surely would have tempered
severity. But the search was left to Francisco de Carvajal, an old hunting dog of a man who sniffed the air for a scent and came to the kill
with zest. Furthermore, he had a habit of destroying his prey before
presenting it to his master. And the hunter now followed a warm
scent, for news had reached him that Captain Garcilaso lodged with the
Dominicans. Thus he came one day and, without success, gave the
convent so thorough a search as to indicate that he had left no spot uncovered. But he knew innately, if not otherwise, that hidden in some
undisclosed corner of that edifice was the man he sought. So he came

again and again, five times in all, and he searched all nooks and corners, even within the sacred recesses of the high altar. And though in one instance he arrived within an inch of discovering the Captain, he was forced each time to depart without his prey.[5]

Four hazardous months Captain Garcilaso lay concealed in the dismal crypts of the Dominicans. He was aware that old friends were interceding for his forgiveness; yet he knew that such a pardon, if obtained, could mean little more than a compromise with Fate until the desires of the King were made manifest. At length, however, Pizarro softened to the extent of altering his death decree to a petulant type of personal banishment—an order demanding that Captain Garcilaso never again be so bold as to appear in his presence. But then, two days later, he reconsidered and, summoning the Captain, commanded that he never again be so bold as to leave his presence. For many months, therefore, Sebastián was to maintain a peculiar relationship with Gonzalo Pizarro, one which, though softened by undefinable bonds of friendship and chivalry and expedience, was presumably a state of captivity. It was a relationship which has never been satisfactorily explained.

Referring to this epoch, the Captain's son afterward declared that until the day of the decisive battle of Sacsahuana his father was not permitted to leave Pizarro's house or even his tent when on the field of battle, and that his instructions always were to take his repasts at the Governor's table. The first of these restrictions, Gómez said, sprang solely from Pizarro's desire to prevent escape; the second found its origin in his generosity, consideration, and affection. For the truth is that Captain Garcilaso had not the means to obtain food, and to make mandatory his appearance at the Governor's board simply was to spare a proud cavalier the mortifying necessity of appearing as a suppliant at the board of his friends. An hidalgo of the ilk of Captain Garcilaso, accustomed as he was to dispensing largess and nourished in the tradition of the degradations of penury, would have preferred, when confronted with such a reversal of circumstances, to mortify the flesh rather than debase his rank and give injury to his spirit. Strangely,

[5] *Ibid.*, Pt. II, Bk. IV, Chap. 20; Fernández, *Historia del Perú,* ed. Odriozola, Pt. I, Bk. I, Chap. 17.

though Pizarro so recently had deprived Garcilaso of his riches and once may have been willing to deprive him of his head, he now was moved to shield him against less permanent though more humiliating distress, and this in the face of the fact that he must have known that his captive would depart again when circumstances and the code of chivalry made it possible for him to do so. Furthermore, Pizarro's reversed command very well may have been motivated by a strong desire to protect his captive comrade from an ever-impending personal danger. For the passions of Francisco de Carvajal had not been assuaged by his master's sentimentality, and he still yearned for the life of the cavalier who so many times had successfully eluded him. As a man of acute perception and vast experience in the theaters of war, Carvajal was aware always of the dubious chivalry of those whose loyalty had been forced by fear, greed, or adverse circumstances; and in judging the character of Captain Garcilaso his wisdom appears always to have been more sober than that of the man he now served.[6]

But the insight of Carvajal approached the occult, and he possessed extrasensory abilities which enabled him either to plumb the depth of invisible thought or to perceive a thought in the face and actions of a man. Moreover, in placing his chips on the wheel of fortune, he, while playing with reckless abandon insofar as his present safety was concerned, appears never to have lost sight of the far distant future and the perils it might hold in store. This phase of his nature was revealed in the precaution he took against those who were recording the events of the moment, among whom was the factor and future chronicler, Agustín de Zárate. For almost a year Zárate had been filling his pouch with notes, and he had little or no sympathy for either the quarreling Justices or the ambitions of Gonzalo Pizarro. Evidence that he was aware of the danger of possessing such notes or of making known his own literary ambitions is to be found in his printed history. "To have begun the history in Peru," he said, "would alone have been enough to put my life in jeopardy since a certain commander named Francisco de Carvajal threatened to take vengeance on anyone who should be so

---

[6] Garcilaso, *Comentarios*, Pt. II, Bk. IV, Chap. 20; Bk. VIII, Chap. 12; *Cartas de Indias*, Vol. II, p. 784.

rash as to attempt the relation of his exploits—far less deserving as they were to be placed on record than to be consigned to oblivion."[7] Indeed, historians have recorded that Carvajal went so far as to threaten to hang Zárate to "the tallest tree in Los Reyes if he was discovered writing anything." As a witness to recent hangings Zárate was well aware that such a threat was not made in jest. But of special significance in the present account is the fact that Zárate was cognizant of the dilemma in which Captain Garcilaso now found himself and later in print was to vouch for a loyalty to the King which the Captain up to this point had shown.

Already Garcilaso would have had reason to anticipate escape. Vaca de Castro, confined to a vessel in the harbor, had induced mariners to weigh anchor and hasten off toward what he hoped would be a haven in Spain; and Núñez Vela had proceeded but a short distance into exile when his escort, repentant and fearful of the hazards of conniving against a royal emissary, had shifted his allegiance and deposited the angry Viceroy on the shores of San Miguel, where he immediately initiated efforts to regain his government. The strength of Núñez Vela grew rapidly in the north, and Garcilaso's innate reckoning told him that eventually Peru must fall again, some time and some place, to the authorized representative of the King. Moreover, for some reason he had not abandoned hope of eventually laying claim again to his lost estates. He was in communication with his overseers, who, during the year 1545, managed in spite of perils and mishaps to convey the deed to certain of his repartimientos back to Cuzco, where on December 31 Juan de Alcobaza filed it with the Alcalde Ordinario, along with the request that the latter examine, transcribe, and make it known to the public.[8]

Meanwhile, as the strength of Núñez Vela continued to grow, two ships sailed into the harbor at Callao, one of them bearing the Treasurer of Panama, Gonzalo Martel de la Puente, who was en route to Cuzco with his family to establish a residence;[9] and two days later

[7] William Hickling Prescott, *History of the Conquest of Peru,* Vol. II, p. 471.
[8] Martel-Cabrera expediente, fols. 8–10v.
[9] Garcilaso, *Comentarios,* Pt. II, Bk. IV, Chap. 24.

Pizarro boarded one of these vessels and sailed north in search of the Viceroy. And with him always in his search, seated at his table and, some say, offering advice on strategy, was Captain Garcilaso, compelled now to watch the gradually approaching denouement of Blasco Núñez Vela, mad but sanctioned emissary of Charles V. The end came on November 19, 1546, in a decisive battle fought near Quito. After an ignominious defeat, the Viceroy was felled by a common soldier and then promptly dispatched by a Negro slave of the renegade to whom Pizarro had promised the Garcilaso encomiendas. The role played by Garcilaso at this battle has not been recorded; nor is there evidence that he ever made any further efforts to escape to the ranks of the Viceroy. But when the head of Blasco Núñez rolled in the Andean dust, Captain Garcilaso must surely have been aware that for the time being any hopes he may have entertained for escape must be buried. Gonzalo Pizarro now was the undisputed master of the realm; all he lacked was the sanction of his sovereign, and so justified did his cause appear that there were many who felt that this sanction would be forthcoming.

Indeed, such a possibility was in the offing. On July 27, 1546, while Pizarro lingered in Quito, there disembarked at Nombre de Dios an ugly, ill-shapen religious, a canny and sagacious prelate and former inquisitor named Pedro de la Gasca, to whom the King had entrusted the sedation of Peru and thus the fate of Gonzalo Pizarro. He bore the unpretentious title of President; but he carried writs which gave him the authority of an absolute monarch, and, according to some records, he brought permission from the Crown to sanction the government of Gonzalo Pizarro in the event that there was evidence that the latter held the support of the majority of the people. From the moment of landing, La Gasca began to peruse the chessboard and, with deadly patience, to study his future moves.

During these strange and never satisfactorily explained days of fraternal captivity, Captain Garcilaso managed to come into possession of that most coveted symbol of a gentleman—a respectable mount. He began negotiations for the purchase of the horse by means of a small loan from a trusting friend, but in the end it was Gonzalo Pizarro who paid for this animal, called Salinillas, which was to prove a boon to the rebel and a crux to Garcilaso de la Vega.[10] It therefore was astride this horse, one of the finest in the land, that the Captain rode back into Los Reyes when, during the following September, Gonzalo Pizarro returned to be publicly proclaimed Governor and Captain General of the whole of Peru. Again the occasion was one of splendor, since in addition to a panoply of richly attired men and horses it was blessed by the presence of four lofty delegates of Rome: the Archbishop of Los Reyes and the Bishops of Quito, Bogotá, and Cuzco. When both civil and ecclesiastical rites of confirmation had terminated, Pizarro assumed residence in the palace of his deceased brother, the Marqués, the floors of which still bore stains of blood let by the men of Chile; and with him always, sharing a strange hospitality, was Captain Garcilaso de la Vega.

The largess of Pizarro of course did not spring entirely from either affection or pity. He was aware of the popularity and influence of his royalist captive and of his need for the support of such a man in his current ambitions. Curiously, on the other hand, Garcilaso appears by now to have perceived some wisdom in giving support to, or at least humoring, this man whose insight into the heart and soul of Peru was to be preferred to that of royal emissaries who came with no knowledge of the land and less sympathy with those who had expended their health and fortunes in winning it. After all, Pizarro did hold his authority from the King's Justices and with the sanction of the Roman pontiffs. So already there must have been born in the heart of Garcilaso a deep hope that his captor-friend might obtain the sanction of the King himself. Only such a hope can account for some of his next moves in the present conflict. When in the ensuing days news of La Gasca's arrival reached Los Reyes and men began to talk of imprisonment or death for the new President, Garcilaso joined others in urging that agents be sent to Spain to lay the whole matter before the King and beg royal approval of Pizarro's incumbency. And when on October 14, 1546, a letter was dispatched to La Gasca asking that he remain in

[10] *Ibid.*, Pt. II, Bk. IV, Chap. 20.

Panama or return to Spain, it bore among its numerous signatures the name of Captain Garcilaso de la Vega.[11] Meanwhile, however, La Gasca had sent Pizarro conciliatory letters which did not preclude the possibility of royal sanction for the latter's government but did demand that he respect the authority of his sovereign and refrain from provoking a rash contest that would prove his past actions were motivated by personal ambition. But Pizarro's aspirations had reached a state of unreason, and spurning the advice of counselors he rejected the offer of reconciliation and in doing so openly proclaimed himself a rebel. And now as La Gasca continued to plot his next moves, he undoubtedly began to suspect the loyalty of Captain Garcilaso and question the true nature of those ties which appeared to bind him to his captor.

More than two years had elapsed since Captain Garcilaso had left his concubine and his two offspring in the care of Juan de Alcobaza at Cuzco, and though through the assistance of Indian vassals and kinsmen they had managed to escape starvation, much of that time they had passed in uncertainty and fear. Threats had persisted, and even when Gómez was invited to take one meal each day with a compassionate Spaniard, he could do so only at noon because of the peril attending the unbolting of doors after night had fallen. At one time in 1545, some hope for rescue came with news that Gómez' godfather, Francisco de Almendras, now Pizarro's deputy at La Plata, had been publicly beheaded and that Diego Centeno was organizing forces in the Charcas to defend the Crown. But this hope was quickly replaced by new fears when Carvajal, on his way to the Charcas to wreak vengeance, paused at Cuzco to give warnings. Soon the gallows in the market place exhibited new victims and men either fled the city or trembled behind bolted doors. Again Captain Garcilaso's family was in peril, for Carvajal had never forgiven the Captain's previous defection from Pizarro, and the defections in the Charcas had been sparked by the murder of the Captain's cousin, Gómez de Luna, because of the latter's open defense of the Crown. Eventually, however, Carvajal moved on to the Charcas, where he promptly dispersed the forces of Centeno, and a few months later Gómez and his mother escaped to a plantation about thirty leagues distant. From there they

---

[11] *Ibid.*, Pt. II, Bk. V, Chap. 3. Fernández, *Historia del Perú*, ed. Odriozola, Pt. I, Bk. II, Chap. 33.

awaited the outcome of events in Cuzco, since with news of the arrival
of La Gasca, Centeno had reorganized his forces and was approaching
with an army to liberate the city.

The ensuing struggle for Cuzco, as Gómez was to describe it many
years later, represents a mock-heroic fiasco which would have inspired
Cervantes. The air was rent with much shouting and some musket fire,
but not one man was killed. In fact the major casualties appear to have
consisted of some ripped breeches, a punctured breviary, an injured
thigh, and a devastating annihilation of ego. And the seizure of the
city was accomplished to a great extent with a pack of asses. Having obtained the secret of the defenses beforehand, Centeno affixed burning
brands to the backs of a number of these lowly beasts and prodded
them into the city under cover of night in such a way as to give the appearance of soldiers scurrying through the streets. Then while the defenders made ready to resist, he attacked from the rear and threw all
into hopeless confusion. But the turning point of the battle appears to
have been a hand-to-hand struggle between Centeno and Pedro Maldonado, one of the most corpulent men ever to win the interest of the
mestizo Gómez.

When his attention was first caught by the shouting in the streets,
don Pedro was piously murmuring the office of Our Lady. Clapping
his breviary into his ample bosom and grasping a rusty sword and
halberd, he mounted a jennet and, galloping through his portals into
the plaza, challenged the first man he encountered, who, as fate would
have it, was Centeno himself. With his initial sword blow the fat
warrior dealt his foe a sharp rap on the hand and followed this with a
quick jab at the thigh with his halberd. A crossbar in the form of a
fleur-de-lis prevented the weapon from pentrating deeply into the
flesh; but when don Pedro attempted to disengage his halberd, barbs
of the crossbar caught in the great general's breeches, tossing him
comically to the ground. At that, an avenging fury in the form of one
of Centeno's pages blasted the fat warrior full in the chest and laid him
prone alongside his foe.

The struggle was brief and the victory prompt. Soon the rebel defenders either declared for Centeno or fled. As men scanned the arena
flecked with blood from the victor's thigh, they surely marveled that
Centeno had been preserved from serious injury by a Gallic symbol;

but there were many who would note that the boon of life itself had been bestowed upon Maldonado by none other than Our Lady. Though the ball from the carbine had laid him prone, it had struck the breviary in his bosom, passed through some thirty or forty pages, and halted at the office devoted to the Mother of God.

Six days later, when news of the successes at Cuzco had reached them, Gómez and his mother returned to the city. With them was Captain Garcilaso's youngest brother, Juan de Vargas, who forthwith joined the forces of Centeno. Sent by his mother to pay her respects to the victor, now lodged in the house of the hated Bachicao, Gómez noted a bandage on Centeno's hand and the reluctance of the cavalier to sit because of the wound in his thigh. But he was especially intrigued by the account of the boon of the Holy Virgin, and some time later, when he encountered don Pedro murmuring his devotions in the church of La Merced, he begged the privilege of examining the fabulous breviary. Then tracing the path of a bullet, the boy was convinced of a miracle which, he noted, had been made manifest only a few days after the sacred feast of the Most Holy Sacrament.[12]

In May, 1547, news spread that La Gasca had landed at Túmbez and was calling for loyal soldiers. At once men throughout the land began to pledge allegiance to the President, some, it is said, even daring to walk off in sight of Pizarro at Los Reyes. Such conduct provoked the cynical Carvajal to offer a social comment which demanded little power of perception. These men, he advised his master in colorful words, had pledged their allegiance at a time when they needed his aid in saving their estates, their lives, and their honor, even going so far as to renounce their sovereign and hound his Viceroy to death. But now that the tide had turned and all was secure, they were willing to deny, sell, or abandon their leader completely. They were but typical, he added, of all men throughout the world who adored no god other than their own interests. Meanwhile, much to the amusement of the sage old warrior, the licentiate Cepeda, an oidor who had firmly supported the rebels, resorted to a foolish expedient by which he thought to bind men more securely. Haranguing the citizens of Los Reyes on the liberties they had enjoyed under Pizarro, he offered any one of them the

[12] Garcilaso, *Comentarios,* Pt. II, Bk. V, Chaps. 6–10.

privilege of shifting to La Gasca but demanded that those who remained pledge their lives with an oath of fealty. With their heads thus
in the lion's mouth, Gómez later remarked, none were bold enough to
flee or to evade the oath, which all took and then promptly disregarded.
If Gómez was speaking seriously, one must conclude that his father took
that oath. But even though it was induced by expediency, Sebastián
Garcilaso, descendant of Garcí Pérez de Vargas and Garcí Lasso de la
Vega, could not have disregarded the oath with the same ease as did
his less traditionally chivalric comrades. Only a short time after this
occasion, when Pizarro had abandoned his capital to establish a camp
further south at Pachacámac, Garcilaso and two comrades slipped back
under cover of night to Los Reyes. Their intent is unknown, though
one is said to have been motivated by amorous impulses. Certainly the
occasion appears to have offered an excellent opportunity for escape;
nevertheless, within a brief time all three returned to Pachacámac and
Captain Garcilaso, purportedly to keep him under surveillance, was
put in command of Pizzaro's personal guard.[13]

As commander of Gonzalo Pizarro's personal guard, Captain Garcilaso was well horsed and well armed, and in a position once more to
turn men's minds toward defection, as he eventually was to do. His
previous conduct, therefore, combined with his later declaration
that he never found an opportunity to escape from Pizarro, leaves
some question. It would appear that now, as when he was held captive
by the elder Almagro, he could find no opportunity for escape because
he could not abandon his traditional concept of the sacredness of an
oath. On the other hand, he seems never to have ignored an opportunity to persuade his captor to come to terms with La Gasca and the
King, and his persuasions sometimes were effective. By the time Pizarro's army had left Pachacámac and moved on to Arequipa, Garcilaso
and his anxious friends had wrung from the rebel a promise to seek
reconciliation at the first propitious moment.[14] But then as they fled on
toward the Charcas they found their route blocked in the vicinity of
Lake Titicaca by resolute forces of Diego Centeno. Soon news reached
La Gasca that Centeno had received three letters from the rebel camp.

[13] Aurelio Miró Quesada y Sosa, *El Inca Garcilaso*, p. 35.
[14] Garcilaso, *Comentarios*, Pt. II, Bk. V, Chap. 27.

Two of them, offering promises of reward if he would shift allegiance, bore the signature of Gonzalo Pizarro; the third, carrying an offer to stand as guarantor for the promises, was signed by Garcilaso de la Vega. Though La Gasca passed this information on to the Council of the Indies with the statement that he believed Captain Garcilaso to be held against his will, he still must have harbored some suspicions.[15] These suspicions, of course, would be strengthened by subsequent rumors concerning Garcilaso's conduct in the momentous battle which now was to ensue between Centeno and the rebel commander at Huarina.

[15] *Colección de documentos inéditos para la historia de España,* Vol. 49, pp. 290–292.

CHAPTER THREE

O N OCTOBER 26, 1547, at Huarina, a windswept plain bordering lake Titicaca, the legions of Diego Centeno and Gonzalo Pizarro faced each other in stubborn defiance.[1] This was to be a soul-stirring contest between men who had been forced to a terrible decision as to whether more was to be gained through adherence to a royal emissary of untested sympathies or to a beloved and trusted conqueror who had defied that emissary and in doing so had defied the authority of the Spanish Crown. Gonzalo Pizarro, astride a splendid horse, and tunicked in green and crimson velvet, was flanked by a guard of counselors and aides, among whom would have been Captain Garcilaso. Opposite, Diego Centeno, tortured by a pleurisy, made ready to direct his forces from a litter, while Friar Juan Solano, the militant Bishop of Cuzco, rode among the royalists bestowing benedictions and exhorting soldiers to their duty. Commanding Pizarro's infantry was Francisco de Carvajal, his armor sheathed in a soiled green cloth; and commanding at least one of Centeno's contingents of foot was Captain Garcilaso's brother Juan, who had joined Centeno at Cuzco. When horses and men had been mustered into battle formation, they presented a picture of gleaming copper and steel, streaming banners, and multihued splashes of velvet and taffeta.

[1] El Inca Garcilaso, *Los comentarios reales*, Pt. II, Bk. V, Chaps. 19–22. Because of the importance of this battle in the destiny of the Inca Garcilaso, the details, which are controversial, have been taken from his account.

For a time neither army stirred. Then slowly a friar with upraised crucifix advanced from the rebel ranks with a message demanding passage. He was quickly seized and borne off to the tent of Bishop Solano, and with this gesture the inevitable struggle began. Firing all the while, Centeno's infantry moved forward toward the forces of Carvajal, but the latter, who had been provided with an extra burden of guns, made no move until the enemy came within range. Then opening a deadly barrage they fired again and again, using their additional muskets. The ensuing slaughter was devastating and the royalist infantry fled in utter rout and confusion.

To the right of the footsoldiers and in command of his horsemen, Pizarro was regarding the melee with supreme satisfaction when he suddenly perceived the whole of his enemy's cavalry hurtling toward him in one mad rush; and to avoid interfering with the action of his infantry, he was forced to remain stationary and subject himself to grievous disaster. The impact of his adversaries, augmented by the fury of a long run, could not be withstood, and his horsemen were bowled over like sheep, not ten of them remaining in their saddles. But among those ten, according to Captain Garcilaso's son, was the chieftain himself, who now rode off alone to give aid to his infantry, pursued all the while by three persistent and slashing royalists, one of whom was a cavalier named Gonzalo Silvestre. Particularly vexed by the interference of this man's horse, Pizarro turned in the saddle and with the utmost agility severed the animal's nostrils to the teeth and cut its right eye socket to the skull. Yet before he could reach the safety of his cohorts, his own horse received a slight wound from the sword of Silvestre, who, in spite of the severe wounds to his mount, eventually managed to escape.

History has thrown an enigmatic veil over the whereabouts of Captain Garcilaso during these desperate moments. There were men who claimed that they knew, but their reports are subject to question. As commander of Pizarro's personal guard, he, it must be assumed, was by his captor's side when the latter received the thundering rush of Centeno's cavalry. It is hardly possible that he was one of those trampled in the onslaught. More than likely he fled on the swiftfooted Salinillas. But somewhat damaging to him afterward was the fact

that, though at this point the victory appeared to be Centeno's, Garcilaso, either through intuition or restraint, apparently made no attempt
to bolt to the forces of the King. Be that as it may, it possibly was fortunate that he did not do so. For by the time the royalists had made
their next charge Pizarro had reorganized forces, and before long his
adversaries were racing across the marshes to seek haven wherever it
could be found. Already Centeno, viewing the disaster from his litter, had risen, mounted his steed, and fled without further ado down
the desert road toward Los Reyes; and the Bishop of Cuzco, equally
aware of impending destruction, had seized a horse and scurried post-
haste up the rugged trail toward his Episcopal See. And now as Pizarro and his companions were crossing a marsh toward the tents
of their adversaries to make certain of victory, their attention again
was drawn to Gonzalo Silvestre, who was fleeing on his badly injured
steed from a common soldier whom only a few moments previously
he had spared. Maddened by such ingratitude, Silvestre turned upon
his pursuer and administered such a glorious pommeling that Pizarro, filled with admiration, shouted an invitation for the stouthearted
cavalier to shift his allegiance. But Silvestre sped swiftly on to his tent
to obtain his red cape as well as practical necessities for the road and
then joined a host of stricken humanity who were fleeing for their
lives into the forbidding cold of the Andes.

When the desperate battle of Huarina was over, the banners of the
King once more lay trampled. Across blood-spattered fields came the
agonizing cries of the wounded and the exultant shouts of men sack-
ing the tents of the foe. To arrange for burial of the fallen, Pizarro
now determined to reconnoiter the site personally, and, though his
horse was but slightly wounded, he demanded a fresh mount. At this
point, according to Gómez, his father dismounted and generously assisted the victorious but unforgivable rebel to the back of Salinillas.
This was a simple gesture which found precedent in many accounts
of medieval and Renaissance chivalry; but the circumstances under
which it was rendered strengthened suspicion and subjected Garcilaso
to malicious rumors which could never be completely allayed. Meanwhile, he himself surveyed the carnage, grieving for the loss of both
men and horses; and he found reason for personal grief since among

those who at Huarina had given their lives in the service of the Crown was his brother Juan. As an officer and a nobleman, this youngest son of the Lord of Valdesevilla was buried by his enemies in the most exalted spot the dreary region afforded—a humble sanctuary which had been erected on the windswept plain by regenerated Indians.

In the interim, Francisco de Carvajal, always amused by the sight of flying buttocks, but now heartily miffed by the escape of Bishop Solano, avenged himself by hanging another friar as well as Solano's brother.[2] For Carvajal, like many, felt that the Bishop, instead of serving as Centeno's campmaster, should have been passing his time on his knees, praying for all Christians. Nevertheless, the Bishop had made good his escape, and it came to pass that, shortly after, the inhabitants of Cuzco were startled by the extraordinary spectacle of this holy man and a wild escort flying frantically back through the gates of the city. The haste with which they traveled gave proof of their peril, which indeed was so imminent that the fugitives bypassed the cathedral and came clattering into the courtyard of the Garcilaso dwelling. Though at Huarina they may have questioned the association of Garcilaso and Pizarro, they sensed somehow that the Captain's house at Cuzco, for the time being, offered more positive security for royalists than did the sacrosanctity of the church. Here, while Captain Garcilaso's concubine prepared food, her amazed mestizo watched hungry, frightened men devouring grains of raw maize as if they were candied almonds. All must have listened with curiosity and alarm as these men unfolded the grievous tale of Huarina; but there was little time for the telling, and in the early hours of the following morning Gómez, possibly with some boyish amusement, watched the militant Bishop and his companions in flight as they galloped for their lives down the road to Sausa and on to the camp of La Gasca. Years later this scene surely flashed upon the mind of the mestizo when he pictured a Dominican friar in La Florida racing back and forth in the heat of an Indian battle, his two cowls and his large felt hat flapping in the wind

[2] Diego Fernández, *Historia del Perú,* ed. Odriozola, Pt. I, Bk. II, Chap. 80. Much to Garcilaso's disgust, Fernández reported that Carvajal reconnoitered the field with two Negroes, clubbing to death all of the enemy wounded.

and a pagan arrow piercing his Christian buttocks. The experience, he said, taught that friar a lesson, and he recorded also that Bishop Solano's experience at Huarina taught him that, instead of participating in martial contests, it was better for him to remain on his knees in church and pray for all concerned.[3]

Indeed, the Bishop and his frightened cohorts had ridden out of Cuzco none too soon; for scarcely had they departed when Pizarro's hangman appeared. Once more the city was strangled with terror as avenging ropes fell about the necks of the King's Alcalde and his counselors, and as men waited nervously to see how many more dangling bodies would appear in the market plaza. Soon, however, a festive air began to prevail as preparations were initiated for the triumphal return of Pizarro to the Imperial City. And Gómez, now a curious and astute boy of eight, awaited eagerly the arrival of his father. Three hazard-packed years had passed since he had seen his lord Garcilaso vanish into the night in desperate flight from the man he now was accompanying back to Cuzco as a comrade if not as an aide.

Before abandoning the battle plains of Huarina, Pizarro had assigned many of his enemy's wounded to the individual care of affluent cavaliers, and the fact that Captain Garcilaso was commanded to share in this task is indicative either that he was not altogether destitute or that already he had obtained some assurance of restitution. Significant among those placed in his care was one Diego de Tapia, survivor of De Soto's fiasco in La Florida, who many times was to demonstrate his gratitude to Captain Garcilaso and whose account of his experiences more than once may have captured the attention of the Captain's mestizo. But though his future with Pizarro must have appeared satisfactory at this point, Captain Garcilaso surely was forced to regard it with fearful apprehension, since he would have been acutely aware of the perilous interpretations which now, more than ever, could be placed upon his peculiar association with the rebel chieftain. Thus as the triumphant army proceeded toward Cuzco he joined in a

<hr>

[3] Garcilaso, *Comentarios*, Pt. I, Bk. IX, Chap. 24; Pt. II, Bk. V, Chap. 23; *La Florida del Inca*, Bk. III, Chap. 27.

renewed attempt to persuade Pizarro to honor a promise made at Arequipa—a vow that when a propitious moment arrived he would seek reconciliation with the President.[4] But Pizarro, now flushed with victory, was merely incited to anger by such importunities and provoked by further suspicion to keep closer watch for desertions. Moreover, as the army approached Quespicancha, but three leagues from Cuzco, his ego as well as his assurance were swollen by the sight of a host of people, both Spanish and Indian, who had come forth to acclaim him.

Somewhere in that eager throng was Captain Garcilaso's mestizo, who had traveled a part of the rough terrain on foot and the remainder on the shoulders of vassal Indians. But the boy's return to Cuzco was accomplished in more cavalier fashion; for someone, possibly his father, provided him a horse, and thus equipped he emerged into a blood-tingling procession: long lines of infantry with multicolored banners unfurled, prancing horsemen with glittering armor and lances set, and then the great victor himself, vested in a brilliant tunic, mounted on his noble chestnut and flanked by his personal guard as well as by loyal citizens. When the resplendent procession moved through the ancient, carved portals of Cuzco, adorned now after the fashion of the natives in the time of their great sovereigns, the bells of the city began to peal joyfully, and hundreds of Indians lining the thoroughfares and plazas paid their most profound tribute to the victorious rebel by crying out the revered title of "Inca." Then as the triumphant Pizarro rode on to the church of La Merced to partake of the Holy Sacrament and to humble himself before the Mother of God, there came the familiar and heart-warming sounds of lute and viol and gay laughter.

Each minute part of this entrancing procession Gómez mentally recorded as he accompanied it back to the ancient city astride a horse that had survived the bitter struggle at Huarina. Sixty years later he recalled not only the splendid actors in that glamorous pageant but the horses they rode and the dwellings in which they lodged.[5] Yet there was much more which he was to assimilate during the succeeding

---

[4] Garcilaso, *Comentarios*, Pt. II, Bk. V, Chaps. 25, 27; Francisco López de Gómara, *Historia general de las Indias*, Vol. II, Chap. 182.

[5] Garcilaso, *Comentarios*, Pt. II, Bk. V, Chap. 27.

months as he and his mestizo companions roamed the passion-ridden city and as the visionary world of their Incaic childhood began to recede beneath the increasing and ponderous realities of fratricidal war. Present continually beneath the color of Hispanic chivalry were gaping evidences of the cruelties and disasters of battle, the insecurities of life, and the perils of misplaced confidence. Only a stroll across the plaza revealed the ghastly countenances of former friends and sometimes of fathers staring through lifeless eyes from the scaffold, or the living faces of mutilated warriors. Once they were thrown into fits of laughter by the sight of a strutting little Negro, bedecked with plumes and prouder than a peacock because he had pommeled an unhorsed cavalier at Huarina; and on another occasion they were startled into sobriety by the somber spectacle of a renowned gossip dangling by the neck from a window, her garrulous tongue throttled by the bestial Negro executioners of Francisco de Carvajal. And ever an integral and portentous part of the Cuzco scene during these feverish, enigmatic days was the demoniac Carvajal. His obese thighs laboriously flung across the tired haunches of a pied mule, he moved like an evil spirit through the streets and plazas in a great plumed hat and a purple mantle, laboring day and night and never giving his hand to be kissed, but offering instead some suggestive proverb, or some sarcastic barb, or some unquotable display of wit. All knew the ruthless potentialities of this fearless psychopath, who appeared to be moved less by conscience or even by vengeance than by a voracious thirst for human blood, and he apparently still yearned for the head of Garcilaso de la Vega.

Yet the somberness of the scene was tempered by the more genial nature of Gonzalo Pizarro. In a land and among a people long inured to mutation and tragedy and innately possessed of shifting emotions, it had become natural to live by the day and submerge the lugubrious in the festive. This latter atmosphere Pizarro now encouraged and preserved to the limits he found possible. With his affable personality, he captivated both Indians and Spaniards, and wherever he went, he was surrounded by a company of men who regarded him with both affection and respect. Moreover, he wisely kept a sumptuous table for any who might wish to join him. Here he himself sat between two vacant places and provided at least a hundred seats for guests; and here men gathered to feed their hungry bodies with food, to stuff their insatiable pride with gallant rehearsals of past accomplishments, and to nourish their passionate dreams with visions of what this very able and generous victor might yet be able to bestow upon them.

And had he but pursued a different course with La Gasca, Gonzalo Pizarro might have given to Spaniards in Peru as well as to Peruvians the boon of a wise and just government, a government which indeed could have eliminated some of the hazards awaiting the increasing and increasingly significant racial mixtures of the land. He took pleasure in his own half-caste offspring as well as in those of his brother the Marqués, and during these days he was attracted by Captain Garcilaso's mestizo, treating the lad as if he were his own son.[6] Thus Gómez became a companion of Fernando and Francisco Pizarro, the rebel's son and his nephew, and through this association he often was brought into the presence of the genial commander, who would amuse himself by ordering all three boys to compete in footraces or by feeding them toothsome morsels from his own table. Moreover, Pizarro appears never to have been gravely concerned by the presence of Gómez when conversation grew confidential. The latter was at hand on one occasion when Francisco de Carvajal, mindful of a boy's curiosity, was forced to bend forward and whisper a secret in his general's ear, so that all the boy heard was a "But look, father," as Pizarro, addressing his lieutenant with this curious form of respect, brought the conversation to a close. The scene takes on dimensions if one considers that the secret may very well have involved a warning against Captain Garcilaso de la Vega. These whispering conquistadors had no way of knowing that they were etching their biographies in the pliant mind of a little half-caste boy. And yet Gómez in after years remembered Gonzalo Pizarro, not as the tyrant, thief, and adulterer that some said he was, not as his father's oppressor, but as a great, handsome, and gentle person, a magnificent horseman in both the Moorish and the Spanish saddles, who rode about the streets of Cuzco in fine toggery, receiving the homage of all manner of people, doffing his hat to

[6] *Ibid.*, Pt. I, Bk. VII, Chap. 10; Pt. II, Bk. III, Chap. 9; Bk. IV, Chap. 42.

each and every one, and addressing them as "Your Grace." Moreover, Gómez was never reticent about proclaiming some of the virtues of Francisco de Carvajal.

There was little that the mestizos did not hear; yet in their efforts to comprehend, much remained in question, for the memories of vaunting cavaliers often held contradictions. Thus, even now, Gómez began to receive from his companions conflicting versions of his father's behavior at Huarina, one of which, though potentially dangerous, was at the moment propitious since it emphasized the Captain's loyalty to Pizarro.[7] And this was the hour of Pizarro's triumph. Apparently he did not aspire to a crown, but he did hold tenaciously to his right to the government of Peru; and even among those who hesitated to support him against La Gasca, there were men who hoped that eventually he would rule the land with the King's sanction. Such a hope undoubtedly had prompted Garcilaso when he counseled the rebel chieftain on the road from Huarina, and it is not unreasonable to assume that he fed this hope in Cuzco so long as he could. Nevertheless, Pizarro surely was aware that only when he had obtained the sanction of the Crown would he be able to depend upon the loyalty of Garcilaso de la Vega. Therefore, though he may have permitted the Captain a certain freedom, he did curtail chances of flight by withholding the fleetfooted Salinillas. And Garcilaso not only refused to buy a respectable mount but proudly refrained from begging the return of his own. Instead he trudged about the city on foot, hoping that the sight of a horseless hidalgo might move a Pizarro to compassion and further generosity.[8]

But it was growing late. The forces of La Gasca had rallied, and when notice came that he was moving toward Cuzco, Pizarro resolved to meet him for a conclusive battle at Sacsahuana. This decision he made against the warnings of men, oracles, and omens. The Indians foreordained disaster when on many mornings they found the streets and plazas littered with dead or dying foxes, victims of a scabious scourge that was rapidly depleting the land of its fauna; astrologers

---

[7] *Ibid.*, Pt. II, Bk. V, Chap. 23.
[8] *Ibid.*, Pt. II, Bk. V, Chap. 35.

pointed out adverse signs in the heavenly nebulae; and Francisco de
Carvajal, moved by diviners, by messages in the wind, and by an innate distrust of an army which included more than three hundred men
recruited from defeated royalist forces, pled with his general to avoid
Sacsahuana and retreat to the south. Yet Pizarro stood adamant, and
one April morning a panorama of bronze cannon, burnished mail, and
unfurled banners moved slowly over the hill of Carmenca toward
Sacsahuana.

Gómez witnessed the departure of that seemingly invincible force
with something more than childish fascination, for he knew the men
who rode in greatest splendor, and he knew the horses. He saw the
licentiate Diego de Cepeda mounted on a magnificent beast, its neck,
chest, and buttocks sheathed in a protection of elegantly adorned,
black-dyed cowhide; he saw the corpulent Carvajal with plumes and
purple mantle, his great weight burdening a little chestnut that bore
the lyric name of Boscanillo—an old horse now, but strong still and
nimble, and one which the boy himself had ridden; he saw the Commander with red cape and slashed velvet, gracefully managing as
fine a mount as could be found in Cuzco; and he saw his lord Garcilaso splendidly vested and astride as magnificent a horse as could be
found in all the realm. It was Salinillas. On entering his supposedly
empty stables one day, Captain Garcilaso had discovered that his horse
had been returned by Pizarro, who, surely moved by an unusual affection, had been touched by the sight of an old comrade humbled.

It is difficult to comprehend what appears to have been a renewed
and naive confidence on the part of Gonzalo Pizarro, though, as historians have recorded, one of his primary weaknesses notoriously lay
in his inability to judge realistically the extent of a man's loyalty. Time
and again he had placed trust and even given strategic assignments to
certain men, among them Garcilaso's intimate friend Martín de Robles,
only to have them abandon him at the first opportunity. Could he have
forgotten a similar journey only four years previous when he had ridden in full faith to Sacsahuana with Captain Garcilaso, who even as
they departed had been contemplating desertion? Obviously some
clever dissimulation or some deft gesture on the part of the Captain,
or perhaps his exaggerated respect for an oath and his previous hesi-

tancy about trying to escape, had renewed and strengthened Pizarro's faith, for in the present instance Garcilaso apparently not only was well mounted but was fully armed for combat. Yet as that cavalcade of men and horses vanished in the dust of the Chinchasuyu, Garcilaso again was plotting escape, and when they came once more to the scene of his former desertion he completed his plans. First he made a survey to determine the securest route for flight. Then, aware that he would be under some observation, he instructed his Indian lance-bearer not to obey when called upon for arms so that there might be an excuse for separating from those who watched. This done, he awaited the conflict, which fell on the ninth day of April, 1548.

When a semblance of peace had come again to the land, Captain Garcilaso told his son of that debacle. Fronting what appeared to be the invincible forces of Gonzalo Pizarro was the wily La Gasca himself, supported not only by valiant men of war but by three high emissaries of Rome, the Bishops of Quito, Los Reyes, and Cuzco, the last of whom must have forgotten the lesson he had learned at Huarina. Then, when all forces had assembled and captains were deploying their men, Garcilaso seized the occasion. Audibly protesting that his arms had not been delivered, he directed his steps toward the river, calling all the while to his vassal Indian. As soon as he was concealed by the barranca, he turned in the direction of the King's forces, and when he had crossed a small morass lying between the two armies he speedily ascended and, in full sight of both armies, presented himself to La Gasca. The latter received and embraced him with a show of satisfaction, yet with words which faintly suggest some suspicion as to the Captain's past behavior. "My Lord Garcilaso," he exclaimed, "I have always hoped that Your Grace would render such service to His Majesty." But the returning prodigal gave a prompt explanation designed to allay doubts. "My Lord," he replied with the assuring grace of the cavalier, "being a prisoner and without liberty, I previously have not been able to serve either His Majesty or Your Lordship, though I have never lacked the desire to do so." Ostensibly, with these few well-chosen words Captain Garcilaso managed to allay some of the President's suspicions. But it would take more than these words to erase from the minds of many others the fixed impression that this cavalier had indeed ignored previous opportunities for flight, and their convictions no doubt were strengthened by the fact that among them were many who had contrived to escape Pizarro as well as by the circumstance that Captain Garcilaso apparently had ridden to forgiveness on a horse named Salinillas.

The clever and hasty departure of Garcilaso left Pizarro much troubled and enraged, though to avoid discouraging his men he concealed his emotions. Yet on encountering one of the Captain's cousins, another Gómez Suárez de Figueroa, the rebel chieftain gave vent to his wrath: "Garcilaso has abandoned us," he roared. "What advantage do you think he will have gained in the event that we are the victors?" Flashing back through his mind surely were visions of all the opportunities previously foregone to dispose of this man and all of the unheeded advice of Francisco de Carvajal concerning him. Nevertheless, in this desperate moment Gonzalo Pizarro, though still able to dissemble, must have been aware that the flight of Garcilaso was more than a flight. It was a signal for a host of deserters to follow suit, and it marked an initial step in the crumbling of his army. If he did not realize it now, the fact soon became manifest. For the contest at Sacsahuana was to evolve into possibly the most ludicrous fiasco in the Peruvian civil wars.

The dominating picture which the Captain's son has left for history to judge is a scene of backsides, of scurrying men and galloping horses, all hastening in one general direction. Garcilaso soon was followed by the licentiate Cepeda and other men of import, and then by troop after troop on horseback and on foot.[9] Thirty arquebusiers rode out ostensibly to skirmish, and when far enough separated, took flight; thirty horsemen, feigning pursuit of the arquebusiers, merely followed their example; then came forty more arquebusiers, defying pursuit; and finally the pikemen simply threw down their weapons and departed. Meanwhile La Gasca, aware that eventually all would come, merely sent out cavaliers to assist the repentants across the marshes and into

[9] *Ibid.*, Pt. II, Bk. V, Chap. 35; Bk. VIII, Chap. 12. Both López de Gómara and Zárate recorded that Cepeda deserted first. Garcilaso's contention was backed by La Gasca and Fernández. See *Colección de documentos inéditos para la historia de España*, Vol. 49, pp. 378–379.

the fold. And throughout it all, the old demon Carvajal, enraged at his master for refusing advice, bawled out in ribaldry and cynicism, "Ah, madre, the wind is whisking off my little hairs two by two." Then spurring the stronghearted Boscanillo, he himself took flight—in a new direction. Nevertheless, he immediately was pursued and shortly brought back by some of his own men who thought to buy their lives with this fat prize.

And now Gonzalo Pizarro, essentially alone and scornful of the idea of dying like a Roman in the arena, turned his noble steed and rode haughtily toward the tents of La Gasca.

"This was the battle of Sacsahuana," Gómez afterward recorded, "if one may term a battle that in which there was no sword blow, no encounter of lances, no exchange of arquebus fire between enemies, and no fighting whatsoever other than what has been related. And the ruination of Gonzalo Pizarro was so brief that more time will be consumed reading this chapter than was spent in the passage of the events related within it."[10]

It was now ten o'clock in the morning, and the inhabitants of Cuzco waited tensely for news of the drama taking place but a few leagues distant. Soon they perceived fugitive Pizzarists racing over the horizon, closely pursued by men who aspired to do them justice. Then all knew that Peru had been returned once again to the hands of the King, and that Gonzalo Pizarro and Francisco de Carvajal were preparing for their last scene. Great throngs thereupon began to move down the Chinchasuyu—officers and citizens, Spaniards, Indians and metizos— all rushing to Sacsahuana to view the moving spectacle, which promised to be a classic drama of noble death enacted with the comic relief of that great, cynical buffoon, Francisco de Carvajal. Some said afterward that the old demon made bold to slap the Bishop, and then when confronted by Centeno, who had sought to protect him from an avenging mob, sardonically refused to recognize his defender. "To whom am I indebted for this protection?" he had mockingly asked, and when Centeno expressed surprise at being unknown to a man who had pursued him through so many leagues of mountainous wilderness, the

[10] For Garcilaso's account of this battle, see *Comentarios,* Pt. II, Bk. V, Chaps. 35–43; Bk. VIII, Chap. 12.

barb-witted old warrior replied that having seen nothing but Centeno's arse for so long, he had forgotten his face. These were stories which Gómez could never countenance even against a man he had reason to hate and fear. But Gómez did not accompany that curious mob to Sacsahuana, though a number of his mestizo companions did and on the following day gave him the details of what they had seen and heard. They told of the old demon spilling comically upon the ground as his obese body was dragged in a hamper, and of his last Latin responses spiced with Spanish ribaldry as thirty soldiers hoisted him to the gallows. And they told of the spectacular exit of the rebel chieftain when, as the afternoon shadows were falling across the plains, he draped himself in a splendid mantle of yellow and gold, mounted a debasing mule, and rode without shame to the scaffold.

Gonzalo Pizarro had begged to be dispatched after night had fallen so that no man might witness his terminal agony. Denied this courtesy, he played his role histrionically and well. Surrounding him were hundreds of men whom he had known long, most of them gazing upon him with open faces, and yet many wearing masks lest they reveal their shame or other emotions. Clasping an image of the Holy Virgin, he faced his audience and, surely with some specific allusion to Captain Garcilaso, spoke earnestly of past conquests shared together, of the spoils with which both he and his brother the Marqués had enriched the coffers of many who had abandoned him, and of the present low state of penury to which he had been reduced since even his fine livery must fall now to his executioner; and he begged his debtors to buy his soul's peace with redeeming masses. Then with a "My Lords, may God be with you" and a final orison, he turned to the awaiting headsman and besought him to perform his art without bungling. Lifting a round-trimmed beard, the latter, with one quick slash, sliced off his head as neatly as if it had been lettuce; and while the lamentations of both Spaniards and Indians filled the air, he prepared to seize his sartorial fee.

In this manner the final curtain descended and the host of spectators began moving back down the road to Cuzco for the postlude, which would be enacted in the main plaza where one had the best view from the house of Garcilaso de la Vega. There, on the ensuing day, the mestizo Gómez joined a motley throng to witness a terrible spectacle. Men were hanged, drawn, and quartered, tongues were torn from gullets, and while amazed Indians gazed in bewilderment upon this strange exposition of fratricidal vengeance, more than a hundred victims were stripped naked, placed on some lowly beast of burden, and lashed pitilessly through a gauntlet before being labeled for the King's galleys. Then, in keeping with the penal tradition, the houses of Gonzalo Pizarro were demolished and the ground on which they had stood was rendered sterile with a goodly sprinkling of salt.

As the deep-toned bells in churches and convents tolled the dead, the decapitated bodies of both Pizarro and Carvajal were brought from Sacsahuana. That of the former was placed in the church of La Merced alongside the remains of Diego de Almagro and his unfortunate mestizo—not naked, but clothed still in his noble vestments which had been redeemed for him by Diego Centeno, the man he so humiliatingly had defeated at Huarina. And it was said that for many years afterwards the people of Cuzco piously and affectionately purchased masses for the pilgrim soul of this magnificent rebel.

The iron spikes of the city now displayed new heads to warn those tempted to pit their wits and strength against a Spanish King. But the heads of Pizarro and Carvajal were reserved for Los Reyes, where they remained exposed until long after corroding elements had erased their earthly identity. Yet Cuzco was to harbor a grim memorial of Carvajal. For his obese body, torn into four parts and denied burial, was moored to pikes at the four entrances of the city. Thus whether one traveled the highroads to Cuntisuyu, Collasuyu, Antisuyu or Chinchasuyu,[11] he found ever before him these putrifying reminders of the perils which confronted men who placed their allegiance rashly and then refused to play the role of weaver.

It was the cynical and realistic old Carvajal himself who coined the term "weaver" for men who shuttled their loyalties with the unpredictable winds, and whenever occasion came to do them justice he refused to consider poetic retribution. And today, looking back across the centuries, one often is puzzled by the ease of conscience with

---

[11] These were the four regions of Tahuantinsuyu, which translated literally as "the four corners of the world." See Glossary.

which a cavalier could shift allegiance. But the conquistador in his frontier ethics possessed a remarkable genius for convenient rationalization. Alleging always his fealty to the King, he could make a shift without any feeling of guilt and usually with an overtone of altrusim. Observed from a point of detachment, the picture sometimes appears mock-epical; and the snubs and irritations with constant desertions and retributions often suggest that such men were emotionally immature. Yet behind this seeming naiveté was something fundamental. For the pioneer world, with all its chivalric veneer, was a world of "dog eat dog," a desperate struggle for survival and fortune when quick decisions were demanded and repentance generally tolerated. In such a world, "weaving" very readily became a psychological weapon with a dual thrust. Always when one found that he had placed his allegiance unfortunately, he could shift to the winner and lay claim to the dubious glory of having helped to restore the realm to its rightful owner, the King. Moreover, forgiveness could be anticipated, since an astute commander knew that often success depended upon his ability to persuade the cohorts of an opponent to shift their loyalties. So weaving, like concubinage, though it could never quite detach itself from some ignominy, often was condoned and encouraged, and even rewarded, in one fashion or another.

The role played by Captain Garcilaso throughout the Pizarro rebellion does at times strongly suggest a man who trifled with friendship and permitted the fickle winds to shuttle his loyalties. The charge of weaving has never been cleared from his name and to many he still remains a man of frail loyalty. Yet he can be defended. Having defected once, he was, as his son has recorded, under surveillance, and any unsuccessful attempt to defect a second time would have cost him his life. But it is difficult to believe that Garcilaso was deterred by fear or even by a lack of opportunity for physical escape. A more reasonable explanation for his conduct appears to lie in the assumption that he sincerely loved and admired Gonzalo Pizarro, thought him the most justified and capable man to rule Peru, felt that he eventually might win the sanction of the King, and until the day they marched out of Cuzco, hoped that the rebel might become reconciled with La Gasca and submit to the will of his sovereign. When this hope failed alto-

gether, he, regardless of any personal oath he might have taken with
his respected captor, was forced to clarify his fealty. In the scale of
his loyalties, always that which weighed heavier than allegiance to a
friend was a traditional chivalric concept of allegiance to one's sovereign. His second flight at Sacsahuana, like his first, was a flight from
sedition. He of course witnessed the execution of Pizarro with deep
and genuine though stoic grief, and one may be sure that over the
years he dropped gold into ecclesiastical coffers to ease the purgatorial
pangs of an old and beloved comrade. But he never would have felt
that he erred in abandoning that comrade, and he would have been convinced that in doing so he had performed a service for his King.

Soon again in Cuzco the lugubrious was replaced with the festive.
One heard gay music and the shouts of men racing splendid horses
across the plaza, baiting bulls, or hurling canes in colorful tournaments.
La Gasca wisely encouraged such festivity, often leaving his lodging
with Tomás Vázquez to regard the scene from the greater advantage of
Captain Garcilaso's balcony.[12] Here Gómez watched the shrewd old
man one afternoon, a gaunt figure, all legs and scant of body, who,
spiderlike, had patiently woven a lethal web about Gonzalo Pizarro,
and who, even at the moment, was subtly contemplating the complex
problem of dealing with those men who raced beneath him in the
plaza. For La Gasca knew that behind each deceptive mask of merriment one thought lay uppermost. What was to be the reward for having given golden Peru back to the King? And it was easy now for all to
persuade themselves that they had shared in the giving. Though many
had at one time or the other in the recent rebellions misplaced their
fealty, they had returned eventually, though in some cases embarrass-
ingly late, to the man who represented the King. The problem of La
Gasca, as ever with the distributor, lay in the facility with which each
man could over-appraise his own conduct. Often the least worthy
yearned for and could persuade himself that he deserved the best repartimientos, and the expectations of the really deserving were almost
beyond satisfying.

One can only conjecture as to the true attitude of La Gasca concern-

---

[12] Garcilaso, *Comentarios*, Pt. II, Bk. V, Chap. 2; Bk. VI, Chap. 1.

ing the loyalty of the cavalier whose balcony he now shared while regarding the Cuzco scene. On December 27, 1547, scarcely six months previously, he had reported to the Council of the Indies that in his opinion Garcilaso was being held against his will, and on May 7, 1548, less than a month after the battle of Sacsahuana, he again wrote the Council that on that occasion Garcilaso not only had been the first to come to him but he had offered valuable advice as to how victory could be attained.[13] Yet La Gasca possessed incriminating documents which bore Captain Garcilaso's signature. Moreover, he knew that in the recent rebellion this cavalier had ridden a fine horse, carried a lance, and counseled Pizarro, and such knowledge made it reasonably difficult for him to believe that the captain had seized the first opportunity to elude his captors. In reporting the events of Sacsahuana to the Council, he spoke of his certainty that some men came to him out of fear rather than loyalty to the King, since there had been many opportunities for them to have done so previously. Surely, therefore, to this shrewd and calculating President, what Garcilaso had referred to as captivity must have appeared more than once to have been nothing more than a cautious decision to joust with the most favored quadrille until there could be some certainty as to which side was more likely to win. And surely this impression now would be strengthened in Cuzco where men sometimes referred to the Captain as "el leal de tres horas," or the one who is loyal for only three hours.[14] It was generally known that La Gasca had planned his distributions before coming to Sacsahuana, and the story has survived that the only reward he had had in mind for Garcilaso de la Vega was punishment.[15] Thus even in these moments when he was accepting that cavalier's hospitality he may have been attempting to decide whether or not to alter some of his plans.

Indeed there were strong reasons for Captain Garcilaso to be apprehensive, and standing out among them was the fact that there persisted

---

[13] *Colección de documentos inéditos para la historia de España,* Vol. 49, pp. 290–292, 378–379.

[14] *Cartas de Indias,* Vol. II, p. 784.

[15] Fernández, *Primera parte de la historia del Perú,* ed. De la Torre, Vol. I, Appendix, p. 267.

still in Cuzco a damning story concerning Huarina. It was the story of a man and a horse and a chivalric gesture. But as told now this gesture had cost the King a victory by bringing to Diego Centeno a humiliating defeat. For it was said that in the second stage of the conflict, when Centeno's cavalry had charged en masse and with irrestible force, Pizarro himself had not remained in his saddle but had been hurled to the ground and his horse slashed into pieces, and that it was not after the battle but at this point, when victory for the King appeared most certain, that Garcilaso had turned the tide by proffering his mount to the rebel chieftain. This version, long common gossip, was what Gómez had heard from his garrulous mestizo companions, and his father possibly had given it little thought at the time Pizarro was dominating the scene. But it was perilous now for such a tale to circulate, because Pizarro lay mouldering in his sepulcher and La Gasca not only was alert to each wind of rumor but was passionate for justice. The old story was a menace and must be dispelled, this time by the signatures of men whom the President could trust. In order to do so, Captain Garcilaso now appeared before a justice, made an affidavit, and presented twenty-two reputable witnesses, all adherents of Diego Centeno, who swore that when Pizarro requested Garcilaso's horse, there was not within half a league a single royalist with whom to fight, and who declared that the wound inflicted upon Pizarro's horse was so slight that, had it been necessary, the animal could have continued in the struggle throughout the entire day. Moreover, Captain Garcilaso provided evidence to prove that rumor had confused the slain horse of another soldier with the slightly wounded animal of Pizarro, and that the latter animal had died of a spasm twenty-two leagues from Huarina and some days after its wound had healed.[16] Present in Cuzco at this time was Gonzalo Silvestre, who had inflicted that wound and thus may have been one of those who gave testimony, though he is said to have avoided the subject of Pizarro's horse whenever possible on the pretense that people might think his sword arm as inoffensive as the injury bestowed.

[16] *Cartas de Indias,* Vol. II, p. 784; Garcilaso, *Comentarios,* Pt. II, Bk. V, Chaps. 20, 23. The Inca Garcilaso knew personally the stableboy who had been responsible for the death of Pizarro's horse.

The signatures of twenty-two such witnesses, legally sworn by, should have put an end to the rumor if it were false. Yet men believed it; and persisting, it left the Captain suspect. Even more fatally, it gained the credence of men who were recording the annals of Peru and who could convert the story into ruinous evidence. In all probability La Gasca was tempted to accept it as the truth. Nevertheless, at some time during these critical days he was convinced of the political expediency of rewarding Garcilaso with riches rather than punishment. Consequently, when on August 4, 1548, emissaries of the President announced new distributions at Cuzco, Captain Garcilaso found himself in the midst of an uproar sufficient to give him further apprehension.

There was a surge of angry voices. Men cursed and gave vent to seditious mutterings. As the days passed they formed cabals and entered into ominous consultations. Some proposed slaying the Archbishop, Gerónimo de Loaisa, whom they suspected of meddling; others proposed bringing the unjustness of La Gasca before the Council of the Indies. For, they said, he had but half rewarded those who were most deserving, and in many cases had given riches to men who merited no more than the right to live. Pedro Sánchez del Castillo, a cavalier who had accompanied La Gasca from the time he landed, received nothing; Diego Centeno, defeated hero of Huarina, received but half of what he felt he deserved; Pedro de Hinojosa, who for a time had commanded Pizarro's fleet, was given the richest repartimiento; and Martín de Robles, who even jested that he was the first man to seize the King's first Viceroy at Los Reyes, was bewildered by the excess of his reward.

According to a eulogy pronounced soon after his death, Captain Garcilaso, as a boon for having restored Peru to the King at Sacsahuana, received from La Gasca a repartimiento of Indians worth thirty thousand ducats of income. And certainly from this time forward he once again was in possession of his vast encomienda of Huamanpallpa and Quechuan Indians which Pizarro had promised to the renegade Pedro de Puelles. It is safe to assume that La Gasca authorized the restoration since in a report to the Council of the Indies on May 7, 1548, he stated that, as a reward for services to His Majesty, he had restored all Indians to those who had been dispossessed.[17] It is for the reader to decide whether or not the Captain had given Peru back to the King. Many in Cuzco refused to think so.

The damaging version of the Huarina story eventually reached the Council of the Indies, and even now Diego Centeno, who already may have divulged it to La Gasca and certainly was one of the most capable to affirm or deny it, was formulating plans to carry complaints against La Gasca to the King. But Centeno never reached Spain. For when he persisted in his resolution, he was fed a Borgian dose so neatly that he is said to have expired without so much as one rumble of the bowels. Meanwhile the flames of wrath and indignation smoldered and sparked in Cuzco, and as men congregated in dark streets and corridors one saw frequently among them Francisco Hernández Girón, a morose cavalier who now stood out above others as a malcontent, first because he had been rewarded without merit, second because his maldictions were full mouthed and especially seditious, and finally because he was an egomaniac who consorted primarily with common soldiers and dreamed of leading another rebellion against the King. Eventually the Cabildo sent him to Los Reyes to present his complaints before La Gasca, but he left Cuzco with a resolution to return and carry out his evil ambitions.

[17] Garcilaso, *Comentarios,* Pt. II, Bk. VI, Chaps. 2–3; Bk. VIII, Chap. 12; also *Cartas de Indias,* Vol. II, p. 784; *Colección de documentos inéditos para la historia de España,* Vol. 49, p. 390; Martel-Cabrera expediente.

CHAPTER FOUR

I N THE MIDST of this strange carnival of life and death, mirth and despair, lust, uncertainty, triumph, and defeat, this swift and treacherous game in which one simply waited to discover where the winning numbers were to fall, Gómez passed an incoherent childhood. During his first ten years, spent mainly in his native Cuzco, he continued to regard the scene for the most part through the eyes of his Indian relatives, who in their bafflement and grief kept alive in the boy the basic elements of their own culture. Circumstances had placed him primarily under their training and care, and though he rapidly was assimilating the Castilian language, he clung still to the tongue which made it possible for him to comprehend Incaic wisdom. Permitted to witness ancient pagan ceremonial rites, some of which the Spaniards had forbidden, he half-believingly watched old Indians as they surreptitiously sacrificed lambs to read omens in palpitations and pulsations of hearts, lungs, and entrails; he ran with the little Indian boys when they followed a pancuncu, or burning torch, as it floated down the stream intersecting the city, bearing with it all the evil spirits which it had swept from the ghost-haunted streets; and he witnessed with respect the ritualistic exercises performed when young Indian nobles entered maturity. He learned of significant signs revealed in the twitching of an eye, the itching of an ear, or a sneeze; and he learned the value of traditional medicinal herbs. As time passed, vassal Indians carried him about the land on their shoulders, up the narrow, steep, and treacherous inclines, pausing at times to construct thanksgiving mounds, and then over the thread-like bridges of osier which spanned bottomless chasms. They taught him how to cross streams in lightning-swift balsas which traveled at such breathtaking speed that one dared not look upward in the journey lest he be dizzied and overcome by a mirage of sky meeting earth. And sometime, somewhere, in those years, the Indians disclosed to this small mestizo the secret of perusing and unraveling that strange tangle of multihued and knotted cords, the quipu, by which, from ancient times, the Incas had guarded accounts of their arms, their laws, their populations, and all concrete things.[1]

The self-appointed native tutors of Gómez were multiple; and yet it was principally from the Incas assembling weekly in his mother's quarters that he acquired knowledge of both the bitterness and the triumphs of Incaic history. Here were the persisting quipucamayus and amautas, the desolate voices of the past, who refused to permit the glories of their realm to be forgotten. The aged Cusi Huallpa, whose deep memory reached beyond the time of Túpac Yupanqui, poured into the boy's mind the legends of ancient kings, their conquests and their rich descendency, and he filled it with living pictures of the more recent reign of Huayna Cápac and the birth of Huáscar, which was celebrated with the fabrication of a great golden chain. His mother and her brother Francisco Huallpa, as well as other eyewitnesses, spread before him the bleeding fields of Yahuarpampa and the ensuing hopes which ended with the destruction of Atahualpa and the Hispanicization of Tahuantinsuyu. All emphasized the infamy of the Inca usurper, on whom they persistently placed the onus of their eventual destruction. Even in the crowing of the Spanish cocks they interpreted a divine effort to insure the shame of Atahualpa, recognizing in the cacophonous call of a barnyard fowl the name of the hated tyrant. Thus they taught the little Indian and mestizo boys of Cuzco, on hearing the curious crowing of this alien bird, always to echo in derision the tongue-twisting names of Atahualpa and his despised generals.[2]

[1] El Inca Garcilaso, *Los comentarios reales*, Pt. I, Bk. VI, Chap. 9.
[2] *Ibid*, Pt. I, Bk. IX, Chap. 23. At Túmbez, when the Indians first heard a cock

And yet, bitter memories of the role played by Atahualpa in delivering the realm to the Spaniards could not erase from semi-pagan minds an eternal faith in an ancient prognostication. Often present among the assembled Indians were two former captains of Huayna Cápac, Juan Pechuta and Chaucha Rimachi, who enlightened Gómez as to his mestizo origin with tear-drenched accounts of how their realm had been foredoomed. Once when Cusi Huallpa had completed a rehearsal of the events of Cajamarca, the curious boy ventured to inquire as to how it was possible for an empire so rugged and so teeming with such warlike and powerful people to succumb as swiftly as it did to a handful of Spaniards. Turning in anger as if his people had been accused of cowardice and weakness, the old auqui again explained the augury and admonition of Huayna Cápac and then added: "These words which our Inca uttered and which were the last that he spoke to us were more influential in the subjugation and deprivation of our empire than the arms which your father and his companions brought into this land."[3] Always, as the boy passed in and out of these cheerless assemblies, listening to accounts of the Incaic past, he witnessed the same scene of weeping and resignation and bitter regret that a people who once had reigned now were reduced to shameful vassalage.

Significantly, as these ruminant Incas continued to curse the memory of their defeat and humiliation, their bitterness increasingly encompassed not only the Inca usurper but the strangers to whom he had delivered the realm. Since the initial days of the conquest, much of their belief in the divinity of the viracochas had faded, and they had come to reinterpret the import of the old augury as one of punishment rather than reward. Baptism, whether voluntary or forced, had brought but little comprehension of Catholic mysticism, and they had never emerged completely from the shadows of paganism. Though unified in Cuzco to some extent under the leadership of the regenerated Cristóbal Paullu Inca, many had not severed their relations with the pagan heirs to the throne who still kept Incaic fires smouldering in Villcapampa. During the Pizarro rebellion, the Inca Manco, when on

---

crow, they clapped their hands and asked what it was saying. See William Hickling Prescott, *History of the Conquest of Peru*, Vol. I, p. 276.

[3] Garcilaso, *Comentarios*, Pt. I, Bk. IX, Chaps. 14–15.

the point of sending aid to Blasco Núñez, had received a fatal blow from a bowling ball hurled in anger by a renegade Spaniard who enjoyed the pagan's hospitality. But Manco had left at least three sons and heirs, the eldest of whom, Sayri Túpac, was the offspring of a favorite wife whom the Spaniards had foully slain soon after the siege of Cuzco. Thus from the misty throne at Vitcos there emanated a contempt for the invaders which was shared by many of the more passive Indians of Cuzco. This contempt is especially notable in the retorts of Cusi Huallpa, never mentioned with a Christian name, who in explaining to Gómez not only Incaic history and myth but the finely regulated laws and government of the vanished empire, did so with an effective tone of odious comparison. As the boy grew and the years passed, his questions sometimes irked this bitter old man, whose replies were to shade with some bias the mestizo's memories of Tahuantinsuyu as well as his conception of those who had destroyed it.

And always before Gómez and his companions were visible proofs of the grandeurs of their Indian heritage, convincing traces of which they encountered when wandering about the vicinity, searching for adventures in the endless labyrinths of the fortress of Sacsahuamán or the house of the Chosen Women, or among the multiple half-mutilated remains of ancient Incaic masonry which had survived the siege. Along the worn trails extending from the city they found mute memorials which quickened in their imaginations the myths of pagan god-heroes. At Chita they saw the green fields where an Inca prince reputedly had dozed and encountered a specter deity; at Sacsahuana they saw the legendary white stone relics of succoring sons of the Sun; at Cacha they gazed with wonder and respect upon the massive image of the god Viracocha; and on the desolate road to Muina they beheld great painted condors which the Inca Viracocha had left to perpetuate the cowardice of his blood-weeping sire. And through their Indian eyes they regarded these relics with at least a half-faith. Yet with the assistance of a somewhat indolent and indifferent clergy they were merging their pagan concepts with the equally mystic concepts of Christianity. This fusion they found so easy that Gómez later expressed his regret that in the beginning the Spaniards, principally because of their ignorance of Quechua, had failed to comprehend the facility with which the Catholic faith could have been superimposed as a mere extension of pagan myths. To these boys the Indian Zúpay could readily become a Christian Beelzebub; the mysterious succor which an ancestral prince received from the heavens could be attributed as easily to the Virgin and Santiago as to the god Viracocha; and the great image of an Inca god at Cacha could be regarded with some credence as a replica of the blessed San Bartolomé. Slowly encroaching upon their Indian concepts was the culture of Spain.

Nevertheless, as they gradually awakened to their Spanish heritage, they were forced to view it with some bewilderment. Over the glittering Christian panoply of men and arms and horses there hovered always the specter of greed, uncertainty, deception, and retribution, and the dark shadows of the scaffold from which came the putrifying stench of Spaniards so recently seen alive and walking the streets of Cuzco. Their most vivid memories encompassed the pageantry of Gonzalo Pizarro and Carvajal, but it was a pageantry which had deprived some of them of fathers. They now beheld men who had abandoned Pizarro praying for his soul in the Church of La Merced; and always before them at the entrances of the city were the ugly quarters of Carvajal. Once when romping in a field on the outskirts of Cuzco several of them came upon a great green thigh swollen with corruption. There followed a series of bravadoes and challenges until at length one little mestizo edged forward and plunged a small finger into the loathsome flesh. Meanwhile the others fled in terror, crying out that the demon Carvajal would destroy their companion for his audacity. And the penalty for the experiment did indeed increase their dread, for the bold urchin, though he cleansed his hands repeatedly, promptly developed septic poisoning and came near making a supreme atonement for his daring. Their Indian relatives could interpret this experience realistically since over the years they had seen corrupting flesh used to poison the tips of arrows. But they also saw something more metaphysical than chemical poisoning in the process, since they had found pale-skinned flesh particularly venemous, especially if it had sheathed the bones of a redhead.

Though the exigencies of war had kept Captain Garcilaso from Cuzco during these early years, it cannot be assumed that he had regarded his offspring with indifference. Indeed all evidence points to the contrary and suggests an unusual tenderness for both of them. Moreover, the Captain's solicitude had extended to the children of less fortunate comrades, and he had given asylum to a number of orphans, among whom were Pedro and Juan, mestizo sons of his friend Pedro del Barco, whom Carvajal had hanged during those desperate days of flight at Los Reyes. Living also in the same house was Diego de Alcobaza, whose father, in addition to serving Captain Garcilaso as an overseer, had been entrusted with the care and education of the Captain's son.[4] By the close of the Pizarro rebellion, however, Captain Garcilaso had resolved to extend his son's horizons, and Gómez was placed along with other mestizos under the tutelage of certain of the church fathers. Moreover, he was initiated into the cavalier art of handling a horse. Not only did he learn to shoe, bleed, and groom the horses in his father's stables, but he learned to ride with grace and dexterity. Consequently, there became ingrained within him that peculiar Spanish respect for fine horses as well as for those privileged to ride them, and as time passed he came to know not only the names of individual horses but the points which distinguished a blooded animal.[5] Such Hispanic training marked an initial stage in the metamorphosis of an Indian boy, and it provides insight into the emotions of his father. Apparently the cavalier Captain had determined to endow his mestizo with at least the outer semblance of an hidalgo, and in doing so he possibly set an example for a number of his companions.

In this manner the mestizos of Cuzco came to be more than a race of half-breeds, and a new caste was born—a caste which in the social structure of Peru was regarded as superior to the Negro and the Indian and inferior only to the creole and the Spaniard, a caste which was destined to be torn between its sympathy for the race which gave it stigma and its yearning for the recognition of that race which could give it status. And embedded now in the cultural fibers of these boys was a growing sense of the superiority of those whose veins carried noble blood, either Spanish or Inca. Both their biological inheritance and their current social environment rendered such an attitude inevit-

[4] *Ibid.*, Pt. I, Bk. III, Chap. 1; Pt. II, Bk. IV, Chap. 10.
[5] *Ibid.*, Pt. II, Bk. II, Chap. 25; Bk. V, Chap. 22.

able. Perhaps for this reason the mestizos whom Gómez has recorded as among his intimates were comparatively few and appear to have been to some extent selected. In general they were the sons of his father's associates, fabled first conquerors who had participated significantly in the winning and sedation of the realm, and most of them were linked by blood through noble Inca mothers. It is doubtful if any were the progeny of lowborn Spaniards or common Indians. Among them, for instance, were three grandsons of the Inca Huayna Cápac: Juan Serra de Leguizamo and Martín de Bustincia, offspring by different fathers of the Beatriz Coya; and Juan Balsa, son of the ñusta Leonor. And among them were at least three grandsons of Atahualpa: Juan de Betanzos and Fernando Pizarro, offspring by different fathers of the ñusta Angelina; and Francisco Pizarro, whom Gonzalo Pizarro had begotten on another daughter of the tyrant. Then there were Pedro de Candía, Juan de Cellorico, Bartolomé Monedero, Gaspar Centeno, Alonso Fernández de Mesa, Feliciano Rodríguez de Villafuerte, Diego de Vargas, Pedro and Francisco de Altamirano, Juan Arias Maldonado, Diego and Francisco de Alcobaza, and Pedro del Barco. Some irony and some pathos are attached to the circumstance that the fathers of these boys, bound to them by paternal affection and a feeling of responsibility, and no doubt baffled by the novelty of the situation, had begun to cloud their futures with a proud sense of hidalguía while denying them legitimacy. Herein was to lie the source of much of their future misery. Nevertheless the bitterness later to emerge was present now merely in the embryonic seed of a dangerous bewilderment, which, as a matter of course, increased as their Incaic concepts faded and they began to regard through Hispanicized eyes the social horizons of their Indian mothers as well as the personal insecurities to which they, themselves, as the fruit of concubinage, had fallen heir.

In the earlier years of the conquest, concubinage had contributed to the welfare and contentment of both Spaniards and Indians. It is undeniable, for instance, that Gómez' mother occupied a responsible position in the Garcilaso household, that she was served still by vassal Indians, and that she commanded a degree of her master's affection while he in turn was spared the possibility of a wearisome and passionless marital bondage. But a concubinary structure, agreeable as it may have been, could not long brook the light of sincere Catholic dogma without some embarrassment, especially since numerous friars and priests and other such evangels had used it to satisfy their own lusts; nor could it adjust itself without certain problems to the iron Spanish code of awards and succession. Moreover, through the efforts of Las Casas it had burdened the conscience of the Emperor Charles, who in consequence was now urging the conquerors to marry. Yet with the inevitable shift in domestic structure, the concubine rarely became the Catholic bride of the man who had used her, being relegated instead to a less conspicuous position in the demesne or, as in the case of Gómez' mother, given in marriage to someone of less social significance. Thus Isabel Suárez Chimpu Ocllo, after possibly a decade of service as Captain Garcilaso's concubine, was permitted to become the legitimate wife of one Juan del Pedroche. Just when this marriage took place is not known, but circumstances suggest that it may have occurred about 1549 when La Gasca was urging petitioners to improve their fortunes through marriage and when the palla's cousin, Beatriz Coya, former concubine of the conqueror Mancio Serra de Leguizamo and recent widow of the factor Martín de Bustincia, became the bride of one Diego Hernández.

Though Gómez never told of his mother's marriage, he did describe in detail the marriage of Beatriz Coya, and he of course may have done so with the idea of symbolizing the experience of his mother as well as other concubines.[6] He told of the great pressure put upon Beatriz to wed the prospective groom and of her reluctance to do so because of a rumor that this man once had plied the lowly trade of tailor; and he described a somewhat ridiculous marital ceremony in which, because of the Bishop's ignorance of Quechua and the interpreter's inability to adjust Christian concepts to the native tongue, Beatriz' accepted vow of consent had been nothing more than "perhaps I do and perhaps I don't." Though he gave the name of the groom as Diego Hernández, he in this instance, as he had done elsewhere, undoubtedly confused this name with that of Pedro Hernández el Leal, a former retainer of the House of Feria in Spain, who had resided for many years in the Garcilaso household and whom the rebel Francisco Hernández Girón

[6] *Ibid.*, Pt. II, Bk. VI, Chap. 3.

once referred to contemptuously as a tailor. This man may have served the Garcilaso household as such, but it is more than likely that he groomed the Captain's horses. For he owned a swift-footed horse named Pajarillo, which Gómez sometimes rode, and he was highly respected by both the mestizo and his father. Captain Garcilaso undoubtedly had a hand in the promotion of Beatriz' marriage, and since he himself now was contemplating a union compatible with his social station and religious tenets, it is not unreasonable to assume that he simultaneously was urging the Indian mother of his son to become the legitimate bride of Juan del Pedroche.

Little is known about Juan del Pedroche. The fact that his name never appears in any of the chronicles of Peru suggests that he was distinguished by neither rank nor ambition; and Gómez' failure ever to mention either his mother's marriage or her husband's name appears to be ample proof that the occasion was not one in which he could take pride. Because of the Spanish propensity to fuse and shorten names, Juan del Pedroche may have been the Pedro de Roche who later was asked by the widow of Gómez de Tordoya to accompany Gómez to Spain. He may indeed have performed some slight service of merit, if not to the Crown, then to Garcilaso himself; but the presence of both the Vargas and Figueroa names among his grandchildren strongly suggests that he was but a poor relation who represented a part of the sizable menage that Captain Garcilaso continued to support, and that he was willing to accommodate the Captain at a time when the presence of a faithful concubine lay heaviest on the latter's conscience or threatened to delay his own marital plans. Whether the noble Isabel Suárez Chimpu Ocllo approached her marriage with the same proud reluctance as did Beatriz Coya has not been revealed; but she did enter wedlock dowered with fifteen hundred pesos in stamped silver and the same wealth in llamas, as well as some clothing and household furnishings. Captain Garcilaso most probably provided this dowry as well as living quarters in his Cuzco dwelling for his former concubine and her spouse.[7]

[7] Evidence of the palla's marriage and her children by this marriage is to be found in her will. See Aurelio Miró Quesada y Sosa, *El Inca Garcilaso*, p. 251. Speculation as to the time of the marriage is based on the circumstance that in 1548–1549

What arrangements if any Captain Garcilaso may have made for his other known concubine, María Pilcocissa, mother of his mestiza daughter, is not known; and there as yet is no indication that she ever married. Long afterward, a witness in a lawsuit instigated in Mexico declared that María lived for many years in Cuzco and was highly respected; so again it is plausible to assume that both she and Francisca de la Vega had continued to reside in the Captain's house at Cuzco. For there is ample evidence that Garcilaso regarded his daughter with paternal devotion and consideration. As she approached a marriageable age, according to a number of witnesses, he exercised caution in choosing as her legal mate an hidalgo with "clean" blood, being unwilling to bestow her upon anyone with taint of Jew or Moor, and eventually he found for her a suitable groom in the conquistador Pedro Sánchez del Castillo, an intimate friend of Juan Álvarez Maldonado, who had served as the maiden's godfather and who surely took some of the responsibility for arranging her nuptials.

Don Pedro had been esteemed as a gentleman in Salamanca, and in Peru he consorted only with cavaliers. He owned a house at Cuzco, bore arms and wore fine livery, and always, even when horses were expensive, managed somehow to be well mounted. What he lacked chiefly was youth and a fortune, for though he was one of the first conquerors and had served well in the Pizarro rebellion, La Gasca, as has been noted, had given him nothing. But Sánchez' deficiencies Garcilaso, to some extent, was able to remedy. Not only was he prepared to warm the aging cavalier's blood with a maiden of tender age, but when Francisca was married, her father dowered her with a coca plantation that brought an annual income of fifty thousand pesos. Moreover, on the day of her wedding he bestowed upon her godfather a war saddle and a coat of mail worth five hundred pesos.[8]

Once again, thanks to La Gasca, Captain Garcilaso could dispense largess. But his own youth had vanished, and since he had no legitimate heirs, the bulk of his wealth stood in peril of remission at his death to the Crown. The Pizarros, Pedro del Barco, and Diego Cen-

La Gasca was promoting such marriages, and on the fact that by 1571 the palla had two married daughters and at least one grandchild.

[8] Sarmiento Palacio expediente, fols. 265–275v.

teno, all, through some process, had legitimatized their mestizos, and more than once Captain Garcilaso may have contemplated doing the same for his son, though never by the process of marrying the boy's Indian mother. He was not, however, beyond the limits of potency, and both his nobility of lineage and his fortune offset obstacles which otherwise might have been placed upon him by years. In truth, as sometimes happened in colonial Spain, he long since may have betrothed himself to a child with the idea of biding his time until she reached the age of consummation. For living at Cuzco since 1545 was Luisa Martel de los Ríos, a fourteen-year-old maiden whom he now was preparing to lead to the altar.

Born at Panama in January of 1535, Luisa Martel was the eldest child of the King's factor, Gonzalo Martel de la Puente, and his legitimate wife, Francisca Lasso de Mendoza. Her maternal grandfather was Diego Gutiérrez de los Ríos, a corregidor of Potosí who held a family estate at Cuzco; and her paternal grandfather was Alonso Fernández de la Puente, the unprincipled treasurer under Pedrarias Dávila at Darién, who is possibly best known for the despicable role he played in the execution of Vasco Núñez de Balboa.[9] For many years Luisa's father had resided in the sordid city that commanded the entrance to the Mar del Sur, counting and guarding the bullion which poured through the Isthmus into His Majesty's coffers. Though Luisa Martel was unborn when Captain Garcilaso passed through that region of the world, he would have had ample opportunity to observe her in Cuzco as she approached a maturity which in her time came with early adolescence. He was aware of course of the richness of her lineage, some of the roots of which like those of his own extended back to the famed Garcí Lasso of Salado; and he in addition was aware of the practical advantages of such a marriage. On the other hand, Gonzalo Martel de la Puente would not have been unmindful of the material and social advantages to be gained thereby, and he undoubtedly had instructed his daughter in the wisdom of joining in matrimony with a man of noble estate who, according to the law of averages, was

---

[9] Martel-Cabrera expediente. Also Luis G. Martínez Villada, *Los Cabrera*, p. 116. Luisa's brothers and sisters were Alonso Pérez Martel, Pedro de los Ríos, Aldonza de Acevedo, Mencía de Figueroa, and Beatriz de Mendoza.

not too far removed from the sepulcher. This was a common wisdom which had become the subject of serious banter in Cuzco and which Captain Garcilaso's great friend Martín de Robles found profitable when he betrothed his seven-year-old daughter María to the seventy-year-old Pablo de Meneses; for the viejo had died before the marriage could be consummated and the infant widow, now endowed with an appreciable estate, was able, as Gómez afterward expressed it, "to exchange an old pot for a new one."

Be that as it may, on June 24, 1549, the Day of San Juan, when vassal Indians were bringing their tributes to the storehouses and strongboxes of the opulent Captain Garcilaso, he knelt before the Archdeacon at an altar in Cuzco and exchanged nuptial vows with the creole daughter of one of the shrewdest of the King's former factors. Present to sanction the vows were the bride's parents, and on hand to give their signatures as witnesses were several of the Captain's intimate associates, including Diego de Silva, son of the famed Feliciano de Silva, and Pedro López de Cazalla, the President's secretary.[10]

On such occasions, Gómez later recorded, all the people of the city banished animosities, donned their richest liveries, and assembled to rejoice. In the afternoon the great market place resounded with the shouts of cavaliers baiting bulls and racing fine horses in cane tournaments—re-enacting in cold Cuzco the traditional festivities of old Castile; and when evening came the gentility assembled at well-laden tables to feast and gossip until a late hour. Gómez of course participated in the festivities and heard his father's marital vows; yet his reaction could not have been one of deep bitterness since what occurred on that day, though puzzling, was something he had been taught to accept as a natural sequence of the social order in which he lived. Many years later he bewailed a system which exposed to misery and insecurity the half-breed offspring of fathers who abandoned their Indian concubines to wed women of pure Castilian blood. But that was when he had learned more of the inconveniences and injustices which accompanied bastardy in the Spanish code of rewards and successions, and more of the shrewdness of the creole maiden who had just become

[10] Martel-Cabrera expediente, fol. 34.

his stepmother. At the moment he was but ten years of age and she was but four years his senior. Moreover, neither he nor his own mother had been abandoned and would not be so long as his father was alive; and it is highly probable that Captain Garcilaso already had expressed some plans for providing his son with material possessions.

Nevertheless, as the days passed and the rapidly maturing step-mother assumed her position in the Garcilaso household, Gómez with-out doubt was made increasingly conscious of some of the humiliations attending his new situation. There is no evidence as to the attitude taken by doña Luisa toward her husband's former concubines; yet there was nothing in her character to indicate that she would have regarded them with any feeling other than extreme hauteur, not because of their previous functions but because she was creole and they were Indian. She may have tolerated with tranquility their presence in her aging husband's house, but she would have suffered them no privileges beyond those dictated by the social code. And her attitude would not have varied in her treatment of the Captain's mestizos. Each day was to bring to Gómez a new realization of social limitations.

This new wisdom naturally was shared by all the mestizos and pro-foundly influenced their outlook as with the diminishing noise of bat-tle they were brought into closer communion with their Spanish heri-tage. In a manner the effect was twofold. Their chagrin at their own relative position strengthened their mutual bonds and encouraged them to form a definite unit among themselves; and at the same time it forced them increasingly to regard with pity and some disdain the castes considered their inferiors: the Indians, mulattoes, and Negroes. Fortunately their cultural roots were too fixed to permit them to lose completely their veneration for Incaic ancestors or their respect for the royal descendants. But what they knew of their Indian heritage had come to them through hearsay, more often than not accompanied by lamentations; and the mute evidences of the past with its persistent colors of hopelessness and desolation were dimmed now by an Hispanic zest for life which provided space for ambition and dreams. The vi-tality which plagued their youth forbade their continuing to abide on the memories of a conquered people, and they as yet were too young to foresee future obstacles or the sinister limits of their horizons. A certain irony, therefore, lies in the fact that it was during these years when Gómez' sense of the significance of his Incaic heritage was fading that his father placed in his small but sensitive hands a Castilian bridle and a book of Latin nominatives and at the same time permitted him a respected and hopeful place in the vast and complex Garcilaso demesne.

And Captain Garcilaso's estate now was sufficiently princely to dull memories of his ancestral Valdesevilla. Encompassed within it were immense holdings of mines and coca plantations, with towns of Indian vassals supervised by caciques and overlords, all of whom paid him both tribute and allegiance. Twice yearly, in the seasons of La Navidad and San Juan de Junio, Indians filed into Cuzco with tributes and rents for the Captain's counting houses, where they were received and checked by young Gómez, whose ability to manipulate the quipu had won him the confidence of the natives.[11] Meanwhile vassals kept the manorial house in Cuzco serviced with both firewood and food, and in every way administered to the domestic comforts of those who enjoyed the Captain's generosity, among whom always was an appreciable band of armed guards. Such proofs of opulence and power gave the Garcilaso household a significant position in the rapidly developing colonial structure in which social differences were becoming more pronounced and the limits of pride and pretentiousness sometimes went beyond endurance. La Gasca having departed, this new social milieu was provided some additional impetus by the arrival on September 12, 1551, of Antonio de Mendoza, a viceroy who, having served in Mexico since 1535, was in favor of continuing, at least temporarily, the original feudal structure which had been threatened by the New Laws.

In the Cuzco of this time, as in old Spain, a man's social status was gauged to an appreciable extent by the company he kept, by the size and quality of his stables, and by the condition and splendor of the clothes he wore. Captain Garcilaso not only chose his closest associates from among cavaliers and conquerors, but he supported a fine stable with experienced grooms to care for his horses and kept a competent

11 Garcilaso, *Comentarios,* Pt. I, Bk. VI, Chap. 9.

Negro tailor to snip and sew silks, velvets, and taffetas. Therefore Gómez early was made aware of the significance Spaniards attached to such matters; and though he afterwards tended to be critical of excessive pride in personal adornment, he never fully overcame his own admiration and respect for blooded horses and fine raiment. As a boy he often watched his father's tailor at work, and he glorified in the medieval splendor of rich liveries worn on festive occasions. Once during these days, when he was only twelve years of age, he stood on his father's great balcony alongside Francisco de Mendoza, son of the Viceroy, and marveled at the costly, multihued apparel of cavaliers baiting bulls and tilting canes in honor of this dignitary.[12] He was particularly struck by the rich attire of four fabled conquerors who were clad in black velvet embroidered with leaves of crimson and white, and whose turbans were generously flecked with emeralds and other stones of great price. But he was even more impressed by the grandeur of the clothes worn by his father and his father's companions. Sheathed also in black velvet, they wore capes which bore the motto "Plus ultra," outlined by columns of yellow velvet and topped by a yellow crown through which was interwoven a silken twist of blue and gold. It was an unforgettable scene, not only because of the rich beauty of the apparel but because of the grace and dexterity of the horsemen. Moreover, it was a scene in which the courtly Captain Garcilaso could display the splendor which accompanied a noble heritage. But it was a fatal and cruel splendor destined to awaken vain dreams in a mestizo whose Indian heritage later was to isolate him from the social structure so picturesquely reflected.

Always present now were the brilliant and colorful splashes of Castilian zest for life, marking a sharp contrast to the strange, primordial gloom which shrouded the Indian world; and always as Gómez emerged into adolescence his reverence for Incaic lore was submerging beneath a swift infiltration of the legends and traditions of Spain. For among that motley assembly of fortune seekers passing in and out of the golden mecca of Cuzco there appeared men who had traveled the multiple highways of adventure: men who had fought the King's

¹² *Ibid.,* Pt. II, Bk. VI, Chap. 17.

battles in Italy, France, and Flanders, who had followed the Portuguese to the great Horn and on into east Indian and China seas, and who had penetrated all the remote reaches of the New World. There were few corners in the Imperial City that could not produce an adept spinner of tales. Yet it was never necessary for Gómez to pass beyond the walls of his father's house to hear an enchanting story. Lolling about the Captain's board and enjoying his sumptuous repast were world-seared cavaliers and common soldiers whose experiences were fabulous and whose tongues were unbridled. They told of a strange wind from the east which once blew the flimsy vessels of Alonso Sánchez from the Canaries to an island in the Indian seas, making possible a map which afterward charted the route of Cristóbal Colón; they told of Pedro Serrano, a Spanish Crusoe with sun-thickened skin and trailing beard who wandered the limits of Spain and Flanders with a tale of seven lean and melancholy years passed on a Caribbean island without name; they told of the bold antics of Pedro de Alvarado in old Seville and New Spain, of Hernán Cortés among the Aztecs, of Vasco Núñez de Balboa striding with his mastiff Leoncillo into the turbulent waters of the Mar del Sur; they told of Hernando de Soto hewing a path through the emerald wilderness of La Florida and on to the great river where eventually men lowered his fever-ridden body into deep and murky waters; and they told of Francisco Vázquez de Coronado, deceived by a lying friar into a vain search for the golden pueblos of Cíbola. And when they had exhausted their accounts of far places, they retold the story of Peru—of brave starving men at Gallo and Gorgona, of fierce lions reduced to tranquility at Túmbez by a Christian Cross, of the militant apostle and the resplendent Virgin at Cuzco, and of all the glorious feats which marked the conquest of Tahuantinsuyu. Then again, when weary of such tales many surely turned to lyrical accounts of the conquests of ancient Spain, and from these men as well as from his father, Gómez would hear repeated the fabulous records of two of his most respected ancestors, Garcí Pérez de Vargas, who had scorned to defame a timid warrior, and Garcí Lasso de la Vega, who had salvaged the honor of the Virgin at Salado.

Many of the stories which came now to Gómez as he approached adolescence were foredoomed to be sheathed in a veneer of poetry; for in addition to being innately credulous and continually subjected to a rapidly unfolding world where miracle oftentimes took precedent over fact, his sources long had fed their imaginations and their self-delusions on the lying histories and the books of chivalry, a number of which had of course accompanied them to the Indies. Such books, therefore, represent some of the earliest and most pleasing literary morsels to fall into young Gómez' hands, and he was fated to enter adolescence in the amazing company of such fictional heroes as Amadís, Clarian, Lisuarte, and Florisel de Niquea. He would not have been discouraged from such delights by either his father or his preceptors, the latter of whom, though they may have secreted such literature beneath canonical robes, often became as addicted to them as the famed Knight of La Mancha. But surely Gómez received much of his encouragement in this genial pursuit from Diego de Silva, son of Feliciano de Silva, who to the six accounts of the adventures of Amadís already published had added four more, and in addition had published a continuation of the sordid but popular story of Celestina. Long a friend of Captain Garcilaso, Diego de Silva lived lavishly in a gaily decorated house at Cuzco; and when the Captain's mestizo was admitted to the rites of Catholic confirmation, this son of a famed romancero stood as the boy's godfather and assumed responsibility for the welfare of his soul.[13]

There is not space here to catalogue the names of those men whom Gómez afterward specified as authorities for the stories poured into his receptive mind. But significantly, during this period, when he was but twelve or thirteen years of age, he came under the spell of Gonzalo Silvestre, that spirited hidalgo whose sword arm had wounded Pizarro's horse at Huarina, and whose ability to spin a tale of adventure must already have begun to charm both men and boys at Cuzco. A native of Herrera de Alcántara in the province of Cáceres, Gonzalo Silvestre was no more than twenty-eight years of age when on February 27, 1538, he was granted permission to accompany the Adelantado Hernando de Soto to La Florida as a master of arms. After four years with that ill-fated expedition, he had escaped to the City of Mexico with little to show for his pains but a golden and inexhaustible memory

---

[13] *Ibid.*, Pt. II, Bk. V, Chap. 25.

of glorious adventure. Then passing on to Peru, he had joined Diego Centeno when the latter first took up arms against Gonzalo Pizarro and throughout the rebellion had remained loyal to the Crown, though apparently without tangible reward. The circumstances of this hidalgo's first encounter with Captain Garcilaso's son, Gómez apparently never recorded, but in a memorandum made only a few hours before his death he declared that his friendship with Silvestre dated more or less from the year 1552.[14] Thus as a boy approaching adolescence, with dreams which already penetrated beyond the horizons of the Andes, his fate cast him fortuitously into the path of this spellbinding raconteur, now in his early thirties, a lusty cavalier with an eye for a willing wench as well as fine horseflesh, who wove the fabric of his stories from the woof of both imagination and experience and colored it with romantic hues. He must have fed often at the Garcilaso table, and he must have paid as often for such hospitality with bewitching tales, stories which echoed the music of trumpet and drum and moved to the rhythm of galloping horses. And though he strayed at times from the truth, he unraveled his experiences with a joyous courage and gave substance to the visions of a mestizo who some day would record them. In this felicitous rapport between a boasting New World Quixote and an aspiring Peruvian boy are to be found the seeds of the Inca Garcilaso's account of Hernando de Soto's exploration of those vast regions north of Mexico which Spaniards since the discoveries of Ponce de León had referred to as La Florida.

[14] Document dated April 22, 1616, Archivo de Protocolos de Córdoba, Oficio 29, Protocolo 35, fols. 505–507; document dated January 12, 1558, Archivo General de Indias, Patronato 101, R. 18, 1558, Peru; Cristóbal Bermúdez Plata, ed., *Catálogo de pasajeros a Indias*, Vol. II, p. 267. Silvestre appears throughout Garcilaso's *La Florida* and his *Comentarios*, Pt. II.

CHAPTER FIVE

UNDER THE SPELL of quixotic adventurers and their complement of chivalric literature, Gómez was weaving a cocoon of illusion and developing a romantic perspective which inevitably would leave its imprint on his later histories. But, as previously stated, at least a part of Captain Garcilaso's ambition had been to endow his mestizo with some of the formal training which he himself had received in Spain. At first this training apparently had been entrusted altogether to his overseer, Juan de Alcobaza, and then by the close of the Pizarro rebellion had been delegated to various religious who were primarily interested in material rewards. Gómez has recorded that he and about eighteen of his companions, all but two of them mestizos, had been placed under a succession of five clerical tutors, each of whom approached his task with little interest and quickly abandoned it on finding more lucrative employment elsewhere. At length, however, Juan de Cuéllar, who in 1552 was installed as the ninth Canon of the Cuzco Cathedral, voluntarily undertook the instruction of these boys and continued to labor with them for some time.[1] The substance of their training can only be surmised by scattered references and by what is known of common procedures, which indicate that in addition to the

---

[1] El Inca Garcilaso, *Los comentarios reales*, Pt. I, Bk. II, Chap. 28; Eugenio Asensio, "Dos cartas desconocidas del Inca Garcilaso," *Nueva Revista de Filología Hispánica*, Año VII, Nos. 3–4, 1953, pp. 583–593.

customary processes of mastering prescribed passages of Latin Scriptures they were rigorously subjected to the rudiments of Latin and Castilian grammar. Gómez' ability to interpret Quechuan music in Spanish terms and forms, added to the fact that Juan de Cuéllar assisted with the services of the Cathedral choir, indicates also that Captain Garcilaso's mestizo, like the sons of most Spanish noblemen, was instructed in the mysteries of musical notation. He was enchanted by both Quechuan and Spanish music and once told of his regret at the loss to Cuzco of some strolling minstrels who after the battle of Sacsahuana were sent away to Spain, on what turned out to be a somewhat festive voyage, to serve in the galleys of the King.

Meanwhile, as was normal, Gómez' curiosity continued to penetrate beyond the scope of his preceptor's interests to the multiple attractions of his visible world. Even as he was absorbing the mythical lore of his Inca progenitors, he was storing up knowledge of the physical aspects of the land they had ruled, its flora and fauna and all of its geological distinctions. In consequence the records he left for posterity have become a veritable storehouse, not merely of social, political, anthropological, and linguistic wisdom, but of ornithological, horticultural, and geological data. It follows, therefore, that at this point his curiosity should be quickened by all novel accessions from Spain. The arrival of each new agricultural product, each new bird or beast from the Old World inflamed his interest. Wheat, grapes, asparagus, canary birds, Spanish fowl, camels, cows, and asses, each provided a lively incident in his boyhood adventures. He later recalled that his father bought the first donkey brought to Cuzco for the purpose of breeding mares to produce mules, and he remembered even the names of the first three bullocks ever put to the plow in his native city. To see them at work he had abandoned his classes, a delinquency for which he paid with twelve stripes from his father and twelve more from his tutor.

Neither Captain Garcilaso nor Canon Cuéllar was content to permit natural phenomena or mundane attractions to interrupt formal training, since both placed unusual faith in the intellectual possibilities of the mestizos. So impressed was the Canon with the ability of his charges that he expressed a hope of seeing them someday seasoning their intellects in the scholarly cloisters of Salamanca; and his opinion undoubtedly initiated or at least substantiated Captain Garcilaso's ambition to extend his son's Spanish horizons. Certainly the encouragement of this kindly and sincere prelate can be regarded as pivotal in Gómez' later pleas for the education of the natives of Peru as well as his persistent efforts to establish a conviction that they were capable of comprehending the most profound wisdom that Spain could offer. Such confidence on the part of Juan de Cuéllar stimulated both curiosity and pride in all the mestizos, and while inclining them toward further social isolation and introspection, awakened within them a feeling that in the total scheme they too, in spite of ironbound social codes, merited consideration. But men like Canon Cuéllar were rare and most of these mestizos were destined to receive little more than the rudiments of formal training, since with the rising turmoils which were to culminate in the revolts of Sebastián de Castilla and Francisco Hernández Girón, they, according to Gómez, were forced to abandon the classroom for the saddle. Once again, Satan had seized upon the benevolent frenzy of Bartolomé de las Casas and the detested New Laws as a provocation for insurrection.

On the departure of La Gasca for Spain, the administration of the realm had fallen temporarily to the four cantankerous Justices of the Audiencia, who foolishly made known that they now intended to enforce the New Laws, and serious trouble had been averted only by the arrival of the Viceroy, Antonio de Mendoza, who had wisely proposed suspending these odious decrees until further discussions with the King. But by 1552 the Crown was insisting so strongly on enforcement that the Audiencia, no longer held back by the Viceroy, who was too ill to offer effective resistance, again published them, though with the insertion of some illicit changes in order to stave off public indignation. Nevertheless, though Mendoza had actually succeeded in weakening the decrees, this indignation was inevitable and of course there were men ready to fan it to the point of insurrection. Some warnings of impending danger at Cuzco came when men with ulterior motives began to stir up antagonism by circulating stories of illegitimacy in the bloodlines of certain well known citizens, stories which in the wake of legal threats might have proven economically disastrous.

Reticent always to defame, Gómez afterward estimated the appreciable number of persons involved without mentioning the names of any of the injured; but conspicuous among them, undoubtedly, were some of the offshoots of the Cabreras and Bobadillas, powerful and interrelated Spanish families whose blood was interlaced with that of the Figueroas and Mendozas, and who had not always exercised caution about either racial purity or legitimacy. Living in Cuzco now were at least two sons and a daughter of Miguel Gerónimo de Cabrera, Lord of la Torre de Palencia and great nephew of the famed Andrés de Cabrera, first Conde de Moya. Some years previously, after marriage to Leonor Ponce de León y Figueroa, granddaughter of the first Conde de Feria, don Miguel had scandalized Seville by his unconcealed adultery with María de Toledo, who was said to be the wife of a local tinker. Also in Cuzco were at least two sons and one natural daughter of Guillén Peraza de Ayala y de Rojas, Conde de la Gomera, who was a great nephew of the wife of Andrés de Cabrera, doña Beatriz Fernández de Bobadilla, first Condesa de Moya, and thus closely related to the wives of Pedrarias Dávila and Hernando de Soto. To many Spaniards in Peru the prolific amorous caprices of don Miguel and don Guillén had been the subject of common gossip, and it stands to reason that the offspring of such noble prodigals should become involved in the lives of Gómez and his father, who numbered some of them among their kin.

Pedro Luis de Cabrera, for instance, legitimate son of the adulterous Miguel and his wife Leonor, kept a house adjacent to that of Captain Garcilaso, accompanied him on many missions, and used the services of his tailor. Having left an indolent wife in Seville, he now as lord of a vast Andean repartimiento lived lavishly, regaling his friends with bouncy stories and a well laden table, and all the while adding pound upon pound until his great belly waxed so enormous that he could no longer fit it into a short-stirruped saddle. The front tree, Gómez quaintly remarked, simply would not consent to it. Indeed, his doublets were so large that Gómez and four or five of his companions, all ten or twelve years of age, one day fitted themselves simultaneously into one of these veritable tents without any semblance of crowding. Gómez cherished his visits with this merry mountain of a man, bending double with mirth over the jokes he played on lackies; in him he found a man with a gift for life and a splendid manner of living as well as a sense of compassion and understanding. For don Pedro was proud to be a blood relative of both Captain Garcilaso and his son, and he always addressed Gómez as "nephew," thus unreluctantly identifying him with the noble Figueroas of the house of Feria. There is no evidence, however, that this same cordiality existed between either Gómez or his father and don Pedro's half-brother, Gerónimo Luis, whose mansion in Cuzco also proudly displayed the Cabrera arms. A bastard son of María de Toledo, this Cabrera when little more than a child had come to the Indies as a royal ensign in the King's armada and had continued in that capacity for ten years before settling in Cuzco in 1538. He had served loyally in civil turmoils and was to play a significant role in the settlement of the Charcas; but though his name appears from time to time in the accounts of other historians, it is never to be found in the accounts of Captain Garcilaso's son. This circumstance is understandable, however, for by the time Gómez was telling his story, his father was dead and his father's widow had become the wife of Gerónimo Luis de Cabrera.[2]

These two sons of an adulterous Cabrera in old Seville, as well as his natural daughter, Leonor de Zúñiga, wife of the conquistador Rodrigo de Esquivel, were surely subjects of the current scandals. But equally interesting to those who hoped to promote turmoil in Cuzco would have been two sons and a daughter of the lascivious Conde de la Gomera: Baltasar and Sebastián de Castilla, both of whom may have been illegitimate, and Leonor de Bobadilla, who indeed was illegitimate. For Sebastián was to lead the next insurrection, and the wedding festivities of Leonor's daughter were to provide the scene for the initiation of the revolt of Francisco Hernández Girón, a major rebellion in which Baltasar de Castilla was to be garrotted.

The earlier experiences of Leonor de Bobadilla, which Gómez years

---

[2] Don Pedro's mother was the granddaughter of the first Conde de Feria; Sebastián's mother was the granddaughter of the Conde's brother. In 1554 María de Toledo obtained permission to pass to the Indies with her two youngest children by Cabrera, but at Arenas Gordas her ship was wrecked and all were drowned. For a full account of the Cabreras see Luis G. Martínez Villada, *Los Cabrera;* also José Vélez Picasso, *La Villa de Valverde del Valle de Ica;* Manuel de Mendeburu, *Diccionario histórico-biográfico del Perú,* Vol. I, Appendix, pp. 254–256.

later was to reveal in print, must often have been the subject of loose talk among those in Cuzco who had accompanied Hernando de Soto to La Florida. When the great Adelantado had passed through the Canaries with his wife, Isabel de Bobadilla, doña Leonor, already beautiful and but seventeen years of age, was permitted after much persuasion to join doña Isabel as a lady in waiting. So pleased was the latter with this young kinswoman that she formally adopted her, and the happiness of De Soto himself was so manifest that some have thought he had designs on the maiden's virtue. But before reaching their first port, Leonor had been seduced by De Soto's vice-admiral, Nuño Tovar, who married her secretly when it became evident that she was pregnant. Furious, De Soto reduced the rank of Tovar, who, nonetheless, continued with the expedition and died on the banks of the Mississippi. Meanwhile, Leonor had borne him a daughter, María Sarmiento de Castilla, and now at Cuzco, fourteen years later, this maiden was on the eve of marriage to the conqueror, Alonso de Loaisa, a nephew of the first President of the Council of the Indies and also of the present Archbishop of Los Reyes, the latter of whom many hated because he was suspected of having influenced La Gasca in his recent distributions. Among Gómez' boyhood companions was Gonzalo Mejía de Figueroa, a son of Leonor by her second husband, Lorenzo Mejía de Figueroa, whose name suggests that he too may have been a Garcilaso kinsman.[3]

When the fury at Cuzco over malicious rumors had reached a point of danger, Marshal Alonso de Alvarado, whose haughty creole wife was renowned for both pride and cruelty, proceeded at the orders of the Viceroy to punish the guilty. Among those who joined him in his mission was Gerónimo Luis de Cabrera, and for some reason which could not be explained, Leonor's brother, Sebastián de Castilla, slipped off secretly in the night for the Charcas. Soon the bodies of several

[3] Garcilaso, *Comentarios*, Pt. II, Bk. V, Chap. 8; *La Florida del Inca*, Bk. I, Chaps. 8, 12; Bk. V, Pt. II, Chap. 7. The Conde de la Gomera married María de Castilla, daughter of Leonor de Bobadilla, her carnal aunt. Neither Baltasar nor Sebastián de Castilla is listed among their legitimate children. María Sarmiento de Castilla, daughter of Tovar, was referred to by her half brother as María de Ayala. For information about the Conde de la Gomera and the Bobadillas see Alberto y Arturo García Carraffa, *Enciclopedia heráldica y genealógica hispano-americana*, Vol. 17.

scandalmongers were displayed in the plaza; but more was involved than met the eye. Alvarado had scarcely brought the offenders to justice in Cuzco when news came that Sebastián de Castilla had assassinated the Governor of Potosí and was raising a general rebellion in the Charcas. The lords of great manors thereupon began to arm and Captain Garcilaso was preparing to lead out a contingent of horse when reports came that Castilla had been slain by his own men. Alvarado now sped to the Charcas to punish rebels, and Cuzco awaited nervously, for by July of 1552 Antonio de Mendoza was dead and the realm again was completely under the Justices of the Audiencia, who continued to threaten with the New Laws.

Passing from La Paz and Potosí to La Plata, Alvarado punished with prodigality and coolness, declaring all the while that when he had trimmed off the branches of insurrection in the Charcas he intended to return and destroy its roots in the Imperial City. Such warnings produced consternation at Cuzco, and as citizens began to take measures for security, the Indians, relying for their knowledge upon the behavior of the elements, warned loudly and openly of the presence of a traitor in their midst. Gómez watched them early one morning in 1553 when he had wandered into the plaza to see what preparations had been made for the religious processions of the day. Aroused to a frenzy by the sight of a great luminous comet sweeping across the heavens to the accompaniment of thunder and lightning, they filled the air with shrill cries of "auca, auca," their word for tyrant or traitor. Gómez heard their warnings with respect because he still held much faith in their ability to read the language of the heavens; but imbued as he was with the concept that any civil dissension in Peru was but an extension of the eternal conflict between God and the most mutinous of his angels, he saw significance in the fact that this terrible display of Divine wrath had occurred on the day of the Feast of the Most Holy Sacrament.[4] But he knew, as did many people in Cuzco, whom Satan had designated to lead his cohorts, since among them there was one citizen whose conduct past and present rendered obvious his seditious ambitions. He was Francisco Hernández Girón.

---

[4] Garcilaso, *Comentarios*, Pt. II, Bk. VI, Chap. 29.

Soon after the departure of La Gasca, Hernández Girón had returned to Cuzco purportedly to raise troops to conquer the Charcas but in reality to plot a new rebellion. He had filled the city with despicable recruits, whom nervous citizens were forced to feed at their tables, and when at length efforts were made to hasten the departure of these adventurers, they had petulantly barricaded themselves in the dwelling of their leader. In the several perilous days that followed, Captain Garcilaso three times had served voluntarily as a hostage and Gómez as a messenger between hostile factions while officials bombarded Girón with persuasions.[5] And though Hernández Girón eventually had been returned to Los Reyes and his troops dispersed with gunfire, he now was back in Cuzco surrounded with his usual following of common soldiers, whose lusts and ambitions could be depended upon whenever there was an opportunity for a quarrel. Aware of course that he was one of the objects of Alvarado's threats, Hernández Girón continued to plot secretly and by November 13, 1553, was ready to strike.

On this day, all of Cuzco was preoccupied with the marriage of the daughter of Leonor de Bobadilla to the nephew of the Archbishop of Los Reyes, and the usual enmities had been laid aside for the festivities.[6] In the afternoon the customary games and races took place in the plaza, and in the evening the revelers gathered to feast at the home of the bride's uncle, Baltasar de Castilla, the men in the great hall near the entrance and the ladies in the salon to the rear. When the hour was late and gaiety had reached a climax, there was a loud summons at the doors and almost immediately Francisco Hernández Girón swept in with a small band of armed men to proclaim his rebellion, suggesting as he did so that he was merely taking the lead in a movement in which others had been involved. Panic now ensued, and in the initial struggle

[5] *Ibid.*, Pt. II, Bk. VI, Chap. 14; also Diego Fernández, *Historia del Perú,* ed. Odriozola, Pt. II, Bk. I, Chap. 5.

[6] Alonso de Loaisa, who had fled with Sebastián Garcilaso at Sacsahuana, was a nephew of Gerónimo de Loaisa, Archbishop of Los Reyes, and also a nephew of García de Loaisa, Archbishop of Seville, who as first president of the Council of the Indies had opposed the New Laws. For the story of the beginning of the Hernández Girón rebellion, see Garcilaso, *Comentarios,* Pt. II, Bk. VII, Chaps. 1–4. See also Fernández, *Historia del Perú,* ed. Odriozola, Pt. II, Bk. II, Chap. 24.

several men were brutally slain, though the majority hastily departed through the most available exits. The Corregidor shamefully took refuge in the salon with the ladies, and Captain Garcilaso fled with a group to the rear where they found a ladder that provided escape to an adjacent courtyard and from thence to the streets. Before ascending, however, the Captain three times returned to persuade the Corregidor to hasten with them to the main plaza and use his rod of authority to put down the rebellion. But the Corregidor, fearful that all, including Garcilaso, might be plotting, refused to budge, and eventually Garcilaso, after joining his companions, slipped through the streets to the house of his brother-in-law Antonio de Quiñones, from whence, after hasty preparations, he set out with a few companions for Los Reyes, some going first to the plantation of López de Cazalla and others to the rural retreat of Pedro Luis de Cabrera.

During the nuptial festivities, Gómez, while observing the sports from the top of a nearby wall, took note of the brooding countenance of Hernández Girón, who had not joined the players; and in the evening he had just arrived at the wedding feast to accompany his father and his stepmother back to their home when Hernández Girón struck. Thus he saw the whole doleful event from a point of vantage. In the ensuing turmoil he remained with his father, scaling the wall, and then preceded the little group, whistling at street intersections to indicate that passage was safe. Later, as he crept from the Quiñones house to fetch a horse from his father's stables, he noted three well caparisoned horses tended by Negro lackeys in front of the house of Tomás Vázquez, a circumstance which when reported troubled Captain Garcilaso exceedingly, since it led him to suspect that this old friend and neighbor had joined the rebels. This suspicion Gómez soon afterward confirmed when, as he wandered about the plaza, he not only saw Tomás Vázquez doing the rebel's bidding, but with him Juan de Piedrahita, another of the Captain's friends. Three days later when Hernández Girón came to search for Captain Garcilaso, Gómez heard his young stepmother inform the rebel leader, in language befitting the stouthearted woman she was to prove herself to be, that her husband had not returned home since the night of the wedding; and Hernández Girón quickly sensed what many afterward were to discover, that Luisa

Martel de los Ríos was a woman who could not easily be intimidated. Meanwhile, Captain Garcilaso fled on to Los Reyes in the company of his brother-in-law and López de Cazalla; but Pedro Luis de Cabrera, wishing to know more of the true situation at Cuzco before taking flight, resorted to a stratagem which deceived few and left room for future charges. Dispatching messengers to Hernández Girón who in truth were no more than spies, he declared his desire to see the rebel made Governor General of the realm but warned that the latter could expect no aid from Antonio de Quiñones or Garcilaso de la Vega since he had usurped the leadership of a revolt which they themselves had been plotting. Hernández Girón gave no credence to the message, but some men did, and it eventually was accepted as substantially true by the chronicler Diego Fernández de Palencia, generally known as "the Palentino."[7] Moreover, there was to persist a rumor that Garcilaso at one time did indeed contemplate joining the rebels, a rumor which must have pained the Captain considerably because of the contempt with which he regarded Hernández Girón and his lowborn associates.

Once more Cuzco lay under a shroud of fear and death. Many others now attempted to emulate Captain Garcilaso in flight. Some succeeded and some failed. Among the latter, to Gómez' sorrow, was Baltasar de Castilla, son of the Conde de la Gomera and brother of Leonor de Bobadilla; soon his naked and headless body was left exposed in the plaza as a warning. And now since security was not to be found in quality, rank, or even innocence, those intimidated citizens who were unable to escape reluctantly accepted Hernández Girón as a Procurator General and, accompanied by a motley contingent of common soldiers as well as a unique regiment of colorfully-vested Negroes, they followed the rebel out of the city to challenge the forces of the King.

In this new panorama of arms and horses, turmoil and confusion, Gómez had little time for formal instruction or the perusal of romances. All about him a new drama of cold reality was demanding his attention.[8] Presently he saw the splendid forces of Marshal Alonso de Al-

---

[7] Garcilaso, *Comentarios*, Pt. II, Bk. VII, Chap. 5; also *Cartas de Indias*, Vol. II, p. 784; Fernández, *Historia del Perú*, ed. Odriozola, Pt. II, Bk. II, Chap. 25.

[8] For the story of the Hernández Girón rebellion, see Garcilaso, *Comentarios*, Pt. II, Bk. VII, *passim*.

varado enter the city, their horses arrayed in the rich silver trappings of Potosí; and he watched them depart for Chuquinca, where they were to suffer a miserable defeat which would mark the beginning of a lethal lypothymia for their great general. He saw the rebels heap new fruit on the gallows as fleeing men were trapped and returned to face eternity. He saw them robbing the neighboring courtyards of hastily buried treasures; and he watched them removing the great iron bells from the churches of Cuzco—one from the church of Nuestra Señora de la Merced and another from that of the Dominicans, but only two of the five from the Cathedral before the Bishop checked them with threats of eternal damnation. Then one morning he watched with relief as they departed for Yúcay to join their leader; and at noon of the same day, his heart was lifted by the sight of his father, who had joined Alvarado with two hundred soldiers after the rout at Chuquinca and now was returning to the city with friends to ascertain what in their absence had befallen their families and property.

Fear reigned on that and the succeeding night. Streets were barricaded and sentinels placed, and while Captain Garcilaso and others lay concealed in the house of a neighbor, Gómez conveyed messages back and forth between sentinels and citizens. He was but an insignificant mestizo, but because of his insignificance he could perform a service for the forces of the King. On the following afternoon, while standing in the courtyard of his father's house, he heard a clatter of hooves flying across the cobbles and on looking up beheld Pedro Hernández el Leal dashing through the portals on the swift-footed little Pajarillo. Seized with joy, the boy rushed to his father with the news, and when Captain Garcilaso had greeted his friend with a warm embrace, Hernández regaled them with another thrilling tale of flight from death. Captured and sentenced by Hernández Girón to be hanged, he said, he was already kneeling to receive the halter when his hangman was interrupted by a question from a companion. Seizing the opportunity, the miserable captive sprang to his feet and departed with all speed to beg mercy of Hernández Girón, who, though he regarded the petitioner as no more than a vile tailor, granted it. His tale of further flight must have delighted his listeners exceedingly, and it offers an amazing and colorful example of Spanish modesty and chivalry. His generous captors simply had granted this man of extravagant loyalty license to secret himself behind the rugged landscape while performing an obligation to nature, and once more sensing an opportunity, he had dashed away to perform an obligation to his sovereign. What a loyal man was don Pedro, and what a swift-footed horse was "the little sparrow," Pajarillo! Soon all the King's forces returned to Cuzco and the plazas rang with the sound of trumpet and drum as men raced back and forth rehearsing battle maneuvers. Then a few days later, they were gone, off now for Pucara and a decisive struggle which took place on October 8, 1554.

The efforts to stem the rebellion of Francisco Hernández Girón had been somewhat inglorious and more than once the forces of the King had suffered defeat. The Justices of the Audiencia had continued to quarrel among themselves, Santillán and Mercado siding against Saravia, and all bickering over who was to marshal the forces. And when this important post was divided between the pompous Archbishop of Los Reyes, Gerónimo de Loaisa, and the licentiate Santillán, many came to feel that His Holiness could have passed his time more profitably on his knees praying for Christians and that the lawyer might have done just as well if he had remained at home stretched out on his bed. Indeed, gossipmongers spread word that the Archbishop wasted interminable hours playing chess while the lawyer occupied himself with unlimited siestas, and their unprofitable activities eventually were immortalized in some jolly doggerel which their cohorts chanted with profane zest.[9] And the termination of the rebellion presented as sorry a spectacle as its beginning, for it too was distinguished mainly by confusion and weavings. The missiles from the rebel cannons were of course ineffective since, as it was believed, they had been molded from the sacred bells of the Imperial City; and as the gloom of night fell, many of the King's men were peppered in the rear by their own musket fire, it being too dark to distinguish between a loyal buttock and that of a rebel. Then the weavings and flights began. Tomás Vázquez

---

[9] The Justices were Melchor Bravo de Saravia, Fernando de Santillán, Diego González Altamirano, and Pedro Mercado de Peñalosa. See Garcilaso, *Comentarios*, Pt. II, Bk. VII, Chaps. 7, 19; also *Gobernantes del Perú*, Vol. I, pp. 272–273; *Colección de libros y documentos referentes a la historia del Perú*, Ser. II, Vol. IX, p. 22; and the Introduction to Fernando Santillán's *Relación*, pp. xli–xlii.

and Juan de Piedrahita, undergoing a swift and judicious shift in conscience, fled to the forces of the King; Hernández Girón's chief lieutenant gathered a small group and vanished into the wilderness; and at
length Hernández Girón himself, fearing death at the hands of his
own men, called for his horse and slipped off into the night. Before
long, however, the rebel was apprehended at Sausa. With him to the
last and refusing to desert him was Captain Garcilaso's rebellious
cousin, Gómez Suárez de Figueroa, who had been one of the last to
remain with Gonzalo Pizarro at Sacsahuana.

While the hounds of justice were pursuing the conspirators, Captain
Garcilaso and the Justices of the Audiencia and all who had lifted a
hand had remained at Pucara to contemplate the spoils; and here at the
scene of triumph the Captain began mapping his future with astuteness.
He kept a well-provided table and won men's fealties by filling their
stomachs, and doubtlessly he entertained at his board at least some if
not all of the Justices who had witnessed the recent struggle. Afterward, when the victors returned to Cuzco, the licentiate Fernando de
Santillán, who years later was to defend Garcilaso's loyalty, lodged at
the house of the Captain's repentant friend, Tomás Vázquez, and the
licentiate Mercado Peñalosa, who formerly had been a member of the
Council of the Indies, accepted the hospitality of Garcilaso himself.
Soon Tomás Vázquez could boast of a royal pardon as well as a bounte-
ous estate, and Captain Garcilaso, by a decree executed on November
16, 1554, was named Corregidor of Cuzco and assured of an emolu-
ment befitting his rank and station.[10]

In explaining the appointment of Garcilaso to such a responsible
position, as well as other similar appointments throughout the realm,
the Justices declared that they had sought to fill these positions with
citizens who were both illustrious and rich, since such men were more
capable of executing the laws and gave greater promise of bringing
tranquility to the land. Yet the appointees had not responded to the
honor without bargain and, because of the expenses involved, had demanded that the corresponding emoluments be made equally honor-

[10] Garcilaso, *Comentarios,* Pt. II, Bk. VII, Chap. 30; Bk. VIII, Chap. 12; *Cartas
de Indias,* Vol. II, p. 784; letter of Oidores to Council of Indies, Feb. 5, 1555,
Colección de documentos inéditos del Archivo de Indias, Vol. III, pp. 321–325.

able. According to the Justices, the remuneration of Captain Garcilaso amounted to three thousand pesos, but according to the Marqúes de Cañete, who suspected some connivance, it was a repartimiento which had belonged to Francisco Hernández Girón and was valued at twelve thousand pesos.[11] Nevertheless, there was one thing about which the people of Cuzco could be certain: the gay and rich Corregidor would spend at least a portion of his wealth endowing the city once again with some of the splendors of sunny Castile.

On December 7, 1554, approximately thirteen months after the beginning of his revolt, Francisco Hernández Girón was hitched to the tail of a lean jade at Los Reyes and dragged to the executioner's block. His head, on being severed, was fixed to an iron pike in the main plaza to form a triumvirate in death with the heads of Francisco de Carvajal and Gonzalo Pizarro; and his noble widow, whom Gómez had admired in Cuzco, now retired to the loneliness of a nearby convent. Again the realm had rejected a crusader for rebellion, but another somber spectacle of punishment would not yet serve to discourage ambitious and inflamed spirits. Cuzco remained a bed of smoldering coals, and the delicate task of keeping them from bursting into flames lay with the new Corregidor, Captain Garcilaso de la Vega. During the two succeeding years, therefore, Gómez, even more intimately associated now than previously with his father, was to see the Captain bring at least a semblance of peace out of turmoil.

And so the years sped by like giant leaves twisting in the winds, whirling in circles and revealing multicolored hues to a wide-eyed mestizo. As his wisdom increased he became even more aware that the deeds of Spaniards were performed with an eye on both the past and the future. Glorying always in their traditions, which emphasized that noble acts were an evidence of rich blood, they now recorded their present accomplishments with the same zeal that they had recorded the past. Even in the battle arenas there were men who found time, if not in the mad heat of combat, then in the mad heat of post-battle boasting, to write down what they had seen and heard. There were men who scribbled for the sole purpose of preserving their experiences for the

---

[11] Cañete to the King, Sept. 15, 1556. See *Gobernantes del Perú*, Vol. I, p. 272.

entertainment of friends and relatives; and there were men who set down in miserable ink and costly but perishable paper both facts and rumors with an ambition to enter and swell the ever-growing ranks of chroniclers. Moreover, in a milieu of such magniloquence and heroics it often was difficult for both actor and recorder to separate fact from fiction, and since few conquerors were unaware of the extent to which their fame and security lay with the men who wielded the pen, sops and emoluments sometimes were utilized to persuade chroniclers to conceal or color the truth. Yet within the souls of these busy historians there lay a fine talent for "doublethink," and each found it easy to convince himself that his account of this New World adventure was the "true one." Certainly Gómez and his father at one time or another had come in contact with most of these men who were busy with the quill. With the Captain in his flight to Arequipa had been Pedro Pizarro, who kept a diary of events, though possibly with no idea of publication; associated with him to some extent during the Pizarro rebellion had been Agustín de Zárate, who did plan to publish; present at the battle of Sacsahuana when he finally escaped from Pizarro was Pedro de Cieza de León, whom La Gasca very soon afterward appointed as a royal chronicler and who in 1549 and 1550 was in Cuzco questioning a number of the Captain's friends, including his brother-in-law, Antonio de Quiñones;[12] with Alonso de Alvarado when he came to Cuzco to punish scandalmongers and throughout the Hernández Girón rebellion was Diego Fernández de Palencia, the Palentino, who was recording with an eye to publication;[13] and witnessing the whole of the Peruvian conflicts was Pedro Gutiérrez de Santa Clara, a man of obscure origin whose voluminous records give evidence that he hoped for a more widespread audience than that of relatives and friends.

Now, as the civil turmoils of Peru were drawing to a close, accounts of these struggles were beginning to find their way to the printers of

---

[12] Cieza de León undoubtedly was closely related to Sebastián Garcilaso's good friend Pedro López de Cazalla. Both were from Llerena. Cieza's mother was Leonor de Cazalla and his father was Lope de León; he had a brother named Rodrigo de Cieza, and López de Cazalla had a brother named León, who lived at Cuzco.

[13] William Hickling Prescott, *History of the Conquest of Perú*, Vol. II, p. 473.

Europe. Ironically, the first of the professed historians to convert the more recent annals of the Peruvian conquest into print was Francisco López de Gómara, already a scholar of renown, who, though he enjoyed high court favor and served as chaplain for Hernán Cortés after the latter's return to Spain, had never set foot in the New World. López de Gómara's history of the conquest of the Indies was first published in 1552, and new editions appeared in 1553 and 1554. Meanwhile Cieza de León had been laboriously arranging his mass of manuscripts into an extended chronicle, and the first part, which dealt primarily with the Incas and the land they inhabited, was published in 1553 and again in 1554. But three books which he had written on the civil wars of Peru, he was afraid to print because of the scandal that might ensue and because certain people might resent what these histories contained. In his last will, dated June 23, 1554, he specified that these books were to be kept under lock and key until fifteen years after his death. Furthermore, Zárate, back in Spain and no longer menaced by Carvajal, had prepared an account which detailed the affairs of Peru from the time of its discovery until the close of the La Gasca mission. Still fearful of embroilment or of hurting living persons, Zárate on finishing his history had stipulated that it not be published for nine years, and he later extended his specification to ninety years. But Prince Philip, while on his way to England to wed Mary Tudor, became so impressed with Zárate's account that he urged its immediate publication and it appeared in print in 1555.

Of significance at this point is that any account of the conquest and the civil strifes in Peru would record some of the actions of Captain Garcilaso de la Vega; and though in general the historians pictured him in an honorable role, they all persisted in burdening him more or less with the stigma of Huarina. In describing the battle, López de Gómara had written: "Pizarro would have been in peril had not Garcilaso given him a horse." And Zárate, though he prudently omitted the cavalier's name, attested that indeed it was in the heat of the battle and not afterward that Pizarro was in need of a horse when he wrote: "The horsemen, seeing the route of the infantry, assailed the adversaries and did them much damage. They slew the horse of Gonzalo Pizarro and hurled the rider to the ground without injuring him." What Cieza de León had to say of the incident, if anything, did not appear in his 1553 publication; but Gutiérrez de Santa Clara wrote:

Being present, Garcilaso de la Vega, Captain of his guard, dismounted hurriedly and gave his horse to his master, telling him to give courage to his men, who had believed that he had been killed, and he did so, and Garcilaso took another horse which was running loose there and followed after his master. Thus when Gonzalo Pizarro found himself mounted, he joined the loyal ones, with four men on horse and six arquebusiers who followed them, and he began anew to fight with a fine-edged sword, wishing to avenge the offense they had done him in knocking him off his horse.

And finally, Fernández de Palencia was to insert in his manuscripts:

Pedro de los Ríos and Antonio de Ulloa, instead of attacking the infantry as they had been ordered to do, attacked the cavalry from the opposite side and in such a manner as to hurl them all to the ground, not ten of them remaining in the saddle; and as men who held their victory assured they began to plunder their adversaries and to subdue and deprive them of arms. Gonzalo Pizarro was thrown to the ground in this encounter, and Garcilaso (who had remained in the saddle) dismounted and gave him his horse and helped him to mount.[14]

It would be several centuries before the manuscripts of Gutiérrez de Santa Clara were published and almost two decades before those of the Palentino appeared in print. But even as Captain Garcilaso, at the apex of his career, was entering upon his duties as Corregidor of Cuzco, the shadow of Huarina was lowering.

[14] Garcilaso, *Comentarios*, Pt. II, Bk. V, Chap. 23; Francisco López de Gómara, *Historia general de las Indias*, Vol. II, Chap. 181; Agustín de Zárate, *Historia del descubrimiento y conquista del Perú*, Bk. VII, Chap. 3; Pedro Gutiérrez de Santa Clara, *Historia de las guerras civiles del Perú*, Vol. X, Chap. 58; Fernández, *Historia del Perú*, ed. Odriozola, Pt. I, Bk. II, Chap. 79. Though Cieza's comments on Huarina have not been found, he did speak favorably of Garcilaso's role elsewhere. See Cieza de León, *Guerras civiles*, Vol. II, Chap. 55.

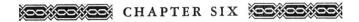 CHAPTER SIX

G ÓMEZ WAS FIFTEEN YEARS OF AGE when in November of 1554 Captain Garcilaso entered upon his official duties as Corregidor of Cuzco. Mounting evidence of his son's intelligence had served to increase the Captain's affection, though it also had brought some apprehension as to the uncertainty of the boy's future. Just what stipulations, if any, he had made by this time for Gómez in his will is not known. But one of the Captain's first gestures after assuming his administrative office was to bestow equally and irrevocably upon Gómez and a cousin, García Suárez de Figueroa, a coca plantation in the fertile valley of Havisca.[1] Thus, even as an adolescent the mestizo began to receive some personal profits from the riches of Peru. Meanwhile he served his father in a variety of roles. He is known to have traveled widely throughout the surrounding regions, and because of his knowledge of the quipu he surely continued to aid in counting the vast and varied tributes that were brought to the Captain's storehouses. Furthermore, because of his formal training he was able to assist the Captain as a scribe at a time when men who could write seldom were readily

[1] Havisca was in the region of Antisuyu to the east of Paucartambo. Later references make it reasonable to assume that this cousin was the same as Garcí Sánchez de Figueroa. El Inca Garcilaso, *Los comentarios reales,* Pt. I, Bk. IV, Chap. 16; Pt. II, Bk. VII, Chap. 4; also documents dated August 19 and 27, 1574, Montilla, Archivo de Protocolos, Escribano Juan Martínez de Córdoba, fols. 555–557; 581–582.

available.[2] In this manner he was brought into closer communion with his father and given the opportunity to become unusually cognizant of the affairs in which the latter was involved while serving as Corregidor of the turbulent city.

In general, what is known of the government of Captain Garcilaso comes from the records of his son and consequently is biased.[3] Yet few would have denied that after the previous mutinous years, the appointment of the Captain was fortunate for all. In addition to possessing the authority and comparative immunity of both rank and riches, he had a remarkable insight into the minds and personalities of people of all races and classes. He was a quiet man, soft-spoken, even-tempered, and deliberate, who over the years had directed his career through perilous situations by the sheer force of diplomacy and cavalier charm. He possessed a remarkable ability to admire all potentially honest men and to appear to understand them regardless of their politics, an ability strengthened by sincerity and strangely effective whether dealing with an opponent or a friend. His method as Corregidor, as his son recorded, was paternal rather than judicial, and preventive rather than corrective.

But Captain Garcilaso was unwilling to rely altogether upon his natural prudence in handling men or even upon experience acquired in the Indies. Aware of his obligation to the Crown and of his own comparative ignorance of the intricacies of Spanish legal ethics, he set about reading not only those laws which pertained to the Kingdom and its far-flung colonies but those which bore upon himself personally. Moreover, he selected as his assistant the able licentiate Juan Ruiz Monjaraz, and he welcomed the counsel of this man as well as that of other men of exceptional erudition. Conscious, however, of the perils of a divided administration, he foresightedly insisted that his lieutenant be responsible to the Corregidor rather than to the Judges of the Audiencia, whose renowned dissensions Garcilaso knew could impede the processes of justice. But though cautious to know the law, he exercised his own discretion in applying it, tempering it in accordance with his understanding of Spanish character. Having imperiled his own

[2] Garcilaso, *Comentarios,* Pt. II, Bk. VIII, Chap. 6.
[3] *Ibid.,* Pt. II, Bk. VIII, Chap. 12 *et passim.*

life and fortunes to gain new dominions for Spain, he regarded with sympathy the disappointments of those who had done the same without just reward; and though he apparently under no circumstances condoned armed rebellion against his sovereign, he was reluctant to condemn men who, having appeared to err in this manner, had repented propitiously.

The first test of Captain Garcilaso's administrative talents came in the early days of his government when news reached him secretly that Francisco de Añasco, an energetic young cavalier, had assembled a small army with the intention of throwing the city once more into anarchy. Concealing his knowledge, the Corregidor, much to the suspicion and terror of the citizens, merely invited Añasco to his house and offered him both board and bed. Meanwhile the embryonic army was dispersed, and the misguided young cavalier, after forty days of guarded hospitality and persuasion, was sent as an exile to Quito, grateful and repentant, with three hundred pesos and a fine horse, gifts of the Corregidor. Thus Captain Garcilaso, through mere prudence and foresight, averted another revolution and won praise from the Audiencia.

And yet though forebearing in judging civil matters and the petty personal animosities which arose constantly between easily irritated citizens, Captain Garcilaso, utterly intolerant when it came to deeds that reflected on the Church, zealously guarded the tradition and semblances of piety. Once when an irate hidalgo with drawn sword pursued the object of his wrath to the very high altar of a sanctuary, the passion of the Corregidor flared. Who was this man, he asked, who would profane God's temple; and how, indeed, would the natives regard men who preached one code and practiced another? And when this defiler of sanctuary came to the Corregidor pleading for remission of the fine imposed, he indignantly doubled the amount and admonished the culprit to be grateful for not having received the garrote.

Church discipline Garcilaso imposed first upon himself, adhering rigidly to the demands and precepts of Catholicism. Not only did he attend ecclesiastical rites with solemn regularity, but ever solicitous for men's souls, whether on earth or in transit, he purchased masses generously for those who might need the additional boost into Paradise.

Two hundred ducats of his gold went each year for the celebration of one particular religious feast, and his ample and pious patronage could be relied upon always for the various orders of religious who sought a foothold in the Inca capital. When the Franciscans thought to establish their convent nearer to the great plaza they enlisted his aid, and he soon was able to put them in possession of sufficient funds for an appropriate edifice. They in turn assigned him a choice sepulcher beneath the high altar of their church, placing over it the arms of his illustrious family.

A constant witness to his father's piety and a receptive scholar in the discipline of the prelates, Gómez, as he matured in the Roman faith, searched always for manifestations which could be explained only by miracles. His never-dying faith in such traditional and orthodox Catholic lore as the miraculous intervention of Santiago and the Holy Virgin in pagan-Christian conflicts is understandable. But his persistent faith in less orthodox concepts appears at times incredible, though it was not uncommon. He believed always that the Devil ceased speaking through pagan oracles after the first Christian sacraments were said in Peru, and he held firmly that men who blasphemed eventually were punished with oral wounds, and to prove his theory he could cite horrible examples. But of uncommon interest is his credence in a supra-sensory perception to be found in dumb animals, a kind of spiritual communication with their maker which rendered them capable of some unusual transactions. This faith is to be seen in his later stories of canine intelligence in La Florida and in his account of the fierce lions at Túmbez who were converted immediately into fawning and lovable creatures by the sight of a Christian cross. Such examples of Christian marvels of course had come to him as hearsay, but now in Cuzco, in these years when he was responding so eagerly to the pageantry accompanying the multiple feasts designated by the Church calendar, he was to witness a spectacle which apparently wrought heavily on his naive and willing credulity.[4]

It happened, so he said, on the occasion of the feast of San Bartolomé, a colorful celebration in which the featured actor was a flower-festooned bull. All the clergy and confraternities of the city as well as

[4] *Ibid.*, Pt. II, Bk. VIII, Chap. 2.

a host of other people had gathered to solemnize the occasion, and the bull, tame and gentle as a lamb, walked in their midst without the slightest sign of disturbance. On arrival at the church, which was too small to accommodate the multitudes, the Indians and persons of less importance remained outside but formed a lane through which the procession could pass. The Spaniards, in turn, on entering the church, left a passage to the chancel for the blessed bull, which ambled forward in all tranquility directly in front of the prelates. But having passed three or four paces within the portico, the animal suddenly lunged at a Spaniard named Salazar and with well directed horns tossed the man unharmed from the church. Such an unprecedented performance of course threw the frightened multitude into confusion; but the sanctified bull, in an unusual display of serenity, merely returned to its alloted place of honor and proceeded with infinite gentleness to the altar. In utter amazement, witnesses to the occasion diligently set about trying to penetrate the mystery; and their search, according to Gómez, was not without reward. On strict examination it was discovered that a few months previously Salazar, having made the error of instituting a lawsuit against the prelates, had incurred a penalty of excommunication from which he had never been absolved. But with this incident, all noted, the wretched man punctually declared his intention of never again committing such a contumacy and pled for absolution.

The vigilance of prelates concerning their worldly resources was to become a subject of ribaldry in sixteenth-century Spain, and one cannot be sure that in recalling this event many years later Gómez did not do so in the same spirit as Cervantes, who more than once suffered the inconvenience of excommunication for attempting legally to invade the storehouses of the priesthood. But to the credulous mestizo in Cuzco, who had been trained by both Spaniards and Indians to look for signs in natural phenomena, the incident of the pious and resolute bull was subject to but one interpretation, and it increased his alertness for miracles in the mystic rituals of Catholicism.

Always eager to transplant to the Indies the pageantry of Spain, the conquerors with the encouragement of the clergy had spared no pains in making their religious processions as ostentatious as those which through the years had been consecrated in the homeland; and at Cuzco Captain Garcilaso as Corregidor would have urged the embelishment of such occasions. Among the most significant festivals was that of the sacred Feast of Corpus Christi, during which sturdy vassals and penitents conveyed through the streets and plazas the carefully adorned litters of both Indians and Spaniards who vied with each other to produce the greatest splendor. On these litters, which were ornamented with fringes and embroideries of silk and gold, studded with emeralds and other precious stones, were placed large images of Christ, the Virgin, or some particular saint, so that in all respects they resembled those used by the confraternities of old Spain.

But what gave these occasions a novelty not to be found in the most grotesque processions of the homeland was the participation of the natives, who, though ostensibly converted to Catholicism, clung still to much of their pagan culture. Caciques residing near the city came with their kindred and the nobility of their provinces, and since they arrived vested in the apparel formerly used to celebrate their own traditional feasts, there as ever was reason to suspect that they simply were worshipping old gods under new names. For even in their costumes and disguises multiple pagan and primitive concepts were depicted. Some wore lion skins with the head of the beast serving as a cap; others appeared as angels with long, extended wings taken from the sacred condor; some wore clothes which bore paintings of rivers, fountains, lakes, mountains, caves, and many other natural phenomena which they regarded as sources of their being; some were adorned with strange pagan devices of gold and silver; some appeared as monsters, their hands being the claws or paws of wild beasts taken in a jungle struggle; others pretended to be fools and idiots, endeavoring in every way to divert their superiors, while still others feigned riches and grandeurs or feigned misery and penury. But unavoidable was the truth that while purporting to enhance a Catholic and alien solemnity, these confused people unconsciously, and sometimes consciously, revealed that their faith was not a conversion but an amalgam. Thus a celebration designed to be grotesque in its mysticism became, in its heterogeneousness, supra-grotesque.

On one such solemn occasion during the government of Captain Garcilaso, the Spanish population of Cuzco was given an opportunity to fathom the memory of a conquered race and to test the durable pride of a lost people.[5] In a golden coffer resting on a scaffold in the church-yard lay the Holy Sacrament while alongside, in addition to the Corregidor and his aide, sat church officials, citizens, and remnants of the Inca nobility. Meanwhile, Indians of various districts had assembled in their pagan finery and were parading their litters through the streets with hymns of thanksgiving to both their Pachacámac and their conquerors for the gift of Christianity. But when they began to ascend the scaffold to adore the Host, there suddenly burst into their midst a mysterious, mantled figure whose accompanying litter bore four panels depicting struggles between Spaniards and Indians, and who bore in his right hand the counterfeited head of an Inca. Disrobing until he stood naked before all, this revolting character revealed himself to be Francisco Chillchi, unprincipled leader of the lowborn and despised Cañari Indians of Cuzco and especially odious to the memory of all Incas who had participated in the unsuccessful siege of the Inca Manco. Then when angry Incas had hurled him from the scaffold with cries that the traitorous dog had come to quicken odious memories and not to celebrate a feast, the Cañari reminded them of a day when in that same plaza he, with the sanction of Christians, had met and cut off the head of an Inca challenger because no one of the besieged Spaniards would dishonor himself by contending with an Indian in single combat. And since the four panels of his litter, he said, represented battles in which he himself had fought alongside Spaniards against Indians, his boasting of feats of arms performed in the service of Christians should present no occasion for surprise.

Again shouting dog and traitor, an enraged Inca, in a reply designed for both Spaniards and Indians, reminded the Cañari that he and all his lineage once had been slaves of the Incas, and that his previous triumph had not been due to his own strength but to the intervention of the Pachacámac before whom all at the moment stood. And now that all were Christians, he said, let the Cañari arm himself again and retire to the market place, where one of the lowliest of the Inca slaves

[5] *Ibid.,* Pt. II, Bk. II, Chaps. 25–26; Bk. VIII, Chap. 1.

would meet him in a new combat and slice him into pieces. Then detailing the great number of Spaniards the Incas had slain during the siege, both in Cuzco and along the road to Rímac, and declaring that the siege had been lifted only when the Inca Manco beheld the miracles wrought by Pachacámac in favor of the Christians, he ironically asked if it would not have been appropriate for the Incas to bring to this present feast the heads of those Spaniards, including that of Juan Pizarro, who had been slain at the fortress above where they all now stood. Having thus vented his rage, the proud Inca faced the officials and begged that they render appropriate punishment and not force his people to suffer insults from those who once were their slaves.

The despicable Cañari was ordered to surrender the provocative symbol at once, and all Indians were forbidden under pain of death to treat of such matters either publicly or privately. Nevertheless, as the procession moved forward and regenerated pagans knelt to adore the sacred Host, the familiar Indian cry of "auca, auca" was raised and passed with subtle meaning from one Indian to another until it resounded throughout the Imperial City. The shades of Santiago and the Holy Virgin still kept watch over that storied plaza, but the Sun deity moved eternally through the Andean heavens; the Pachacámac of the Incas had failed to merge entirely with a Hebraic Jehovah.

The Corregidor of Cuzco was in need of no additional demonstrations to increase his awareness of the extent to which Incaic fires still smoldered; for at nearby Vitcos, the Inca Sayri Túpac, un-Christianized and unrelenting, clung obstinately to a shadow throne, and each week many of his relatives continued to gather in the dwelling of Isabel Suárez Chimpu Ocllo to keep alive memories of the past. Still frequenting those curious occasions, noting the persistency with which confused Indians clung to ancient pagan concepts, was the mestizo who someday would record them. Moreover, as Gómez observed other Indians in Cuzco and in the outlying villages of his father's domain, he saw them performing pagan rites both openly and secretly. At their tables, he saw them dip their fingers into an intoxicating maze before holding them to the Sun as a token of thanksgiving; at great heights to which they had borne their burdens along wearisome Andean paths, he saw them turn their eyes to the heavens and then demonstrate their gratitude by offering some valued article, possibly a hair plucked from an eyebrow, a wad of coca from the mouth, or, if nothing better, sometimes a stick or a stone or a clod of earth as a mere token; and in their dark temples where the "Zúpay" or Indian Devil was purported to speak, he saw them offering tokens of adoration and affection to some pagan idol. Once when awakened from his sleep in a province of the Quechuas, he saw great crowds with banners and the clothing of a dead leader hastening to the fields to carry out the pagan rites with which at each phase of the moon they still honored their departed leaders. In numerous places, on observing the natives carefully preserving nail parings or plucked hairs in some niche of a wall, he was moved to question them in regard to this strange custom. "Know that all who have been born in this world must return and live in it," they invariably replied, revealing a strange concept of immortality and resurrection, "and their souls must ascend from their sepulchers with their bodies complete. Lest our souls be detained by having to search for their hairs and fingernails (for on that day there will be much bustle and clamor and haste) we assemble them here in this place. Thus they may be retrieved more quickly, and if it were possible we would always expectorate in the same place." Years later when Gómez exposed this startling concept in one of his manuscripts, he was ordered by the Jesuits to remove it.[6]

It was only natural that as Gómez continued to observe these evidences of a lingering paganism, even among Christianized Indians, he would be affected by a spirit of evangelism which was strengthened not only by maturing Catholic convictions but by the pious efforts of his father. For Captain Garcilaso, contrary to many who manifestly regarded the conversion of the Indians as a somewhat tedious and worthless task, appears to have considered this an integral part of his mission. Whether moved by the dictates of the Crown, which always had demanded evangelism in making awards, or simply by his devotion to the Church and a sincere desire for the well-being of the Indians, he did take unusual precaution to provide teachers and preachers for the dissemination of the Faith among the Indians of his encomienda. And at times when the spiritual needs of the natives surpassed the ability or the

[6] *Ibid.,* Pt. I, Bk. II, Chap. 7.

zeal of priests to assist them, Gómez himself undertook to perform the rites of baptism.[7] Furthermore, when Church Fathers found themselves unable to interpret Christian mysteries in Quechua, Gómez assisted them. In doing so he strengthened a belief, long since emphasized by Las Casas, that the Indian as a rational human being should be Christianized by reason rather than by force. But he was aware that the processes of reason inevitably were impeded by linguistic ignorance, and he never ceased to stress that the fate of Peru and its people often had rested in the hands of incompetent and sometimes vicious interpreters, and to plead the tremendous necessity for Spanish evangels, both lay and ecclesiastical, to learn Quechua.

This same linguistic ignorance, Gómez knew to have contributed to the failure of Spaniards to comprehend the nature of the Incas as well as their past achievements. Over the years his own encounters with pagan traditions and customs had been so frequent as to fade into the commonplace; but as he grew older and regarded with keener perception the paradoxical arguments and changing attitudes of Spaniards concerning Indians, he became increasingly aware of the significance a comprehensive and true picture of the past civilization of the Incas might have in shaping their future. Having lived through the turmoils engendered by the New Laws, he of course would have been quite familiar with current Aristotelian arguments for Indian enslavement as well as popular attempts to justify Spanish exploitation of the Incas on the theory that in the past the Incas themselves had been little more than marauders. And though he appears to have been indoctrinated early by both Incas and Spaniards with a classic and permanent concept of the justice of human slavery, that concept embraced the idea that in the past, Inca emperors, like current Christian crusaders, had enforced their culture and laws and their system of slavery upon a less fortunate people in a spirit of benevolence and in accordance with a divine ordinance. Certainly by the time Gómez had become so intimately associated with his father in the affairs of Cuzco, he was beginning to feel a sense of regret that such vital knowledge of his Inca ancestors was to be had only through the oral recitations of the diminish-

[7] *Ibid.,* Pt. I, Bk. II, Chap. 8.

ing survivors of the vanished realm or through Spaniards forced to rely on interpreters. Thus moved, he one day, when approximately sixteen years of age, wandered into the abode of his mother and listened with renewed interest as the aged Cusi Huallpa was reiterating the deeds of his royal ancestors.

"But Inca, my uncle," the youth exclaimed, "since it is through writing that memory of things is preserved, and since you have no written language, what recollections do you have of the origin of our Emperors? Since the Spaniards and their neighboring nations are in possession of both human and divine histories, they know when their kings and the kings of others began to reign and how some empires gave way to others, and they know even how many thousands of years have elapsed since God created the heavens and the earth, for all of this and much more they have ascertained through their books. But you, who have no books, what recollection have you of your antiquities? Who was the first of your Incas, what was his name, what was the source of his lineage, how did he begin to reign, with what people and arms did he conquer this great empire, and what was the origin of our great achievements?"[8]

At that the face of the ancient was filled with piteous and contemptuous eagerness, and admonishing the youth to preserve in his heart forever the things he now would hear, he began that so often rehearsed tale of primitive beauty which linked the mestizo and the whole of the Incaic race with cosmic forces, that tale which, penetrating the mists of the past, told of how at least four centuries previously the Sun deity and his sister-queen, the Moon, brooding compassionately over the Andes, had sent two of their offspring through the dark womb of the fathomless Lake Titicaca to bring peace and prosperity and civilization to the miserable barbarians of that desolate region. Ascending to the rim of the world, he said, Manco Cápac and Mama Ocllo, the first Incas, had wandered northward with a golden scepter, searching always for a spot where the reluctant earth should be willing to swallow this glittering symbol of their mystic origin. Such a site they eventually discovered in an emerald valley cradled in peaks of shim-

[8] *Ibid.*, Pt. I, Bk. I, Chaps. 15–17.

mering ice and snow; and here they founded the Imperial City of Cuzco and fulfilled the benevolent mission of the Sun. From these two direct offspring of the Moon and the Sun, he declared, all Incas, including themselves, were descended, and it was they, he added with a tone of accusation and bitterness, who had owned that vast, rich and renowned empire of which Gómez's father and his father's companions had robbed them. And then the aged auqui concluded with that sob of despair common to a people who sang of what they had lost. "I believe that I have given you a full account of what you asked and have answered your questions," he said, "yet lest I should move you to weep, I, in reciting this history, have not permitted the tears of blood to flow from my eyes that do flow in my heart because of the grief it brings me to see our Incas no longer ruling and our people bereft of an empire."

The faith of the conquering Christians had been imposed by now upon Gómez' childhood conceptions of semi-divine origin, and his preceptors long since had substituted in his mind a new poetic concept for the old, robbing him of primitive though magnificent illusions. He would believe now that the first Incas were merely exceptional men who in exceptional times had utilized their illusions to strengthen their sway. Nevertheless the Incaic past was a part of his bone and marrow, and though the canopy of Castilian splendor and the strength of his Catholic faith had come to shield him against some of his Indian heritage, it had failed to purge his heart of a conception of the magnificence of these sovereigns whom he believed to be his ancestors. The questions presented his uncle were asked with the half-facetiousness of a mestizo youth who now was viewing the world through Castilian eyes, but, as he later admitted, he heeded the response with a raptness not previously experienced. Though he afterward declared that while in Peru he never contemplated recording any of the history of the Incas, surely as the sonorous words of an old Inca sage poured forth in a language that was vanishing with the empire, this youth who understood the heart of that language saw the beginning of a dream that was to result in his becoming a classic and sympathetic defender of the Incas.

All such interests in the welfare of the Indian were further encouraged by the exceptional attention which Captain Garcilaso gave to the material comfort of his vassals as well as the wretched Indians of Cuzco. He lowered their tributes, gave them llamas to bear their burdens, paid them for services by discounting amounts for foodstuffs they were to bring him, and whenever he found them ill took them into his own dwellings until they recovered. Upon the cacique García Pauqui he lavished especial attention, since it was this man who in the perilous days of the Pizarro rebellion had saved the Garcilaso household from starvation. In Cuzco he gave asylum to many orphaned Indians, and he left a monument to his efforts in a hospital for natives, the construction of which was initiated on July 13, 1556.[9] In behalf of this institution and its church annex of Nuestra Señora de los Remedios, he himself solicited funds with the assistance of his son, and the Franciscans were so pleased with this manifestation of piety that they gave a special blessing to the project. In time even wealthy Indians begged to pass their dying hours in that abode, hoping thereby to find an easier entrance into Paradise. Thus with his own Indians Captain Garcilaso was able to establish a species of vassalage which was not devoid of loyalty and affection and which conformed very well with the demands of the Crown. And with other Indians he came to be regarded as both a protector and a liaison.

The stable white population of Cuzco consisted still of approximately eighty citizens, primarily men who had arrived with the first conquerors, though of course there had been more recent additions. And yet mingled with the privileged who constituted the social structure of the city were still to be found the human driftage of the Renaissance world—the continual flow of adventurers and fortune seekers of Christendom. To these men Captain Garcilaso represented the courtier Spaniard, but an unusually acceptable one; for his wisdom and values did not emanate from the too frequently biased, ignorant, and invidious communications to and through the Council of the Indies. He had gained his knowledge from the wilderness alongside ruffians and common soldiers as well as the highborn. But what in this Corregidor appealed particularly to all Spaniards in Cuzco during his government

[9] *Ibid.*, Pt. I, Bk. VII, Chap. 12; Pt. II, Bk. VIII, Chap. 12.

was that, in his almost quixotic love of pageantry, he never ceased to link their present and oftentimes drab existence with the remembered merriment of their homeland—to seek to bring to the cold and doleful regions of the Andes a touch of the gaiety of Castile. Thus the gallows in the market places began to be less in evidence, and the Captain, in addition to encouraging ecclesiastical festivals, filled the plazas with all manner of secular gaiety. Whatever the opportunity, he himself would mount a blooded horse and join an organized race through the streets while Indians, always fearful of horses, scampered for cover in some opportune portal; or he would join with his comrades in baiting a bull or unfolding the colorful panorama of a cane tournament. And when the season of the Blessed Nativity fell upon the Andes, he would spice his spiritual ecstasy with the more mundane exultation of the gaming table, inviting his friends to make their wagers and cast their dice in his own home, and sometimes joining in the game himself. Moreover, he often displayed his faith in compatriots by going abroad without his verge of authority, though admittedly he managed to keep it within easy reach.

The concern of the Corregidor for splendor and well-being extended especially to the mestizos, whose Spanish heritage continued to weave more closely about their Indian fibers. They now became an integral part of the Hispanic scene, assuming a role more ennobling than debasing. No longer were they mere messengers, pages, and stableboys. Their caste permitted them to don splendid raiment, ride the finest horses, and participate along with the most distinguished citizens in races and games; and their fathers, having trained them in cavalier arts, took pride in their equestrian prowess. A record in the Cabildo of Cuzco reveals Gómez at this time as a member of the quadrille of the noble Antonio de Quiñones in a game of canes; and in one instance he himself told of how his mestizo companion, Pedro de Altamirano, racing through the plaza on a spirited horse, became so dazzled by the beauty of a damsel peering from a nearby balcony that he gave a wrong signal to his mount and in consequence was hurled to the cobbles. Just as in Spain, the women who occupied corridors and balconies during such sports became an essential element in the chivalric scene; and since the same amorous urges that had tormented their

fathers now were awakening in the mestizos as they raced into adolescence, one may be sure that they were becoming increasingly conscious of such allurements. During these days of Captain Garcilaso's
government, Pedro del Barco, whom the Captain had reared in his own
house, was seduced by a creole maiden and forced to marry;[10] and before long two of Gómez' companions were involved in a shameful case
of rape. The extent to which Gómez himself was affected by such
emotions is not known, but the record of his later achievements is indicative that he was not devoid of amorous impulses, and one finds it
difficult to accept that at this point his piety would have eradicated
desire. Certainly any twinges of conscience which may have accompanied the awakening of sexual passion in the mestizos would have
been allayed by what they had witnessed in the conduct of their fathers
as well as that of some of their spiritual mentors, for it was to be almost two decades before the Viceroy Toledo began efforts to purge
the colonial clergy of its immorality.

Ever more in evidence now in the Corregidor's house was the open
table with its strange collection of adventurers whose only fee for admission was an ostensible loyalty to the host and perhaps a talent for
telling an arresting tale. The repast had become more than a source
of physical nourishment. It was a means of reimbursing a command of
soldiers, of gathering information about friends and enemies, of gaug-
ing feelings and scenting danger of uprisings. According to records
Captain Garcilaso provided both board and bed regularly, and sometimes lent horses, to a hundred and fifty to two hundred soldiers during his term as Corregidor of Cuzco.[11] He as a matter of course felt
the need for such protection, not only for his own safety and that of his
domain, but for the security of the land and the people who had fallen
to his care. And though he had contributed handsomely toward the
comfort as well as the gaiety of the residents of Cuzco, initiating such
projects as the construction of an aqueduct to convey pure water into

[10] Document dated May 22, 1559, Archivo de Protocolos de Córdoba, Oficio, 37,
Protocolo 23, fols. 932v–933v.
[11] Garcilaso, *Comentarios*, Pt. II, Bk. VIII, Chap. 12; Martel-Cabrera expediente,
passim; Sarmiento Palacio expediente, *passim*; also letter from Cañete to the King,
September 15, 1556, in *Gobernantes del Perú*, Vol. I, pp. 272–273.

the city from the surrounding slopes and permitting the erection of buildings over the little arroyo which separated the two main plazas, he was too wise for complacency.[12] Petitions for rewards had never ceased, and the Justices of the Audiencia had persisted in holding claims for a new viceroy to settle. Consequently danger lurked always. Once a critical point was reached when Garcilaso received orders from the Audiencia to confiscate all weapons in Cuzco and only the gentility and soldiers of proven loyalty were willing to yield to the demand without reimbursement. Eventually he persuaded the Justices that such a situation left the city at the mercy of the bourgeois and the malcontents, and the order was rescinded. Yet when the Corregidor returned the weapons—secretly, as ordered—he was accused of providing the citizens with arms for a revolt.

It would require more than the generosity and understanding of Captain Garcilaso to eliminate the covetous spirit ever seething beneath the gay panoply of Cuzco. Even so, though aware of the peril, he fed it to some extent by a certain stubborn allegiance to comrades who at one time or another had appeared seditious, among them Tomás Vázquez and Juan de Piedrahita. It was well known that these men had deserted Francisco Hernández Girón only after the latter had refused the sole course which they felt would carry them to safety. Nevertheless, they had received the King's pardon as well as respectable estates for having helped restore Peru to the Crown. Humbled now and supposedly repentant, they passed most of their days in outlying repartimientos; but when they made occasional journeys to Cuzco, they, according to rumor, were received hospitably by the Corregidor. Therefore, when news came that the Emperor Charles finally had succeeded in locating a viceroy who was willing to assume the government of Peru, Garcilaso was aware that though he could present a record of achievement and tranquility, there were men ready to claim that he had harbored the seditious and kept an armed band of soldiers in anticipation of furthering his own ambitions.

Andrés Hurtado de Mendoza, second Marqués de Cañete and third Viceroy to Peru, was a haughty nobleman whose immediate kinsmen

[12] Garcilaso, *Comentarios*, Pt. I, Bk. VI, Chap. 4; Bk. VII, Chap. 11; Pt. II, Bk. II, Chap. 27.

had wielded power in the courts of Spain. His maternal grandparents, Andrés de Cabrera and Beatriz Fernández de Bobadilla, the Conde and Condesa de Moya, had exerted a robust influence over Ferdinand and Isabel; one of his mother's brothers, a Dominican friar, had abandoned his order and become one of the most fearsome corsairs of his time, though later, on absolution, he had commanded the galleys of both the Pope and Charles V; his father had served Charles V as Viceroy to Navarre; and his son Diego had accompanied Philip II to England.[13] No sooner had Cañete arrived at Paita on June 20, 1556, than he set about asserting his authority by means of letters to each corregidor in the Kingdom, letters in which he arrogantly saluted these proud men as they sometimes saluted their servants and inferiors. His superscription simply read "To the noble Lord, Corregidor of such and such a place," and in the body of the letter each governor, regardless of rank, was addressed in the familiar second person. Captain Garcilaso apparently received his communication with his customary imperturbability, but others more sensitive detected a sinister sign in this inexcusable breach of protocol, and it provided an occasion for men ever eager for rebellion to fill the air with threats and maldictions. In La Plata, Martín de Robles, who at Los Reyes had been the first man to seize the first Viceroy, Núñez Vela, remarked, more in jest than otherwise, that should this third Viceroy visit the Charcas the people of that region would lose no time in teaching him some of the regulations of good breeding. But Captain Garcilaso was ever wary of excuses for rebellion, and when questioned by sensitive spirits as to how he could brook such an insult, he merely replied that he could bear it very well since Cañete was not writing to Garcilaso de la Vega but rather to his minister, the Corregidor of Cuzco; and he prophesied that shortly he would receive a letter of a different color. Then dictating an answer, he gave it to his son, who served as his scribe for all the messages the Corregidor sent to other parts of the realm.[14]

Soon there came rumors which strengthened the Captain's confi-

[13] Roger Bigelow Merriman, *The Rise of the Spanish Empire*, Vol. IV, p. 580; Alberto y Arturo García Carraffa, *Enciclopedia heráldica y genealógica hispano-americana*, Vol. 17, pp. 166–169.

[14] Garcilaso, *Comentarios*, Pt. II, Bk. VIII, Chap. 6.

dence and stimulated his ambition. It was said that the Viceroy planned to set up a cabinet of the four most capable men in the Kingdom—the most impartial and unbiased who by long experience and ancient practice were best qualified to render an account of each man's service and merits—and two of the names mentioned were those of Antonio de Quiñones and Garcilaso de la Vega. Such rumors brought much flattery to Garcilaso, for both clergy and secular now declared that any of these four men would be capable of governing the entire empire alone if such became necessary; and his happiness was more replete when reports came that even before arriving in Los Reyes the Marqués was manifesting generosity in the matter of rewards. Many went so far as to declare that this Viceroy must surely have been Heaven-sent.[15]

All things now pointed to a more glittering future for the Garcilaso household, and it appeared that soon the Captain was to reach an apex of which he had never dreamed. On June 25, 1556, Cañete arrived at Los Reyes with his Marquesa and a splendid retinue of ladies as well as gentlemen to establish the kind of court for which cavalier Spaniards had yearned, and such social aspirations were strengthened by knowledge that the whole of Spain now was under the authority of a new and more youthful sovereign. Scarcely six months previously, Charles V, old, sick, and burdened with a heavy conscience, had retired to a convent at Yuste and left the Kingdom to his son, who as Philip II was to guide its destiny for more than four decades. While the Marqués was sworn into office at Los Reyes, festivities in that city were duplicated at Cuzco, and once more Gómez joined in the jousts and games which signaled the beginning of what all hoped was to be a golden era. And at some time during this period the Marqués wrote a second letter to Captain Garcilaso, addressing him this time as "The Very Magnificent Lord Garcilaso de la Vega," and in the body of the letter treating him with the cordiality usually accorded a younger brother. Indeed, through the veins of both men there did flow kindred blood, since far back in their lineage loomed the figure of the old hero of the vega who had salvaged the honor of the virgin.[16]

    [15] Ibid., Pt. II, Bk. VIII, Chap. 4.
    [16] Ibid., Pt. II, Bk. VIII, Chap. 6. Both men could trace their lineage back to Leonor de la Vega, who married Diego Hurtado de Mendoza, High Admiral of

Seventeen-year-old Gómez, serving as his father's scribe, read the letter and penned the answer to it as he had to the previous one. He never revealed the nature of its contents—whether its substance was flattering, deceiving, or conciliatory; whether it carried a forboding undertone of meaning or a flat statement of the Viceroy's new decisions; or even whether the well-mannered title was followed by that of "Corregidor of Cuzco." But from this letter or one that would have had to follow shortly after, Captain Garcilaso was to learn that he was being replaced as Corregidor and that it was not an apex but a nadir that he was approaching in his career. Already the Marqués de Cañete was removing his mask, and what many of the conquerors were to discover behind it was not pleasant to behold.

Castile. Sebastián's wife, whose mother was a Mendoza, is said to have been related to Cañete, and within her immediate family appears the name of Figueroa.

 CHAPTER SEVEN

Andrés Hurtado de Mendoza, Marqués de Cañete and grandson of a Cabrera whose own Hebraic blood had not deterred him from harrying the heretic Marranos at Seville, had arrived in Peru with a pouch of authorizations, multiple suspicions, and a determination to investigate and punish. As dissembling as La Gasca, though possibly not so shrewd, he had conciliated petitioners with promises while traveling from Paita to Los Reyes, lulling them into a false sense of well-being while probing into their previous histories, much of which he already would have known before leaving Spain. He was suspicious of the quarrelsome Justices of the Audiencia, and this suspicion naturally carried forward to their rewards and appointments. Moreover, he was forewarned and displeased by reports concerning the key cities of his new jurisdiction, especially those on Cuzco, which he regarded, not without reason, as the wellspring of sedition. It was presented to him now as a refractory center of armed and overambitious men, fed and encouraged by an affluent Corregidor whose record had led some to regard him as a man of fragile loyalty. And combined with these feelings was a common viceregal weakness, an overwhelming urge to distribute the wealth of Peru among relatives and favorites.[1]

[1] Possibly among the first of his relatives Cañete was to favor was the Conde de la Gomera, who by October of 1556 was making plans to go to Peru to claim the re-

On July 23, 1556, the Marqués de Cañete issued a decree authorizing the licentiate Bautista Muñoz to replace Garcilaso de la Vega as Corregidor of Cuzco.[2] Muñoz he knew to be free from previous entanglements since he had accompanied the Viceroy from Spain; and when, shortly after, Muñoz set out for Cuzco, he took with him six assistants, all appointed by Cañete, as well as official instructions to execute punishment upon Tomás Vázquez and Juan de Piedrahita "within a brief time and with cunning." And in exercising this cunning, the licentiate no doubt was instructed to keep his eyes open for any further evidence of sedition, for in a message to the King some two months later, Cañete declared that he yearned to cut off the heads of "all these people," and that under the guise of fiestas he was making preparations against war.

Such was the delegation which Captain Garcilaso met when he and a number of citizens went forth to receive the incoming Corregidor. As the Captain placed in the hands of Muñoz the white verge of authority, the latter confronted him with a petty question that gave ample forewarning to all who heard it as to what they could anticipate. What fees, the new Corregidor asked of his predecessor, had he charged for affixing a signature to documents? And when Garcilaso replied that he had never required any such fees, he was openly rebuked. No official, Muñoz declared, should ever relinquish any of his privileges, regardless of how insignificant the nature. Those standing by thereupon murmured in disgust that it was nothing unusual for this man to want to know what in addition to a salary he could extract from his office, since such men were in the habit of coming from Spain to the Indies with the sole purpose of getting what they could without expending energy. Here was a refrain which, as the years rolled on, would be augmented and repeated with increasing bitterness—one which echoed through the memories of Gómez when, as an old man, lamenting his own losses, he reminded his readers that the wealth flowing continu-

---

partimientos left vacant by the death of his son Baltasar in the Hernández Girón rebellion. See *Colección de documentos inéditos del Archivo de Indias*, Series II, Vol. XV, p. 194.

[2] El Inca Garcilaso, *Los comentarios reales*, Pt. II, Bk. VIII, Chap. 4; also Cañete to King, Sept. 15, 1556; *Gobernantes del Perú*, Vol. I, pp. 272–273.

ously into the King's coffers had not been won by beribboned knights who fed on marchpanes or Utrera buns, but by naked and starved men who had hewn and fought their way through the devastating and debilitating wilderness.

The new Corregidor's rebuke on this humiliating occasion carried the tenor of the accusations he was to make in the customary residencia or investigation required for all outgoing officials—the Captain had been cavalier about his use of authority. It all mounted up in the end to the charge that while Corregidor, Garcilaso had betrayed the dignity of his office by gambling and playing darts and canes with his constituents, by oftentimes laying aside his ensign of authority when going abroad, and finally by using a scribe for communications which must go outside the city without first having observed the judicial formalities required in such cases. To these charges, the Captain made ready answer, explaining the expediency of encouraging men to do their gambling where he could observe and arbitrate, and propounding the uselessness of carrying a verge each time he attended a neighbor who respected his authority with or without that symbol. The scribe, who in all probability was his mestizo son, the Captain declared he appointed without knowledge of what the law demanded in such matters, but with the belief, always justified, that that person would be loyal. Moreover, he added honestly, Cuzco afforded few people who could perform such an office. But in referring to the matter of jousts with darts and canes, the Captain broke his customary serenity. This was a traditional cavalier pastime, he retorted, in which he had engaged throughout his life and would continue to enjoy as long as he lived, even though he were placed in a position of far higher dignity and honor than the one he had just quitted.[3]

To condemn Garcilaso for such attitudes and conduct was to condemn him for his Hispanicism, and the inquisition ended painlessly. But Muñoz' persecution did not terminate here. He apparently was

[3] Garcilaso, *Comentarios,* Pt. II, Bk. VIII, Chap. 5; Arthur Franklin Zimmerman, *Francisco de Toledo,* pp. 147–148. Toledo found that some corregidors with little knowledge of legal procedures employed others to conduct lawsuits and that those employed frequently overcharged for titles to property and then gave worthless papers.

convinced and was prepared to encourage Cañete in the latter's conviction that back of Garcilaso's conviviality and amiability lay sinister ambitions.

One can only speculate as to the origin of the Viceroy's distrust of Captain Garcilaso. It may have originated in Spain where reports poured continuously into the Council of the Indies. It may have begun in Panama where an inquisitive governor could always hear rumors of Peru, or at Paita where Cañete was beseiged with complaints and petitions. And it may have begun at Los Reyes when the Viceroy examined the official papers of the Audiencia. Later, on September 15, 1556, he wrote the King that some of the confessions emanating from the recent rebellion made clear that Garcilaso de la Vega was seditious;[4] and among those papers at Los Reyes he most surely would have found a letter from Pedro Luis de Cabrera, informing Francisco Hernández Girón that the latter had merely instigated a move long plotted by Garcilaso de la Vega. This letter, standing without explanation, was damning.

But whatever its beginning, the suspicion of the Viceroy could have been sustained by reports which he saw in the multiple memorandums of Diego Fernández de Palencia, who had continued to follow the recent rebellion from its beginning and at all leisure moments to record what he had seen and heard. So impressed was Cañete with this man's knowledge and ability that he named him an official chronicler of Peru, gave him access to royal documents, and encouraged him to include in his project an account of the rebellion of Gonzalo Pizarro as well as that of Hernández Girón.[5] The nature of the manuscripts of Diego Fernández can be detected only by what he published later and much of this information, especially his account of the battle of Huarina, as has been noted, did not throw a favorable light on Garcilaso de la Vega.

Strengthening the suspicions Cañete already harbored were reports which now reached him from Bautista Muñoz and from men perfectly willing to corroborate these reports, if not to save their own necks, then

[4] *Gobernantes del Perú*, Vol. I, pp. 272–273.
[5] Diego Fernández, *Historia del Perú*, ed. Odriozola, Pt. II, "Proemio."

to enrich their estates. Not only did this Corregidor emphasize the Captain's cool violations of the spirit and letter of some of the New Laws, but he spoke of his intemperate and epicurean entertainment of an armed contingent of suspect men and especially of his genial and harmonious relations with such repentants from the Hernández Girón rebellion as Tomás Vázquez and Juan de Piedrahita.[6]

Arrogant, emotional, and utterly devoid of any firsthand comprehension of the Indies, the Marqués de Cañete could not regard with sympathy the desires and changing attitudes of men who had won the wilderness with little aid and less personal consideration from the ever-demanding King. From the iron head-cages suspended on the gallows beneath his palace windows loomed the corroded visages of ambitious rebels who had imperiled the empire and destroyed a viceregal predecessor; and he could neither understand nor forgive a man who had provided hospitality and sympathy for those who had supported these rebels, even though some of them now held pardons bearing the seal of the King. And since he exaggerated and enlarged upon the personal ambitions of Garcilaso, Cañete with each report became more convinced that the Captain was not to be trusted.

Nor did Garcilaso alleviate this distrust when, shortly after, Tomás Vázquez was ferreted from his country estate and cast into the town prison; instead, he boldly offered to provide bail for Vázquez until proper charges could be ordered. Muñoz, however, acted under an authority which demanded no further evidence, and one dark night he secretly executed both Tomás Vázquez and Juan de Piedrahita. Soon news spread from other parts of the realm that among the multiple victims whom the Marqués later boasted of having destroyed was Martín de Robles, a first conqueror whom Garcilaso numbered among his intimate companions. Too aged and feeble to wear his own sword, which he entrusted to a lackey, this noble conqueror had been executed by Cañete's new corregidor in the Charcas, secretly and without charge. He had been a man of great wit and much charm, though vainglorious to excess. Some claimed now that he simply had paid for his

---

[6] Cañete to King, November 3, 1556, *Colección de documentos inéditos del Archivo de Indias*, Vol. IV, pp. 111–123. See also Cañete to King, September 15, 1556, in *Gobernantes del Perú*, Vol. I, pp. 272–291.

collaboration with Hernández Girón in the recent rebellion, but the winds whispered that death was the reward for his jest about improving viceregal manners.[7]

Meanwhile, as his lieutenants continued a program of extinction in other parts of the land, Cañete was scheming to rid himself of fractious petitioners in Cuzco who, undeterred by recent hangings, continued to nettle him for repartimientos. Falling back upon the King's provision for married settlers, he now offered to compensate those who would consent to wed certain females whom he had brought from Spain, many of whom were reputed to be common strumpets. But when he came to assign these drabs under pretense that they were women of virtue, the intended victims, still connoisseurs of Spanish bitchery in spite of their long absence from the Peninsula, stood aloof from the bargain and were promptly accused of being out of tune with their Sovereign's wishes. Then luring the recalcitrants to Los Reyes, the Viceroy seized their arms and hustled them off to Spain, to his later damage and regret, without charges.

To these men such a fate could be worse than death, or possibly even that of being wed to a Castilian harlot, because their fortunes had been consumed in the service of the King and they could anticipate little more than a humiliating life of poverty in their homeland. Among those included in this strange banishment was Gonzalo Silvestre, who, as he afterward reported to the Council, had asked for five thousand pesos of income and a repartimiento of Indians, and had received a promise of the same under the specified matrimonial conditions. But though this stouthearted cavalier would have felt no timidity about occupying the bed of a whore for a limited time, he was unwilling to be tied to that bed by a noose so eternal and inextricable as a sanctified nuptial vow. Thus it was that this loquacious Andalusian, who could convert an ordinary adventure into a quixotic enchantment, passed for the time being from the world of the mestizo Gómez, as did also the beloved Pedro Luis de Cabrera. The wife of the jolly don Pedro was

[7] Garcilaso, *Comentarios*, Pt. II, Bk. VIII, Chaps. 5–6; Cañete to King, November 3, 1556, *Colección de documentos inéditos del Archivo de Indias*, Vol. IV, pp. 111–123. For documents concerning the execution of Vázquez and Robles see Martel-Cabrera expediente.

beckoning from Seville, and Cañete had brought orders from the King to return Cabrera to his spouse. Soon don Pedro, who found it as difficult to fit his corpulence into the cramped quarters of a galleon as into a short-stirruped saddle, was tossing miserably back over the rolling seas to a cramping domesticity.[8]

The hysterical zeal of the Marqués de Cañete had taken its toll from among the ranks of those who ordinarily might hope for immunity, first conquerors and cavaliers as well as men who had thought to find sanctuary in a King's pardon; and many had been dispatched without benefit of charge or trial. Captain Garcilaso, therefore, could not have failed to be aware of his own mounting insecurity. Surely he must have known, through rumor or otherwise, that by the closing months of 1556 Cañete had written the King that Garcilaso de la Vega had connived with the Justices for his appointment as Corregidor; that he had demanded an excessive salary which he wasted on the feeding and housing of from one hundred and fifty to two hundred soldiers, all of them guilty either in the Hernández Girón rebellion or previous ones; that he had offered his hospitality to Tomás Vázquez and Juan de Piedrahita, arch rebels; and that he was regarded as the most suspect of the men of Peru. Moreover, unable to purge his name of the stigma of Huarina, Captain Garcilaso must have listened with unusual trepidation to the report that at noon of the same day on which Tomás Vázquez had been executed, Cañete had ordered hanged a man named Pavía, a slave with a gentleman's sense of chivalry, who, after being captured by Hernández Girón, had pledged himself to serve his captor until he was retaken in fair combat by his own people. The crime of this man was not novel; it was simply that in the heat of the battle of Pucara he, on finding Hernández Girón unhorsed, had dismounted and given him his own horse, thereby preserving the latter's life.[9] An awareness of these circumstances accounts at least in part for the reso-

---

[8] Garcilaso, *Comentarios,* Pt. II, Bk. VIII, Chaps. 4, 7; Cañete to King, November 3, 1556, *Colección de documentos inéditos del Archivo de Indias,* Vol. IV, pp. 111–123; *Gobernantes del Perú,* Vol. I, pp. 292–301; Silvestre expediente, January 12, 1558, Seville, Archivo de Indias, Patronato 101, R. 18, Peru.

[9] Cañete to King, November 3, 1556, *Colección de documentos inéditos del Archivo de Indias,* Vol. IV, pp. 111–123; also Garcilaso, *Comentarios,* Pt. II, Bk. VII, Chap. 25.

lution of Captain Garcilaso to return to Spain. Even before the close of the year 1556, it would appear, he petitioned the King for permission to do so without loss of encomienda, "for personal reasons," he explained, and thereby drew a veil over his real intentions.

Significant changes had occurred in Captain Garcilaso's immediate family during the almost thirty years of his absence from Spain. His mother and father were dying or already dead; three of his sisters had taken vows and were passing their days in the piety of a convent at Zafra. Two other sisters were married, Beatriz de Figueroa to the well-known Captain Fernando de Guillada, and Isabel de Vargas to Alonso Rodríguez de Sanabria, a gentleman of noble lineage. His youngest brother, Juan, had perished at Huarina, as has been noted, and his eldest brother Gómez had married and as Lord of Torre del Águila y el Tesorero ruled his domain from Badajoz.[10] But it was the fortunes of his favorite brother Alonso which now possibly interested Sebastián most, and which begin to loom significant in the present story because of the role this cavalier was to play eventually in the destiny of the Captain's mestizo.

For many years Alonso de Vargas, under the appellation of Francisco de Plasencia, had pursued a colorful career fighting the battles of Charles V in both Europe and Africa, even serving as a member of His Majesty's Council of War. Moreover, when in the autumn of 1549 the Prince Regent, Philip, set out with the young Conde de Feria, the Príncipe de Éboli, and other notables to present himself before his Flemish subjects, don Alonso, now using the name under which he must have been baptized, accompanied this tournament-studded progress from Genoa to Flanders as a personal aide. He therefore had experienced both the splendors and dangers involved in the Emperor's complex political tilts, and when in 1553 he was compelled by age to retire from military service, he was rewarded by the Crown with an annuity of two hundred ducats per year on property near Jerez de Badajoz and permitted those tax exemptions always regarded as the privilege of an hidalgo. But Alonso de Vargas apparently did not return to Spain at once and in all probability was at Brussels on Oc-

---

[10] Garcilaso, *La Descendencia de Garcí Pérez de Vargas.*

tober 25, 1555, when the Emperor officially abdicated his throne in favor of his son Philip, for in this year and at Brussels the retired Captain is known to have extended an appreciable loan to a highborn kinsman, Alonso Fernández de Córdoba y Figueroa, who according to report found himself in need of cavalier raiment. In return Alonso de Vargas received a writ of redeemable annuities on the hacienda of Montalbán and its aggregates in the vicinity of the Andalusian village of Montilla, which lay a few leagues south of Córdoba.[11] This transaction was to bring him into a permanent economic relation with Figueroa kinsmen who represented two of the most powerful seigniories of Spain—the marquisate of Priego and the condado or earldom of Feria.

Alonso Fernández de Córdoba y Figueroa was third of the four sons of Lorenzo Suárez de Figueroa, deceased third Conde de Feria and second Marqués de Priego through his marriage to Catalina Fernández de Córdoba y Aguilar, heiress to the Priego marquisate. Although he eventually was to obtain both title and power, don Alonso's possibilities at this point apparently were slight. But his brother, Gómez Suárez de Figueroa, who through the death of the eldest son and heir to both titles, Pedro Fernández de Córdoba y Figueroa, had inherited the title of fifth Conde de Feria and had laid plans to become the fourth Marqués de Priego by betrothing himself to his niece, Catalina Fernández de Córdoba y Figueroa, now heiress to the Priego marquisate. Moreover, he for some time had been one of Prince Philip's most trusted confidants and had played a significant role in the Prince's marriage to Mary Tudor. Alonso de Vargas, as a descendant of the first Lord of Feria, claimed close ties with this branch of the Figueroas. But at the moment he surely must have been aware that the security of his new claims at Montilla demanded that he be on hand to husband them and rested

[11] Garcilaso to King, January 19, 1586, attached to preface of León Hebreo, *Diálogos de Amor*, trans. Garcilaso Inca de la Vega; also document dated December 11, 1559, Archivo de Protocolos de Montilla, Escribano Rodrigo Páez, Año de 1559, fols. 459–464v; also two documents issued by Luis de Góngora, December 31, 1591, Archivo de Protocolos de Córdoba, Oficio 22, Protocolo 41, fols. 2493–2497. On the death of Pedro Fernández de Córdoba, third Marqués, the marquisate of Priego fell to his daughter Catalina. One of this man's brothers, Lorenzo Suárez de Figueroa, took monastic vows, relinquished to his mother all titular claims, and eventually became Bishop of Sigüenza.

almost wholly on the honesty and good will of Catalina Fernández, the widowed Marquesa de Priego and Condesa de Feria, and mother of the youth to whom he had extended the loan; for it was to be seven years before she would personally ratify the loan. Ostensibly, therefore, at least in part for the purpose of guarding and administering his assets, Alonso de Vargas now decided to establish himself at Montilla, seat of the seigniory of Priego.

But other interesting circumstances were involved in which Alonso de Vargas' Figueroa relatives may have had a hand. On March 8, 1557, he purchased a house at Montilla on which the young Conde de Feria held liens, and in this same year he married a lady of that village, who, one suspects, had been unduly abiding a profitable opportunity. She was Luisa Ponce de León, daughter of Alonso Fernández de Argote, deceased alcalde of Córdoba, and his wife, Leonor de Angulo, who at the moment was residing at Montilla. Though suspiciously beyond the bloom of youth, or at least in full bloom, Luisa Ponce could claim a clean lineage, and she came to her nuptials with an appreciable dowry as well as a promise of additional rents on property in the event that she bore offspring.[12] Tamed now into a comfortable domesticity after almost forty years of martial experiences, Alonso de Vargas was living the life of an hidalgo, collecting his annuities and rents and accepting those common privileges accorded a cavalier and a gentleman.

This was the situation among the immediate relatives of Captain Garcilaso when he asked to return to Spain for reasons that were personal. Possibly he was moved by nostalgia to renew old associations in Castile; possibly he wished to make plans for an illegitimate daughter, Leonor de la Vega, now in Spain, or for his mestizo son, or for the legitimate offspring he was expecting since his wife at last had proven fecund. Possibly he desired to plead the cause of deceased or exiled friends or to attempt to salvage a fast-fading spirit so essential

---

[12] For letter of sale of house see Archivo de Protocolos de Montilla, Escribano Martín de Castro, año de 1557, sin foliar. A document dated December 20, 1556, indicates that Luisa Ponce was not yet married and another dated September 26, 1557, shows her married. For further information concerning her see writ dated August 6, 1577, Archivo de Protocolos de Montilla, Escribano Luis Fernández, fols. 1003–1005; also her will, dated April 9, 1586, Escribano Gerónimo Pérez, fols. 112–116.

for the progress of Peru. But it is even more likely that he wished to appear at Court and with the aid of influential relatives clear his name of aspersions, seek additional awards and security, or pursue the flattering rumors that had preceded Cañete to Los Reyes. The new intimacy of his brother with powerful Figueroa kinsmen very well could have inspired him to hope for their support against the Viceroy who had reduced him to humiliation. There were some months of delay, but on March 6, 1557, Philip II, now King of both Spain and England, signed a decree permitting Captain Garcilaso to return with his wife to Castile for the customary period of three years without forfeiture of Indians.[13] Yet when the permit was placed in his hands, Captain Garcilaso, for some reason, did not use it.

It is easy to assume that Captain Garcilaso was deterred by changes in his domestic affairs. In May of 1557 his wife bore his first legitimate offspring, a daughter whom they named for her paternal grandmother, Blanca de Sotomayor,[14] and the presence of a legal heir may have rendered the Captain more reluctant to leave his estate to the whims of a Viceroy with such scant regard for the King's mandates. But the most plausible reason for his reversal of plans appears to lie in the fact that he was ill, both physically and spiritually. He was no longer young and his body of course bore some of the scars of his years of wilderness toil. Yet more significant is the fact that he suddenly found himself consumed by a disillusionment which long had eaten at the entrails of his comrades, and he was overcome by the curious and bitter sadness which had been sweeping over the whole of Spain since the succession of Philip II. As a man of noble lineage with a name which for centuries had resounded throughout Spain, he always had enjoyed a certain immunity on the Peruvian political scene. But recent experiences had forced him to the realization that a new social and political atmosphere now prevailed and that neither his name nor his deeds could avail him much in a system which was disposed to ignore the men who had won the land and to favor with

---

[13] Seville, Archivo General de Indias, Audiencia de Lima, Leg. 567, Lib. 8, fols. 231v–232.

[14] In the Martel-Cabrera expediente, multiple witnesses said Blanca was about two years old at the time of her father's death; if so, she was born about May 18, 1557.

both goods and preeminence those who had suffered no hardships, were ignorant of the psychology of the conquest, and were dominated by self-interest. He had watched the dying fires of a spirit which had inflamed men to world conquest, and his own agony may have been greater than that of his fellow conquerors because of the very fact of his nobility. For whereas they had set out with neither name nor goods to lose, he had set out with both and now stood in danger of losing all. Consequently, as he observed the ruthless procedures of Cañete he succumbed to an affliction common to his century and his environment.

An interesting clue to Garcilaso's present condition is to be seen in a letter directed by Cañete to the Council of the Indies on March 26, 1557, only twenty days after the King at Valladolid had given authority for Garcilaso to return to Castile. After describing five madmen whom he kept chained in a house at Los Reyes, men who had lost their sanity because of "having seen what they had never thought to see," Cañete added: "And they write me that in Cuzco, Garcilaso de la Vega suffers the same affliction, having never been himself again since he learned that Martín de Robles was executed."

There are no further records in evidence as to just how psychopathic was the nature of Captain Garcilaso's affliction; but the date which Gómez later gave as the beginning of his father's fatal suffering coincides appropriately with the date of the execution of his friend Martín de Robles.[15] It was described as an illness which struck with regularity while leaving its victim with intervals of apparent health and physical strength. Under the circumstances it very well may have been a disease of the soul, but it has been diagnosed by some, though possibly without sufficient evidence, as a malady of the liver or kidneys. It is in the tradition of the Latin to attribute much emotional woe to these overworked and oft-assailed organs, classic fountains of yellow and black bile that color the humors which plague the soul; and it was ever in the nature of the Renaissance cavalier, as many case histories re-

[15] Ernesto Schafer, *El Consejo Real y Supremo de las Indias,* Vol. II, p. 36. Robles was executed in the fall of 1556 and Garcilaso recorded that his father's illness began about two and a half years before his death, which occurred in May, 1559. See Garcilaso, *Comentarios,* Pt. II, Bk. VIII, Chap. 12; also Martel-Cabrera expediente.

veal, to suffer gravely and oftentimes mortally from splenetic and psychic wounds. He could turn on a fit of melancholia and sink into a lypothymia as easily as one now turns on a faucet, and he would drown himself in it, precipitately or protractedly, according to his whim. The less sympathetic and less understanding reader has a tendency to view such an affliction through the penetrating eyes of Sancho Panza, who, when standing at the deathbed of the immortal Quixote, cried out:

"Woe is me, my dear Master's worship! Don't die this bout, but e'en take my council and live on many a year; 'tis the maddest trick a man can ever play on his whole life to let his breath sneak out of his body without any more ado and without so much as a rap o'er the pate or a kick of the guts, to go out like the snuff of a farthing candle and die of the mulligrubs or the sullens. For shame, Sir, don't give way to sluggishness, but get out of your doleful dumps and rise."[16]

One may be sure that the malady of Captain Garcilaso was no ordinary case of the mulligrubs or the sullens; its sources were too grave, and this cavalier demands a more serious diagnosis, as did Quixote, who still prods the curiosity of literary psychoanalists. But whether stricken by a melancholia or an organic disruption or a mere decree from Heaven, the Captain remained nontheless stricken. And during the coming months Gómez witnessed in the decline of his father a process of cavalier dying which he surely recalled later when detailing the demise of other conquerors. Once abed, Captain Garcilaso fell more and more into the hands of those ever-present friars and prelates who utilized the customary methods of helping him purge his conscience and bolster his confidence. Accordingly, he increased his prayers and devotions, his purchase of masses and his almsgiving; and he called more and more for his confessor, Friar Antonio de San Miguel, Franciscan. And when life held to him tenaciously and he fretted or wondered at the delay, he was assured that God had decreed him a lingering illness that he might be able to make his dispositions without haste.

Meanwhile, as the months moved slowly into 1558, he witnessed

---

[16] From the Peter Motteux 1865 translation of *Don Quixote*.

the passing of two comrades who along with himself represented the lingering remnants of the early conquerors: one, Juan Julio de Hojeda, son-in-law of Gómez de Tordoya, and the other, his former commander, Alonso de Alvarado, who after forty days of agony was terminating a lypothymia that began with his defeat by Hernández Girón at Chuquinca. Most of the first knights of the western crusade had made their exits traditionally on horseback in the heat of valiant or vainglorious deeds, or again possibly more or less histrionically with their well-trimmed beards suspended over the edge of a chopping block. But these two noble cavaliers had died abed. It may have been this insufferable thought which inspired Captain Garcilaso from time to time to abandon his bed and mount his horse for a ride about the city. Yet when in such burning moods, there was always the unguent of Fray Antonio's oft-repeated and pious admonition that the Captain, even when unable to sally forth and accomplish worthy deeds, still could do universal good by thrusting his ungauntleted fist into a well-lined purse. And as the Captain continued to increase his devotions and almsgiving, so one of the Franciscans has recorded, he succeeded in attaining serenity.[17]

Though perhaps induced by pious sedatives, this increasing calm may have been prolonged by rumors of new attitudes at court concerning colonial policies and administration. The Marqués de Cañete no longer was luxuriating in the grace of the Crown. Philip had not been pleased with the highhanded maneuvers of his Viceroy, and His Majesty was ever averse to permitting too much power to fall into the hands of one family. Not only had Cañete lavished forced vacancies upon his kinsmen and favorites but in January of 1557 he had awarded his son, García Hurtado de Mendoza, the government of the rich though perilous regions of the Charcas. Even in February of the same year, the very month in which the Viceroy was boasting of his exterminations, he had received a rebuke from his sovereign, and now Juan Sarmiento, long a member of the Council of the Indies, was joining others to recommend that the Marqués be brought back to Spain on the charge that he was seeking to usurp the prerogatives of the Crown.

[17] Garcilaso, *Comentarios,* Pt. II, Bk. VIII, Chap. 12.

Moreover, Philip had listened with a sympathetic ear to the complaints of those whom Cañete had dispatched to Spain without a written charge, among whom had been Gonzalo Silvestre. Even as Captain Garcilaso lay stricken, some of these men were returning to Peru with permits and annuities from the Crown that would render them immune to the whims of the Viceroy. Such new evidence of the King's sense of justice had encouraged a clamor, not merely for restitution and status, but for the punishment of those who so carelessly had executed cavaliers without charge. For when a man was condemned under the stigma of treason, he not only forfeited for his heirs and their descendants whatever repartimientos they might have succeeded to, but he set up for them almost insuperable social and political barriers. Such suits, therefore, were expedient for the cleansing of both a name and a lineage, and among the plaintiffs now were the widows of Tomás Vázquez and Martín de Robles. Whether Captain Garcilaso gave testimony in these suits is not known, but he would live to see the honor of his old comrades restored, a circumstance which must have given him satisfaction.

By January of 1558 Cañete received another communication from the King which, if not in the nature of a rebuke, at least demanded some explanation. In his reply of February 28, 1558, Cañete with some bitterness described the situation that had confronted him in Peru. Among other things he told of the difficulties he had encountered because of the activities of Pedro Luis de Cabrera along the coast, of Martín de Robles at La Plata, and of Garcilaso de la Vega and his friends Piedrahita and Tomás Vázquez at Cuzco. And he added that considering the nature of the problem, the King should regard its solution as satisfactory.[18]

The changing personal fortunes of Cañete served to soften his nature and to induce some tranquility during the remainder of his government. But other elements of discontent at Court, had they been known, would have conveyed additional hope to Spanish colonials. Not only had the inadequacies of viceroys been brought to the attention of the King, but the question of the adequacy of the members

[18] *Gobernantes del Perú*, Vol. I, p. 319.

of the Council of the Indies also had been raised by contemporary critics. In this year of 1558, when Philip was to make his first appointment to that august body, Francisco Briceño urged him to place on the Council at least three members who had served from seven to eight years in the New World and to appoint as President either Cristóbal Vaca de Castro or La Gasca. Only with such experience, Briceño declared, could an oidor judge the infirmities of a province and the information emanating therefrom since a shepherd unacquainted with the sheep he protected was not a "buen pastor" or good shepherd. And he added that the present Council, not having been in the Indies, knew nothing about those lands except what was told, and that this process of obtaining information amounted to no more than reading a book of chivalry. To Briceño's communication Philip affixed a characteristic marginal note to the effect that some things within it were not without reason but that they must be reserved for the future.

Had Briceño's suggestions been heeded, the destiny of Captain Garcilaso and especially that of his son might have been considerably altered. But La Gasca, though frequently consulted by the Crown concerning the affairs of the Indies, had been returned to his episcopal functions and was serving as Bishop of Sigüenza. And Vaca de Castro, after release from a long confinement in 1558, had been rewarded with the promise of a repartimiento in Peru for his son Antonio and with an appointment, not to the Council of the Indies, but to his former seat in the Council of Castile. Moreover, when in the same year Philip made his first replacement on the Council of the Indies, he named a man who according to Briceño's standards was not a "good shepherd." He was Lope García de Castro, formerly of the Council of Valladolid.[19] It was an evil stroke of fate that this man who was to weave such an inextricable web about the future of the mestizo Gómez should assume his position on the Council when Peru was under the authority of a Viceroy who regarded Gómez' father with almost fanatic suspicion and was not in awe of that cavalier's lineage.

Toward the middle of the year of 1558 Captain Garcilaso began to show signs of recovery, and for some time it was thought that he had

[19] Schafer, *El Consejo Real y Supremo de las Indias,* Vol. I, pp. 113, 142.

regained his health completely. Soon he was seen riding his horse through the streets of Cuzco in good spirits and executing the demands of a normal existence. Further evidence of his vigor became apparent in the condition of his wife, who once more was with child. Nevertheless, after the lapse of several months and near the termination of the year, he was back again on his bed, too stricken to do much more than continue his search for spiritual solace. Even when the city was thrown into an orgy of rejoicing over the capitulation and conversion of the Inca Sayri Túpac, the Captain was unable to participate.

The decision of the Inca Sayri Túpac to abandon the ghost throne at Vitcos and submit to the authority of Spain represented an accomplishment for Cañete; yet it was brought about primarily through the intervention of the Inca's relatives at Cuzco. Long embittered against the Spaniards, he had resisted the efforts of both La Gasca and the Marqués to lure him into vassalage. Yet in 1557, though warned by pagan diviners against putting faith in the promises of the invaders, he yielded to the persuasions of regenerated relatives led chiefly by his aunt, Beatriz Coya, who was assisted by her mestizo son Juan Serra de Leguizamo and by Juan de Betanzos, husband of a daughter of Atahualpa. In January of 1558 the Inca sovereign, accompanied by his wife and year-old daughter, was borne in a royal litter to Los Reyes, where, in return for an oath of allegiance, he received a pitiful allotment which he contemptuously described as but a thread of the cloth, the whole of which his people once had owned. Then amid festive processions he passed on to the Imperial City, where he lodged with Beatriz Coya in houses immediately to the rear of the Garcilaso mansion. At once all of the blood royal hastened thither to pay their respects, and the loyal Isabel Suárez Chimpu Ocllo, still essentially pagan, sent her mestizo to beg the dethroned emperor's permission to come personally and offer an obeisance.

The sight of Sayri Túpac, his red llatu adorned with two black and white feathers from the royal and symbolic corequenque bird, reawakened in Gómez that mystic sense of the divine man, the legitimate son of the Sun, a sense so deeply planted in his subconscious that it could never be completely erased, just as it never could be eradicated entirely from the hearts of his adult Indian relatives. Sayri Túpac, in turn, being more than favorably impressed with his mestizo kinsman, detained him for some time with questions concerning his life and activities, and expressed his regret that Gómez had not come for him at Vitcos instead of the church fathers who did. Furthermore, he made known his respect for the mestizo's royal mother by offering to call upon her at her own dwelling; and when Gómez, on begging permission to depart, honored the now powerless Inca with an obeisance customary among natives, the latter was emotionally touched and bade the youth to pay him frequent visits.

All caciques in the vast region between Cuzco and the Charcas had now gathered in the city to celebrate with solemn and magnificent fiestas. Some they performed with great joy because of the presence of their prince; and some with sorrow and lamentation because of the state to which they had been reduced. When during the ensuing celebrations Sayri Túpac asked for the sacrament of Christian baptism, he begged that Captain Garcilaso stand as his godfather as he had done in the case of the Inca's two uncles, Cristóbal Paullu and Felipe Titu; but the Captain's illness forbade him the privilege, and the responsibility for this Indian soul fell to another conqueror. Nevertheless, the pagan chieftain was spiritually cleansed along with his wife, Cusi Huarque, a very beautiful woman who would have been even more beautiful, Gómez explained, but for her swarthy skin. And when it came time to assign a Christian name to the regenerate, he expressed his preference. In times past, his father, the Inca Manco, and his father's captains had told of an auspicious moment in blood-drenched Cuzco when the clouds rolled back and a militant apostle brought succor to the viracochas. It was the name of this resplendent warrior that Sayri Túpac now wished to bear. Thus on this day he became Santiago or Diego Sayri Túpac, and the citizens of Cuzco honored him with a Christian fiesta, entertaining him with bull baiting and cane tournaments performed in their finest liveries; and among those who hurled canes on that occasion was the mestizo lad whom the Inca sovereign had regretted not seeing at Vitcos. Yet there were skeptics who questioned the extent of the triumph, and when during the ensuing days Sayri Túpac knelt in reverence before the Holy Sacrament in the church of the Dominicans, where once had stood the temple of the Sun, they declared that he did so merely to adore his ancestors whose bodies had lain in that place sacred to all Incas. Such skeptics, like Las Casas and even Gómez himself, lacked faith in the efficacy of swift and compulsory conversions. It was no matter of surprise therefore, when shortly after, Sayri Túpac, while contemplating the balance of his losses and gains, fell into a lethal melancholia.[20]

It is noteworthy that Gómez, during late adolescence, when both his intellect and his character were taking on permanent traits, should experience this intimate contact with a surviving Inca sovereign. It was to give new strength to his Indian fibers, which so rapidly were being strangled by cords of Hispanicism, and deepen the emotional conflict which eventually was to engulf him. He would encounter the chieftain often and surely in his mother's dwelling, where the Inca had promised to visit and where his Indian relatives still assembled with regularity to sob over what they had lost. To the bitter memories of these people Sayri Túpac could add the woes of his personal experiences, and even on this supposedly happy occasion of his capitulation to Hispanic domination and Catholic Christianity he gave vent to some of his covert feelings. It follows that from this scion of a lost throne Gómez was to learn much of the basic justification of Incaic resentment, and much of the Indian psyche of those pagans who had refused regeneration. And most surely he would learn much of two other sons of the Inca Manco, the illegitimate Titu Cusi Yupanqui and his legitimate half brother, Túpac Amaru, whom Sayri Túpac had left at Vitcos, and whose eventual murder Gómez was to record as one of the most tragic and unjustifiable events in the subjugation of the Incas.

Meanwhile, as the Indians of Cuzco, revitalized by the presence of a living sovereign, continued to bewail their vassalage, the emperor whose cohorts had vanquished and bled Tahuantinsuyu lay dying in a convent at Yuste. As the tormented soul of Charles V struggled morbidly but picturesquely for serenity and release, he was soothed at times by Francisco de Toledo, a Garcilaso kinsman,[21] who was fated to

---

[20] Garcilaso, *Comentarios,* Pt. II, Bk. VIII, Chaps. 8–12.
[21] Toledo was a great-grandson of the first Conde de Feria. His mother was María

extinguish the last vestiges of the shadow throne at Vitcos. For Toledo, contrary to the opinion of Las Casas, held strongly to the theory that the Spanish conquest of the Inca realm could be justified on a securer basis than the donation of a Borgian pontiff. And it was during these same dreary months that there appeared in Cuzco a strange and often-times despicable adventurer and future historian who possibly more than anyone else was to assist Toledo in his attempts to give founda-tion to his theory. He was Pedro Sarmiento de Gamboa, who hated Las Casas with a passion, and who only recently had been driven from Mexico on a charge of having practiced "sympathetic magic."

As the painful days of the new year of 1559 ebbed into weeks and months, Captain Garcilaso, confident of the approach of death, again became concerned about his estate and the heirs whom he must leave behind. Though married for ten years, he had but one legal offspring and that a female, and he held no hopes of living to see the outcome of his wife's present conception. Yet the very fact that Luisa Martel was pregnant made it advisable to alter his will. It may be that this expediency alone accounted for his taking such action now; or it may be that he was encouraged to do so by an increasing consciousness of the urgency of providing additional security for his natural offspring, and especially for his son Gómez.

Twenty years of age now, Gómez was well groomed in cavalier skills, and his prowess in the saddle as well as with his nominatives was outstanding. The circumstance of his bastardy in no manner could have served to temper the affection or weaken the interest of his father; for the annals of Spain, both civil and ecclesiastic, are replete with the names of favored sons and "nephews" who owed their existence to some prearranged or chance tumble. But in spite of his cavalier semblance, the boy was a mestizo; and his peculiar social caste in the Indies as well as the presence of his dark blood in an age which often-times linked such with Jew or Moor constituted hazards.

Already Captain Garcilaso had seen enough injustice to sense the fatal insecurity of the mestizos as they waxed in years and as, with the passing of the first conquerors, they came under the scrutiny of less

---

de Figueroa y Toledo. See Guillermo Lohmann Villena, "La Ascendencia Española del Inca Garcilaso de la Vega," *Hidalguía*, No. 29, Julio-Agosto, 1958, p. 691.

sympathetic forces. He was aware, as his will reveals, that after his death Gómez could anticipate little security with his creole stepmother and that there would be even less should she remarry. Moreover, he was aware of the boy's natural affinity not only with the groaning Indians but with those mestizos who were becoming increasingly resentful. Such circumstances undoubtedly pervaded his mind now as he prepared to declare his last will concerning the future of his son. And yet one would like to think that the dying conqueror, seduced and flattered by the astuteness, youthful charm, and tenacious affection of his mestizo, was even more influenced by an old dream of seeing Gómez pit his intellectual skill against the aspiring scholars of Castile, and that possibly the urge came first when an ardent priest and preceptor had built a dream fabric of mestizos at Salamanca. The encouraging words of the Canon Cuéllar, which had woven themselves deeply into the boy's memory, undoubtedly intruded into his discourses with a dying father; and Sebastián Garcilaso unduly burdened now with his conscience, may have visualized an opportunity to expiate some of his past sins of fornication by offering up a natural son for the priesthood. Certainly by now Captain Garcilaso had determined to remove his son, at least temporarily, from the hazards presented in the boy's native land and to make it possible for him to pursue the less perilous career of a scholar.

By March 3, 1559, Captain Garcilaso had concluded his dispositions, and on this day, tormented by fear of death, he sent for a curate and a scrivener, as well as for those men he had chosen to witness his signature. Placing a document in the hands of the scribe, he declared that it was indeed his ultimate testimony, that it had not been executed under duress, and that its stipulations were to be given precedence over any others previously expressed.[22] Then, his earthly possessions disposed of, he settled back again to the melancholy tedium of dying.

Yet his soul clung stubbornly to his weakening flesh, and he lingered. March faded into April, and with April came further disappointment. All hopes he may have held for a legitimate male heir vanished when in this month doña Luisa travailed and delivered her

[22] "Documentos sobre el Inca Garcilaso de la Vega," *Revista del Archivo Histórico del Cuzco,* Año II, No. 2, 1951, pp. 11–15.

second child, a daughter whom they named for her maternal grand-mother, Francisca de Mendoza.[23] But the father apparently was too ill to bother. His thoughts were on the sepulcher which yawned in the convent of the Franciscans and upon the purging he must undergo before entering Paradise. He kept constant contact with his confessors and laid plans for his obsequies, which he hoped would be in keeping with the austerity of a penitent cavalier. And in these terminal hours, when his thoughts drifted back to the happy and capricious days of his youth, he must surely have expressed a yearning that someday his mortal remains might be removed from chill Cuzco and placed with the Franciscans somewhere in sunny Spain. Possibly it came as a nostalgic cry uttered in a delirium or as a feeble whisper in the ears of a curate; or possibly it was a promise exhorted from a grieving mestizo youth whom he was sending back with love, and hopes, and dreams, to his own homeland.

[23] A number of witnesses swore that Francisca de Mendoza was from twenty to twenty-three days old at the time of her father's death. See Martel-Cabrera expediente.

CHAPTER EIGHT

S EBASTIÁN GARCILASO DE LA VEGA terminated his wilderness crusade on May 18, 1559.[1] It had been a rewarding adventure from
a material point of view, and having sown the seeds of Spain and
Catholicism among the most destitute pagans, he could anticipate adequate intercession at the gates of Paradise. Yet the encounter with his
last grim and unconquerable adversary was without splendor; when
it occurred he was unhorsed, unhelmeted, and prone on his bed. Still
it would not have been lacking in the pious pageantry which inevitably
accompanied a cavalier in his demise; for the moment of death, regardless of where it occurred, was the supreme moment of drama and was
seldom private. Whatever madness the Captain had suffered during
the past months had vanished and he had attained serenity. So in his
great, melancholy bedchamber, while curates droned litanies for the
dying, he calmly made his confessions and yielded up his soul.

On May 19, presumably preceding burial, Juan de Salas, Alcalde
of Cuzco, gave orders for the opening of the Captain's will. It is not
known who was present on this occasion, but when the dispositions
of the deceased had been officially disclosed, Sancho de Orive, a public
scribe and member of the Cabildo of Cuzco, gave them the authority of

[1] The date given by the court and testified to by a number of witnesses in the
Martel-Cabrera expediente. See also El Inca Garcilaso, Los comentarios reales, Pt. II,
Bk. VIII, Chap. 12; also Garcilaso's letter to the King, January 19, 1586, in the
Prólogo of Pt. II.

a seal and his signature. Today this will lies hidden still in some musty archive or, more than likely, has been destroyed. All knowledge of its contents must be obtained from fragmentary copies of the original to be found in the archives of Cuzco and Seville.[2] The length of these fragments, combined with the recorded fact that the original encompassed but four and a half pages, leaves some assurance that not a great amount is missing. On the other hand, both sides of the pages are known to have been written upon and the paleography may have been small. Moreover, much does not appear that ordinarily is encountered in contemporary wills and that is suggested in the existing fragments. Missing, for instance, are customary specifications concerning the disposal of remains, masses to be said for departed souls, provisions for unpaid debts and collections, and the many bequests which a man of generosity usually made for retainers and faithful menials. In the existing fragments, no mention is made of the Captain's natural daughter, Francisca de la Vega; and a definite reference to his other natural daughter, Leonor de la Vega, indicates that there may be a missing item concerning her. Furthermore, a description, later published by Gómez, of the Captain's instructions concerning his funeral procession makes clear that these instructions had appeared first in the Captain's will, though they are not included among the copied fragments.[3]

The lost items of course could be replete with nuggets of interest, for often in a man's more obscure and insignificant legacies are concealed some of the curious and revealing data of his biography. But the extant fragments are of inestimable value because of the light they throw upon matters which henceforward were to involve the destiny of Gómez. Of negligible interest is the preamble, stereotyped as a Te Deum, which merely spelled out the solemn litany of Captain Garcilaso's faith and identity. But there is a shining item which confirmed the father's affection for his son as well as his plans for the boy's future. "To Gómez Suárez," the dying Captain had dictated, "I bequeath four thousand pesos of gold and silver, assayed and stamped, that with

[2] Copies of parts of this will can be found in the Archivo Histórico del Cuzco, Protocolo No. 755, año de 1595 del Oficio Notorial de Juan de Olave, fols. 99–101; copies of other parts can be found in the Martel-Cabrera expediente.

[3] Garcilaso, *Comentarios*, Pt. II, Bk. VIII, Chap. 12.

it he may proceed to Castile for the purpose of study; and I order that in the Kingdoms of Castile, they be entrusted to him in revenues conformable to the advice of Señor Antonio de Quiñones whom I beg to do me the favor of looking after my son; and I order that neither the money nor the revenues from it be placed in the power of the said Gómez Suárez before he has come of age. . . . . The previously mentioned four thousand pesos which I bequeath to the said Gómez Suárez, my natural son, I order and desire that he receive from the best portion of my possessions; and this I desire because of the love I hold for him, being as he is my natural son, and as such I name and acknowledge him and leave the money for him in the best legal manner and form."[4]

Buried within this item is a mention of Leonor de la Vega, "my natural daughter who is in the Kingdoms of Spain," and the money her father had bequeathed her "in this my testimony." The item specifying the amount she was to receive has never been found, but in a document at Montilla, half-consumed by rats, mutilated fragments indicate that her legacy amounted to approximately one thousand ducats and that she was to receive it on condition that she not become a religious.[5] Of further interest is what appears to be an order that in the event she bore no offspring the next in line for her legacy was to be Gómez Suárez. Thus the cavalier Captain, by the time he expressed his last desires, apparently had endowed his mestizo not only with irrevocable property at Havisca and appreciable funds for study in Spain but with the possibility of additional resources. It was both a gesture and a compensation for having denied him a succession which could have been made possible through legitimization. That succession now must fall by the King's decree to a legitimate offspring.

Other fragments reveal that Captain Garcilaso had named as universal heirs to his "landed estates and movable properties" Blanca de Sotomayor, her mother Luisa Martel, and the unborn child which the latter was carrying in her womb. Should this second child prove to be a male, he was to succeed to the Garcilaso Indians, and an additional

---

[4] "Documentos sobre el Inca Garcilaso de la Vega," *Revista del Archivo Histórico del Cuzco,* 1951, No. 2.

[5] Document dated September 16, 1561, Archivo de Protocolos de Montilla, Escribano Rodrigo Páez, Año de 1561, fol. 3.

fifth of the Captain's goods was to go to Blanca. If the child proved to be female, Blanca was to succeed to the Indians and the additional fifth be given to her sister.

Subsequent events suggest that Captain Garcilaso had left little to his widow and that her legacy did not even include her dowry. He had named her, in addition to Antonio de Quiñones, Diego de los Ríos, and Juan de Alcobaza, as an executor of his will, and he had specified that she should be curator and guardian of his legitimate children. But possibly with some forewarning, he had taken the caution to add that "should, God forbid, the said doña Luisa die or change status during the said charge" it should fall to Antonio de Quiñones, the trusted brother-in-law in whose hands, as has been noted, the Captain had placed the custody and security of his two illegitimates, Leonor and Gómez.

The final paragraph of Captain Garcilaso's testimony discloses that he had made previous wills which shifts in fortune and in feelings had compelled him to alter. One can account for his failure to add codicils concerning his newborn daughter, Francisca de Mendoza, only by the supposition that in the brief interval between her birth and his demise, he was too ill to concern himself with the matter—and, after all, the existent document was adequate. And though, perchance, on this melancholy occasion of May 19, what he had dictated was received with mingled and some mangled emotions, feelings would be suppressed temporarily; for the Captain's body must yet be borne to the cold crypt of the Franciscans, and most of Cuzco awaited the procession.

Twice around the great market place, where in times past he had witnessed the mutable pageantry of Peru, mourning friends now bore their burden before turning up the narrow lane to the convent. And as the cortege passed through throngs of sorrowing Indians and paused at specific sites for Te Deums, the Captain's remains were permitted to rest, not upon the customary tall and ostentatious scaffold, but upon a simple black cloth spread upon the ground. Thus his crusade was closed as he had requested in his will, with the austerity befitting an exemplary cavalier; and it is recorded that the onlookers were so filled with admiration for these simple rites that a new fashion in obsequies was established in the Imperial City.[6] When the body was placed finally beneath the high altar of the Franciscans, the Indians and mestizos of Cuzco were aware that they had lost an advocate; and Gómez grieved for the loss not only of an affectionate father who represented a material security, but of something less tangible. To him, though he may not have been as yet fully conscious of the fact, his father had been a source of higher wisdom and ambition, a promise that the Renaissance world still could offer splendid opportunities even for mestizos.

Many years later, as a tribute to his father, Gómez published a eulogy which had been delivered at some time during this period of mourning by a pious friend whom he had been forbidden to name.[7] This tribute, primarily because of its burden of doxologies and rodomontades, has met the scorn of critics who have failed to perceive how effectively it illustrates the lachrymal luxury and false passion of a civilization which still found some emotional release in a funeral orgy. Of particular interest to the mestizo, who took inordinate pride in his noble lineage and now was looking with hope toward Spain, must have been a passage in which the orator represented the virtues of Sebastián Garcilaso as superior to those of his famed ancestor Garcí Pérez de Vargas. Garcí Pérez, this eulogist declared, had served his king in the conquest of only one province whereas Garcilaso had served in the conquest of the world. Garcí Pérez had risked his life driving the Moors from Andalusia, but Garcilaso had abandoned his homeland, traversed great seas, hewn his way through dense forests, explored lands, and dominated ferocious, barbarous, and unlimited multitudes in order to subject them to God and the King and to cast out demons and eliminate the worship of demons in many realms. Garcí Pérez had assisted in gaining Seville, the wealthiest city in Spain, but Garcilaso had aided in the conquest of an empire which was not only the richest in the world but one from which wealth had flowed to the entire universe. Furthermore, the aid which Garcí Pérez had received from God and the apostle Santiago had been bestowed likewise upon

---

[6] Garcilaso, *Comentarios,* Pt. II, Bk. VIII, Chap. 12.
[7] *Ibid.,* Pt. II, Bk. VIII, Chap. 12.

his descendant, Garcilaso de la Vega. And in the end, the pious eulogist declared, Garcí Pérez, by marrying into the royal family, had emblazoned his escutcheon with the arms of Castile, whereas Garcilaso, while embellishing his arms with his own blood and the blood of Incas, had not deigned to form nuptial ties with the imperial family of Tahuantinsuyu. This last assertion, though of little comfort and possibly of some humiliation to the boy most injured by the circumstance, may have represented an obsequious sop for the highborn creole who now was entitled to rule the Captain's household and guard at least a portion of his estate.

Though but twenty-three years of age, the widowed Luisa Martel, as a daughter of the shrewd Gonzalo Martel, was adequate for the course which lay ahead of her. She knew well the perils which accompanied wealth in the treacherous colonial policies of Philip II, and she could anticipate and face these perils with cunning and temerity. Moreover, she was surrounded by powerful relatives whose allegiance would have been strengthened by their knowledge of the nature of the woman.

Thus, during the ensuing days, few changes were in evidence in the daily affairs of the Garcilaso household. Young adventurers and destitute orphans continued to feed, at least temporarily, upon the largess of the deceased, though one may rest assured that soon they were asked to become more practical and less ornamental. The faithful Juan de Alcobaza remained as overseer, and the natives continued to serve the household as formerly, providing food and firewood as well as other necessities. And when on the Day of San Juan the Indians from the outlying districts plodded into the city to convey their tributes and rents, they came as usual and as well laden to the collecting houses of the late Captain to deposit their burdens to the credit of the Captain's infant heir, doña Blanca de Sotomayor. It may be that Gómez, as previously, recorded the tributes on the quipu; but these assets doña Luisa would have guarded with vigilance.

During the succeeding days, the cunning of the Captain's widow became even more manifest. She was much discomforted by the fact that though the rents and tributes rolled in, she could not reach them legally except through her daughter. She could not even claim the dowry with which she had enriched the Captain's coffers. Yet her husband's will had designated her as legal guardian of his heir, and doña Luisa was aware of the significance and the possibilities of the appointment. She therefore very promptly, even before she had reached the legal age for the position, summoned custodians of the law to her chambers, and in the presence of reputable witnesses made sure that the guardianship was ratified and recorded. Then, certainly through no want of maternal tenderness, she brought suit against her ward, not only for the coveted dowry, but for sustenance.

Though at first it may appear strange, there was one significant legal step which the widow ignored. She did not, in accordance with the King's mandates, arrange for the investiture of her daughter into succession. In colonial Peru, such a step was commonly disregarded without adverse consequences, though the explanation which doña Luisa later made, when urged by an emergency, was that the child had not been of legal age for investiture. But the omission must simply be regarded as a shrewd act of foresight. If not formally invested, the child could always answer any threat with the plea of regional custom, since repartimientos were valid for two lives and succession was understood; on the other hand, if formally invested, her repartimiento, in the event of her death, would irrevocably fall into the hands of the King. But there was a third possibility which undoubtedly pressed itself upon the well-informed mind of the Captain's widow. Should doña Blanca die without formal investiture, a claim for succession could be made by her legitimate sister or, if the latter also were dead, by the widow herself. Death was a common occurrence in Cuzco, and in the chill, thin air of the Andes, children of pure Spanish descent often found it difficult to survive. Blanca was scarcely two years old at this time and Francisca was but a few months. Subsequent events indicate that the health of both children was precarious. Indeed, members of the household, observing the delicacy of the elder child, often were heard to breathe an anxious hope that God in his mercy would protect doña Blanca since with her demise all would be "spilled."[8] And apparently the general welfare of many who had benefited by the Captain's will did hang upon the frail thread of this child's existence, since in it presumably

[8] See Martel-Cabrera expediente.

was constituted the second and terminal life of the Garcilaso encomienda.

Any resentment Gómez may have felt at the maneuvers of his stepmother could have been measured only by his ability to penetrate her
crafty nature and to anticipate her long-range plans. Yet he undoubtedly did resent the woman herself, innately and as a cog in a caste
system which, as he emerged into young manhood, was looming more
and more as a source of insecurity and misery. It is hardly possible that
he ever seriously felt that she had supplanted his mother in his father's
affections; he would have been too acutely aware of the significance of
rank and the insignificance of affection in Spanish marital arrangements, and he would have been equally aware of the exact nature of a
cavalier's relations with his concubine. But he had seen his Indian
mother humbled and reduced to an even more menial position or at
least to what he of a certainty considered a more humiliating one; and
in these bitter days when he grieved for his departed father, he at least
would have been further saddened by the injustice of a system which
had forced his father to give this creole woman preference over himself
in matters of succession. Moreover, even this early he may have detected in his stepmother visions which added bitterness to his grief.

There was an old story, heard often in Cuzco, which told of a retinue
of scheming Spanish women with Pedro de Alvarado at Guatemala
who prattled of marriage with rich but aging conquerors. Contemplating the prospects with revulsion, one of the more fastidious wenches
had protested: "Must we wed these rotten old men? Let those do so
who wish, but I certainly have no intention of wedding any of them.
Frauds of the Devil! They are so maimed that they appear to have escaped from Hell. Some are crippled and others have but one arm; some
are without ears, and others have but one eye; and still others have but
half a face, and he who has fared best has had his face slashed once,
twice or even more times." To this obstinate outburst a shrewd damsel
offered a reply designed to soothe with its practicality. "Ah, we are
not going to marry them for their winsomeness but to inherit their
Indians; since they are old and weary, they soon must die, and then we
will be able to select whatever young man we may wish to replace the
old one, just as a person customarily exchanges an old and broken pot

for one that is new and whole." And it was said that an aged and unnoticed cavalier, overhearing the prattle, first excoriated the wenches
with insulting words and then, having warned his comrades of what
they might expect, hastened to his house, called a priest, and wed a
noble Indian woman on whom he already had begotten two natural
children. This generous cavalier, Gómez later remarked in reviewing
the story, was moved by a desire to legitimatize his offspring so that
they might inherit his Indians and not become the servants or slaves of
some swain whom his widow might choose to enjoy what he himself
had labored for. And Gómez added, undoubtedly with some emotion:
"There were some men in Peru who did likewise, marrying their Indian women, but they were few. Most of them became the victims of
such counsel as that woman expressed, and their children will testify
as to how accurate she was, since from the asylums in which they now
live, they can see the offspring of strangers enjoying what their own
fathers had gained with the assistance of their native mothers and relatives."[9]

These words were written when many years had fled and Gómez
was enjoying greater security than his stepmother, but their intensity
suggests that the feeling which inspired them was born early. The story
of the scheming women with Alvarado was not apochryphal, and the
colorful metaphor of exchanging an old pot for a new one, a metaphor
which Gómez was to use at least twice in his histories, had sufficient
basis in reality to become a colonial proverb. The extreme youth of
Luisa Martel at the time of her marriage to a man three times her age,
and her comparative youth at the time of his death, surely left some
speculation among mourners as to whether she would prove a "sister
under the skin" of those scheming females of Guatemala. There was
an ancient Spanish adage that a widow smiles with one eye while
weeping with the other, and possibly this early Gómez had detected
a suspect twinkle. Still living in Cuzco was Gerónimo Luis de Cabrera,
an unwed cavalier of fine figure who enjoyed the favor of his kinsman, the Marqués de Cañete, and whom Luisa Martel long had regarded with an admiration that promised interesting possibilities.

A social system which gave unjust material advantages to his step-

[9] Garcilaso, *Comentarios*, Pt. II, Bk. II, Chap. 1; Bk. VI, Chap. 21.

mother and increased his own insecurity naturally augmented Gómez' resentment of Luisa Martel, and this feeling could not have been lessened by any of her subsequent actions. In her veins flowed the blood of one of Spain's most callous and vigilant emissaries, and into the very fabric of her nature was woven the inimitable hauteur of the creole. She had little concern for her husband's bastards, and had he not provided for them, she would have abandoned them to the fate which the circumstances of their birth so frequently ordained. Yet there is no evidence to suggest that she as an executor of her husband's will ever made any effort to impede his desires concerning his son. The boy had the interest and protection of powerful relatives in both Peru and Spain, and the amount he would take from the whole was negligible. In truth she may have been pleased with the arrangement and actually have encouraged it, for the presence in her household of a youth of his astuteness could provide a let to her plans and an obstacle to her fortunes.

The fact is that many of the citizens of Cuzco were beginning to regard the mestizos with some concern. As quick-witted and spirited boys romping through the streets, they had provided novelty, but as intelligent young men, many of them more erudite than their fathers, they were beginning to constitute an element of colonial society to be reckoned with. Slowly through the years their boyish excitement and puzzlement over the intrigues and escapades of their fathers had emerged into a full comprehension of Spanish colonial abuses, and as their conqueror fathers began to die, the sons became poignantly aware of a personal insecurity. Conscious of their rich heritage and unfortunately gilded with a veneer of Old World hidalguía, they were not content to cry out from the asylums of the poor or to serve the new consorts of their fathers' widows. All had been schooled by example in the expedient, perilous as it was, of resorting to intrigue when justice was denied, and this early they must have discussed among themselves the possibility of turning to the King for favor on the basis of their fathers' services and the patrimony due their mothers. This was a plea and a claim which was to ring in the ears of kings and to aggravate viceroys down through the years, and the seeds of mestizo discontent which later were to blossom under García de Castro and Toledo already were in the soil and slowly germinating. Among those carefully nourishing these seeds were several of Gómez' most cherished friends. Indeed, it was about this time or certainly not long afterward that the mestizos of Cuzco, bound always by blood and caste and camaraderie, and yet apparently feeling the need for a more compact organization, formed a brotherhood to which membership was forbidden both creole and Spaniard. As their patron, they chose San Bartolomé, whose image, they claimed, adorned the Inca temple at Cacha. But this image, all but the most credulous knew, represented Viracocha, the famed apparition which had guarded the welfare of ancient Incas. Consequently, when the mestizos knelt, supposedly to adore and supplicate a Christian saint, some Spaniards murmured, and possibly with reason, that these youths were surreptitiously paying their respects to a pagan ancestor and revitalizing their faith in a lineage which found its origin in the Sun.[10] Unquestionably, many of the mestizos, whose earliest interpretation of the world about them had come to them as infants and in Quechua, were as mixed in their religious concepts and loyalties as they were in blood.

Both spiritually and politically, then, the mestizos were suspect, and their potentialities were rendered more ominous not only by the peculiar justness of their claims for security and favor but by their innate affinity and influence with the Indians, both pagan and Christian, who groaned continually about their lot and no doubt at times voiced the opinion that their lost empire could be restored by a new viracocha— one in whose veins coursed the blood of two races. Such circumstances could account for an apochryphal though not unreasonable story to the effect that the long journey to Spain which Gómez soon was to undertake was being forced upon him because of a fear that the Indians had set him up as a symbol in their efforts to resuscitate an ancient realm.[11] Such a fear, if it existed, could have been enhanced by the fact that there still were men in Cuzco and still a Viceroy at Los Reyes who in the past had suspected the loyalties of Captain Garcilaso. The story, on

[10] Garcilaso, *Comentarios,* Pt. I, Bk. V, Chap. 22. Usually San Bartolomé was painted with a demon tied at his feet.
[11] Gustavo Barroso, "Garcilaso de la Vega, el Inca," *O Cruzeiro* (Edición Internacional), May 1, 1957, pp. 44–45.

the surface, and in the light of Captain Garcilaso's will, appears hardly to merit consideration and no doubt represents a confusion. Yet not to be ignored is the fact that on the eve of his departure from Peru, Gómez numbered among his most intimate companions mestizos who in the near future were to revolt against viceregal authority, and throughout his life he regarded with intense admiration Diego de Almagro, that mestizo youth who had died defending his claims in Peru. That strange cord of cavalier loyalty which had bound Captain Garcilaso to his sovereign, he had bequeathed to his son, but the son had seen it weaken more than once when exposed to the inclement weather of Spanish colonialism. Moreover, the cord which now bound that son to an alien sovereign had twisted into it fibers which tied him inexorably and emotionally to a people who writhed under the heel of injustice. He still joined regularly with these people when they gathered in his debased mother's quarters to bewail their miseries, and as they did so, these fibers grew tauter. Though tender and sensitive, they were to become the tough and everlasting sinews of the cord; and to the Indians, in this year of 1559, the mestizo Gómez Suárez de Figueroa may very well have represented the beginnings of the symbol which he later was to become.

For, even now, trained as he had been in Spanish refinement and hauteur, and yearning for a half-mystic process which would merge him, in spite of his blood and caste, into the Spanish family and tradition, he did not reject the Indian in himself. His pity for his mother's people was mingled with an inextinguishable pride, and within the compass of his Indian family he included the whole of the Incaic line—not just the washed and baptized of Cuzco, but all of those unredeemed worshippers of the Sun who gathered about the ghost throne at Vitcos to dream of a new empire and a revitalization of their pagan culture. All who carried within their veins the noble blood of the Incas were his kinsmen, even those unfortunate offspring of the bastard Inca tyrant, at least one of whom still lived in Cuzco in bitter isolation and loneliness.

Thus when, but a few months before his departure from his native city, Gómez learned of the death of young Francisco Atahualpa, he paid this handsome youth the honor of his grief; and when, on the day following, the Indians gathered with his mother for what he expected to be an outburst of sorrow over the passing of a relative, he was distressed to find that they had come to rejoice over the extinction of another seed of the beast who had harrowed the bleeding fields of Yahuarpampa and given their empire to aliens. Too far removed from the horrors of that attempt at genocide to comprehend such frigidity of heart, Gómez, turning to the ancient Cusi Huallpa, boldly questioned this lack of concern over the death of a kinsman. Whirling upon this young apostate who soon was to abandon his native Tahuantinsuyu, the old Inca, his mind wormed with memories of terrifying days when he had barely escaped extinction, seized the hem of his mantle, ground it in rage between his teeth, and with glaring eyes began a series of withering excoriations.

"Then you must be related to a traitor, to the son of a treacherous despot who annihilated our empire, slew our Inca, consumed our blood, destroyed our lineage, and perpetrated so many of those cruelties that are alien to the Incas, our fathers! Give me this youth, dead as he is, and I will eat him raw and without pepper. For his father, that deceitful Atahualpa, was not a son of our Inca Huayna Cápac, but rather of some Quito Indian whom his mother permitted to make a cuckold of our emperor. Had he been an Inca, he not only would have refrained from the cruelties and abominations which he committed, but he would never have imagined them since the tradition of our ancestors was to do much good for all and not harm anyone, not even enemies, much less relatives. Therefore, do not say that he who was so different from all of our ancestors was a kinsman of ours. Take heed that in calling us relatives of that ruthless tryrant who made vassals of kings and of those few of us who escaped his barbarities, you offer great affront, not only to us, but to our ancestors and to yourself as well."[12]

These few words, Gómez afterward declared when reporting them, were but samples of the aged man's fury as he recalled the evils and desecrations of Atahualpa, and in consequence the occasion which had been designed to be festive was converted into an orgy of howling and lamentation, not over the untimely death of a wretched and lone Indian youth, but over what had been suffered and what had been lost.

---

[12] Garcilaso, *Comentarios,* Pt. I, Bk. IX, Chap. 39.

By means of an irritating query, the mestizo had brought upon himself a rebuke which conveyed sharply again to his memory those everlasting stories wherein his mother and her kinsmen long ago had unfolded to him the exploits of his Inca forebears, the splendors she had known as a palla in a golden city, the tortures and terrors she had witnessed at Yahuarpampa, and the escape down the long trail which led to Christianity, concubinage, and abasement. Soon the physical cries of these people would fade from his ears, but their echoes would ring always as he listened from across the Ocean Sea to the ever-recurring accounts of their hopelessness and despair.

In this tumult of feeling which now enveloped the mestizo Gómez, there still remained the hope derived from the shining clause of his father's will. For the Captain had extended his son's horizons beyond Peru to a land which ironically inspired in the youth dreams as fabulous as those of his father when the latter first contemplated the harvest of souls and minerals offered by the Indies. The pursuit promised to carry him to the mines of wisdom and to the wellsprings of chivalry; and the thought was warming. So there were exciting days as goods were auctioned and silver collected, and as relatives in Spain were informed of the death of Captain Garcilaso as well as reminded of the role they most surely already had agreed to take in the education and protection of his mestizo son. For until he reached his majority the youth was to remain under the protection of the Captain's two living brothers, Gómez Suárez de Figueroa y Vargas and Alonso de Vargas, who also were to receive and invest his legacy, doling out to him periodically the income necessary for his meager existence.

The months fled swiftly through the year 1559. Out of deference to the memory of Captain Garcilaso, the triumphal feast of Corpus Christi, which fell on May 25, was allowed to pass without ostentation;[13] but with the approach of the season of the Nativity, the great plazas of Cuzco again assumed a festive air as the spirit of the Holy Mother and the Blessed Child settled over the Imperial City of the Incas. And yet, mingled still with the exaltation of Christians were the persistent voices of paganism, and Catholic saints were forced to share honors with the shades of departed Incaic sovereigns. At some time

13 Martel-Cabrera expediente.

during the closing weeks of the year, the Corregidor, Juan Polo de Ondegardo, who already had begun an account of Incaic civilization, had unearthed from secret pagan recesses relics which set the spirits of the Indians aflame. Thus it happened that one day when Gómez had gone to bid farewell to this official, he was invited into an adjoining room to view the discoveries. Here he found himself in the presence of august death, facing a grim and memorable evidence of transient glory and mutability. Before him, posed as in life, were the embalmed and hoary-haired remains of some of the most renowned sovereigns of Tahuantinsuyu. Here, according to his recollection, was the Inca Viracocha who as a prince tending the flocks of the Sun at Chita had come face to face with the deity whose name he bore; here was Túpac Yupanqui, the mestizo's great-grandsire, who had rounded out the four corners of the realm; and here was Huayna Cápac, most splendid of Incas, who had doomed the kingdom with a prognostication and a bastard son; and alongside them in death, equally hoary of hair, were their sister-consorts. This was the final chapter to the stories of past grandeurs which the boy had heard from his mother and her kinsmen, from the quipucamayus and the amautas. In curiosity and reverence he reached out his hand and touched the finger of Huayna Cápac. It was so dry and brittle that the Andean winds could have wafted it into oblivion; and it was cold. But when later these fragile and sacred symbols were turned over to the Indians, they gave way to a heated orgy of feasting and celebration which emulated their ancient festivals. The quipucamayus were busy again with their tales and the amautas with their songs, and memories became so inflamed that eventually an alarmed viceroy seized the embalmed pagan sovereigns and gave them permanent burial at Los Reyes.[14]

There were hurried visits now, anguished conversations and farewells with mestizo companions and Indian kinsmen, and messages from nostalgic Spaniards to be conveyed to relatives in Estremadura and Andalusia. Among those whom Gómez saw last was María de Chávez, widow of Gómez de Tordoya, who burdened him with three hundred pesos and gave him power jointly with a man of Cuzco named

---

[14] Garcilaso, *Comentarios*, Pt. I, Bk. V, Chap. 29; Bk. VIII, Chap. 8. Other historians differ with Garcilaso as to which Incas were represented.

Pedro de Roche to transact business for her near Badajoz. Her specification that Pedro was to retrieve the pesos in the event that Gómez
should perish before reaching his destination in Spain strongly indicates that the two were to travel the whole journey together. Then on
January 18, 1560, Antonio de Quiñones, securing transcripts of Captain Garcilaso's will, empowered Ruy López de Torres and Alexis
González Gallego, merchants of Cuzco and Los Reyes respectively, to
transfer four thousand pesos in silver bars to Francisco de Torres,
brother of Ruy López, at Seville, where they were to be held for collection by the Captain's brothers.[15] This apparently was to be the mestizo's sole source of income in Spain. The coca plantation of Havisca
he now owned in full since in 1559 he had purchased the portion belonging to García Suárez de Figueroa, possibly with a promissory note,
as records reveal that this cousin was to enjoy half the income from the
property during Gómez' absence in Spain. The remaining half he assigned to his mother, who in exchange gave him a small quantity of
gold.[16] Some pathos lies in the fact that this meager but necessary assistance came to him, not from the haughty creole who by royal decree
and a twist of fate might be entitled to succeed to his father's estate,
but from the Indian woman who in the beginning had helped Captain Garcilaso to win his American domain. And when her mestizo son
last cast eyes upon this woman, she was no longer the pagan Inca palla,
Chimpu Ocllo, but Isabel Suárez, the drab Christian spouse of Juan
del Pedroche, to whom by now she undoubtedly had borne two mes-
tizas, Ana Ruiz and Luisa de Herrera.

Either on January 20, 1560, or the day following, Gómez mounted
his horse and for the last time climbed the Hill of Carmenca.[17] When
he had reached the rim of the ancient city, he is said to have paused and
sadly contemplated the scene, his hopes and his spirit of high adven-

---

[15] See writs published in *Revista del Archivo Histórico del Cuzco*, No. 2, 1951,
pp. 15–23 and No. 3, 1952, pp. 257–259.

[16] Document dated August 19, 1574, Archivo de Protocolos de Montilla, Escribano
Juan Martínez de Córdoba, Año de 1574, fols. 555–557; see also Aurelio Miró Quesada y Sosa, *El Inca Garcilaso*, p. 100.

[17] In many instances Garcilaso gave the date of his departure from Cuzco as 1560.
The document of María de Chávez shows him in Cuzco on January 19, and he re-
corded that he arrived at Marcahuaci, nine leagues distant but over rough terrain, on
January 21. See his *Comentarios*, Pt. I, Bk. IX, Chap. 26; Pt. II, Bk. VII, Chap. 4.

ture marred by something unspoken and intangible. Spread out beneath him in a nest of snowy peaks lay the debauched and betrayed city of the Moon and the Sun, a city which to him had now become a mother to aliens and a stepmother to its own. With this parting twinge of pity and nostalgia for his melancholy Indian world, he goaded his horse forward and set out down the long road toward Los Reyes and Spain. And though because of his Indian blood he began that journey with some trepidation, he also began it with the confidence of a youth in a renascent and rapidly changing world. He knew that his Indian blood was princely and that mixed with it was some of the richest blood of Spain; and from the time he had parsed his first Latin noun and mounted his first horse, there had been engendered within him a firm sense of hidalguía. Already he had felt the first pulsations of a New World humanism which found its inspiration in an ancient and frequently forgotten concept that true nobility rested not merely on noble blood but on the more solid foundation of noble deeds, and he was departing from Peru with an unshakable belief that among the noblest of the early conquerors of that land, in both blood and service, had been Garcilaso de la Vega, Cavalier Captain of His Majesty in the Indies. Moreover, he definitely was departing with the understanding that he someday would return better equipped to assist in the progress of the confused and despondent people whom his father in good faith had helped to conquer and subdue.

 CHAPTER NINE

On THAT CHILL JANUARY MORNING of 1560, when Gómez, in a confusion of emotions and ideals, bade farewell to his native Cuzco and set out down the trail to Los Reyes and the sea, he was not alone. With him was an anonymous companion who was carrying a valued mastiff puppy to a relative near Los Reyes,[1] and unless plans were altered, he also was accompanied by Pedro de Roche. Moreover, he would have found the narrow paths and mountain passes congested here and there with slow plodding trains of llamas and asses laden with precious ore, for the broadmasted ships at Callao were loading their burdens for Panama and the convoys of the King's Armada lay in the roads at Havana, awaiting the vast treasures of Mexico, Tierra Firme, and New Castile. But the city of Los Reyes was one hundred and twenty leagues and at least ten or twelve days distant from Cuzco, and he knew the journey there to be burdensome. Not only must the treacherous paths rising and descending through Andean peaks and forges be accomplished, but there lay ahead the frozen and forbidding wastes of the sierras awaiting with bone-freezing winds unfortunate victims caught in the night, and in addition the interminable and scorching coastal sands with myriads of blood-sucking insects. Furthermore, there were no tambos, or inns, and travelers along that desolate route either sought shelter from natives or friends or, in the icy

1 El Inca Garcilaso, *Los comentarios reales*, Pt. I, Bk. IX, Chap. 21.

regions, huddled hopefully together in the darkness, both man and beast, to draw what life-giving warmth they could from each other. But the rugged and devious route which Gómez now followed from Cuzco to the harbors of the New World and on to those of the Old was one with which he already had become familiar through the proud and vaunting tales of both Indians and Spaniards who had forged it, and years later when recounting their adventures he outlined his own course in some detail. Traveling first through nine leagues of rugged terrain and historic battlefields, he came on January 21 to Marcahuaci, the repartimiento of Pedro López de Cazalla, where his father had found haven on that first bitter night of the Hernández Girón rebellion, and where he himself now encountered only a Portuguese overseer, who laid before him a vision of a vast vineyard but offered him not one pip of a grape. Moving on, he crossed the raging Apurímac, and then, after passing over the crest of the Andes at Huaquirca, descended to the sandy wastes of Ica. Turning north through the pampa of Villacurí, he reached the valley of Huarcu, where he was welcomed by one of his father's former servants, Garcí Vázquez, who was anxious to send information of his New World achievements back to relatives in Spain. And then, after continuing up the shores of the great southern sea, the weary youth came at length to Pachacámac and soon after to Los Reyes, his flesh mortified by the pricks and stings of voracious gnats, which busied themselves night and day, and which, he had heard, could pierce a Cordovan boot. And Los Reyes offered scant relief, for though dwellings were screened they provided little protection.[2]

Yet for a number of reasons this capital which Francisco Pizarro had founded in honor of three Oriental kings represented a novel world for an altiplano mestizo. Indeed, the very name of the city appealed to his romantic piety, and though already common soldiers and ordinary citizens were beginning to refer to it as Lima, a careless perversion of Rímac, the name of the river which watered the surrounding valley, Gómez, like the first conquerors and the Peruvian hidalguía, persisted always in calling it Los Reyes or "the City of the Kings."

[2] *Ibid.*, Pt. I, Bk. IX, Chaps. 26, 29; Pt. II, Bk. II, Chap. 17; also Aurelio Miró Quesada y Sosa, *El Inca Garcilaso*, pp. 80–83.

Yet as he now approached, anticipating colorful towers and battlements, he beheld only flat dwellings with mud roofs typical of Spanish coastal architecture. Houses were commodious and situated on streets of great breadth with encompassing tropical gardens, but enveloped in heat—heat that corrupted dead flesh quickly and brought a stench from the iron head-cages in the plaza where still could be seen the sadly decomposed visages of bold men he once had known well in Cuzco: Francisco de Carvajal, Gonzalo Pizarro, and the despicable Francisco Hernández Girón. He could identify them now only by their name tags; and yet it was to be four more years before a compassionate citizen, stealing forth under cover of night, removed these grim mementos of sedition and gave them concealment in the convent of the Franciscans. So just as he recently had witnessed the dessicated mummies of fabled ancestors who had conquered and ruled Tahuantinsuyu, he now was witnessing the decaying remnants of once impassioned Spaniards who had dreamed of holding sway over that land. And all about him lay poignant reminders of his father's perilous days at Los Reyes—the ghostly streets through which the Captain had raced in the night for safety, the solemn crypts of the Dominicans where he had eluded the wrath of the Demon of the Andes, and the great viceregal palace where he had acted out a strange captive role and where now resided the haughty emissary who during the past few years had hurled him from envious summits of fortune into the depths of humiliation, madness, and defeat. The Marqués de Cañete would have felt little concern now for the mestizo offspring of a cavalier he had ruined, and Gómez has left no record even of having caught a glimpse of this Viceroy while passing through the capital. But already retributive justice had fallen upon Cañete, and he was preoccupied with his own disappointments; orders had come for his return to Spain, and his replacement even now was approaching the shores of Tierra Firme.

There would have been little to detain Gómez in Los Reyes and more than likely during the first days of February he boarded a ship at nearby Callao and departed for Panama. As he traveled up the Peruvian coast toward Trujillo and Paita, his attention was drawn to the movement of marine birds—long, thin ribbons winging in from a distance and swooping into the green sea depths for fish with such phenomenal success that he was forced at times to pause and marvel at God's providence. But at Cape Passau on the equinoctial line, where his vessel paused three days to take on firewood and water, he once again became conscious of the forces of Satan as he watched the natives diving for fish—naked, bestial men who filled him with aversion because of their tradition of sodomy, indiscriminate sexual relations, and other manifestations of social filth. And then from this point he began a most hazardous journey through the perilous winds and channels of the Mar del Sur, a sea which few Spaniards who traveled those turbulent waters would have mocked with the name by which it is known today—the Pacific. As the great, rapid ocean current raced south along the coast, it was countered by a powerful wind blowing north so that speeding waters sometimes were walled by two slow-moving currents. Thus the miserable passengers spent some days in abject terror, since their ship was constantly in danger of being sucked into whirlpools or into currents so frenzied as to cast up earth and slime from the very depths of the sea. At one point near the island of Gorgona, when they were blown close in to land and becalmed, their situation became so precarious that all gave up hope of escape, and Gómez undoubtedly began to suspect that they journeyed under a curse. For their vessel was owned by two brothers who, so the pilot informed him, several years previously had taken advantage of a scarcity at Los Reyes and extorted an exorbitant price from prelates for a cargo of sacramental wine. At length, however, the frightened travelers arrived at the city of Panama, gateway to the great southern sea, where it was customary for cargoes to be unloaded and packed on the backs of mules for transportation across the isthmus either by a dangerous and sometimes impassable land trail or by the equally hazardous Chagres River.[3]

Twenty-five years previously a solitary traveler passing through this dreary tropical port had arrived on the eve of the Feast of the Magi at the dwelling of Gonzalo Martel de la Puente and found great rejoicing over the birth of a daughter who now was the stepmother of the lonely mestizo awaiting passage across the isthmus. Whether or

[3] *Ibid.*, Pt. I, Bk. I, Chap. 7; Bk. VIII, Chap. 19; Bk. IX, Chap. 8.

not Gómez paused at this time to contemplate the role which Panama
had played in his own destiny, he never recorded, just as he never recorded the name of Luisa Martel. But one memory of this miserable
settlement which never left him encompassed a vision of poisoned rats,
hundreds of them lying dead along the shores of the turbulent sea,
indeed such vast numbers that one could not walk in the area without
treading upon them. Rats had moved with Europeans into the western
world to form a plague and a pestilence and often a formidable peril
to men left sick and without protection in the night. Gómez could
recall more than one story of men found dead and without arms, legs,
and faces, victims of these voracious creatures whose terrible strength
lay in their limitless numbers; and he may have recalled now, as he
did later, that the first rats had entered Peru with the first Viceroy,
Blasco Núñez Vela.[4]

Abandoning the city of Panama, Gómez now pushed on through
eighteen leagues of tropical mountains and deadly swamps to Nombre
de Dios, where merchant vessels were loading and making preparations to join the armada and its convoys at Havana. This fever-ridden
settlement, cursed by God and man, was replete with avaricious trad-
ers, soldiers, sailors, priests, friars, and diplomats, and as sulky mule
trains came trudging in from Panama, men could be seen unloading
silver in the market place, where it would lie like stones until transferred to vessels. Here in this fetid outpost of Hell, in which it was
said the Devil reigned and puppets danced alongside a yawning grave,
Gómez was to encounter the Devil's piper; already Diego López de
Zúñiga y Velasco, Conde de Nieva and fourth Viceroy to Peru, had
arrived at Tierra Firme, and this lascivious nobleman, as was soon
proven, had come to the Indies primarily to enrich himself, his relatives, and his favorites without regard to justice. Indeed, the Conde's
hunger for gold was exceeded only by his lust for women of flexible
virtue, a passion soon to be made conspicuous by a seraglio set up for
his comfort on the outskirts of Los Reyes. Forming a part of the new
Viceroy's retinue at Nombre de Dios was Antonio Vaca de Castro, to
whom the King had promised a rich encomienda to be chosen from

[4] *Ibid.*, Pt. I, Bk. IX, Chap. 22.

whatever repartimientos might fall vacant in Peru. It was the father of this young nobleman who had so bountifully enriched Captain Garcilaso after the rebellion of Almagro the Lad, and ironically don Antonio soon was to receive some of the same wealth which Gómez, because of the circumstances of his birth, had been denied.

Although he was to mention the incident, Gómez left no details of his encounter with these two dignitaries.[5] But incoming viceroys usually took advantage of any opportunities offered to obtain advance information on Peru; and one suspects that at this point if not earlier the Conde was told of those ill-mannered and inflaming directives with which some years previously the arrogant Marqués de Cañete had humbled Sebastián Garcilaso and other corregidors of Peru and the Charcas. For the communication which Nieva shortly dispatched to the man he was replacing subjected the latter to a similar humiliation. It is said that when Cañete heard of the approach of the new Viceroy's emissary, he prepared to receive him with gifts of gold, silver, and jewelry. But the sumptuous gifts were never bestowed. When Nieva's message was placed in the hands of the Marqués, he noted that its superscription contained nothing more respectful than the simple words "Your Lordship," and having utilized this same means of relegating men to their proper stations, Cañete was well aware of the seriousness of its implication. He fell immediately into an abysmal melancholy and declined so rapidly as to die before the arrival of his successor at Los Reyes. But by this time the mestizo whose quill had penned the answers to those first haughty communications to his father from Cañete was riding a high-decked and full-masted galleon across the deep and troubled waters of the great Ocean Sea.

In making the return voyage from Tierra Firme to Spain most vessels followed a generally established route, going first to Cartagena, where treasure-laden ships customarily assembled from sundry parts of the Spanish Main, and then moving swiftly through the Yucatán Channel to unite at Havana with the Mexican fleet for a long and perilous journey by way of the Bahama Straits to the Azores. Such voyages were made painful by restricted quarters and on the whole were tedious,

---

[5] *Ibid.*, Pt. II, Bk. IV, Chap. 23; Bk. VIII, Chap. 15.

though monotony often was broken by mock bullfights, cockfights, illuminations, shark fishing, and religious festivals. Also some excitement was constantly engendered by the anticipation of corsairs, and even before reaching the Azores passengers were instructed to clear out staterooms and berths and put ships in fighting trim. Gómez is known to have disembarked at Cartagena, and later at Fayal, Terceira and Lisbon. Since ships ordinarily were forbidden to come into port between the Azores and Spain, and since these waters especially were infested with corsairs, his landing at Lisbon may be assumed to have been made necessary by some mishap or emergency. Such an assumption is supported by his declaration that when approaching the shores of the Old World for the first time, a magnanimous Portuguese saved him from perishing. This unelaborated statement taunts one with visions of such piratical encounters and marine disasters as he afterward described in recounting the adventures of Hernando de Soto; but more important in the progress of his story is a simultaneous assertion that at this time the people of the Azores as well as those at Lisbon treated him with kindness and charity, offering him the utmost cordiality and greeting him as a native son.[6] Thus in a moment when his heart was heavy with memories of what he had left behind and when his soul anticipated with the sharp anxiety of an alien the treatment which he might receive in the uncertain world of his father's people, the Portuguese placed him under an obligation which he could never forget. As a Peruvian mestizo yearning to merge into the great Hispanic family, he had been received by these hospitable people, not as a half-caste or an alien, but as one of their own; and such an experience of course extended the limits of his hopes.

Over the near horizon and but a relatively few miles of well-trodden Portuguese road lay the city of Badajoz and the kinsmen Gómez eventually must encounter; and he would have longed to abandon the cramped quarters of a clumsy vessel and continue by the less dangerous land route to his goal. Yet because of smuggling and traffic in contra-

---

[6] Garcilaso, *Comentarios*, Pt. I, Bk. I, Chap. 13; *La Florida del Inca*, see the dedication to Teodosio de Portugal. For the accepted and most traveled routes to and from the Indies, see Francisco López de Gómara, *Historia general de las Indias*, Vol. II, Chap. 222, pp. 250–251. Ordinarily the journey required about three months.

band, few travelers from the Indies were permitted that route; and this Indian youth, whose legacy of silver had been assigned to Seville and possibly accompanied him in the same vessel, was no exception. It would be necessary for him, like all others, to enter Spain under the vigilant eye of the Casa de Contratación, and to do so he soon would board ship once again and move down the gray, rock-bound coast of Portugal to the Bay of Cádiz and the long stretches of sand which guard the mouth of the Guadalquivir.

It surely, therefore, must have been at this historical site that Gómez received his first glimpse of old Spain, and the picture would have been enchanting to a youth of romantic imagination whose life had been passed below the equinoctial line in the chill regions of the Andes. It was a vision of warm blue seas, sapphire skies, and white houses dotting an emerald landscape, while all up and down the broad river rode the ships of the Renaissance world, treasure-laden vessels moving to and from China, India, Africa, the Canaries, and all the known ports of Europe and the great Ocean Sea, a varicolored medley of mainsails, many bearing on their canvases the brilliantly painted likenesses of protectors and saints. Passing slowly now through this ebb and flow of color and adventure, the dark-featured son of Sebastián Garcilaso de la Vega soon would step ashore at Seville, where more than thirty years previously his father presumably had set forth with the gay caravels of Pedro de Alvarado to spread the seeds of Spain and Catholicism while garnering some of the silver and gold of the Indies.

The long journey from Cuzco to Seville had simply added to the rich deposit of knowledge and experience which was to form the basic source of a classic history. Gómez now had traced in reverse the trail which many conquerors had followed in their search for fulfillment, and he had become a firsthand witness to additional hazards they often had encountered while en route to the mines of wealth and dreams. This knowledge was to lend authenticity to his later records of voyages in which he had not actually participated. Already he had attained a vast wisdom of men, lands, and seas which eventually enabled him to create a reality from the mottled fabric of his experience and his imaginative genius.

It apparently was in the late summer or early fall of 1560 that

Gómez arrived at Seville. The bustling old port, with its background of Roman, Gothic, and Saracenic memories shining through the hubbub and confusion, the splendor and the dirt of a Renaissance mart, held him enthralled. Many of its ancient legends he already knew, and he now regarded with both pride and respect the storied portals from which corroding years had almost succeeded in erasing the celebrated tribute to Julius Caesar, Ferdinand the Holy, and Garcí Pérez de Vargas. He wandered through the malodorous Alameda, at this time a pestilential lagoon into which drained continually the filth and rotting refuse of the city; and he observed the teeming manswarm flowing through narrow streets along which many an adventurer and dreaming conqueror had trod—fine liveried cavaliers and gentlemen, merchants and peddlers, sailors, montebanks, charlatans, prostitutes, gypsies, and thieves. And as he beheld multiple shops lining the crooked thoroughfares, he marveled at the emeralds and pearls which had poured into the city from the far reaches of the western world. Yet when this proud and aspiring mestizo made his first purchase, it was not an object from an Indian world but a symbol of Hispanicism and affluence—a pair of Cordovan boots.

At this point his record grows dim, and the chances are that he soon proceeded to Estremadura to complete the mission entrusted to him by María de Chávez, to visit the ancestral seat of his father's family, and timidly but hopefully to encounter the elder of the two guardians of his legacy. If so, at some time during the closing months of 1560 or the early months of the following year he entered Badajoz and sought out his uncle, Gómez Suárez de Figueroa y Vargas, proud Lord of Torre del Águila y Tesorero, and, significantly, the only one of the sons of Alonso de Hinestrosa de Vargas whose nobility rested solely on lineage and patrimony and had not been bolstered by martial accomplishments. The appearance of the traveler at this crucial time unfortunately must be left to the imagination of the reader. Assuredly he was vested in the livery of a gentleman, and there was nothing especially astonishing about his mien and behavior. But in spite of various poetic conceptions, it is difficult to believe that this first-generation mestizo did not combine with a certain resemblance to Captain Garcilaso many of the striking physical characteristics of the Peruvian Indian—the high, majestic, and finely molded cheekbones, the dark slanted eyes, and the copperhued skin of the children of the Sun. A friend who knew him in his old age did record that he was a man of medium stature and that his complexion was swarthy; and even in succeeding years when his Spanish culture might have erased some traces of his origin, his physical features made it impossible for Spaniards to disassociate him from the Indian.

Alonso de Hinestrosa de Vargas and Blanca de Sotomayor Suárez de Figueroa, highborn paternal grandparents of this mestizo, lay entombed in the vaults of the Franciscans at Badajoz and thus were spared the shock of witnessing this evidence of their blood mixed with that of a strange and dark race.[7] Their eldest son, the proud Lord of Torre del Águila, apparently had accepted or resigned himself to some responsibility for the well-being of his errant brother's mestizo offspring, but there is no evidence to show that he and his wife and children ever regarded the task as anything other than an expediency. Most likely a similar attitude was shared by Sebastián's sisters, though Isabel de Vargas may have proven an exception since there is reason to believe that she and her husband had assumed some responsibility for her brother's illegitimate daughter Leonor. Somewhere Gómez now may have encountered this half sister, who at least shared with him the common legacy of bastardy as well as some of her father's silver. But a conception of Spanish hauteur and racial bias in an age of discovery forces a melancholy picture of the mestizo's reception at Badajoz, and the picture becomes more dismal if one accepts the possibility that Gómez was accompanied to Estremadura by a poor Vargas cousin or at worst a "son of nobody" who had married Captain Garcilaso's concubine, mother of the youth the Figueroas and Vargases now were asked to received. Undoubtedly, as soon as feasible Gómez was encouraged if not urged to seek out his second guardian uncle, Alonso de Vargas, in the Andalusian village of Montilla.

During these trying months, when sufficient time had elapsed for

---

[7] Sebastián Garcilaso stated in his will that his mother and father were dead; their burial place is disclosed in the will of Sebastián's oldest brother. Archivo Histórico Provincial de Badajoz, Escribano Marcos de Herrera, Año de 1563, No. 1, fols. 477–480.

news to arrive from Cuzco, and when he must have been sick with longing for information of what had transpired in his homeland, Gómez would receive reports which were both disconcerting and discouraging. Even while he was crossing the vast Ocean Sea, both of his legitimate half sisters had died, Blanca de Sotomayor on May 8, 1560, and Francisca de Mendoza seventeen days later. The bodies of both girls were placed alongside that of their father in the vault beneath the high altar of the Franciscans.[8] But when on June 24 the Indians came with their tributes, Luisa Martel accepted them as if there had been no break in succession. Ten days later, however, the Officials of the Royal Exchequer at Cuzco put an end to her collections and the Garcilaso repartimientos reverted to the Crown. But these men were to have reason to reckon with Captain Garcilaso's shrewd widow, who already could anticipate the assistance of an experienced cavalier of Cuzco, Gerónimo Luis de Cabrera.

An ancient Spanish adage advised a widow to marry before she had cast off her weeds; and Luisa Martel, even while Captain Garcilaso was dying, may have been contemplating the superior virtues of Cabrera. She now was but twenty-five years of age and he was a comparatively young man of charm and some wealth who for his part could not have been unaware of the advantages she could offer. Certainly during the precarious months of her widowhood, especially after the seizure of the Garcilaso repartimientos, she responded warmly to the advice and consolation of Gerónimo Luis de Cabrera, and at some time in September or October of 1560 she married him.[9] Then on October 7 of the same year, with the approval and assistance of her new husband, she began a suit before Juan Polo de Ondegardo, Corregidor of Cuzco, for the return of the Garcilaso encomienda with all tributes collected in the interim since what she termed its illegal seizure.

[8] Information concerning the deaths of these two girls and Luisa Martel's subsequent actions is to be found in the Martel-Cabrera expediente.

[9] In two documents issued on Sept. 10, 1560, she referred to herself respectively as the wife of Garcilaso de la Vega and the widow of Garcilaso de la Vega. In a document issued at the close of the first week in October, 1560, she identified herself as the widow of Garcilaso de la Vega and the wife in second nuptials of Gerónimo Luis de Cabrera. Archivo Histórico del Cuzco, Escribano Gregorio de Bitorero, Año de 1560, Reg. nos. 3 and 4, Ata. no. 827. Published in *Revista del Archivo Histórico del Cuzco*, No. 3, 1952, pp. 255–257. Also Martel-Cabrera expediente.

Immediately the Royal Officials, refusing to recognize any claims or charges, declared that the Garcilaso Indians, having been given for but two lives, had reverted legally to the Crown at the demise of the Captain's successor, Blanca de Sotomayor. In reply doña Luisa insisted that her daughter had never succeeded to the Indians since she had never reached the age specified for corporeal investiture, and that since both daughters had died without succeeding, the encomienda had fallen to herself legally as the widow of the original encomendero. Afterward, when confronted with an accusation that she as legal guardian had collected tributes in her daughter's name, she denied the charge and asserted that she had collected them in her own name, since, according to a precedent set by the Marqués de Cañete, property remained in the possession of a guardian until the heir had legally succeeded. When the Corregidor appeared to favor the Cabreras, the Officials declared that corporeal investiture had never been customary in Peru, that an heir succeeded immediately on the death of the father, and that since the case was not a mere petition for protection of rights but a suit on Indians, it could be settled only by the King's representatives at Los Reyes. So Polo de Ondegardo, against loud opposition from the Cabreras, remitted the plea to the Audiencia. Then, at the close of the year, the Cabreras learned to their dismay that several months previously the Conde de Nieva had conferred a vast portion of the litigated encomienda upon Antonio Vaca de Castro, son of the man who originally had bestowed it upon Captain Garcilaso, and that the remainder had been given to Melchor Vázquez de Ávila, Governor of Quito, whose brother, Juan Vázquez de Arce, was a significant member of the Council of the Indies.[10] But the fortune at stake was too enviable to relinquish, and the Cabreras still could claim that the new awards were illegal since they had been bestowed while the Indians were under litigation. So the suit was continued tediously at Los Reyes through the ensuing year, until eventually the Audiencia, against the passionate protests of the litigants, resolved to place it in the hands of the Council of the Indies.

News of these activities most certainly confronted Gómez during

[10] Martel-Cabrera expediente; Garcilaso, *Comentarios,* Pt. II, Bk. IV, Chap. 23; *La Audiencia de Lima,* Bk. I, pp. 312–313.

his first year in Spain; but the extent to which it affected him can be ascertained only in part through some of his later assertions. The suit, even if won, could not have nullified his legacy of silver and there is much to suggest that this silver was already in Spain. The question of his plantation of Havisca is more puzzling since it had represented a part of the original Garcilaso encomienda; but somehow and in some way Captain Garcilaso had managed to bestow it upon him irrevocably. The same, however, may not have been true of the coca plantation with which the Captain had dowered his daughter Francisca de la Vega, for at some time during these years she and her family are known to have suffered a loss of income. With the evidence at hand, one can only assume that somewhere among the vanished clauses or codicils of Captain Garcilaso's last testimony there is a request that his natural children share part of the revenue from the Garcilaso Indians. Gómez later declared that with the termination of the "second life" of his father's encomienda (which meant precisely with the death of his legitimate half sister, Blanca de Sotomayor) he and the remaining children were left unsupported.[11] In the light of what is known this statement remains more or less enigmatic. But one can be sure that at this point, regardless of the depth of their destitution, neither Gómez nor his sisters could have hoped for any succor from their stepmother even though she were lucky enough to win her suit. Nevertheless, the progress of the Cabrera litigation did surely have some bearing on the actions Gómez shortly determined to take, the presentation of his own pretensions before the Council of the Indies.

By September of 1561, Gómez had joined his other uncle at Montilla.[12] Alonso de Vargas and his austere wife lived still in their manorial dwelling in the upper part of the town and continued to enjoy cordial relations with the Figueroas who represented the ruling houses of Feria and Priego. Devout in his faith, don Alonso maintained close bonds with the curates of the church of Santiago, whose baptismal records abound in instances wherein both he and his wife, Luisa Ponce, stood as godparents to sundry infants of the parish. Though the Cap-

---

[11] Garcilaso, *Comentarios*, Pt. II, Bk. V, Chap. 23.
[12] Document dated September 16, 1561, Archivo de Protocolos de Montilla, Escribano Rodrigo Páez, Año de 1561, folios illegible.

tain was almost sixty years of age at marriage, his bride had been young enough to expect children; but by now both ostensibly had begun to despair of progeny. As early as 1559 don Alonso had drawn up his will, and the fact that it had met the approval of his wife indicates that in the event there were no offspring, many of the Captain's assets were destined to fall to Luisa Ponce and her relatives.[13] Of more than passing interest, therefore, is the circumstance that this year of 1561, which marked the arrival of don Alonso's nephew at Montilla, also marked the birth at Córdoba of his wife's nephew, Luis de Góngora y Argote, first-born son of her brother Francisco de Argote and destined to become one of the great poets of Renaissance Spain.

A paternal yearning, therefore, combined with an old warrior's admiration and respect for his brother's career in the Indies, accounts to some extent for the warmth with which Alonso de Vargas now received his young kinsman from Peru. To the youth, this hospitable uncle represented another colorful picture of Spanish grandeur and chivalry as well as a new source of hope and security. He listened with rapture and faith to the cavalier's accounts of splendid experiences and noble accomplishments in the Old World campaigns of Charles V and Philip II;[14] and don Alonso, impressed by the intelligence, cavalier refinement, and dark but noble mien of this astute mestizo, was equally enthralled by what he now heard firsthand of a gallant struggle in the New World where his younger brothers had given their lives in the service of the same sovereigns. Between the two there developed a congeniality which could not have existed between the mestizo and his elder uncle at Badajoz. Very promptly the aging grandee drew his nephew into his own sphere of activity, motivating his participation in lay duties at the ancient church of Santiago, bringing him to the attention of local scholars, and utilizing his splendid knowledge of horses, for of late the Crown had put pressure on the Town Council and on the ruling house of Priego to improve the strain of horses at Montilla.

---

[13] Archivo de Protocolos de Montilla, Escribano Andrés Baptista, Año de 1559. The document has been lost, but its existence and the fact that it was approved by Luisa Ponce is disclosed in Baptista's "Índice."

[14] For one such story see Garcilaso, *La Florida del Inca*, Bk. II, Pt. I, Chap. 25.

His equestrian prowess alone was sufficient to have won for Gómez both the curiosity and the admiration of his Figueroa kin, for finely groomed as he was in the art of handling a horse "a la jinete," or in the short-stirruped Moorish saddle, he could vie with the lords of the land in their traditional sports. Indeed much of his training in horsemanship had been received at the hands of Pedro Hernández el Leal, who before going to Peru had served in the Feria household; and the present Conde de Feria, perhaps attracted by Gómez' expert knowledge of horseflesh, eventually was to put a portion of his stables under the management of don Pedro's son, Martín Leal, who had been born and reared in the Garcilaso house at Cuzco.[15] Had Gómez been able to overcome the racial consciousness and the inherent haughtiness of the scions of Feria and Priego, his future in Spain might have been considerably altered. For the Conde de Feria had continued as a trusted Crown diplomat, playing a shrewd role in Philip's vain attempts to marry Elizabeth Tudor and in his recent marriage to Isabel de Valois. In 1560 the Conde, having attained release from his betrothal to his niece, had returned to Spain with an English bride, Jane Dormer, a first cousin to His Majesty's godson, Sir Philip Sidney, and now ruled his earldom from a formidable palace at nearby Córdoba. Meanwhile, his brother, Alonso Fernández, had gained the title of Marqués de Priego by marrying the jilted niece and was guarding his interests from the family seat at Montilla. But the admiration of these highborn noblemen for the cavalier skills of their kinsman from Cuzco apparently stopped short of taking pride in blood ties with an Indian, as their future relations with him were to reveal.

On the other hand, the mother of these grandees and her granddaughter in line of succession apparently were not reluctant to bestow upon Gómez some of the respect he felt his due as a Figueroa and as a grandson of the deceased Lord of Valdesevilla. Both of these women, he declared, were paragons of Christian virtue who revealed the magnanimities of princes and by their examples exposed to shame all who did not attempt to emulate them.[16] The primary purpose of Gómez' voyage to Spain had been to secure an education and he may

[15] Garcilaso, *Comentarios*, Pt. II, Bk. VII, Chap. 18.
[16] Garcilaso, *La Descendencia de Garcí Pérez de Vargas.*

even have planned, in accordance with the dream of Juan de Cuéllar, to pit his mestizo intellect against the scholars of Salamanca, though nothing has been uncovered to indicate what plans he had in this respect. But the process of his Spanish education surely was begun at once at Montilla under some of the eminent scholars patronized by the kindly old Catalina, Condesa de Feria and Marquesa de Priego, whose intellectual interests were as well known as her piety.

By September of 1561 Gómez' half sister Leonor was dead, and with the aid of his Uncle Alonso he filed claim for her portion of their father's legacy.[17] Furthermore, because of the economic hazards which arose with the demise of his half sisters, Blanca and Francisca, he certainly by now had begun to formulate serious plans for seeking favors at Court. Indeed this idea may very well have been present in his mind for some time and possibly had been suggested first or even urged by his foresighted father. Certainly that pollen of social and economic ambition which had fallen upon the emotions of all Peruvian mestizos whose fathers had endowed them with the semblances of hidalguía had been on the verge of producing a bitter flower even as Gómez departed from his native Cuzco, and undoubtedly his comrades had bidden him farewell with secret understandings and with some determination to regard his progress in Spain as a suggestion of the horizons to which they might aspire. Only recently the King had given evidence of an inclination to favor mestizos, and now in 1561 Pedro del Barco, though imprisoned at Córdoba for attempting to murder the vixen who had seduced him into marriage, had such a petition before the Council of the Indies. Yet Gómez would have been poignantly aware that this mestizo comrade whom Sebastián Garcilaso had succored and protected throughout his boyhood could make a claim denied most mestizos; his father had been one of the few conquistadors who had been sufficiently considerate to legitimize his offspring. Even succession, therefore, had been within his reach.

It must be emphasized, however, that Gómez did not and could not seek succession. He was forced to accept the fact that his father's encomienda had terminated with the death of Blanca de Sotomayor. Yet

---

[17] Document dated September 16, 1561, Archivo de Protocolos de Montilla, Escribano Rodrigo Páez, Año de 1561, fol. 3.

the recent efforts of Luisa Martel to abrogate that legal resolution by exceptions may have suggested new hopes, and he was sensitively conscious that his moral right to what his father had gained and what his Indian mother had helped his father to gain was as profound as that of his stepmother and her recently acquired spouse. Furthermore, he felt that in accordance with his understanding of the Spanish social structure, a request on his part for favor at Court was both legal and ethical since his lineage was noble and "clean," and since the services of his father and his father's brothers to the Crown had been loyal, worthy, and generous. Such thoughts were not absent from his mind when he made his decision to seek favor at Court, and though he recorded that this decision was due to destitution resulting from the termination of his father's estate, it undoubtedly was made with a hope of social stature and with a faith in the justice of Spanish nobility, a faith in a concept, apparently long forgotten in Spain, that a plinth of chivalry was to be found in the chivalric virtues of honor and good deeds. This faith he had received from a father whose ancient chivalry had been enriched by democratic concepts breeding in the New World, and by his sponsoring uncle who for almost forty years had watched the progress of kings.

At some time during the closing days of 1561 Gómez left Montilla and set out upon the well-trodden road which led through the heartland of Spain to Madrid.[18] Thus it was that in the early days of 1562 this visionary youth from the Imperial Capital of the Incas found himself in a city which only the previous year had been designated as the imperial capital of all the kingdoms of Spain.

[18] On November 24, 1561, Gómez appeared as a godfather at Montilla. See Archivo de la Parroquia de Santiago de Montilla, Libro de Bautismos No. 3, fol. 124v. He himself recorded that he left at the close of the year. Garcilaso, *Comentarios*, Pt. II, Bk. IV, Chap. 23.

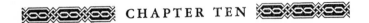

CHAPTER TEN

Madrid often had been favored by the Emperor Charles and for many years had claimed the title of "la villa imperial y coronada"; yet when in 1561 Philip II designated this old city as his new capital, it was the least imposing of the eighteen emulous cities privileged to send parliamentary representatives to the Cortes de Castilla. But Philip's benediction gave Madrid an impetus for rapid growth. Soon multitudes of people of all trades and classes began to flow through its mud-choked streets, and new edifices of imposing dimensions arose above its ancient structures. Nerve center of this turbulent social and political mecca was the Alcázar Real, which now served not only as the residence of the King but as the seat of his judicial councils, whose most minute affairs he insisted on supervising. And in this year of 1561 the courts of Madrid were heavily burdened with fortune seekers and petitioners for royal favor, many of them old conquerors who had survived the hazards of the New World and had helped to make its resources available for the multiple needs of the Spanish Crown.

It therefore was a bustling and turbulent Madrid which the mestizo Gómez encountered when during the festive season of the Nativity he entered the ancient gates of Philip's new capital; and as he mingled with the motley crowds of this city whose population within a few decades was to soar beyond one hundred thousand, he was struck by the splendor of the scene and by the fact that much of this splendor had its source in the rich veins of Tahuantinsuyu. On all sides he saw gold, silver, and gems from the Indies; and he noted an even greater profusion of pearls here than he had seen at Seville. In the inn where he lodged he was attracted to a young devotee of pearls and gambling who had arrived in Madrid with nothing and was attaining wealth by transporting gems from the Indian world; and in his devotions he was struck by the richness of an image of the Virgin of Guadalupe, an image favored by a sovereign prone to utilize gems for pious purposes. Not only was the altar beneath encrusted with pearls, but the mantle and skirt of the Holy Mother were embroidered in a chessboard pattern with squares of rubies and emeralds set in gold. It did credit, he thought, not only to the artificer who designed it, but to the great Christian Prince who was willing to dispose thus of his treasures. And yet, even in these hopeful moments before he had developed any of the melancholy skepticism which later was to engulf him, he was sensitive to the fact that only the Emperor of the Indies had the means for such an expenditure.[1]

All around him now Gómez encountered men whom he had known in Peru, a cyclorama of old men, mostly, whose lives had touched that of his father, and who in far-off days had helped to twist the fate of Tahuantinsuyu.[2] Here was Hernando Pizarro, massive, red-nosed aristocrat of the Pizarros, who had married his mestiza niece and, now a hundred years old, was seeking reimbursement and favor, after twenty-three wearisome years of imprisonment for his role in the tragic denouement of the elder Almagro. Here was Cristóbal Vaca de Castro, who had vanquished the younger Almagro, and who, after having passed eight empty years of mild confinement in Spain, had been restored to the Council of Castile. Here was Juan Suárez de Carvajal, Bishop of Lugo, whose brother Illén had fallen prey to the maniacal rage of Blasco Núñez Vela, and who had opposed the reforms of Las Casas. And here was Bartolemé de las Casas himself, eighty-eight years of age and still hovering over the courts with an undying zeal for the

---

[1] El Inca Garcilaso, *Los comentarios reales*, Pt. I, Bk. VIII, Chap. 23.
[2] *Ibid.*, Pt. I, Bk. VII, Chap. 10; Pt. II, Bk. II, Chap. 6; Bk. III, Chap. 20; Bk. IV, Chaps. 3, 23; Bk. VII, Chap. 5; Aurelio Miró Quesada y Sosa, *El Inca Garcilaso*, p. 88.

welfare of the Indians and with a long memory for men who previously had opposed him. More than a decade had elapsed since his heated controversy with Sepúlveda, but he now was rounding out a vast history of the Indies on which he had labored for forty years. When young Gómez approached to kiss the hands of this venerable prelate, he was received with warmth, and then suddenly the air grew chill. This strange shift in atmosphere, Gómez curiously attributed to the bishop's realization that the obeisant mestizo was a Peruvian rather than a Mexican. Indeed, though Las Casas' enemies possibly were as abundant in Mexico as elsewhere, he did hold a special disdain for those conquerors who had permitted the New Laws to convert Peru into a holocaust; and he now was in the presence of the son of one of those conquerors, a mestizo of cavalier mien and conscience who ostensibly was not seeking relief for the common Indian but for favors which might make him a master of Indians. Las Casas' intimate association with the court as well as his long preoccupation with the affairs of the Indies would have acquainted him with some of the suspicion that colored the activities of Sebastián Garcilaso; and Sebastián's son surely was not far enough removed from the scene of Gonzalo Pizarro's rebellion to have approached the zealot without some unconscious emanation of resentment. Though their concepts eventually were to coincide in some respects, there existed at this point a significant gulf between the ideals of the mestizo Gómez and the fanatical Bishop of Chiapas.

The spectacle of body- and soul-scarred adventurers, hungry ghosts of an old conquest, now haunting the courts of the King whom they had helped to enrich, echoed the whole of the turbulent story of Peru from the time of its invasion until the present. Many of them had reason to remember Captain Garcilaso with admiration and affection, though there surely were some who still thought of him as one who was "loyal for but three hours." Conspicuous among the former was Pedro Luis de Cabrera, the fat old cavalier who always addressed Gómez as "nephew" and who now, after having obtained a reassignment of his Peruvian estate, was at Madrid seeking an extension of time on his allotted period of absence. One may be sure that he offered valuable information and encouragement to the timid and bewildered mestizo. They are known to have discussed don Pedro's mother, Leonor Ponce de León y Figueroa, through whom they were related, and this subject would lead naturally to that of his bastard half brother, now married to the mestizo's stepmother and assisting her in her efforts to regain the Garcilaso Indians. At this point the Cabrera suit must have loomed significant at Madrid since it undoubtedly was being followed closely by two of the King's chief magistrates, Cristóbal Vaca de Castro and Juan Vázquez de Arce. Moreover, it was demanding what Gómez now was preparing to ask of the Council of the Indies—an investigation of the loyalty and the services of Captain Garcilaso de la Vega.

During these days the Council of the Indies occupied three large rooms in the northeast corner of the first floor of the Alcázar Real. Their windows overlooked the palace gardens, and they had a separate entrance which led through the patio to the salas of the King. Here, under the watchful eye of a cautious and prudent sovereign, they followed a strict schedule, on Mondays listening to appeals, on Tuesdays and Thursdays examining the visitas and residencias of upper functionaries of the Indies, on Wednesdays deliberating matters which concerned the Royal Treasury of the Indies, and on Saturdays judging criminal cases and hearing the pleas of prisoners or the suits of the poor. In one of these busy and crowded rooms, the very antechambers of the King, and at some time in the early part of 1562, the mestizo son of Sebastián Garcilaso, now almost twenty-three years of age, made his appearance with a petition for the pecuniary recognition of his father's services and the restitution of his Indian mother's patrimony. He may have had legal council, since he had not reached his majority, and the fact that he returned once to Montilla during the course of the year indicates that Alonso de Vargas at least was watching with interest the progress of his nephew's suit.[3] But there must have been intermittent appearances as the days dragged on and evidence was accumulated or witnesses summoned. No proof as to who was called upon is extant, though among them must surely have been some of the conquerors whom Gómez afterwards mentioned as having encountered at court. Most helpful would have been Vaca de Castro, but his high position

[3] Raúl Porras Barrenechea, *El Inca Garcilaso en Montilla*, p. xx.

on the Council of Castile may have precluded his participation as a personal witness; and equally favorable would have been Pedro Luis de Cabrera, but by March this genial kinsman was dead. There is, however, highly creditable evidence that Gonzalo Silvestre was at court at this time, and he, so Gómez has recorded, often was called before the Council as a witness. But the assistance which Gómez would sorely need before final judgment was rendered was that of some of his highborn Mendoza and Figueroa kinsmen, those who formed a part of Philip's more or less personal coterie of counselors and frequently were appointed by the King to special juntas dealing with matters concerning the Indies: the Duque del Infantado, the Conde de Feria, and the Príncipe de Éboli, husband of Ana de Mendoza.[4] Yet there is no indication that any of these men ever spoke a word in favor of their equally highborn Indian relative, and there is much to indicate that they did not. The Mendozas may have known nothing of either him or his pretensions; but the Figueroas did know, and could have been regarding his suit with some personal concern. For Alonso de Vargas may already have formally adopted his nephew and declared him an heir; and even as Gómez was initiating claims at Madrid his uncle was strengthening claims on Figueroa rents. On January 7, 1562, the aging Marquesa de Priego had ratified her son's debt to Alonso de Vargas, and in doing so she sealed a contract that was to affect the fortunes of the mestizo Gómez and to prove irksome to some of her own heirs for years to come.[5]

Unfortunately, many of the memoranda accompanying such suits as Gómez was presenting were destroyed in the process of the appeals, and at this point there is no certainty as to the exact nature of the inquiries made of him. Yet a similar suit made by his stepmother and another by his niece strongly indicate that pivotal questions would have involved such matters as legitimacy, cleanness of blood, loyalty, and services rendered the Crown.[6] In all such matters, Gómez could have offered substantial and favorable evidence, with the exception of course

[4] Ernesto Schafer, *El Consejo Real y Supremo de las Indias*, Vol. I, p. 166.

[5] Authorization made by Luis de Góngora, December 31, 1591, Archivo de Protocolos de Córdoba, Oficio 22, Protocolo 14, fols. 2493–2497.

[6] Martel-Cabrera and Sarmiento Palacio expedientes.

of the first. In this it would be necessary to place himself at the mercy of judges who may have had little sympathy with or understanding of the significant role played by concubinage in the initial stages of the conquest. To questions concerning loyalty and services, he could have mentioned, as he is known to have done in later suits, the records of two of his uncles as well as those of his father. And in addition to his testimony as well as that of other witnesses, the Council already would have seen or have had access to favorable reports on Captain Garcilaso, among them the records of Vaca de Castro and La Gasca. On the other hand, they also possessed records that were damaging. Embedded among them was the bitter correspondence of the Marqués de Cañete which had proclaimed Garcilaso's suspected perfidy and declared him insane, and even among the reports of La Gasca there were suggestions that the Captain's association with Gonzalo Pizarro was at times open to question. Again, as has been noted, both Zárate and López de Gómara had printed slight allusions which needed only enlargement and substantiation to make them harmful. This enlargement was to be found in the unpublished manuscripts of Cañete's protégé-chronicler, Diego Fernández de Palencia, which undoubtedly had been seen by some members of the present Council. The Palentino himself has written that on his return to Spain he placed his manuscripts in the hands of Francisco Tello de Sandoval, whom he identified as President of the Council of the Indies, along with a petition to publish a history of the Girón rebellion, which he at that time had finished; and that he had been encouraged by the Council first to complete his account of the Pizarro rebellion, for which he already had obtained material in Peru.[7]

The records of the Palentino, published less than a decade later, indicate the tenor of the reports which he had seen and heard in Peru concerning Garcilaso de la Vega, and which of course formed a part of his original manuscripts. Among other things, he mentioned with-

[7] Diego Fernández, *Historia del Perú,* ed. Odriozola, prefaces to Pt. I and Pt. II. Merriman says Tello became President of the Council in 1559, though neither Schafer nor León Pinelo gives him this post before 1565. As the oldest member of the Council in both age and tenure, he possibly served as President Interim between 1560 and 1563 when there was no official President. See Roger Bigelow Merriman, *The Rise of the Spanish Empire,* Vol. IV, p. 202; Schafer, *El Consejo Real y Supremo de las Indias,* Vol. I, pp. 351–366; also Antonio León Pinelo, *Tablas cronológicas de los Reales Consejos,* pp. 1–13.

out explanation Pedro Luis de Cabrera's statement that Hernández Girón in his major rebellion had merely usurped plans already laid by Garcilaso and his brother-in-law, Antonio de Quiñones; and, as has been shown, he gave a damning version of Garcilaso's association with Gonzalo Pizarro. The Palentino was not yet a recognized historian and he had been sanctioned by a Viceroy whose bias and passion were common knowledge in Peru if not in Spain. But the confidence of the Crown ostensibly had been bestowed upon him when he was granted permission to examine official documents, and his concept of the loyalty of the cavalier in question would be respected by at least some of the members of the Council.

To present a petition at court required an expenditure of time as well as funds. Judgments often were delayed interminably and before handed down required the signature of the King. As Gómez tarried in Madrid he would have an opportunity to witness an orgy of hagiolatry attending efforts both public and private to save the life of Prince Carlos, who presumably was dying of a head injury at Alcalá, and he surely would have regarded with some faith the macabre and miraculous incident which added another name to the hierarchy of saints and, according to general credence, prolonged the existence of this ill-fated heir to the Hapsburg throne.[8] And throughout the remainder of this year of 1562, as he awaited his turn in the antechambers of the Council of the Indies, Gómez would continue to meet familiar petitioners, among them the revolter cleric, Baltasar de Loaisa, who had risked the wrath of Carvajal in the Pizarro rebellion, and Melchor Verdugo, a renowned bully of Potosí. Moreover, he may have encountered Pedro del Barco, to whom in June, 1562, the Council had awarded a repartimiento of Peruvian Indians.[9] But the very plethora of petitions was serving to lessen Gómez' own opportunity. The salaries of councilmen long had been a source of complaint, and when only the previous year Philip had yielded to demands for an increase in these salaries, he had

---

[8] After all other cures had failed, the mouldering remains of a pious friar, dead a hundred years, were placed alongside the dying Carlos, and from that moment, so it was said, the Prince began to recover. At Philip's behest, the friar was beatified.

[9] Garcilaso, *Comentarios*, Pt. II, Bk. IV, Chap. 12; Bk. V, Chap. 2; Order of King to the Viceroy of Peru, June 21, 1562, Seville, Archivo General de Indias, Audiencia de Lima, Legajo 568, fols. 268–268v.

specified that the funds must be taken from the few vacant reparti-mientos remaining in Peru. Furthermore, at this moment, Gómez' stepmother still was pressing claims on the services of his father, and by the latter part of the year the Council undoubtedly had been ad-vised that her suit was to be remitted to them, a circumstance which surely inspired those inquisitors to peer more attentively at the record of Garcilaso de la Vega. Indeed, but for a twist of fate, and a second thought on the part of a Viceroy, Gómez' suit might have been brought to judgment simultaneously and in the same tribunal as that of his stepmother, for by the beginning of 1563 Luisa Martel's husband had formulated plans to defend his wife's rights in person at Madrid. Such an interesting possibility, however, failed to materialize when the Conde de Nieva, fearful of the turmoil and confusion and personal loss which might arise with a Cabrera victory at court, arranged a com-promise on January 18, 1563, by which Luisa Martel was to receive an annuity of four thousand pesos from the Royal Treasury at Cuzco so long as she relinquished all claims to the Garcilaso Indians. This con-tract, of course, would demand the approval of the Council and the Crown, both of whom were regarding all actions of the lascivious Nieva with such acute displeasure that they already were formulating plans to replace him.[10]

Ironically, this was the situation when in 1563 Gómez approached the Council for a final judgment on his petition. Nevertheless, he ap-proached with hope since the indications were that he had convinced its members of the justness of his claims. The occasion would not have taken place in the crowded anterooms of the Council but in one of the great salas that led to the chambers of the King. The tribunal was headed by the licentiate Lope García de Castro, Philip's first appointee to the Council in 1558, and according to regulations at least three members of the Council would have been present. Just who did attend is not known, but some idea of those who had reviewed the petition may be obtained from the roster of councilmen for 1563. In addition to Lope García de Castro there were Gómez Zapata, Gerónimo de Val-derrama, Francisco Fernández de Llevana, Alonso Muñoz, Juan Tomás,

---

[10] Martel-Cabrera expediente.

Diego de los Cobos, Juan Vázquez de Arce, Juan Sarmiento, who once had demanded that Cañete be returned to Spain, and possibly Francisco Tello de Sandoval, who had seen and approved the Palentino's manuscripts.[11] All were men of dignity and maturity, and all, as the King demanded, were persons of distinction. Yet some question can be raised as to the quality of their judgment and their ability to decide dispassionately matters of such vital consequence to the conquerors and the sons of conquerors of the New World. In the main they were the same men whom Francisco Briceño in 1558 had disqualified so picturesquely, and as yet none of them had ever approached the Western World unless it were Tello de Sandoval, who had announced the New Laws in Mexico but whose actual presence on the Council at this time is debatable. Furthermore, Vázquez de Arce's brother was holding under litigation some of the controversial Garcilaso Indians, and García de Castro already may have been eying Peruvian distributions and the petitions of Peruvians with a foreknowledge that he soon was to replace the Viceroy at Los Reyes.

It was before such men as these that the mestizo son of Sebastián Garcilaso made his final plea. One can see him now, a well-groomed young man twenty-four years of age, proud, hopeful, and enmeshed in dreams of hidalguía—all the Castilian in him surging forward to submerge the Indian—his cavalier heritage on the point of realization, the very room itself reflecting the heritage he so desperately wanted to establish. Draperies of crimson and green silks and velvets lined deep windows overlooking the flowering gardens of the Alcázar, while rich tapestries of corresponding colors covered tables. And before him on benches trimmed with velvet sat his inquisitors, grandees of overpowering dignity. It was an appropriate setting for the recognition of a proud and ambitious descendant of Garcí Pérez and Garcí Lasso. He had proven his blood ties with the fabled rulers of Tahuantinsuyu, and he had proven that his father had been instrumental in winning Peru for the sovereigns of Spain. And he clung still to a strong but naive faith in Spanish justice. The question with which he undoubtedly was confronted now was one which apparently he already had answered

---

[11] Schafer, *El Consejo Real y Supremo de las Indias,* Vol. I, pp. 351–366; León Pinelo, *Tablas cronológicas de los Reales Consejos,* pp. 1–13.

with confidence during the preceding years, but the fact that this question should arise again indicated that it had not been answered to the satisfaction of some of the members of the Council. Did Captain Garcilaso de la Vega during his services in Peru remain ever loyal to the King and did he at any time traffic or have friendly relations with the rebellious?

This was a difficult question to answer before effete judges with such scant knowledge of the code of the Indies and of the intricate passions of those men who had won the wilderness. How could they comprehend the actions of men who while opposing and even destroying incompetent emissaries never ceased to proclaim and honestly feel loyalty to their sovereign? And where could they encounter men in Peru who had not consorted at one time or the other with those who had given evidence of sedition? His father's loyalty the mestizo again would proclaim in complete faith and confidence. But he was an unknown youth from an alien land and, even to some of his relatives, no more to be considered than an Indian. The answer to the question, apparently already heard and accepted by the Council, was provided by the judge of the tribunal before which Gómez now stood.

It involved an old ghost of a story told many years ago in Cuzco and denied in sworn statements that still could have been found in official records—a story of a noble horse named Salinillas which had borne Gonzalo Pizarro from defeat to victory on the wind-tortured plains of Huarina. Once more, blame for the humiliating rout of Diego Centeno was placed on the shoulders of Captain Garcilaso de la Vega, and this time in the anterooms of Philip II. Hurling this indestructible and persistent story at the anxiously awaiting mestizo, Lope García de Castro now demanded: "And what favor can you expect from His Majesty since your father assisted Gonzalo Pizarro as he did in the battle of Huarina and thereby gave him such a great victory?" And when Gómez replied that his judge had received false testimony, he was met with the chill retort: "Historians have recorded this; do you deny it?"[12]

There is little evidence that the mestizo was shown the testimony referred to, but the chances are that he was; many years later, when he

12 Garcilaso, Pt. II, Bk. V, Chap. 23.

refuted the story in print, he quoted three chroniclers whose statements concerning the incident at Huarina could have been used: Agustín de Zárate, Francisco López de Gómara, and Diego Fernández de Palencia, the Palentino. In reading the printed histories of these authors, one encounters multiple instances of Captain Garcilaso's loyalty and services; yet, though there may have been other unfavorable witnesses, it apparently was the isolated passages of these historians concerning Huarina, where Sebastián's youngest brother had perished in the service of the King, that Lope García de Castro employed to destroy the hopes and pretensions of a worthy and aspiring mestizo. Moreover, none of these authors, unless it were the less offensive Zárate, could have witnessed the event in question. They were recording hearsay, and in utilizing their records García de Castro was substantiating the previous claims of Briceño as to the inadequacy of councilmen who were reduced to depending upon reports sometimes as unreliable as the books of chivalry. The picture becomes gloomier when one considers that, though there could have been unfavorable testimony from authoritative eyewitnesses, the uncertain future of the mestizo apparently was allowed to rest upon the decision of a councilman who accepted without question the reports of royal chroniclers and whose subsequent history reveals him to have been possessed of deep passions and prejudices. This decision represented a finality more bitter and more far-reaching than could have been anticipated.

As to what ensued in that meeting after García de Castro's crushing denunciation, the mestizo has left no record other than to say that because of the sin ascribed to his lord Garcilaso, he himself was forced to do penance without there having been any guilt, and that he thereby was robbed of his pretenses and all doors were closed on any claims he might have hoped to make later for either his father's or his own services.[13]

It was an hour of impenetrable darkness. He had journeyed to Madrid in search of further sustenance for himself, his debased mother, and the mestizo descendants of Captain Garcilaso de la Vega. More-

[13] *Ibid.*, Pt. II, Bk. V, Chap. 23.

over, as a mestizo trained in the outward semblances of the cavalier and imbued with a faith in the richness of his lineage, he blindly had aspired to the hidalguía of Renaissance Spain with all the glitter that it offered; and since he had sought the restitution of his mother's patrimony, he may even have envisioned himself someday as the recipient of a repartimiento which would make him the feudal lord of a Peruvian estate of Indians. What he had gained after more than a year of tedious and anxious waiting was humiliation, frustration, and despondency. He had heard his father proclaimed seditious in the high courts of Castile, and though Captain Garcilaso was dead, his son was aware that to that cavalier loss of honor would have been more bitter than loss of life itself, and that the charge of disloyalty would fall like a blight upon all of his father's descendants. Years later, when life was ebbing fast, he still reflected the sorrow which he had suffered at court. "Forgive me these impertinences," he wrote when describing his experience at Madrid, "for I have uttered them out of grief and resentment over what in this particular instance my evil fortune has wrought me." He may even have contemplated appearing once more before those august judges to offer further evidence of what he felt to be the truth about Huarina, but if so, he undoubtedly was overcome by timidity and despair. For all the historians quoted had written under royal protection and with unlimited documents at their disposal, and, he afterward declared, it was useless for a mere mestizo youth to contradict the testimony of such acknowledged authorities. People simply would not believe him.[14]

But Gómez was acutely aware of the fallibility of these authorities, and his own opinion weighed more with him now because it was backed by personal experience. Though the distressing accusation hurled before him in the velvet-lined courts at Madrid may have shaken some of his previous conceptions, it had failed to rob him of the ideals and values he had found in the man who had sired and protected him. Thus, even in these dark and doubting moments, he would begin to erect in his mind a somewhat naive and compulsive defense which

[14] *Ibid.*, Pt. II, Bk. V, Chap. 23.

he was to echo many years later when bitterness had been tempered to some extent by piety and fortune. He of course had been fully conscious of his father's personal affection for Gonzalo Pizarro, and he himself always and forever had felt and would feel a deep-rooted admiration for the ill-fated rebel. And though holding still to the falsity of the rumor concerning Salinillas, there now slowly was to seep into his mind a new conception of ethics which placed a noble gesture and loyalty to a friend above loyalty to the unqualified emissaries of an indifferent and ungrateful sovereign. It was the budding of a seed unconsciously sown in the heart of a bewildered though awakening mestizo by old warriors in Peru, a bud which someday would emerge into full blossom. The accusations hurled before this aspiring youth in the antechambers of Philip II had started a small fissure in a respected image, but the image was that of a king. Moreover, it had strengthened in him a long-sleeping realization of the shabbiness of Spanish colonial polity. Most surely at this moment he recalled an utterance often heard in turbulent Cuzco: "Wretched are we who must perish while striving to gain remote empires and kingdoms, not for ourselves or our children but for others." This galling thought, first uttered by Gonzalo Pizarro, had become so commonplace that many conquerors attributed it to themselves. It was an angry and epidemic complaint which emphasized a New World concept of the rights of the individual, and it was a theme which Gómez in later years was to weave into his chronicles in such a fashion as to render them inflammatory.

Accompanying such thoughts now, surely, was the equally significant realization of a need for chroniclers with a sound knowledge of, and a keen sense of honesty and sincerity in reporting, matters of such grave consequence. Having seen many of these men at work with their quills in Peru, Gómez was well acquainted with the dimensions of their inspiration. In his records he has left a statement which to an extent exonerates certain historians for their accounts of Huarina. But if at this time he was aware that the Palentino's manuscripts had been used against him, he was also aware that this chronicler had begun his history under the direction of Cañete and even now was continuing it under the sympathetic eye of the Council of the Indies. Time and again he has hurled accusations of ignorance, carelessness, and lying against this chronicler. In one instance he expressed his profound regret that the Palentino should condemn or at least put under suspicion men who had won a great and wealthy empire which had enriched the whole world and who were guiltless of any offense against His Majesty. In another place he accused this chronicler of holding such a deep-rooted prejudice against the inhabitants of Cuzco as to blame them when they were not guilty; again, he wrote that this man had gone to Peru late and heard many fables that had been invented to suit the passions of their authors, and that he was guilty of flattering some while maligning others. And one of his less choleric indictments is that the Palentino plagiarized such a careless historian as López de Gómara, whose account the mestizo was to declare unreliable since López de Gómara had written so far from the actual scene.[15]

Perhaps in the teeming medley of court gossip Gómez by now had learned that only three years previously, in Guatemala, Bernal Díaz del Castillo had begun his history of the conquest of New Spain, ostensibly to correct the biased and directed errors of López de Gómara; and in a court still so shadowed by the eternal ghost of Las Casas he surely had absorbed some of the contempt which led this aging prelate to proclaim over and over that López de Gómara was a liar. Surely by now the mestizo had acquired some acceptable firsthand proof that the statements of this royal historian were at times questionable. "It so happened," he wrote many years later in regard to a rumor which defamed Carvajal, "that one of the outstanding and most famous soldiers of Peru, who had arrived in Spain shortly after López de Gómara's history was issued, accidently encountered this author in Valladolid and in some discourses with him on this matter asked why he had written and printed such a manifest lie when no such thing occurred. And to this he added several other words that cannot be included here. In response López de Gómara said that the error did not lie with him but with those who had given him accounts that were generated in passion. To this the soldier retorted that it was the duty of a discreet historian not to accept such reports and not to write extensively without a thorough investigation lest in his work he defame those who de-

15 *Ibid.*, Pt. II, Bk. V, Chaps. 21, 39; also Bk. VII, Chaps. 1, 24 *et al.*

served complete honor and praise. At that López de Gómara departed confused and depressed."[16]

The anonymous soldier here referred to undoubtedly was Gonzalo Silvestre, who had been ordered back to Spain by Cañete only a year after the third edition of López de Gómara's history was published, and who in 1558 was at Valladolid for the purpose of presenting an account of his services to the King and the Council of the Indies. A copy of this edition of López de Gómara's *Historia*, copiously annotated in two handwritings, that of Gómez and that of another whom reliable evidence points to as being Gonzalo Silvestre, eventually became a part of Gómez' library. The margins of this book are replete with interesting indictments; and alongside López de Gómara's account of Sebastián Garcilaso's questionable action at Huarina, Gómez has written a note which proves beyond doubt that he attributed to López de Gómara some of the unfortunate consequences of his suit at Madrid. "This lie has taken food from me," he wrote, and then added piously, "perhaps for the better."[17]

There is much to suggest that during his sojourn at Madrid, Gómez once more encountered Gonzalo Silvestre, the picturesque warrior who was to play such a significant role in the conversion of the mestizo into a chronicler. Years later, in the preface to his *La Florida del Inca*, he wrote of his principal source, who without question was Gonzalo Silvestre: "Many times I saw the Royal Council of the Indies call upon him as a man worthy of confidence to verify acts that had occurred in that expedition to La Florida and in other expeditions in which he served." And though some argument can be offered to the contrary, in all probability it was this same cavalier to whom he referred when he declared that a Silvestre González told him of being called before the Council of the Indies at the close of Hernando Pizarro's imprisonment, twenty-three years after the battle of Las Salinas in 1538, to testify as

---

[16] *Ibid.*, Pt. I, Bk. I, Chap. 3; Pt. II, Bk. V, Chap. 40; Lewis Hanke, *Bartolomé de las Casas*, p. 49. In 1553 the Council of the Indies ordered that the works of López de Gómara not be permitted to go to the Indies.

[17] Silvestre expediente; Porras Barrenechea, *El Inca Garcilaso en Montilla*, pp. 219–235. In his *Comentarios*. Pt. II, Bk. II, Chap. 21, Garcilaso cited a copy of López de Gómara's history which had included marginal notes made by "that old conquistador whom we have mentioned in another place."

LA TRADVZION
DEL INDIO DE LOS TRES
Dialogos de Amor de Leon Hebreo, hecha de
Italiano en Eſpañol por Garcilaſſo Inga de
la Vega, natural de la gran Ciudad del Cuzco,
cabeça de los Reynos y Prouincias
del Piru.

DIRIGIDOS A LA SACRA
Catolica Real Mageſtad del Rey don
Felipe nueſtro ſeñor.

Angulo.

Gre libro es de
Benito de
ſotto

EN MADRID,
En caſa de Pedro Madrigal.

M. D. X C.

1. Title page of *La traduzion del Indio de los tres Diálogos de Amor de León Hebreo.*

LA FLORIDA
DEL YNCA.

HISTORIA DEL ADELANTA-
do Hernando de Soto, Gouernador y capitan general del Reyno de la Florida, y de
otros heroicos caualleros Españoles è
Indios; escrita por el Ynca Garcilasso
de la Vega, capitan de su Magestad,
natural de la gran ciudad del Cozco, cabeça de los Reynos y
prouincias del Peru.

*Dirigida al serenissimo Principe, Duque
de Bragança.&c.*

Con licencia de la santa Inquisicion.

EN LISBONA.

Impresso por Pedro Crasbeeck.

Con priuilegio Real.

2. Title page of *La Florida del Inca.*

PRIMERA PARTE DE LOS
COMMENTARIOS
R E A L E S,

QVE TRATAN DEL ORI-
GEN DE LOS YNCAS, REYES QVE FVE-
RON DEL PERV, DE SV IDOLATRIA, LEYES, Y
gouierno en paz y en guerra: de fus vidas y con-
quiftas, y de todo lo que fue aquel Imperio y
fu Republica, antes que los Efpañoles paffaran a el.

Efcritos por el Ynca Garcilaffo de la Vega, natural del Cozco,
y Capitan de fu Mageftad.

DIRIGIDOS A LA SERENISSIMA PRIN-
cefa Doña Catalina de Portugal, Duqueza
de Bargança, &c.

Cou licencia de la Sancta Inquificion, Ordinario, y Paço.

EN LISBOA:
En la offcina de Pedro Crasbeeck.
Año de M. DCIX.

3. Title page of *Primera parte de los comentarios reales.*

HISTORIA
GENERAL DEL,
PERV.

TRATA EL DESCVBRIMIENTO DEL,
y como lo ganaron los Efpañoles. Las guerras ciuiles
que huuo entre Piçarros, y Almagros, fobre la partija
de la tierra. Caftigo y leuantamiento de tiranos: y
otros fuceffos particulares que en la Hifto-
ria fe contienen.

ESCRITA POR EL YNCA GARCILASO DE
la Vega, Capitan de fu Mageftad, &c.

DIRIGIDA A LA LIMPISSIMA VIRGEN
Maria Madre de Dios, y Señora nueftra.

Año   *Mariam non tetigit*   *Primum peccatum.*   1616.

CON PRIVILEGIO REAL.

En Cordoua, Por la viuda de Andres de Barrera

4. A 1616 title page of the *Historia general del Perú*.

HISTORIA
GENERAL DEL
PERV.

TRATA EL DESCVBIMIENTO DEL,
y como lo ganaron los Españoles. Las guerras ciuiles
que huuo entre Piçarros, y Almagros, sobre la partija
de la tierra. Castigo y leuantamiento de tiranos: y
otros sucessos particulares que en la Historia se contienen.

ESCRITA POR EL YNCA GARCILASO DE
la Vega, Capitan de su Magestad, &c.

DIRIGIDA A LA LIMPISSIMA VIRGEN
Maria Madre de Dios, y Señora nuestra.

Año   *Mariam non tetigit*   *Primum peccatum*   1616.

CON PRIVILEGIO REAL.

En Cordoua, Por la viuda de Andres de Barrera.

5. A variant 1616 title page of the *Historia general del Perú*.

HISTORIA.
GENERAL DEL
PERV

TRATA EL DESCVBRIMIENTO DEL,
y como lo ganaron los Eſpañoles. Las guerras ciuiles
que huuo entre Piçarros, y Almagros, ſobre la partija
de la tierra. Caſtigo y leuantamiéto de tiranos: y
otros ſuceſſos particulares que en la Hiſto-
ria ſe contienen.

ESCRITA POR EL YNCA GARCILASSO DE LA
Vega, Capitan de ſu mageſtad, &c.

DIRIGIDA A LA LIMPISSIMA VIRGEN
Maria Madre de Dios, y Señora nueſtra.

MARIAM NON TETIGIT

PRIMVM PECCATVM.

CON PRIVILEGIO REAL.

❡ En Cordoua, *Por la Viuda de Andres Barrera, y á ſu coſta.* Año, M.DC. XVII.

6. Title page of the 1617 issue of the *Historia general del Perú*.

7. The execution of Atahualpa. An illustration by an unnamed artist in Sir
Paul Rycaut's translation of *Los comentarios reales*, 1688.

8. El Apóstol Santiago (Saint James the Greater). A colonial painting in the Museo Nacional del Cuzco.

9. Francisco Pizarro. From a painting in the Palace of the Viceroys in Lima.

10. The Garcilaso house at Cuzco. A nineteenth-century drawing by the French traveler Laurent Saint Cricq (pseud. Paul Marcoy).

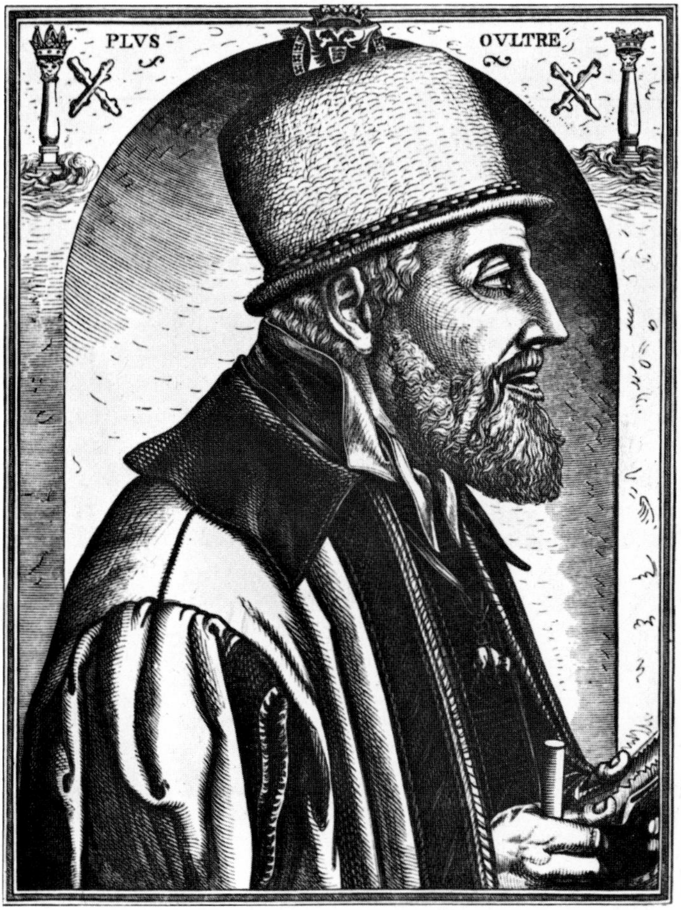

11. The Emperor Charles V. A woodcut by Melchior Lorch.

12. The Cuzco earthquake of 1650. From the painting known as the *Monroy Panorama* in the church of El Triunfo.

13. Reclining effigy of Don Juan de Austria. The tomb of the Prince in the Escorial.

14. The execution of Túpac Amaru. A drawing by Felipe Huamán
Poma de Ayala.

15. The church of Santiago at Montilla.

Courtesy don José Cobos Jiménez

16. The house of Alonso de Vargas at Montilla.

17. The coat of arms of the Inca Garcilaso, from *Primera parte de los co-mentarios reales*.

y de Doña Blanca de Sotomayor fue Gutiérrez dela Vega
mi señor y padre. El qual empleo treynta años dlesu vida
hasta que sele acabo en ayudar a conquistar y poblar el
Nueuo Mundo principalmente los grandes reynos y prouincias del Peru. Donde con la palabra y el exemplo enseño
y doctrino a aquellos Gentiles nuestra Santa Fe catholica:
y numero y magnifico la corona de España tan larga-
via, y poderosamente. que por solo aquel Empetiro que entre
otros possee se teme oy todo lo restante del mundo. Huuo
me en una Yndia llamada Doña Ysabel Chimpu Ocllo. Son
dos nombres propios el Christiano, y el Gentil porque las
Yndias e Yndios en comun, principalmente los dela sangre
Real han hecho costumbre de tomar por sobre nombre despues
del bautismo el nombre propio o apelatiuo que antes del
tenian. Y estas muy bien por la representacion y memoria
delos nombres y sobrenombres reales que en sus magestrales
antiguos solian tener. Los quales Renombres no podia poner
selos nadie sino los de la sangre Real hombre o muger des-
cendiente por linea de varon: y assi selos ponen toda uia
... que elletos han quedado.
Doña Ysabel Palla Chimpu Ocllo fue hija de Huall
pa Tupac Ynca, hijo legitimo de... Ynca Yupanqui, y
dela Coya Mama Ocllo su legitima muger y hermano de
Huayna Capac Ynca ultimo Rey natural que fue en aquel

imperio llamado Peru, como en la dedicatoria de mi Leon
Hebreo lo dixe largamente ala Magestad Catholica. y se
dira mas largamente en la propria historia del origen y
descendencia de aquellos Reyes Yncas, en la qual si Dios
nos da salud y la vida fortuna no nos persigue que aun
fin me a contentia en lo que mas desseo passaremos adelante
luego que quietemos la mano desta historia.
El quarto y hermano delos sobre dichos se llamo Iuan
de Vargas caso en Badajoz con Doña Maria de Silua, tu
tuuo hijos. passo al Peru y aunque llego tarde que fue
despues de su descubrimiento y conquista recibo temprano
segun el refran comun. porque al fin de ocho o nueue
años que en seruicio de su Rey auia gastado entre en la
batalla de Huarina dela parte de Diego Centeno por la
parte de infanteria en la qual se dieron quatro arcabuzajes
deque falleçio.
A estos assi ochenta años que mi padre y dos her
manos suyos siruieron ala corona de España quiero aña
dir los mies essos pocos e inutiles que en la moçedad serui
con la espada y los mas inutiles de aora con la pluma, para
me jntar y Vānot de aquestos y mirado en el serui a Dios
Rey siguiendo por galardon del seruicio la gloria de aure...

18. Two manuscript pages of Garcilaso's *Relación de la descendencia de Garcí Pérez de Vargas*. The complete manuscript is in the Biblioteca Nacional at Madrid.

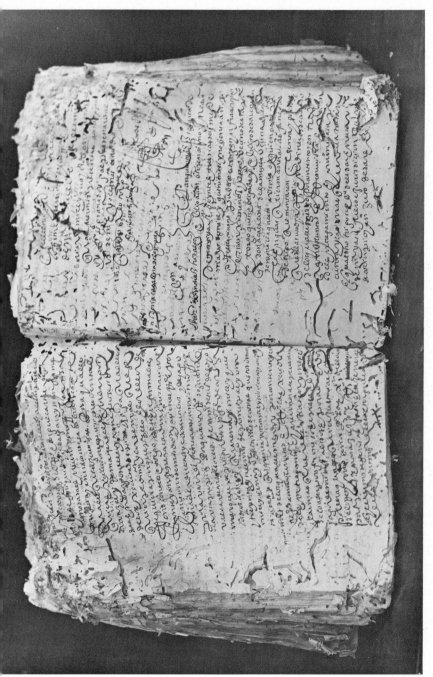

19. A manuscript dated 1590 and bearing Garcilaso's signature. In the Archivo Municipal de Montilla.

20. Chapel of the Blessed Souls of Purgatory in the Mosque-Cathedral at Córdoba.

to whether or not Pizarro had been known in Peru as a coward. As has been shown, Gómez not only was at court at this time but while there he also encountered Hernando Pizarro.[18] It is not difficult, therefore, to conjure up a vision of the embittered mestizo, lamenting the inaccuracies of accepted and protected chroniclers and germinating plans for new, trustworthy, and "true" accounts not only of the conquest of Peru but of the ill-fated expedition of Hernando de Soto to La Florida.

With the rejection of his own pretenses at Madrid, Gómez also was made poignantly conscious of the melancholy prospects for all mestizos, of the hopelessness which lay like a pall upon this foredoomed caste, denying them succession and leaving them to insecurity and misery. Having already received personal snubs from certain of his Spanish kinsmen, he could not have dispelled from his mind a feeling that the failure of his claims had been due, at least in part, to the fact that to most Spaniards he was but an Indian. There surely swept over him now in his despair the conviction that his aspirations to Hispanicism must give way, that in spite of obstacles he must seek his fortune somewhere other than Spain. One thing is certain: during these days, either just before or immediately after his disappointment at Madrid, he filed another petition with the Council of the Indies, this time for permission to return to Peru.

The petition itself has not been uncovered and the motives and feeling back of it are obscure. It may of course have been filed in a moment of confidence when Gómez dreamed still of returning to Peru to enjoy favors he hoped to receive from the King. There is no indication that he had planned to remain permanently in Spain, and already three years had elapsed since he had left his native land. Yet more than likely the request was made in a sick desire to flee all that Spain represented, to abandon his pretenses at Hispanicism and accept his lot as an Indian. The granting of his request, dated June 27, 1563, is a matter of record, and it suggests that the embittered youth thought to find consolation in the habit of a religious, for it appears as a portion of a document in which His Majesty gave license to an insignificant cleric

---

[18] Garcilaso, *Comentarios*, Pt. II, Bk. II, Chap. 37. The argument to the contrary is that Silvestre was not at the batle of Las Salinas, and the name here is Silvestre González. The confusion could be scribal, however.

and a priest to depart for the Indies, as well as an instruction to the archbishop of Los Reyes to take care to examine the morals of clerics before permitting them to return to Spain.[19] Though Gómez, as an illegitimate mestizo, at this point may have been denied aspirations for any high ecclesiastical orders, he could have labored as a missionary among the Indians, and already his closest boyhood companion, Diego de Alcobaza, doubtlessly had begun just such a career.

The chances are that the King's permit found Gómez still in Madrid and that with it he turned despondently south to consult with his guardian relatives. His eldest uncle apparently was dying, and in his final testament, drawn up on May 14, 1563, he acknowledged a debt to his nephew in the following item: "I declare that I owe to Gómez Suárez de Figueroa, my nephew, son of my brother, three hundred ducats more or less, and for the payment of them I have made a writ before Rodrigo de Almendras. They are to be paid in eight years from the royal grant on the town of Almendral y la Torre de Miguel Sesmero, as is contained in the writ." Though an added codicil shows that this uncle was still living on July 16, a document issued on October 6 indicates that by that date he was dead.[20] But surely by then Gómez was again in Montilla, preparing to take passage with the autumn armada which was scheduled to sail soon for the Indies.

In November these gallant vessels began that long journey, going by way of the Canaries, where a storm forced them to return to Spain. But Gómez was not with them. His absence has been attributed by some to the fact that aboard one of the vessels was Lope García de Castro, whom Philip on August 8, 1563, had named, not as Viceroy but as Governor, to replace the lecherous and irresponsible Conde de Nieva.[21] Any hopes Gómez may have harbored for peace or success in his native Peru under the authority of this man who had humiliated him at Madrid would have dwindled; and undoubtedly this shift in circumstances contributed to a decision to remain at least temporarily

[19] Seville, Archivo General de Indias, Audencia de Lima, Legajo 568, fols. 357–358.

[20] Archivo Histórico Provincial de Badajoz, Escribano Marcos de Herrera, Año de 1563, No. 1, fols. 477–480; also No. 3, fol. illegible; and No. 4, fol. 642.

[21] Garcilaso, Comentarios, Pt. II, Bk. VIII, Chap. 15; Schafer, El Consejo Real y Supremo de las Indias, Vol. II, p. 46.

in Spain. But there were other contributing circumstances. Not to be forgotten is that the bulk of his worldly goods was invested in Spain, for though he nominally still was in possession of Havisca, the income from that estate was negligible. But more important, it would appear, is that he had not completely abandoned hopes for vindicating his father and making further claims at Madrid; and the very absence of Lope García from the Council may have given him courage. The tug toward Spain and social stature, though temporarily stifled, was still very much present, and undoubtedly he was strongly supported by his Uncle Alonso, who could point out to him further means to his goal and who surely encouraged him now to weaken his ties with Peru by changing his baptismal name. Certainly by the closing months of 1563 Gómez was contemplating just such a change, for on November 17, when he appeared as a godfather in the Church of Santiago at Montilla, he was entered in the baptismal records as Gómez Suárez de la Vega, a combination which linked the surnames of his father and mother. But when five days later he appeared again in the same role, he was recorded as Garcilaso de la Vega.[22]

Various explanations have been offered for the mestizo's desire to change his name. Plausible is the theory that he wished to avoid confusion with those of his lineage who were reluctant to acknowledge him, a confusion which surely had resulted in his being identified locally by the clarifying but at this point humiliating title of "the Indian." Thus he dropped the Figueroa and then the Suárez, names particularly associated with the scions of Feria. Equally plausible is the suggestion that awakening aspirations were creating within him a desire to bear a name famous in past and current history for deeds of both sword and pen. He long had gloried in the accomplishments of that Garcí Lasso who on the plains of Salado had won an *Ave María* for the family escutcheon; and certainly by now he had developed an exalted respect for his father's second cousin, the Renaissance poet, Garcilaso de la Vega, whose deeds in battle and whose lyric pen already had won him a permanent place in the martial as well as the literary annals of Spain. But Gómez' eventual decision to adopt the name Garcilaso de

[22] Archivo Parroquial de Santiago de Montilla, Libro de Bautismos, No. 3, fols. 198–199.

la Vega surely was inspired by an intense devotion to his father and was made in a passion of defense and pride. Under the name which Lope García de Castro had sullied he would attempt to forge a new route to fame and fortune, and he would wear it proudly when he renewed his pretensions at Madrid. Be that as it may, from this time forward Gómez referred to himself always as Garcilaso de la Vega, though when clarification demanded he frequently added "who was known in the Indies as Gómez Suárez de Figueroa." And then as the years passed and he began to awaken to the former glories and the current miseries of his mother's people, the mestizo, again in a passion which mingled both pride and defense, embellished his adopted name with "el Indio" or "el Inca."

PART TWO

EL INCA
GARCILASO DE LA VEGA
Who was known in the Indies
as Gómez Suárez de Figueroa.

 CHAPTER ELEVEN

B Y THE YEAR 1564, the Peruvian mestizo Garcilaso de la Vega, who had been known in the Indies as Gómez Suárez de Figueroa, was twenty-five years of age, and, having reached his majority, was master of his resources. He had been in Spain for more than three years, and he often must have felt an urge if not a compulsion to return to his native land; but in moments of indecision both reason and some lingering hopes would have deterred him. He was aware that whatever claims he might now make for justice and even security in Peru would have to be made before the man who had denied his pretenses at Madrid, for in February, Lope García de Castro had sailed once more to assume the authority of the Conde de Nieva, who, even as his successor journeyed westward, was found murdered in the streets of Los Reyes. Soon Lope García would be harassed in Peru by the claims of Garcilaso's creole stepmother, whose conciliatory contract from Nieva had never received the approval of the Crown, and who by now must have been informed of the charge of sedition the new Governor had made against her deceased husband in the Council of the Indies; he would learn that living in Cuzco still was Garcilaso's Indian mother, whose patrimony he had denied at Madrid; and he would begin to hear the persistent and threatening voices of a number of Garcilaso's mestizo companions, whose fathers also had won the land with the help of their Indian concubines. Most of the early conquerors were now dead, and with them had vanished not only all security for their mestizos but in addition an optimism and an epic pioneer spirit which had flourished under the Emperor Charles and had been slowly fading since the succession of his son. Peru in 1564 still presented a melancholy picture of exploitation and slavery, and as the years passed there would be little variation in the tone and color of the picture. Meanwhile, her wealth would continue to flow back across the Atlantic to provide substance for the political and religious struggles of Philip II.

For more than five decades now, Garcilaso was to live in the Spain of Philip II and his successor, Philip III, known respectively as "the Prudent King" and "the Picture King." During these years he would see the evolution of a golden age of literature and the rise of Spain to a political zenith; but he also would see the descent of the realm into a political twilight and the disintegration of its proud aristocracy into a condition of effeteness and impotence. He would be witness to the persistent struggle of Spanish Catholicism against the rapid encroachments of Protestant reformers and the ever-abiding perils of Islam; and in the multiple efforts to staunch the inroads of religious and political heresy he would reflect the rise of a new humanism, much of it based upon a system of reasoning which held up mirrors to rulers of state and often placed moral and ethical rights of men above the long-accepted rights of magistrates. Before his maturing vision now were to pass further stages of a universal struggle to cast off the shackles of feudalism and to come closer to a state of social, spiritual, and intellectual independence; and as he watched the changing times, his character was to be slowly and painfully molded into the symbol by which he is best known today, the voice of the creole, mestizos and Indians crying out for an opportunity to prove their worth in a world which had denied them human dignity and justice.

By 1564, Philip II was well launched in his role as King of Spain and defender of the Catholic world against the onslaughts of Moslems and heretics. England, France, the Low Countries, and especially Turkish Islam offered constant threats, and within Spain itself there were continual onsets from apostates, both ecclesiastical and lay, whose relapses Philip tended to blame on the Hebraic blood which had infiltered the nation. In his own household, the hope and felicity he had attained through his marriage to Isabel de Valois had been marred by the conduct of don Carlos, his son and heir, who already was giving evidences of spiritual and political degeneration; and by now he may have detected some radical inclinations in his magnetic and handsome half brother, Juan de Austria, who long had eyed with distaste the sacerdotal career commonly designed for the unlawfully begotten sons of noblemen and kings. And still among the most intimate and respected advisors of Philip II in domestic as well as political affairs were the Duque del Infantado, the Conde de Feria, and the Príncipe de Éboli, men who were tied by blood or marriage to the famed Garcí Lasso de la Vega.

Records of Garcilaso's activities during the year 1564 are scant, and some have assumed that he was engaged in military exercises either in Navarre or in contested regions of the Italian penninsula. Such conjectures, however, cannot be supported, and a more plausible surmise is that he passed a portion of this year at Seville perfecting his Latin with the scholar and theologian, Pedro Sánchez de Herrera. He was familiar with this Andalusian port, for which he always expressed great admiration, and it could have been that here he became imbued with the changing culture of the nation, which in this country was merging continually with that of Italy. Furthermore, in this gateway to the western seas he would have had quick access to all rumors from the Indies, which to him at this point were both significant and essential. And finally, it could be that at this time he was arranging for the return of his father's remains to Spain; but though they are known to have been permitted by Papal bull to be buried in the little church of San Isidro at Seville, the records of that church have failed to yield information as to the date of the transaction or the exact place of interment.[1] Certainly in February Garcilaso was collecting his uncle's rents at Jerez de Badajoz, and at the termination of the year he again was at Montilla, serving as a godfather and negotiating with Gonzalo Silvestre for the purchase of a female slave.[2] It seems reasonable, there-

---

[1] El Inca Garcilaso, *Los comentarios reales*, Pt. II, Bk. VIII, Chap. 12. In 1954 the author personally searched the records of the church of San Isidro with the aid of a priest but nothing concerning Sebastián Garcilaso could be found.

[2] Archivo de Protocolos de Montilla, Escribano Rodrigo Fernández, Año de 1564, fol. 104; Escribano Andrés Bautista, Año de 1567, fols. 329v–331; Archivo de la

fore, to assume that he spent much of 1564 in economic transactions and that by the final months of that year, if not earlier, he had resolved to make his home at Montilla, where he was to pass more than twenty-five years, and where he was to begin the writing of those chronicles with which he has gained increasing fame.

The village of Montilla occupied an elevated position on the soft slopes of the Andalusian mountains in a region rich in both Roman and Saracenic history. It was one of the sites which marked the struggle of Caesar and Pompey and for years had been under the direct authority of the caliphs of Córdoba from whom it was liberated on the Day of Santiago in 1240 by the Holy Ferdinand, who so frequently was assisted by the militant saint and by the intrepid Garcí Pérez de Vargas. Dominating its horizon was the church of Santiago and the ruined battlements and walls of the ducal palace of Aguilar, distinguished as the birthplace of Gonzalo Fernández de Córdoba, "el Gran Capitán." In Garcilaso's day, Montilla represented but one of several towns encompassed in the Marquisate of Priego, whose feudal climate had changed but little with the passage of years. The life of the town was subject to the ruling Marqueses and there was seldom if ever any show of individual or communal independence. Civil authority was represented by a cabildo, but always its enforcements and agreements required the ultimate approval of the liege lord.

Within the feudal structure of Montilla, Garcilaso found several distinct social classes. Those delegated to sit in places of judgment were the clerics and friars of the parish, the members of the local Augustinian, Franciscan, and Jesuit monasteries, the physicians and licentiates, certain citizens of high merit, and specially designated functionaries of the Marqués. Highest in social rank were the hidalgos or men entitled to certain annuities of income as well as a quota of salt and tax exemptions on meat and fish. Next were the affluent tradesmen and those men known as caballeros contiosos, whose income exceeded one hundred thousand pesos and who were required to maintain the same military accoutrements as gentlemen of lineage as well as to assist the

---

Parroquia de Santiago de Montilla, Libro de Bautismos, No. 3, fol. 249v. In 1558 Silvestre had asked the Crown for two thousand permits to sell Negro slaves. See Silvestre expediente.

King in time of war. The lowest social order comprised some three thousand laborers who worked the neighboring vineyards and olive groves or served as artisans. In addition there of course were itinerants and slaves.

After his tumultuous and perplexing youth in Peru and his recent disappointments at Madrid, Garcilaso was to find the pastoral atmosphere of Montilla congenial. The feudal vassals of its great lords were hospitable and affectionate, and in the leagues of orchards, vineyards, and olive groves which spread over the gently sloping landscape there was ample opportunity for his long-developed horticultural interests. And always there were the horses, fine-blooded animals of Arabic strain which could test a man's skill and in the handling give him a sense of hidalguía. He groomed them, trained them, and rode them, and at one time is known to have advanced forty ducats to his uncle for the construction of suitable stables. Moreover, there were religious festivals and parades, gypsy fairs and carnivals, strolling minstrels, bagpipers, pitch shows, and possibly ventriloquists with garrulous canines, and with them all the gaiety of a little village famed for hearty laughter and fine wines. And here as in Peru there were those ever-present attempts to delve into the occult, a forbidden preoccupation which Garcilaso had noted so often among both Spaniards and Indians during his boyhood and which he knew to have been an integral force in the decisions of some of the leading conquerors. Only a few decades previously the Marquisate of Priego had witnessed the day-long trial of the famed religious clairvoyant, Magdalena de la Cruz, who in 1560 died in penance at nearby Andújar; and even now in a faded inn at Montilla there lived Leonor Rodríguez, a renowned sorceress known as La Camacha, who frequently appeared in the pointed hat reserved for criminals and who, rumor would have it, once with the aid of her demon had converted a handsome though illegitimate grandson of the first Marqués de Priego into a splendid horse.[3]

It was an exciting village and one not devoid of human sympathy. Yet even here the mestizo still was forced to accept the position of an

[3] Raúl Porras Barrenechea, *El Inca Garcilaso en Montilla*, pp. 236–247; the Amazúa y Mayo introduction to Cervantes, *El casamiento engañoso y El coloquio de los perros*, pp. 171–177.

alien. He had failed to obtain the stature of an hidalgo, and because of his lack of substance he could not even claim the rank of a caballero contioso. Though noble of blood, he was not entitled to be regarded as either a citizen or a commoner, and because of his mixture of blood he was neither a Spaniard nor an Indian. He was a presentable youth whose intellectual acumen and equestrian prowess made him acceptable in the suite of the Marqueses, but he still was the alien, taught from his early years to aspire but impeded always in his pretensions by the peculiarity of his fortune. Yet here in Montilla there was a noble uncle who yearned to give him affectionate protection, and here there were quiet corners which afforded occasion for pious exercises and the pursuit of knowledge. The lords of Priego continued to foster intellectual pursuits, occasionally sponsoring the publication of learned tracts and sermons, and always, as has been said, employing reputable ecclesiastics and scholars to tutor their children. Thus in Montilla Garcilaso now was able to form close associations with scholars who this early must have encouraged his literary ambitions by providing opportunities whenever possible for reading and study, and by urging him to seek fame with his pen.

Undoubtedly it was during these first few years after his humiliation at Madrid that Garcilaso began to contemplate seriously the possibility of joining the ever-increasing ranks of Spanish chroniclers. The origin of a dream or a yearning is of course never certain. Perhaps this one had its beginning in faraway Cuzco with a mestizo boy poring over the ancient campaigns of the Caesars, or listening to the vaunting tales of Spaniards, or watching with fascination the ever-moving quills of ambitious scribes as they recorded the stirring events of his own ambitious world. Perhaps it had begun on a somber afternoon, long ago, when an ancient and embittered Inca, responding to the taunt of his mestizo nephew, had awakened within the youth for the first time a genuine appreciation of Inca glories and stirred his conscience even more poignantly to the regrettable fact that these splendors had never been preserved in the written word. Garcilaso himself has declared that he had formulated no plans for recording such facts at the time he bade farewell to Peru; but the dream would have been present and would have assumed some form in Madrid when once again he encountered

Gonzalo Silvestre, and when he was made acutely aware of the tragedy which could evolve from inaccurate and biased reporting. The resolution that found origin in his own loss would gain purpose as he surveyed a host of deserving compatriots who were meeting with rebuffs before the Council of the Indies; and his personal enlightenment as to the eccentricities of Spanish justice would augment an old concern for the miserable plight of those whom he had left behind in his homeland. For it is reasonable to assume that his embryonic ambition encompassed the whole vast scope of what was to be his ultimate contribution to Peruvian history. It was enlarged and shaped by shifting circumstances as the years fled, but the basic dream remained the same—to reveal a "true" picture of the Indians of Peru and an honest picture of the circumstances of their subjugation and loss. At the moment, as an unrecognized mestizo in an alien land, it remained for him to find a beginning and a limitation, both of which could be provided by Gonzalo Silvestre and his fabulous memories of the expedition of Hernando de Soto to La Florida.

The mestizo Garcilaso had not come into the world when De Soto's unparalleled armada embarked for La Florida, and he was still but an infant when stragglers from that ill-fated conquest first began to filter into Cuzco. But throughout his boyhood and youth he had heard accounts from various sources of adventures in La Florida, and even now this bewitching Eden, as yet relatively unexplored, provided utopian incentive for men who dreamed. Moreover, both the scene and the plot of De Soto's expedition lay close to the spirit of Italian and Spanish literary romances, and though Garcilaso, like his contemporaries, was beginning to disavow such fabrications, he never could quite shed their influence, which at this point was still potent. Thus in the drama of La Florida he in a sense could relive much of the excitement of the chivalric romances he once had absorbed and now, with some exceptions, eschewed.[4] This he could not have escaped because of the storytelling genius of his ageless source, Gonzalo Silvestre.

[4] Garcilaso in *La Florida del Inca*, Bk. II, Pt. I, Chap. 27, claimed that the condemnation of the books of chivalry offered by Pedro Mejía in his *Historia imperial y cesárea*, published in 1545, took from him the love of these books. As early as 1555 the Cortes at Valladolid had asked for the prohibition of such books. George Ticknor, *History of Spanish Literature*, Vol. I, p. 225.

As early as 1557 a relatively brief, factual, and eyewitness account of the De Soto expedition had found its way into print; but this account had come from the pen of an anonymous Portuguese from the border village of Elvas.[5] Though the story of this fidalgo of Elvas may have aroused some curiosity, no Spaniard as yet had attempted to enlarge upon it, and Spain had continued to disregard its opportunity seriously to pursue further conquests in one of the richest regions of the western world. And now French Huguenots had already begun to infiltrate that land, arousing the anxiety of many Spaniards who professed to regard the purpose of conquest as basically evangelical. The evangelism of the mestizo Garcilaso, combined with his later expressed concern over the general indifference of Spaniards to the perils opened to the heathen by heretics, suggests that even now a part of his interest in recording the De Soto story sprang from a desire to warn the Catholic world of this new menace. Yet when he first contemplated recording that story, Garcilaso's purpose, according to his own declaration, was more patriotic than pious; from time to time he had listened to accounts of the glorious accomplishments of noble Spaniards and noble Indians in La Florida, and as a mestizo he felt an obligation to preserve them in print. Moreover, as he also said, his early literary ambition did not soar beyond the point of serving as a scribe for the distinguished hidalgo who was providing him with these accounts.[6]

To an obscure and alien youth groping for a beginning, this secondary literary role would provide both confidence and authenticity. As yet no mestizo had dared aspire to such a lofty task in the Spain of Philip II, and he needed the authority of an eyewitness and a Spaniard. Furthermore, though his continual declarations of inadequacy and humility ring with an overtone of defense and even obsequiousness as his talent matured, he undoubtedly did at this point consider himself as relatively unlettered, and he was equally aware of the sus-

---

[5] Anonymous, *Relaçam verdadeira dos trabalhos q̃ ho governador dõ Fernãdo de souto e certos fidalgos portugueses passarom no descobrimẽto da provincia da Frolida. Agora novamẽte feita per hũ fidalgo Delvas.* Both Luis Hernández de Biedma, factor of the expedition, and Rodrigo Ranjel, De Soto's secretary, left short accounts but they were not published in Garcilaso's lifetime.

[6] Garcilaso, *La Florida del Inca,* Proemio al Letor and the dedication to Teodosio de Portugal, Duque de Braganza.

picion with which his contemporaries would have regarded his erudition. His native tongue was Quechua; his formal training had been
scattered and disrupted; and though it is evident now that with his
keen penetration and recondite memory, he had arrived in Spain better
equipped intellectually than many of his contemporaries, he was unaware of the extent of his genius, and in a Spain seeking pinnacles in
belles lettres and language, he must have approached a career of letters
with wretched timidity.

It was in this mood that the mestizo now gave ear again to the en-
chantments of Gonzalo Silvestre and they formed a bond. The old
cavalier could narrate the thrilling story of La Florida; but he could
not write it. The mestizo had not witnessed the drama, but he could
save it from oblivion. The two geniuses of La Florida were mutually
dependent; but between them there was a unity of purpose. They both
yearned to find a living flame in the ashes of the De Soto saga. What is
known of the genesis of their accord must be gathered from Garcilaso's
statement that he had conversed with his friend on the subject over a
lengthy period of time and in sundry places and that he often had
urged the plan on the cavalier. Surely, as has been suggested, they had
discussed the matter in Madrid and even again at the close of 1564
when the Peruvian was negotiating with Silvestre for the purchase of a
slave. The slave was delivered and paid for in 1567, at which time
Silvestre appeared in Montilla with a bill of sale and the merchandise,
Juana, a white female, twenty years of age, who bore a brand on her
chin and was guaranteed to be untainted with drunkenness, demons,
or disease. The article appearing satisfactory, Garcilaso parted with one
hundred and fifty golden ducats, and Juana became a portion of his
chattel.[7] By this time the story of La Florida must have been well in
the loom, and the stalwart narrator once more would seize the opportunity to spin his tales while his amanuensis wove them into an everlasting tapestry.

There were similar occasions, as colorful threads of a dead story became a part of a living picture. But before long there were discouraging
interruptions. For ghostly shadows were gathering over Andalusia, and

---

[7] Document dated January 27, 1567, Archivo de Protocolos de Montilla, Escribano
Andrés Bautista, Año de 1567, fols. 329v–331.

soon the story of old and vanished struggles was to give way to the reality of new ones. "Although we both were eager to accomplish the task," Garcilaso wrote later of his project, "we were prevented from doing so by such circumstances as my going to war and the long absences which occurred between us."[8] So the garrulous cavalier retired to Herrera to refurbish his arms and dream of more glorious conflicts, and the mestizo lay down his quill to take up the sword with a renascent hope for recognition. The long oppressed Moriscos were plotting, and the hated Saracens of Africa and the Ottoman Empire had pledged them aid.

The Moriscos were those Moors who had escaped exile from Catholic Spain by ostensibly accepting Christianity. The vast majority of them now inhabited the valleys of the Alpujarras, bare and remote highlands of the Sierra Madre. Here, while developing into a race as stubborn as the rock-ribbed land, they had managed to hold on to much of their Moslem culture by concealing it beneath a veneer of Christianity. The history of their rebellion under Philip II is strangely reminiscent of the events and changes which were transpiring in Peru. For it represented an opposition to another attempt on the part of Catholic Spain to erase the peril of dual loyalties by annihilating a deep-rooted culture isolated within the limits of Spanish sovereignty, an attempt which found its source in fear, cupidity, racial bias, and religion. One of its most tragic aspects lies in the fact that to some extent it was engendered by a political rivalry between Philip II and the Holy Office in Spain.

Aware that outward semblances frequently belied true feelings and that the Moriscos did practice Islamic rites in secret, the Emperor Charles as early as 1526 had promulgated a humiliating and strangling edict against these people. But over the years this edict had been tactfully ignored, and the Moriscos had lived in comparative contentment and prosperity, replacing the exiled Jews in the commercial and industrial structures of Spain. This fact alone, however, had made them an object of the covetous, who, not content with exploiting them, desired their complete eradication. And to Philip the Moriscos represented an element of even greater consequence. Their racial and cultural ties with

---

[8] Garcilaso, *La Florida del Inca*, Proemio al Letor.

the North Africans and the Turks made them a constant peril, and their obvious heresy was both humiliating and dangerous at a time when Spanish Catholicism was being forced to a desperate struggle against the Lutherans and Huguenots of northern Europe and against what some have seen as the beginnings of freemasonry. Consequently, in 1566, Philip, yielding to persuasion, re-enacted the old edict, which now was more vexatious than ever since there was no genuine necessity for it. Among other things, all Moorish names, dress, and ornaments were banned, baths were prohibited, and arms forbidden. All doors were ordered to be left ajar on feast and fast days and special occasions, and all births to be attended by Christian midwives to prevent the performance of Islamic ceremonies. Moreover, each Morisco was commanded to learn the Castilian language within a period of three years, though no provision whatsoever was made for instruction, and all contracts in Arabic were pronounced invalid.

The edict was published at Granada on January 1, 1567, and by Holy Thursday the Moriscos were in open rebellion. There now ensued an orgy of blood lust and bestiality in the Alpujarras. Churches in which Christians had taken refuge were stormed and captives were slain with flails, clubs, sickles, and knives. Eyes were gouged out, noses and ears were lopped off, children were tortured and put to death in sight of their mothers, women were raped and slaughtered in the presence of their husbands and brothers, and in one instance all the friars of a certain monastery were cast into a vat of boiling oil. By the close of the year Morisco bands were roving the whole countryside and threatening all the adjacent villages. But soon the Marqués de Mondéjar, whom Philip had designated to suppress the rebellion, summoned the aid of all Andalusian cities, and by February of 1568, after a campaign of cruelty and violence which equaled that of the Moriscos, succeeded in establishing temporary peace.

Meanwhile, as Philip battled with the problem of Moorish heretics in Spain, he was beset with similar problems which threatened the outposts of his realm while offering some hazard to the security of the Crown. England and France continued to harass him and his opposition in the Low Countries reached a climax. Then word came through the much favored Juan de Austria that Prince Carlos was plotting not only to seize the Netherlands but to take the life of the King. This threat both to the Spanish State and to the whole of the Counter Reformation forced Philip to a definite decision regarding his mentally and physically deficient heir, and the ensuing seizure and death of the Prince burdened Philip with a legend of infamy from which he has never completely emerged. During these days, when desperately in need of funds to combat the enemies of Catholic Christendom both at home and abroad, the King was forced to direct his attention to difficulties arising in a realm which provided much of the royal income. In Peru, as in Spain, revolt was in the air. The promises made by the deceased Conde de Nieva had far exceeded the number of available encomiendas, and growing passions could not be soothed by mere assurances that matters would be brought to the attention of the King. More than once Governor Lope García had been spared serious trouble only by priests who violated the secrets of the confessional to warn of impending intrigues. Lacking other means of appeasement, he now resorted to the old expedient of sending the idle and disgruntled on new conquests, and among those so honored was Gerónimo Luis de Cabrera, who in his discontent already had commissioned a procurator to represent his wife's claims on the Garcilaso Indians before the Council of the Indies at Madrid.

But equally vexatious and possibly more ominous were the conditions which persisted among the natives of Peru. Not only had the unregenerated Indians at Vitcos kept alive their ancient paganism, but the baptized Indians of Cuzco and elsewhere, like the Moriscos of the Alpujarras, had continued to reveal that the veneer of Christianity which sheathed their indestructible native culture was flimsy and that their loyalties were dual. Moreover, they often were abetted in their deep-rooted antipathy for their conquerors by the mestizos, many of whom, having been left with little more than pride and misery and a dubious hope of spiritual salvation, had strengthened their bonds with the pagans who still maintained a semblance of empire under the Inca Titu Cusi Yupanqui, brother of Sayri Túpac. Their obstinate and rebellious attitudes had even been encouraged by the clergy, whose open immorality and lust had become a subject of concern in the New as well as the Old World, and whose willingness to agitate and monitor insurrections several times had constituted a peril. As early as 1567, Lope García de Castro, having warned the King of the potential danger of these half-caste boys who had been brought up as cavaliers and soldiers only to be permitted to starve, begged that they be forbidden to carry arms on pain of death. They had resolved, he said, never to recognize the authority of the Spanish Crown since their fathers had gained Peru at their own expense. And the Governor had given this warning with some apprehension for his personal safety, since only recently he had uncovered a plot to take his life as well as that of other men of authority in Peru.

This plot had been instigated by Garcilaso's mestizo friend Juan Arias Maldonado and his brother Cristóbal, whose animosity was embedded in a frustration deeper than that of a mere denial of pretenses. At some time after the death of Sayri Túpac in 1560, this Inca's small daughter, Beatriz Clara Coya, and her mother were brought from Yúcay and established in the Maldonado household, ostensibly for the purpose of training them in Spanish customs. But the daughter's potential wealth proved too great a temptation. Cristóbal Maldonado, with the intent of forcing a marriage and with the consent of his brother Juan, cunningly raped the maiden before she had reached the age of ten. In consequence, the mother, now sufficiently Hispanicized, insisted on Christian nuptials, and the Maldonados thereby stood on the brink of wealth. Soon, however, they were thwarted by Lope García de Castro, who, on learning that Beatriz Clara had been forced into the union against her will, arranged for the marriage to be annulled, and when in February he wrote the King of the sordid affair he placed the blame on Juan Arias Maldonado. Whether or not this particular frustration of plans was the sole source of the Maldonados' discontent is doubtful. But had not one of the members of the conspiracy betrayed their murderous plans to a Franciscan provincial, they would have slain the Governor, who, on learning of their perfidy, exiled them both with a request that the Council of the Indies bar them forever from Peru. Apparently both youths fled to Chile, where for years to come Cristóbal remained troublesome; but shortly afterward,

Juan Arias was sent to Spain, where from time to time he received the aid and consolation of Garcilaso at Montilla.[9] But already the King was beginning to feel the need of a more competent authority in Peru, and by May of 1568 he had resolved to replace his present Governor with the Viceroy Francisco de Toledo y Figueroa, who was closely related to the houses of Feria and Priego. In May of the following year, Toledo sailed out of San Lúcar de Barrameda with a determination to eradicate all semblances of paganism and heresy in Peru by destroying lingering Incaic concepts and customs, and one of his first actions after reaching Nombre de Dios in June was to send back to his sovereign a vast amount of bullion to be used in eradicating Moorish concepts and customs in Spain. This wealth, much of it from Peru, was to reach its destination opportunely, for the lusts of Christian soldiers in the Alpujarras, like those in the Andes, had never been assuaged, and once more rebellion was fomenting among the enraged Moriscos.

Dissension having arisen among officially designated generals in the Alpujarras, Philip now gave the command there to his ambitious half brother, the beloved don Juan de Austria. The appointment, though encompassing some risks, proved fortunate. Already Spaniards had built a legend about this handsome, blond, and blue-eyed youth who at the age of fifteen had sought to join the Maltese in their valiant struggle against the inhuman Turks. In him they had seen a new champion against the Mohammedan world and a genuine descendant of the Cid. And now when he appeared at Granada, clad in splendid armor and mounted upon a black Arabian steed, the ambitions of the motley Spanish army soared, and many of the Castilian and Andalusian nobility, from boys of twelve to men of seventy, rushed to join his standard. With this beau ideal in command, Philip on October 19,

[9] Rómulo Cúneo-Vidal, *Historia de las guerras de los últimos Incas peruanos contra el poder español*, p. 212; José Pérez de Barradas, *Los mestizos de América*, p. 116; the King to the President of the Audiencia of La Plata, February 15, 1567, *Colección de documentos inéditos del Archivo de Indias*, Vol. 18, pp. 80–81; Memorandum from *Colección de documentos inéditos para la historia de España*, Vol. 94, pp. 297, 387–391; Lope García to the King, December 20, 1567, *Nueva colección de documentos inéditos para la historia de España y sus Indias*, Vol. 6, pp. 210–211. Two other Maldonado brothers, Arias Pardo and Friar Alonso, all sons of Diego Maldonado, had been involved in the conspiracy.

1569, officially proclaimed a war of annihilation against the Moriscos and gave permission for his soldiers to plunder at will. The following January, don Juan gained a brilliant victory at Galera, which was followed shortly by a complete rout at Serón, where he lost his beloved tutor, Luis de Quijada, who was replaced by Francisco de Córdoba, second son of the Conde de Alcaudete.

There is no evidence to support and much to disprove the supposition that Garcilaso previous to this time had raised his sword and standard against the Moriscos of Granada, though like all residents of Andalusia he watched with fearful apprehension the bloody progress of the rebellion and stood in readiness to sally forth when summoned. Nevertheless, from this time forward he did take some active part in the suppression of the uprising, as he has stated, through God's grace and through the favors of Francisco de Córdoba, who had replaced Quijada, and Alonso Fernández de Córdoba y Figueroa, Marqués de Priego, whose mother had died the previous year. As a Figueroa and a blood kinsman of the lords of Priego, Garcilaso undoubtedly yearned to serve them as an honored relative and not as a mercenary. His status in the present struggle he never completely clarified, but apparently he agreed to join the number of auxiliaries demanded of the Marqués, or, surely aware of an imminent increase in his fortunes, assumed the role of a caballero contioso. Certainly, as all evidence suggests, he advanced his own ducats for the privilege of serving both his Figueroa relatives and the King.[10]

By March of 1570, don Juan had written to the King of the futility of attempting to resist the Moriscos with an army as despicable and shameless as the one at his command, and on the fourth day of that month Philip, now at Córdoba, dispatched a message to the Marqués de Priego and other noblemen, asking that they each raise contingents of three hundred footsoldiers to hold in readiness to go to the aid of his "dear and beloved brother."[11] It follows naturally that the Marqués in complying with the request of his sovereign would utilize the talents

---

[10] Garcilaso, *Comentarios,* Pt. II, Bk. V, Chap. 23; also his *Descendencia de Garci Pérez de Vargas.*

[11] Document dated March 21, 1570, Archivo General de Simancas, Cámara de Castilla, 42156, fol. 15.

and services of the Peruvian nephew of Alonso de Vargas. During the succeeding days, therefore, Garcilaso undoubtedly assisted in raising men and providing them with equipment, the nature of which is suggested by his later statement that he manufactured a diabolic species of chain bullets which in Peru had proven particularly devastating at the battle of Chupas. Moreover, he is known to have purchased a quantity of vari-colored fabrics to make ensigns and banners for the arquebusiers.[12] Thus the combat which he anticipated was not to be a mere skirmish or a raid, but one which might provide opportunity for both military prowess and chivalry; and it was to be accomplished under the command of a prince who, though but twenty years of age, already had fired the imagination of Spain. Legends of old crusades must have flashed across the mestizo's memory, and he may even have visualized himself briefly as another Garcí Pérez or Garcí Lasso carrying the Cross against the Crescent and winning the favor he had sought in vain at Madrid. And ever at hand to offer advice and encouragement was the cavalier uncle whose sword arm often had drawn the blood of Islam.

Yet whatever pleasure Alonso de Vargas now found in anticipating his nephew's martial career was diminished by the realization that he himself might never see either the beginning or the end of that career. He was at least seventy years of age, if not more, and his strength was vanishing. As death approached, his mind dwelled more and more upon the disposition of his worldly assets. A decade had elapsed since he had drawn up a testament which surely took into consideration the possibility of offspring of his own. But there had been no such offspring, and the events of the past years had outmoded the old will. Already Luisa Ponce may have contemplated taking into her home and naming as her heir, as she later did, her niece, María Leonor de Angulo, daughter of Francisco de Argote and Leonor de Góngora; and already Alonso de Vargas must have adopted his Peruvian nephew. On March 10, 1570, the old cavalier, fearing the rapid approach of death, summoned his confessor as well as a competent scribe and dictated a new will. How long he had contemplated the items of this will or what domestic conflicts he may have encountered in making them is

12 Garcilaso, *Comentarios,* Pt. II, Bk. II, Chap. 37.

not known. But at this time, while murmuring his confessions and declaring his faith, he cautiously revoked in advance any denials of that faith which he might make later in a moment of irrationality; and he surely expected that conditional revocation to extend to all items of his will. His wife had approved the old will, but she scarcely could have been wholly content with the new one. Though it named her as an executrix and in formal terms of conjugal appreciation left her the usufruct of her husband's assets until her death, it gave her no principle other than the amount of her dowry. Moreover, it gave equal power as executors to the mestizo Garcilaso and a local curate, Francisco de Castro, and it made clear that it was to be her husband's relatives and not her own who in the end were to benefit by what Alonso de Vargas had gained. For in listing his bequests the dying grandee dictated the following significant items:

What remains of my goods and property, both equities and capital, after what I have ordered through this testimony has been paid, I order that after the end of the days of the said doña Luisa, my wife, it be divided equally between my married sister, doña Isabel de Vargas, wife of señor Rodríguez de Sanabria, citizen of Badajoz, and the said Garcilaso, my nephew, a resident of this town, both of whom I leave and institute as my universal heirs to what remains, for I declare that other than my above named sister and nephew I have no obligatory heirs, ascendants or descendants—with the charge, however, that the said Garcilaso, my nephew, be under obligation to pay and give each year from the specified part of the inheritance that thus will be his after the days of the said doña Luisa, twelve ducats of gold that are worth four thousand five hundred maravedís, to doña Leonor de la Vega and doña Blanca, my legitimate sisters who are professed nuns in the convent of Santa Clara at the town of Zafra, during the days of their lives, and through them and in their names to the said convent and its majordomo or majordomos. And at the termination of the days of the said doña Leonor and doña Blanca, my sisters, let the mandate and charge which I make to the said Garcilaso, heir to his specified half, expire, and let him not be obligated to pay them more. This I order in the way and form that is best suited according to law.[13]

[13] Archivo de Protocolos de Córdoba, Oficio 22, Protocolo 52, sin foliar; also Archivo de Protocolos de Montilla, Escribano Juan Martínez de Córdoba, Año 1570, fols. 169–173.

When the will was passed to the dying grandee for a signature, his palsied hand could execute no more than three letters, and the Vicar completed the task. Yet the will was valid, and it is recognized today that but for the generosity and sympathy of this unusual cavalier, the world might never have seen the histories of the Inca Garcilaso de la Vega. Alonso de Vargas had been caught by the mestizo's charms, and his last will bears testimony to the fact that, as Garcilaso has recorded, his uncle had accepted him as a son. Thus from this understanding kinsman he had received a benefit and an honor which even his father had been forced to deny him.[14]

By March 17, 1570, within a week after drawing up his will, don Alonso was dead, and his beloved nephew undoubtedly was present to witness the doleful occasion of his demise as well as to follow the long cortege of priests, friars, confraternities, and lay organizations up the hill to the ancient church of Santiago where the old warrior's body was to lie in a sanctuary designated by his relative and debtor, the Marqúes de Priego. But now don Juan was storming the gates of Tijada and the echoes of battle were growing more distinct. Apparently anticipating an immediate summons, Garcilaso on March 17 and again on March 20 took the precaution of empowering substitute executors to act for him at Montilla during his absence.[15] Then on March 21 the Marqués de Priego received a second command from the King, this time to have contingents of both horse and foot in readiness for forays of from five to eight days; and during the last days of the month there came an order to dispatch a captain with a contingent to Loja for the purpose of joining there with don Juan.[16]

It therefore was approximately during the last days of March or the first of April, 1570, when Garcilaso was approaching his thirty-first birthday, that he bade farewell to Montilla and set out to emulate his famed ancestors among the descendants of their adversaries in the Alpujarras. It was an opportunity to strengthen pretensions at Madrid and to vindicate his father's honor, and he would approach it with a

---

[14] In his *Descendencia de Garcí Pérez*, Garcilaso wrote: "Fallesció don Alonso de Vargas sin hijos de cuya causa me adoptó por tal aunque indigno yo de serlo."
[15] Archivo de Protocolos de Montilla, Escribano Juan Martínez de Córdoba, Año de 1570, fols. 195–196v. Both documents state that Alonso de Vargas is dead.
[16] Archivo General de Simancas, Cámara de Castilla, 42156, fols. 15, 19.

surge of Hispanicism. Moreover, though his services were not to be spectacular, he was to acquit himself honorably. In speaking of his activities he has recorded that he twice was appointed to a captaincy by the King and twice by don Juan de Austria.[17] One is led to believe that the assignments from Philip came in the beginning through the influence of the Marqués de Priego, and that the latter assignments were made by don Juan at the advice of Francisco de Córdoba. Garcilaso has recorded that his appointments revealed an apparent dissension between the King and his brother and that those of the latter were superior. Assuredly this early Philip had begun to regard with some vexation and suspicion the rash ambition of don Juan, an ambition which one day was to grow beyond the limits of toleration. As the campaign proceeded, the Prince, harassed by the inferior quality and greed of the Spaniards, would recognize some superior virtues in Garcilaso other than an ability to give financial support to his contingent. The privilege of military rank offered Garcilaso was no small one, for it not only gave him a specific social status but placed Spaniards under the orders of a mestizo Indian. Moreover, his participation in the contest was notable since it is the first known instance of a native-born Peruvian having served the King in the European arena.

The first sally from Montilla could not have been prolonged. By May of 1570 don Juan, with the assistance of Francisco de Córdoba, had succeeded in arranging a truce with the leader of the Moriscos; and as Turkish and African auxiliaries began to recede from the coast of Spain, the Moriscos gradually retired to their villages. By July 19 Garcilaso had definitely returned to Montilla, for on that date he appeared in the church of Santiago as a godfather, identifying himself this time as "señor Capitán Garcilaso de la Vega."[18] Yet the rebellion was not at an end, since Aben Aboo, the Morisco King, encouraged by rumors of new assistance from Islam, continued to harass the land. Once more the champions of Christendom were forced to reorganize,

[17] Garcilaso, *Comentarios,* Pt. II, Bk. V, Chap. 23; also power dated May 4, 1615, / rchivo de Protocolos de Córdoba, Oficio 25, Protocolo 61, fols. 182–183; also writ dated June 30, 1604, Oficio 29, Protocolo 21, fols. 1265v–1267.

[18] Archivo de la Parroquia de Santiago de Montilla, Libros de Bautismos, No. 4, fol. 144v.

and once more the Peruvian received a summons to serve. At Guadix on August 8 an order was issued, undoubtedly by don Juan, reappointing Garcilaso as a Captain and authorizing him to recruit a company from Córdoba, Aguilar, and Montilla. Affixed to this order is a note explaining that Captain Garcilaso did not answer the summons at once,[19] and his delay, one may suppose, was occasioned by the necessity of guarding some of the minutiae of his heritage. For doña Luisa Ponce now had audaciously seized her deceased husband's clothes with the purpose of bestowing them upon a retainer. This was not a trivial act in Spain obsessed with sartorial splendor, and the mestizo, long aware of the value of cavalier raiment and conscious of his own need for such should he carry his pretensions again to court, resented it. On August 25, 1570, appearing again as "Capitán Garcilaso de la Vega," he appointed an attorney to defend the rights of both himself and his Aunt Isabel against the presumption of Luisa Ponce de León. This done, he once more was prepared to join in the subjugation of the heretics.[20]

Just when the mestizo Captain made his next departure from Montilla is uncertain, nor is there any information as to where he went. In fact, he remained conspicuously silent concerning the details of his activities throughout the entire campaign. He is known to have encountered at some time during the struggle two of his Mérida kinsmen, Alonso and Antonio de Vargas, great-nephews of Gómez de Tordoya,[21] and it appears certain that he did answer the call issued by don Juan on August 8. Possibly he was with the Duque de los Arcos in the final days of sporadic fighting among the mountain regions of Ronda. But he was in Montilla again on September 24 to serve as a godfather.[22] On November 5, don Juan announced that the rebellion was at an end and departed from Granada; and unless Garcilaso served in the after-

---

[19] See document entitled *Relación de los capitanes que se an nombrado a rehacer y a que distritos y los que quedan reformados sin yr a rehacer,* Archivo General de Simancas, Cámara de Castilla, 42154, fol. 322.

[20] Archivo de Protocolos de Montilla, Escribano Juan Martínez de Córdoba, Año de 1570, fols. 471v–474.

[21] Garcilaso, *Descendencia de Garcí Pérez.*

[22] Archivo de la Parroquia de Santiago de Montilla, Libros de Bautismos, No. 4, fol. 151.

math of dispersing the Moriscos, his short career with the sword had come to a somewhat prosaic end.

One seeks to picture the mestizo in the glamorous role of his legendary Spanish ancestors, but he himself has forbidden it. His primary virtue, he insisted, lay not in chivalric feats or even hard fighting, but in his willingness to serve. He saved no sacred banners from the dust of the storied plains, and he possibly terrified no pagans with an intrepid sword. Not once did he behold the militant apostle charging through the clouds on a milkwhite steed, for the cult of Santiago was fading now before the new mysticism of Santa Teresa. Moreover, he must have been robbed of much pious sentiment by a realization that this crusade was not an altogether holy one since in the main it was directed, not against the disciples of Islam, but against a people who, though tainted with ancestral theologies, had accepted, like his own people, the outward semblances of Christianity and Christian culture. And his own dark blood and similar background might have lessened some of his pious idealism and awakened within him at least a modicum of sympathy for the victims when he witnessed their terrible punishment.

Those Moriscos who had rebelled and had been taken in arms were sold into slavery throughout Spain. Those who had not rebelled were removed from the kingdom of Granada and scattered over the realm. Many, unable to endure the climate in Castile, Toledo, and Estremadura, perished; many who had lived in riches now were reduced to poverty; and many were forced to earn their miserable bread by begging in the streets. Even don Juan is said to have paused along the roadside one bitter winter morning and wept as he watched a group of men, women, and children trudging through the snow into exile and slavery. Similar scenes surely awakened pity in Garcilaso; but he had been molded in an age which still accepted the classic theory that a condition of slavery was justifiable if its victims represented the spoils of a righteous war. Already he had purchased three slaves, Juana, Juan, and Marina, at least two of whom had been gained in a "just war"; and a document issued only a year after the termination of the war in the Alpujarras reveals him offering for sale a slave maiden twenty-two years of age whom he himself had named María de Flores.

She was declared to be a Morisca of Granada obtained "in a just war and not in peace," free of any old or new disease, and not subject to note or mortgage. It can be assumed, therefore, that María de Flores represented a portion of the mestizo's spoils from his recent struggle against the heretics of Islam.[23]

But one of the more inglorious aspects of Garcilaso's experiences in the Alpujarras is to be seen in the fact that though he ostensibly had financed his own career, he in the end was neither reimbursed nor rewarded. Don Juan, now in command of the campaign which would result in the victory at Lepanto, did give the King an account of the mestizo's desire to serve, and by 1571 Garcilaso was dreaming of utilizing the Prince's influence at Madrid, either to seek further martial services or to renew his previous pretensions. To appear at court, however, required finances, and in offering an explanation for his failure to do so at this time, Garcilaso declared that his contribution in the recent rebellion had left him so indebted and destitute that he was "unable to return to court and was forced instead to retire to the corners of solitude and poverty."[24] Equally discouraging, however, to the renewal of pretenses would have been the publication in 1571 of the Palentino's *Historia del Perú*, which again fixed in print the damaging version of the battle of Huarina.

By 1567 the Palentino had brought his history to a close but not without some impeding criticism from persons who, as he said, had pressed him to augment his accounts of the disloyal with accounts of their own worthy deeds, as if he had been designated solely to bolster their individual pretensions. Even after this chronicle, begun under the protection of the Marqués de Cañete, was licensed by the Crown for printing, an official censure of it was entrusted to Fernando de Santillán, a former judge of the Peruvian Audiencia whom Cañete had despised, and who had supported the appointment of Sebastián Garcilaso as Corregidor of Cuzco. Santillán thereupon declared that the Palentino's account not only omitted much but contained many lies and perverted facts; and he supported his condemnation with sixty-eight

---

[23] Document dated September 12, 1571, Archivo de Protocolos de Montilla, Escribano Juan Martínez de Córdoba, Año de 1571, fols. 513–513v.
[24] Garcilaso, *Comentarios*, Pt. II, Bk. V, Chap. 23.

objections, in the sixth of which he defended La Gasca's rewards after the battle of Sacsahuana. In answer to this particular objection the Palentino declared, among other things, that Antonio de Quiñones had done nothing in the service of the King and had been rewarded earlier by Vaca de Castro simply because he was a relative of the Governor's wife, and that because of their infamous record in the revolt of Gonzalo Pizarro, both Quiñones and Garcilaso de la Vega, but for political expediency, would have been sentenced to death by La Gasca.[25] His answers to Santillán's objections apparently proved temporarily satisfactory, and when in 1571 the Palentino's *Historia* appeared in print, it bore a dedication to Philip II. Nevertheless, the debate over the Palentino's errors continued and reached such extremes that an official opinion concerning them was asked of the royal chronicler, Juan López de Velasco; and when that august authority declared that because of the Palentino's infamy in reporting the actions not only of men but of cabildos and cities, his history should be suspended, Philip heeded the advice and ordered all copies collected.[26] At the close of a year which marked the official censure of a chronicler on whom he had relied heavily in condemning Garcilaso's father, Lope García de Castro returned to Spain and assumed his former position on the Council of the Indies.

One of the multiple voices raised against the chronicle of Diego Fernández, the Palentino, had been that of Antonio de Quiñones, who had been in Madrid since 1569;[27] and this former guardian undoubtedly was among those friends of Garcilaso who now urged him to renew his claims at court. For, they argued, since Lope García de Castro's sojourn in Peru had given him an opportunity to see at firsthand the bases of Garcilaso's claims, the councilman would be disposed to regard them with some sympathy. But Garcilaso, according to his own words, still was so intimidated by previous disapprobation that he

---

[25] The Palentino's answers can be found in the De Torre edition of Diego Fernández' *Historia del Perú*, Apéndice, Vol. I, pp. 265–268. Vaca de Castro's wife was María de Quiñones.

[26] Aurelio Miró Quesada y Sosa, *El Inca Garcilaso*, p. 224.

[27] Document dated December 31, 1569, Seville, Archivo General de Indias, Audiencia de Lima, Leg. 110; also document dated February 10, 1572, Leg. 270, fol. 1.

dared not revive "old hopes and aspirations or entertain new ones."[28] His reluctance is understandable. Still on the Council of the Indies were several men who a decade previously had witnessed his humiliation and who apparently had accepted without much question the reports made by historians against his father; and though there is conspicuous evidence that Lope García had undergone some changes in perspective, there is more evidence than otherwise that he had undergone but little change in his attitude toward clamoring mestizos or that he wished to rectify his former errors. He still regarded the mestizos with suspicion and for several years he was to be confronted at Madrid by the pretensions of the exiled Juan Arias Maldonado, who only a short time previously had plotted to take the councilman's life. Moreover, though Garcilaso now could lay claims in a different court for his own military services, the recommendations of don Juan surely would have proven of little benefit since the unlimited ambitions of this prince, fired by a recent glorious victory at Lepanto, were being regarded by the Crown with increasing alarm. Yet assuredly one of the most intimidating factors in Garcilaso's present decision must have been news of the fate of his Indian kinsmen, whose nobility of lineage he had emphasized as one of the bases of his claims. The Viceroy Toledo, convinced that there could be no security for Spanish rule so long as the natives maintained a feeling of love and veneration for their former rulers, had persisted in his resolution to belittle and destroy the last semblances of the Inca dynasty. Already at Cuzco he had begun a ruthless persecution which in time Garcilaso was to consider one of the most tragic episodes in the history of his people.

[28] Garcilaso, *Comentarios*, Pt. II, Bk. V, Chap. 23; also Bk. VIII, Chap. 15.

CHAPTER TWELVE

IN OCTOBER, 1570, the Viceroy Francisco de Toledo set out from Los Reyes on a tour of inspection, arriving at Cuzco in time to witness demonstrations of a nature to remind him of the current struggle against Moorish traditions in Spain and to strengthen his convictions that all semblances of Incaic traditions must be eradicated in Peru. For two weeks the city had been engaged in festivities which on the night of the Viceroy's arrival were climaxed with a mock combat in which Christian virgins were rescued from the clutches of a band of Moorish infidels. Midway in the market plaza, where Incas over the centuries had paid obeisance to the Sun, merrymakers had constructed a Moorish castle and surrounded it with real trees, populated with living birds and beasts. And at the edge of this unique forest they had erected a fountain from whose waters the maidens were partaking when they fell victim to Moorish abductors and thereby provided excuse for the courageous efforts of Christian defenders. Mounting a great chestnut with magnificent tail and white-stockinged feet, Toledo himself, in spite of his relatively advanced age, rode three courses in this symbolic tournament before retiring to an adjacent balcony to witness the close of the scene.[1] But it was a celebration of a somewhat different nature which shortly afterwards led the zealous Viceroy on to a more crucial stage in his mission.

[1] Stephen Clissold, *Conquistador*, p. 64.

On Epiphany Sunday of 1571 the Indians had gathered in the Imperial City to celebrate the christening of Melchor Carlos Inca, great-grandson of the Inca Huayna Cápac, and son of Carlos Inca by a creole woman of noble Spanish lineage. Carlos, who resided in the Inca palace of Collcampata, had inherited the leadership of his father, Cristóbal Paullu Inca, and Toledo, shrewdly aware of the significance of this man, had consented to serve as godfather to the newborn mestizo. Royal Incas with attendant vassals had assembled from far and near in their pagan ceremonial robes, and though the occasion ostensibly was a Christian one, the Viceroy must have been quick to perceive that the veneration was Incaic. Somewhat isolated in the midst of this splendid paganism, Toledo stood among a group of dignitaries—an ominous figure, as Sir Clement Markham has described him, tall and stooped in a suit of black velvet and a cloak bearing the scarlet cross of Santiago, a gloomy face with a high forehead and piercing black eyes, through which, like a bird of rapine, he noted every trifle and contemplated the extirpation of his prey. This Viceroy was to see much that he anticipated seeing as during three days of celebration he listened to the boasting and lamentations of royal Incas. But what he apparently missed was the presence of two disguised pagans who had come from Vitcos to mingle with their baptized kinsmen and witness the ostentatious festivities. They were Titu Cusi Yupanqui, recognized emperor of the unregenerated Indians, and his youthful brother, Túpac Amaru, both sons of the Inca Manco. Afterward, when news of their visit was communicated to Toledo, he resolved to decoy these princes into his power.

Meanwhile, in an effort to learn more of the Incas and their past civilization, Toledo utilized the services of Juan Polo de Ondegardo, corregidor-historian, who had shown Garcilaso the mummies of famed Incas, and Padre Blas Valera, whose manuscripts Garcilaso later incorporated into his own histories. Both of these men reported as accurately as they could and without conscious bias; but Toledo was to rely more heavily upon Pedro Sarmiento de Gamboa, who had accompanied him to Cuzco, and whose pen could be attuned readily to the Viceroy's design of diminishing reverence for the Inca dynasty and justifying the presence of Spaniards in Peru. Sarmiento's concurrence with this design is reflected in his later statement that his purpose in writing his histories was to provide a "sure and quiet haven" for His Majesty's conscience in the dispute which raged over the validity of Spanish claims of dominion in the Indies, to show that Las Casas and others appealing in behalf of the Indians had been moved by pure passion and had contended without facts, and to prove that Toledo had been inspired by God to correct their errors. Like most of his contemporary chroniclers, Sarmiento professed to be writing a "true history"; but he of course was aware that he must present the truth in predetermined colors. An even greater hazard to his authenticity, however, lay in the circumstance that because of his ignorance of Quechua he was forced to depend upon the services of official interpreters, chief among whom was the mestizo Gonzalo Gómez Jiménez, generally known as Jimenillo, who proved to be as unreliable and depraved as had been the infamous Felipillo.[2]

It was with a distinct purpose, therefore, that Toledo and his chronicler henchman now eyed the vexatious pagans who kept the fires of Incaicism smoldering in the region of Villcapampa.[3] Thus when the Inca Titu Cusi Yupanqui, impressed by what he had seen at Cuzco and convinced of the expediency of negotiating with the Spaniards, appealed to the Viceroy for baptism, Toledo dispatched a group consisting of two laymen, two priests and a mestizo servant, not only to administer the regenerating waters but to demand that the Inca pretender repair at once to Cuzco and pledge his allegiance to the Spanish King. The mission was only partially successful. The Inca was indeed baptized, but his only immediate indication of sympathy with the demand for obeisance appears to have been a willingness to be reborn as Felipe. Indeed his obstinacy in regard to this matter was so prolonged that at length the embassy departed, leaving him with only Friar Diego de Ortiz and the mestizo servant, Martín de Pando. Then at some time

---

[2] Ibid., pp. 68–71; Philip Ainsworth Means, Fall of the Inca Empire, pp. 123, 125–126.

[3] For accounts of Toledo's extermination of Titu Cusi and Túpac Amaru, see El Inca Garcilaso, Los comentarios reales, Pt. II, Bk. VIII, Chaps. 16–21; Rómulo Cúneo-Vidal, Historia de las guerras de los últimos Incas, pp. 223–301; Means, Fall of the Inca Empire, pp. 111–124; Clements R. Markham, A History of Peru, pp. 149–155.

before October of that year, the Inca fell ill, and when the Indians, encouraged by certain ill-advised boasting on the part of Pando, challenged Ortiz to prove the power of the white man's god by curing their sovereign, the well-intentioned friar not only bombarded his deity with daily orisons but administered such a powerful emetic, a tonic of egg whites mixed with sulphur and pepper, that the miserable regenerate promptly vomited himself to death. Thus the original purpose of the mission may very well have been regarded as accomplished. But the pagans, recalling the humiliating death of the Inca Manco in a game of ninepins, and suspecting their Inca to have been poisoned as well as purged, took a terrible vengeance. For hours they beat and tortured the unfortunate Ortiz, while he, in compliance with their demands, plead vainly with his God for the resuscitation of their Inca. Meanwhile, they forced him, nude and weary, to bear a large cross through the wilderness, and when he cried out in thirst, compelled him to drink a concoction of bitter herbs, saltpeter, and urine. At length, when the sufferings of the friar were relieved by death, the infuriated pagans impaled his body through the anus on a sharp palm branch and buried it head downward in the earth. Vengeance achieved, the Indians now sought out the youthful Túpac Amaru, who had been kept secluded in a convent of virgins, possibly at Machu Picchu, and placed him upon their shadow throne as legitimate sovereign.

Living still in the midst of the accumulating perils which continued to threaten the Indian realm was Garcilaso's mother, Isabel Suárez Chimpu Ocllo, who had never completely relinquished her ties with her royal kinsmen. But beyond the words of her will there is little to indicate what her experiences had been since her marriage to Juan del Pedroche.[4] It would appear that she passed her days in comparative comfort for one of her status, being attended by Indians of lower caste and surrounded by relatives. As her two daughters by Pedroche matured, she had managed somehow to supply them with dowries, and she had seen them married, the one, Luisa de Herrera, to Pedro Már-

[4] The palla's will is to be found in the Archivo Notorial del Cuzco de don Oscar Zambrano Covarrubias, Protocolo de Antonio Sánchez, Año de 1571, número actual 720, fols. 1685–1688. For a published copy, see Aurelio Miró Quesada y Sosa, *El Inca Garcilaso*, pp. 100, 250–253.

quez Galeote, and the other, Ana Ruiz, to Martín de Bustincia, mestizo son of Beatriz Coya. At least one daughter and possibly both had borne children, and the palla's expressed love for her daughters indicates that her family relations were not miserable. Her attitude toward her former concubinage and the mestizo offspring of that relation can only be surmised. A lingering veneration for the dictates of her ancestors and the commands of Fate would have eliminated any feeling of debasement, though her intelligence surely made her conscious as the years passed of the injustice of a circumstance and a system that had deprived her of even her patrimony while rewarding the woman who had supplanted her. Whether she ever was aware of her son's efforts to have her patrimony restored or whether there was any kind of communication between them after he departed for Spain are questions still to be answered. She undoubtedly continued to regard him with a maternal affection but an affection which possibly even from his infancy had been deeply colored by an Indian stoicism. The only instances extant in which she is known to have mentioned him, the following two items from her will, reveal no strong show of affection but a humble supplication for the welfare of her soul and the material welfare of her daughters, for whom in the same document she specifically expressed her love.

I declare that I hold in possession a coca farm which lies in a province of the Andes called Avisca and from which fifty or sixty baskets of coca are gathered each mita. I declare that the said farm belongs to my son, and I order that the debts which I owe be fulfilled and paid from the fruits of this farm, and I order that this being done, the baskets gathered from the said farm be utilized to provide masses for my soul during a period of three successive years. And for this I beseech the approval of my said son who is in Spain and is named Gómez Suárez.

The said farm was left to me by my said son for my sustenance and income when I gave him in exchange certain gold pesos which are worth less than the farm in my charge. I order that when the three years have terminated in which masses are to be said for my soul with the profit of the said farm, my daughters share the profit of the farm equally until my son Gómez shall rule otherwise.

It was on November 22, 1571, that the palla, under the Christian name of Isabel Suárez, drew up her will, proclaiming her daughters and her husband as her universal heirs and specifying provisions for even her most insignificant debts as well as for those masses she could afford for her soul's safety. Aging and sick, she naturally felt death to be imminent, though she may have lived through the first month of the following year since it was not until February 1, 1572, that her two daughters filed a claim as her universal heirs.[5] If her last requests were honored at the time of her death, Cuzco witnessed a cortege of sorrowing Indians led by a priest and a sacristan with a tall candle and bearing the body of this granddaughter of the great Túpac Yupanqui to give it burial beneath the "great church," on a site that once had supported the Temple of the Sun. She had been born during the golden reign of Huayna Cápac, the last great ruling Inca, and she had died on the eve of the *coup de grâce* which Toledo was about to administer to the Inca dynasty. And if her kinsmen, pagan and Christian, had continued to gather regularly in her humble quarters, as they no doubt did, to lament their ill fortunes and nourish their veneration of Inca sovereigns, she would have known before her demise, and even before the news reached Toledo, that the Inca Titu Cusi was dead and that the youthful and fated Túpac Amaru now occupied the condemned Inca throne.

It was some months after the assassination of a second emissary, whom he had sent to Titu Cusi in October of 1571, before Toledo received news of the drastic changes which had taken place in Villcapampa. Provided now with an excuse for invasion, he mustered a large force which was dispatched at once on a mission of vengeance. Among his captains were Martín García de Oñaz de Loyola, nephew of the founder of the Society of Jesus; Mancio Serra de Leguizamo, father of one of the mestizo Garcilaso's boyhood companions; Juan Álvarez Maldonado, godfather to the mestizo's half sister; and the chronicler Pedro Sarmiento de Gamboa, who afterward claimed the honor of having seized the Inca Túpac Amaru with his own hands. The Indians made a show of resistance and then retreated further into the wilderness. In the fall of 1572, however, the timid young emperor, according to reports Garcilaso was to receive, surrendered with the hope that, having committed no crime himself, he would be offered the same cour-

[5] Miró Quesada y Sosa, *El Inca Garcilaso*, p. 102.

tesy that Cañete a few years previously had accorded his brother Sayri Túpac. But Toledo had other plans, and Túpac Amaru had provided means for a stringent warning, not only to those Indians claiming noble and divine descent but to those miserable half-castes spawned by the first conquerors.

Soon this apparently innocent Inca, ephemeral emperor of an ephemeral throne, vested now in his imperial robes and accompanied by his family and chiefs, was led in ignoble triumph back to the Imperial City of his father the Sun to face charges for matters of which he could have had little knowledge. Among other things, he was accused of having ordered his vassals to infest the roads and rob Spanish merchants as they passed upon their lawful business, of having entered into an agreement with caciques to rise up in arms and slay as many Spaniards as possible, and of having received mestizos into his service upon promise that if necessary they would die in defense of his cause. Historians have disagreed as to the justness of his trial. It must be admitted that the youthful Inca's testimony was revealed through a mestizo who was well versed in Quechua; but this mestizo was Gonzalo Gómez Jiménez, and, as was afterward proven, a proficiency in language was not enough to assure reliable evidence.

While the fate of the fallen emperor was pending, all the mestizos of Cuzco were charged with having agreed to assist in the overthrow of Spanish authority, and those over twenty years of age or capable of bearing arms were cast into prison and in some instances tortured for the purpose of substantiating what had been only remotely suspected. At this time, according to Garcilaso, an Indian mother who surely echoed the sentiments of many of her kinswomen hastened to the prison and pled with her mestizo to bear his pains honestly and under no circumstances to make false accusations. Then commenting on the irony of rewarding conquerors of an empire by hanging their sons, she screamed that those mothers who had given the mestizos birth, reared them, and helped their fathers to win the land should also be destroyed. All present circumstances, she cried, had been ordered by Pachacámac as a punishment for the sins of those women who, out of affection for the Spaniards, had been unfaithful to their Inca, his caciques, and his lords. Shouting these statements and others equally bitter, the frenzied woman rushed from the prison and on through the streets, greatly disturbing the Viceroy as well as all others who heard her.

To avoid additional confusion, Toledo now gave orders that none of the mestizos be put to death. But in the case of Túpac Amaru he was unrelenting. Soon a common crier was dispatched throughout the city to announce that the Inca pretender was to have his head removed for having schemed to dispossess Philip II of his authority in Peru and for having drawn into his plot "several Indians who were his creatures together with those who were the sons of Spaniards and born of Indian mothers." The Inca was baffled by the absurdity and injustice of the sentence and continued in every way to give evidence of his loyalty and innocence. He offered to journey to Spain and pledge his allegiance to the King; and when local friars flocked to the prison to instruct him in Christian doctrine and urge baptism, he harkened back to the admonition of his grandfather, Huayna Cápac, and agreed to be reborn under the name of "his Inca and emperor," Felipe. But Toledo was a man with a purpose, and almost immediately the ominous shadows of a new scaffold began to fall across the tragedy-laden stones of the market square. Then, only three days after entering the Imperial City of his Fathers, the condemned Inca, dressed now in humble white cotton and clutching in his hands the bleeding image of an ancient and alien martyr, was brought forth from his prison under the escort of four hundred despised Cañari Indians, mounted upon a mule and led by friars to the great square while a crier proceeded and proclaimed in a loud voice that Túpac Amaru was a traitor.

The terminal scene of this drama, as Garcilaso described it, cries down through history. As the procession edged forward, the Inca pled with friars to make clear that the accusation was false, that he was being led to the scaffold solely because Toledo yearned to see him dead, and that God the Pachacámac was witness to the truth of what he said. On entering the place of execution he was met by a horde of women of all ages, some of them of royal blood, whose lamentations were accompanied by a request reminiscent of their paganism. "Why, oh Inca," they cried, "do they wish to behead you? What crimes, what treasons have you committed to make you deserving of such punishment? Implore your executioners to put us to death along with you, for we belong to you by both blood and nature and would much prefer to accompany you into the other world than to remain in this one as slaves and servants to the lusts and desires of your murderers." Hard pressed for an answer, the miserable Inca now lapsed unknowingly into a slight heresy by explaining to his thousands of devotees that his present fate was the outcome of a curse placed upon him by his mother when he was but a child. He was quickly corrected, however, by church fathers who declared that the evil he was about to suffer was due, not to a mother's curse, but to the will of the god he had just embraced. Such an instance of divine justice, even if it were translated into understandable Quechua, must have been difficult for this quickly converted Christian to comprehend, but Garcilaso recorded that the Inca was convinced and that after repenting his error he asked forgiveness and promised to pray for the Viceroy and his magistrates. If this report is to be credited, Túpac Amaru Inca did indeed approach his demise in the manner of a true Christian.

Apprehensive now lest some insurrection might ensue, nervous officials hastened the Inca to the scaffold, where he was assisted up the stairs by friars and followed by an executioner with broadsword already drawn. And now the lamentations reached such a pitch that nothing else could be heard, for the scene combined both tragedy and insult. Standing ready to sever the head of this fallen Inca was a Cañari Indian.[6] Some memories reached back through the years to the siege of Cuzco when Francisco Chillchi Cañari had humbled the Inca race in single combat; some recalled a day during the government of Sebastián Garcilaso when this same traitorous Cañari had appeared before the Corregidor at this identical site with an image of the severed head of an Inca; some knew that he also had murdered Felipe Inca for the purpose of forcing a marriage with the latter's wife; and all knew that down through the years the Cañari Indians had proven themselves to be without a trace of honor or nobility, serving indiscriminately as spies for both Indians and Spaniards. Surely Toledo in his zeal to destroy the sacred concepts of the Incas had purposely chosen his executioner from

---

[6] In his pictorial representation of the scene, the mestizo Huaman Poma made the executioner a Spaniard.

among the caste they most despised. Even Spaniards were touched, and both priests and friars pled with Toledo to show compassion. But the Viceroy was unmoved and now dispatched an officer galloping through the howling crowd with a command that the Inca's head be severed at once. Then Túpac Amaru, taking one step forward, pointed a raised right hand toward the place from which the noise emanated and lowered it bit by bit until it came to rest upon his right thigh. As the Indians observed this pagan gesture of command, a deathlike silence fell over the city and the Cañari headsman swung his sword. Afterward, while all the bells of the city tolled the death of this new Christian, his mutilated body was carried to the house of Cusi Huarque, widow of the Inca Sayri Túpac.

On the day following, the body of Túpac Amaru was interred in the great church, and for nine days thereafter, requiem masses were piously repeated by sorrowing friars. But Toledo, unwilling to accord such unmitigated respect to a condemned Inca, caused the head to be removed and placed on a pike alongside the scaffold. Then one serene night, just before the hour of dawn, the old conqueror Mancio Serra de Leguizamo, chancing to look from his window onto the market place, beheld a host of silent and kneeling Indians, their sorrowful faces turned in deep devotion toward the impaled head of their departed sovereign. Through the broken clouds above, there fell upon them a nacreous lustre, emanating, not from the Holy Mother of God, but from the pagan and maternal Moon. Pachacámac and the Moon and the Sun still held sway in the hearts of the Indian masses, and there still were quipucamayus and amautas to inflame these hearts in the midst of their desolation. Toledo could never eradicate this veneration for Inca sovereigns so innately conceived of as the lineage of planetary deities; and in so ruthlessly and unwisely destroying Túpac Amaru he had succeeded only in creating another pagan martyr. When told of the nocturnal adoration of the Indians, he ordered the head of the Inca removed from the pike and buried in a Christian ceremony alongside the body. Having sensed further danger, he now continued his harsh measures of eradication.

All male Incas who might possess some claim to the throne, thirty-six in number, Toledo exiled to Los Reyes, where, torn by grief and nostalgia and tormented by an alien climate, they began to perish one by one. When at length only three remained, they were permitted to return to Cuzco, but within three years all were dead. The last to die was Carlos Paullu Inca, whose mestizo, Melchor Carlos, was godson of the Viceroy. Equal in severity to the treatment of the Incas was that of the mestizos. They were simply banished to diverse parts of the Spanish empire, where for years their increasing miseries kept them in a state of mutiny. One bright spot in the whole dark episode, however, is to be found in the fact that Juana Pincohuaco, one of the surviving daughters of Túpac Amaru, after marriage to a cacique of Surinami named Condorcanqui, became the maternal ancestor of José Gabriel Condorcanqui, who two centuries later assumed the name of Túpac Amaru II and instigated a revolt which anticipated the end of Spanish rule in Peru.[7] Furthermore, Beatriz Clara Coya, debauched daughter of the Inca Sayri Túpac, was bestowed upon García de Oñaz de Loyola as a reward for his signal services in the termination of the pagan dynasty. Through this latter princess, the blood of the royal Incas was to enrich that of several of the noblest houses of Spain and to enlace with that of two great Catholic saints: Francisco de Assisi and Ignatius de Loyola.[8]

While Toledo was occupied with his castigation of the Incas and mestizos at Cuzco, his attention was called to a new danger arising in Tucumán. In 1570 he had named Gerónimo Luis de Cabrera as governor of that province with the stipulation that at the completion of three years the office was to be passed on to Gonzalo Abreu de Figueroa. Almost at once Cabrera had begun to show such an eagerness for quick gain that he drew upon himself an official rebuke, and by the termination of his authority rumors had enwebbed him in transactions which were regarded as treasonous. Thus when in 1573 Abreu set out for Tucumán to assume his government, he bore ominous orders from the

[7] For the fate of Túpac Amaru's children, see Markham, *The Incas of Peru*, pp. 297–298; Cúneo-Vidal, *Historia de las guerras de los últimos Incas*, pp. 304–305; Garcilaso, *Comentarios*, Pt. II, Bk. VIII, Chaps. 18, 21.

[8] Garcilaso, *Comentarios*, Pt. II, Bk. VIII, Chap. 20; Means, *Fall of the Inca Empire*, p. 134n; Cúneo-Vidal, *Historia de las guerras de los últimos Incas*, pp. 211–219. After the dissolution of her forced marriage to Cristóbal Maldonado, Beatriz Clara had been betrothed to a son of the deceased Inca Titu Cusi.

Viceroy. Moreover, as a Figueroa, he was sensitive to the circumstances of Cabrera's illegal birth, and on approaching Córdoba de Tucumán, which Cabrera had founded, he is said to have recalled an old scandal and remarked that because of the bad government of his predecessor he had come to put an end to that offspring of a lowborn market woman. This he proceeded to do, ruthlessly and precipitately. When Cabrera, sick and recently bled, came out to pay obeisance, accompanied by his young son, Gonzalo Martel, Abreu, seizing the pennant of Córdoba which the boy bore, struck him and thus inflicted a psychic wound which one day was to fester into a serious rebellion. On the following day, Cabrera was imprisoned and carried off to Santiago del Estero, where he was accused of sedition, tortured, starved, and eventually executed, secretly and without trial. And rumor persists that he was dispatched by the ignobling device of a leathern collar attached to the post at the foot of his bed. By this time Luisa Martel had borne Cabrera at least five children, and she had continued to toil in an effort to increase their power and wealth. She was a mature woman of thirty-eight and had lost none of the confidence and audacity which already had marked her career. The old accusation of disloyalty which long had hovered about her first husband now had fallen upon her second, and she was roused to a pitch of fury not only by the loss of her mate but by the perils which a charge of sedition offered to her own fortune. She promptly appealed to the Audiencia at Los Reyes, denying the charge against Cabrera and placing a countercharge against Abreu; but her suit resulted in little or naught, possibly, as some said, because the original order for Cabrera's eradication had come from the Viceroy himself.[9]

With the dispersion of those Incas who might have laid claim to the vanished throne went the dissemination of reports which sought to defame their lineage. Sarmiento's history was forwarded to the pious sovereign, to whom it was dedicated; but if Philip read it, he found it scant comfort for a conscience which had grown even more troubled

[9] Arthur Franklin Zimmerman, *Francisco de Toledo*, p. 203; Luis G. Martínez Villada. *Los Cabrera*, pp. 23–27, 121–123. Cabrera apparently wished to avoid the scandal of his illegitimacy since none of his legitimate or illegitimate children bore the name of Toledo.

with the execution of Túpac Amaru. The chronicle was not given publication and in time was permitted to be forgotten. And possibly there was good reason. Only a few years later the mestizo Gonzalo Gómez Jiménez, who as an official interpreter had played an important role in Sarmiento's history as well as many of Toledo's reports on the Indians, was discovered dallying with the pages in the Viceroy's own household, and, in terror of the consequences, this sexual deviate unwisely expressed a desire to confess the lies which had constituted the basic charges against Túpac Amaru. Toledo took swift action. Before the naive and depraved mestizo could set his name to a signed statement he was secretly and quietly garroted.[10] News of his treachery and perversion may never have reached the ears of the King; but the chances are that it did, for Philip never forgave Toledo for the execution of Túpac Amaru. And his resentment may have been fostered by Lope García de Castro, since by the time of his reinstallation in the Council of the Indies García had reason to hate Toledo, who in one instance had even informed the King that his predecessor had hoped to lead a rebellion in Peru. Before Toledo returned to Spain the Council of the Indies was to charge him with the murder of Túpac Amaru.

There were a number of sources through whom Garcilaso could have been kept informed of the turmoils in Peru and the reaction to these turmoils at Madrid. As late as 1572 his former guardian, Antonio de Quiñones, still was representing the city of Cuzco before the Council of the Indies; his exiled schoolmate, Juan Arias Maldonado, before going to Madrid to present claims and complaints, had visited him at Montilla and told much of what has transpired in Peru; his cousin, García Suárez de Figueroa, an executor of his mother's will, surely had informed him of his mother's death as well as other events of significance; and since a number of his mestizo companions are known to have sent him information from time to time, possibly he was already in communication with them. But whatever the sources, much of the news which reached him now concerning Peru would have disclosed charges of disloyalty and sedition against the Indians and the mestizo sons of conquerors, and he would have been aware that the

[10] Means, *Fall of the Inca Empire*, p. 123, 137; see also Clissold, *Conquistador*, p. 70.

spirit of revolt which had spread throughout the Spanish realm was keeping the Crown in a state of vigilance. Moreover, he knew that to present his claims again at this point would be to reopen at a delicate time the subject of his father's loyalty. So when his friends urged him to seek aid once more from Lope García de Castro, he could not summon the courage to do so, and, to paraphrase his own words, he decided to abandon the perilous road to wealth and position and conceal himself in the corners of solitude and poverty, the haven of the disillusioned.[11]

Meanwhile, the cries of his Peruvian compatriots continued to vibrate in Garcilaso's ears and to quicken within him a yearning to record the "true" annals of the Inca world, from its origin on down through its travail under the authority of his famed Figueroa kinsman, Francisco de Toledo, who, in his zeal to apply balm to the fevered conscience of a King, had created another Inca martyr.

[11] Garcilaso, La Florida del Inca, Proemio.

CHAPTER THIRTEEN

At this critical point in Garcilaso's career, an epoch in which he was to shift the direction of his ambitions and sympathies, and to intensify his studies as well as his efforts with the pen, he appears on the surface to have reached a nadir of disillusion and despair. Certainly his first decade in Spain had overwhelmed him with a sense of futility, and his gloom had been deepened by the recent culmination of affairs in both Peru and Spain. Outside of his relations with his Uncle Alonso he had found little genuine warmth and security in Spain and he was becoming even more aware that no concrete satisfaction was to be gained in retracing his steps, for much of the Peru he had known had vanished and existed now only as a segment of his memory. Not only had Toledo all but eradicated the gasping Inca civilization, but that social milieu peculiar to the conquerors and their offspring had faded with the expiration of tenure on encomiendas and with the increasing greed and power of viceregal authorities. Moreover, the unbounded hope and zeal which had marked the temper of the early years of renascent Spain had lost its edge, and a spirit of pessimism and criticism prevailed.

But Garcilaso had not yet reached the limits of disillusion and despair, nor had he buried his hopes for wealth and status too deep for disinterment. His professed resolution at this time to abandon with finality all further pretensions and flee from the perils and seductions of a material world was recorded a number of years later in a mood of self-consolation and at a time when age had cooled his worldly ambitions. Such Arcadian clichés became an obsession with him, and in the light of subsequent events they ring with an ironical hollowness. He never ceased completely to seek favor and recompense from the Crown; he never failed to guard meticulously the material assets that had fallen to his lot; he never shut himself off from the multitudes; and though he later joined an order as a minor cleric, so far as is known he never contemplated a monastic vow of poverty.

Even in these early years of his second decade in Spain, Garcilaso was far from destitute, and his use of the word poverty, when applied to his "ill fortune" or his personal affairs, perhaps should be interpreted as "less rich" or as a complaint intended for the ears of delinquent debtors. It would be another decade before the benefits of Alonso de Vargas' generous bequest fell to him, but he had investments of his own in Estremadura and Andalusia; and although he had been unable to collect any of the debt specified by his eldest uncle in his will, he did manage in 1574, three years after the money was due, to collect it from the second wife and widow of this uncle's eldest son, Alonso de Hinestrosa de Vargas y Figueroa.[1] He still possessed at least three slaves, Juana, Juan, and Marina, who in 1570 had borne a bastard offspring. The death of his mother had restored to him a promise of the profits of Havisca, and though he apparently yielded to her plea that for three years these profits be applied to masses for her soul's welfare, he ignored her request that they be passed on at the close of that period to his half sisters, Ana and Luisa. Instead, in August of 1574 he began negotiations for the sale of Havisca. This sale, however, possibly was never realized, for it was to Havisca that he perhaps referred when he later spoke of having been robbed of property in Peru which had been left in the care of a friend. Some suspicion in this instance falls upon the original co-owner of the farm, who had been granted a portion of its usufruct for the period of time that the mestizo was to remain in Spain.[2]

[1] Aurelio Miró Quesada y Sosa, *El Inca Garcilaso*, p. 104.
[2] Archivo de Protocolos de Montilla, Escribano Juan Martínez de Córdoba, Años

Garcilaso continued in the house of his uncle in the Calle del Capitán, sharing its spacious quarters with his aunt as well as the customary retainers. Such proximity, until further evidence is disclosed, must be interpreted as expediency rather than the consequences of cordiality or affection; and it should be observed in the light of a Latin propensity to cluster relatives, rich and poor, under one roof while permitting them to maintain separate households. For Luisa Ponce was a woman of exceeding pride, and, if like some of her kinsmen, of appreciable eccentricity. Already she would have assumed the guardianship of her niece, María Leonor de Angulo, daughter of Francisco de Argote; and her attitude toward her husband's nephew would have been formal rather than congenial. He was past twenty when she first saw him, and though at the time she may have regarded him with some curiosity and esteem, she could not have banished from her mind the fact that he was an Indian and an illegitimate. Thus she normally would have entertained some resentment on perceiving the tightening hold he gained on her husband's affections, and she must have been considerably discomforted by the power which don Alonso's will placed in the hands of the mestizo. As an executor of this will, Garcilaso could provide able assistance, but he also could dull some of her own ambitions. From the beginning he was to learn that the character of this woman demanded that he maintain caution in respect to legal transactions. Her early unauthorized efforts to bestow his deceased uncle's clothing and other household effects upon a retainer had awakened him to this fact, but she later presented him with an even greater contingency by attempting to interfere with the choice of annuities for the support of don Alonso's chaplaincy, a choice which had been legally designated to Garcilaso and the local vicar. Contrary to their opinion, doña Luisa felt that these annuities, having been ordered on the best of the Captain's property, should be derived from the Priego estate; and contrary to specifications she remitted the matter to the Archbishop of Córdoba. Thus she brought the mestizo into legal conflict with high ecclesiastical

de 1573–1574, fols. 555–557; 581–582; El Inca Garcilaso, *Los comentarios reales,* Pt. II, Bk. VIII, Chap. 7.

authorities. Nevertheless, Garcilaso carried the case before the Royal Audiencia at Granada, and in consequence the Priego annuities, surely to the disappointment of the ruling Marqúes, were directed toward a different end.[3]

But what must have proven more vexatious to Luisa Ponce was the fact that though she could enjoy the usufruct of her husband's estate as long as she lived, at her death it must be divided equally between Garcilaso and his aunt, Isabel de Vargas. However, she had property of her own, and when on June 25, 1575, she drew up her last testament, she designated funds for another chaplaincy, the custodians of which were to be her own blood kin. As its successive chaplains she named first her cousin Francisco de Aranda, then her brother Francisco de Argote, and after them, three of her brother's children: Luis de Góngora, the poet "who aspired to be a cleric"; Juan de Góngora y Argote, the youngest son; and María Leonor de Angulo, the eight-year-old niece residing in her home. And as one of the overseers of the endowment she specified Francisco de Castro, who subsequently played a significant role in the publication of Garcilaso's last chronicle. Moreover, as her universal heir Luisa Ponce designated the aforementioned niece, María Leonor. Garcilaso's name appeared but once in the document. He was a mere witness and as such gave it his signature.[4]

The presence of this niece on whom the aging woman had fixed her affections could have contributed nothing to the tranquility of the Vargas household, either for the mestizo or his aunt. For María Leonor was a Góngora y Argote, and she early began to exhibit an insolence and audacity which eventually equaled if not overshadowed that of her brother Luis. By 1579, when she had scarcely reached the age of twelve, her father was forced to come to her defense in court against a charge of jactitation placed by one María Magdalena of Montilla, a former ward of Luisa Ponce's deceased aunt, María de Angulo. But more

---

[3] Archivo de Protocolos de Montilla, Escribano Gerónimo Pérez, Año de 1573, fols. 122–122v; Escribano Juan Martínez de Córdoba, Años de 1573–1574, fols. 139–139v; 148–148v; Año de 1576, fols: 449v–450.

[4] Document dated April 9, 1586, Archivo de Protocolos de Montilla, Escribano Gerónimo Pérez, Año de 1586, fols. 112–116.

significant is the fact that during the decade or more that she passed in the Vargas house at Montilla, the eccentricity of María Leonor ostensibly proved distasteful to the Priegos, who already had reason to suspect her racial purity, and who came to dislike her as intensely as they did her poet brother. Such circumstances surely contributed to Luisa Ponce's growing realization that it would be wise for her to depart from Montilla.

Hence it was not an altogether serene household in which Garcilaso was now residing, and his life was not devoid of domestic vexations as well as others involving legal enterprises. But there remained occupations compatible with the tastes of a gentleman. He continued to increase his spiritual progeny, to consort with canonical scholars, and to pursue those equestrian interests which brought him into contact with the lords of the land. An act of the Cabildo of Montilla reveals that in 1579 one of his blooded stallions, a great chestnut with two stockinged feet and a stripe on its forehead, was chosen in a select contest to throw on the brood mares in the meadows of the Prado or Panchia. The markings of this horse were identical with those of the horse ridden by Gonzalo Silvestre in La Florida, a horse that would thrust its nose to the ground and scent a trail like a bird dog, and Garcilaso in recounting Silvestre's exploits declared that whether found in work horses or ponies, such markings gave more promise of excellence and loyalty than did any others. It was as a breeder of horses that Garcilaso during these years again encountered Martín Leal, who long ago, like himself, had ridden Pajarillo or "the little sparrow," and who in 1579 was employed as a trainer in the stables of the Duque de Feria. Only a year or two later, in response to a plea, Garcilaso was to send a fine horse to Juan Arias Maldonado, who still was confined to Madrid and had recently married; and when Maldonado, after ten years of exile, was granted permission by the Council of the Indies to journey to Peru for a period of three years to settle his estates, he brought his wife Ana to Montilla and begged Garcilaso for some household furnishings. Garcilaso lent the couple silks, taffetas, and linens, which, along with the horse, made them obligated to him to the extent of five hundred ducats.

In recording this transaction with his old mestizo companion, Garcilaso spoke kindly of him, saying that Maldonado had promised to send back two thousand pesos as soon as he arrived in Peru and declaring his faith that Maldonado would have done so had he not died of sheer joy within three days after stepping ashore at Paita. But when Garcilaso made this statement, he was lamenting the plight of the mestizos, and the transaction in reality was not so genial; for a document dated February 14, 1582 reveals that Garcilaso's generosity was tempered with his customary caution. Having learned that Ana Maldonado had died and that her husband still had not left Spain, Garcilaso on this day deputized two men at Seville to collect from Juan Arias Maldonado before his departure, by lawsuit if necessary, one hundred and and fifty yards of vari-colored taffetas, eighty-four yards of homespun linen, some ornamental pillows, and a green bed cover.[5]

So in spite of his augmented estate and his gentlemanly occupations, Garcilaso, as he has admitted, still remained subject to material ambitions and to the perils attending what he called idleness. It follows, therefore, that he as yet had not eschewed worldly seductions and that in this particular period he was not immune to the temptations of the flesh.

Though no records indicate that Garcilaso ever contemplated easing such temptations through matrimony, undoubtedly such a course at one time or another did cross his mind. At least one scholar has suggested an affinity between the mestizo and the arrogant María Leonor de Angulo, basing his assumption on the fact that Garcilaso and a María de Angulo appeared many times conjointly as godparents in the Church of Santiago. Intriguing as is the vision of a romance between the Inca messiah and a sister of the renowned poet Góngora, too many circumstances forbid it. There were several María de Angulos in Montilla, some humble and some exalted, and Garcilaso was serving as a godparent with women of this name before Luisa Ponce's niece was born. In 1575, he did appear at a baptism along with a María Leonor

[5] Document dated March 1, 1579, Archivo Municipal de Montilla, Libro de Actas Capitulares, Años de 1578–1579, Legajo 431, fols. 29v–30; document dated February 14, 1582, Archivo de Protocolos de Montilla, Escribano Juan Martínez de Córdoba, Años de 1582–1583, fols. 113v–114v; also Garcilaso, Comentarios, Pt. II, Bk. VII, Chap. 18; Bk. VIII, Chap. 17.

de Angulo, who is definitely identified as the daughter of Francisco de Argote, but at the time this María was but eight years of age.[6] Moreover, even though while in Montilla this capricious maiden may have allowed herself the sadistic pleasure of encouraging the mestizo, the legends attending her pride of lineage indicate that she, unless out of sheer perversity, never would have permitted the idea of a marriage with him. Shortly afterward, in Córdoba, she is said to have driven to madness and suicide an enamored swain of minor social status whose persistent and revenging ghost she afterward was forced to exorcise with a plethora of masses. On the other hand, even if Garcilaso, now almost forty, ever wildly contemplated such a union, his own pride may have been challenged, since by now he would have learned from the Priegos that the racial purity of the Góngora line was suspect, and though he was alert to the obstacles which attended his hopes of marriage into Spanish hidalguía, in all probability he would have been reluctant to wed into a blood caste which his father evidently had believed and had taught him to believe was inferior to that of the mestizo.

There of course were remedies other than matrimony for soothing erotic urges; and though he already may have contemplated celibacy, neither the social nor the ecclesiastical milieu would have made special demands on his chastity. But whatever yearnings of this nature he may have felt, he never recorded them, and they may never have been divulged except to the understanding heart of some confessor, whose most severe admonition, even then, must have been to avoid the temptations of idleness, which Garcilaso afterward was to describe as the mother of vice, the stepmother of virtue, and the source of all evil. Nevertheless, there now is definite evidence of a relation which produced results difficult to expunge in the confessional or to screen long from public knowledge. At some time during his "idle" Montilla years, possibly in the late seventies or the early eighties, he did beget a son, whom he named Diego de Vargas, upon a woman who is listed in his will as Beatriz de Vega, and in subsequent documents as Beatriz de la Vega. Since no baptismal record of this boy appears in the archives of the church of Santiago at Montilla, he may have been born else-

[6] Archivo de la Parroquia de Santiago de Montilla, Libros de Bautismos, No. 5, fol. 171v, entry dated July 26, 1575.

where and his birth for a time kept a secret. Furthermore, the specific identity and status of Beatriz de Vega have never been discovered. Though her name strongly suggests that she bore Vega and Vargas blood, she just as easily could have been a slave who was given her master's name. Garcilaso, however, never listed her as one of his own slaves, and she appears in his will merely as a favored servant.[7] But this change in Garcilaso's domestic affairs could not long have remained a secret, and to some extent it could have accounted for the fact that in 1580 Luisa Ponce departed with her niece for Córdoba and left the mestizo as overseer of his uncle's great house in the Calle del Capitán.

This tantalizing episode, which only in recent years has come to light, appears to coincide with an increasing interest on the part of Garcilaso in some of the erotic literature which had been expunged or forbidden by the Spanish Inquisition. His delight in amorous lore, however, had long been nourished. Records disclose that he had a mature acquaintance with the chivalric saga and its multiple sequels of Amadis de Gaula, who like himself was begotten out of wedlock on the body of an alien princess. Moreover, he was equally well acquainted with the passion-ridden caprices of the Italian novella; and all of his life he had been enamored of "good poetry," which to him encompassed among others the verse of Ariosto, Boyardo, Boscán, and Garcilaso de la Vega, as well as many of those poems which constituted the popular *Canciones generales,* lyrical outbursts which in general, when not lamenting the fleetingness of life, were detailing the tortures of love.[8] Somewhere in the past he had fallen under the spell of his

---

[7] So far as is known, Garcilaso never mentioned his intimate relations with Beatriz de Vega in any documents; but undeniable reference to this relation is to be found in documents issued over the years after his death. Herein Diego not only is identified as "the natural son of Garcilaso de la Vega," but Beatriz is named as his mother. See documents dated February 14, 1620, Archivo de Protocolos de Córdoba, Oficio 29, Tomo 39, fols. 148–149; March 24 and March 31, 1620, Libros del Cabildo Eclesiástico de Córdoba, docs. 2 and 3 respectively; also Rafael Aguilar Priego, "'El Hijo del Inca Garcilaso," *Boletín de la Real Academia de Ciencias, Bellas Letras y Nobles Artes de Córdoba,* Año XVI, No. 54, Julio-Diciembre, pp. 281–300; Rubén Vargas Ugarte, "Nota sobre Garcilaso," *Mercurio Peruano,* Vol. XX, Enero–Febrero, 1930, pp. 47–50. Íñigo de Córdoba Ponce de León, who had known Diego de Vargas personally, identified him as the son of the Inca Garcilaso.

[8] Garcilaso, *La Florida del Inca,* Bk. II, Pt. I, Chaps. 20, 27.

distant relative, Garcí Sánchez de Badajoz, who, driven to madness by the torments of love, had long stood out as both a symbol and a victim of eroticism, and whom Garcilaso regarded as a "Phoenix of Spanish poets without equal and without possibility of an imitator." Apparently he not only had scanned this man's *Infierno de amor*, which in a Dantesque manner disclosed the agonies of contemporary poets in the hell of love, but at some time before the Holy Inquisition had succeeded in expunging Sánchez' *Lecciones de Job* from all copies of the *Canciones*, the mestizo had managed to memorize these profanations so well that he could recall them at least thirty years later. Indeed, he has confessed that he embedded in his memory all of the works of Garcí Sánchez, and that he was able to recall them later because they were so agreeable to his understanding. The Holy Office could blot out or tear a page from a book but it could not erase it from a memory.

Early in his processes of mature thinking Garcilaso had experienced an urge to see the *Lecciones de Job* returned to circulation, though with the profanations removed and the spiritual sense restored. Thus it was not the erotic elements which held his attention but the beauty of the poetry which Garcí Sánchez de Badajoz had misused to convert a sacred scriptural passage into a profane one, a passage whose spiritual implication must have appealed especially to the mestizo at this period in his career. For he too was a "Man of Uz," meditating his afflictions and contemplating the transcience of life while seeking to cling steadfastly to his faith. The passages profaned were the new lessons now sung in the office of the dead and thus were available in Latin. But Garcilaso wished to see them in the elegant Castilian verse of his poet kinsman. Herein, therefore, he was revealing his desire, often expressed, of seeing Spain rescue from oblivion her glorious accomplishments with both sword and pen, and he was reflecting the ever-growing Renaissance awareness of the glories of the Castilian vulgate. But he was moved further by the fact that in his reading he had discovered lesser poets glorifying themselves by appropriating the exquisite but forbidden lines of Garcí Sánchez de Badajoz. He felt himself unqualified to accomplish the task of purging and renovating the *Lecciones* because of his inadequate knowledge of metrics and theology, but from his memory he could provide for some qualified person the passages so ruthlessly deleted by the Inquisition.[9] It would be an arrangement somewhat in reverse to what he had planned for his story of De Soto's expedition into La Florida.

Garcilaso's sincere or feigned humility, which at times appears obsequious to readers unmindful of sixteenth-century literary manners, makes it easy to read into his life more timidity than actually was present. Such an interpretation is somewhat modified by the none too subtle intercalations which continually accompany his comments on contemporary figures, and it is further weakened by the realization that at a time when the Holy Office and the King were scrupulously supervising everything read and written in Spain, he was preoccupying himself with books that were suspect and with the long-disapproved idea of making available philosophical and theological concepts which in general were forbidden to circulate in the vulgate. One is led to wonder to what extent the *Index Librorum Prohibitorum* had touched Montilla at this time. The machinery of the Inquisition had demanded that a copy of it be placed in each city and village, that ecclesiastical authorities be vigilant in their inspection of libraries and bookshops, and that everyone submit his library for the mutilation or approval of these authorities. Often-times new prohibitions were announced from pulpits and they carried with them threats of confiscation as well as excommunication and even death. Yet possibly even while contemplating a refinement of the condemned *Lecciones*, Garcilaso was drawn to the Neo-Platonic *Dialoghi di Amore* of the renowned humanist, Judah Abarbanal, a Portuguese Jew whose philosophical explanation of the origin of both divine and profane love as early as 1564, if not earlier, had been expurgated in part by the Inquisition. He did not concern himself with the purged Latin translation, and in all probability he was ignorant of the Spanish translation by another renowned Jew, Guedella Yahia, which had been published at Venice in 1568 with a dedication to Philip II. But he occupied himself with the original Tuscan, which he began at once to translate into Castilian.

Garcilaso's interest in Judah Abarbanal, better known by his pseudo-

---

[9] Garcilaso, *La Descendencia de Garcí Pérez de Vargas.* Sánchez' madness sometimes led him to wander naked in the streets. Learned clergymen declared his affliction was God's curse for the poet's profanations.

nym of León Hebreo, may have been aroused first by some member of the Priego household, for a near relative of the Marqueses, Gonzalo Fernández de Córdoba, "el Gran Capitán," had employed the learned Jew from 1505 to 1507 as his personal physician. But whatever its source, Garcilaso made no effort to conceal his interest from canonical scholars, who could have discouraged it, but to their praise they encouraged it. He has recorded that he had scarcely begun his translation of the *Dialoghi* when he submitted it to a number of pious and serious persons, among whom were four eminent scholars: Pedro Agustín de Herrera, a linguist and theologian serving as the preceptor of Pedro Fernández de Córdoba y Figueroa, heir to the Marqués de Priego; Padre Gerónimo de Prado, a Jesuit theologian and lecturer at Córdoba; the Licentiate Pedro Sánchez de Herrera, a native theologian of Montilla now instructing Garcilaso; and finally Padre Fernando de Zárate, an illustrious Augustinian teacher of theology now retired from the University of Osuna. Each of these learned men, he declared, urged him consistently to continue his project and assured him that it would be well received.[10] Such encouragement was sufficient to allay fears of the Inquisition, though Garcilaso must have harbored some apprehension still. He would have been aware of the fate of Alessandro Piccolomini, whom he admired ardently and respected as "an authority on the texts of León Hebreo." One of the first to treat Aristotelian philosophy in the vulgate, the Italian had been rewarded for his efforts with the condemnation of both lay and church critics and with a charge of heresy. Certainly Garcilaso was not ignorant of the fact that he was tampering with a treatise that dealt with theosophic and cabalistic concepts which many regarded as dangerous; yet at the time only specified passages had been forbidden and the book was popular in Spain. In 1584, even before he completed his efforts a second translation into the Spanish vulgate, by Carlos Montesa, was to appear at Zaragoza, and in 1585 Cervantes was to publish *La Galatea*, which carried summaries of some of the dialogues of León Hebreo's classic. Possibly Garcilaso's real daring lay in the fact that his translation was to represent the efforts of an Indian.

---

[10] Garcilaso to Maximiliano de Austria, September 18, 1586, in prefatory material of *Diálogos de amor.*

Though he professed to have begun his translation to escape the pitfalls of boredom and idleness and with no aim at publication, Garcilaso also admitted that in it he was seeking to attain a greater peace of mind than wealth might bring and that he found encouragement and comfort in the "soft and sweet philosophy" of León Hebreo.[11] Disillusioned with a decadent code of nobility and concerned more than ever with social injustice and racial intolerance, he now could find solace in the words of this humanist who was set apart by both his race and the faith of his fathers. It was a philosophy which clarified man's concept of "divine injustice" and revealed the necessity of adversity, which tolerantly synthesized Hellenic, Hebraic, Mozarabic, and Christian concepts, and which revealed all elements of the cosmos as one great cycle emanating from and terminating in the divine purpose of love. In the astro-pantheistic structure of this doctrine, the mestizo consciously or subconsciously could recognize an overtone of the ancient concepts taught him by Indians when as a small boy close to the Andean skies he had contemplated with them the progress of the moon, the sun, the stars, and all the phenomena of the heavens and the earth which lay about them. Submerging himself in the arguments of the famed Hebrew, he could forget some of the rebuffs of fortune, and he could justify his pride in a dual lineage. Here he, as an alien, barred by the forged iron bands of a social code, could find what the half-caste is fated always to seek, a sense of family and a sense of belonging.

Of less significance, but not to be overlooked in a search for motive, is the fact that Garcilaso's interest in León Hebreo again places him in line with contemporary literary trends, especially with the prevalent interest in the art and aethetics of Italy and the desire to reveal these forms in Castilian. The poets Garcilaso and Boscán, among others, had led the way, and though the latter is known to have declared that the business of translating was a "low vanity becoming to men of little knowledge," he, at the request of the former, had succeeded in rendering into Castilian a faithful version of Cas-

---

[11] Garcilaso to Maximiliano de Austria, September 18, 1586, in prefatory material of *Diálogos de amor*. Herein Garcilaso explained his whole purpose and procedure in translating the *Dialoghi di Amore*.

tiglione's *Il Cortegiano*. To the mestizo Garcilaso the art of translation was a gentlemanly exercise, and the fact that he has declared it such indicates not only that he still persisted hopefully in his claim to gentility but that his project carried with it some purpose of polishing his own Castilian, about which he naturally felt humble.

The translator's first difficulty, one might suspect, would lie in an inadequate knowledge of Tuscan. It is vain to attempt to find some excuse to place him at one time or another in the Italian peninsula; and even a quick military expedition into Italy could not have provided the knowledge necessary to master another language. It is wiser to assume that in past years he had taken advantage of the knowledge of his Uncle Alonso, whose experiences had carried him often into Italy, or of those ecclesiastical scholars who from the beginning had encouraged him in his translation. Moreover, in a Spain so engrossed in the aesthetics and literature of Italy there would not have been lacking among his acquaintances many who knew at least a modicum if not much of the Tuscan language, and by 1583 Cristóbal de las Casas had published his *Vocabulario de las dos lenguas toscana y castillana*. But Garcilaso was himself a natural and enthusiastic linguist with keen appreciation of syntactical nuances and with a better knowledge of his nominatives than he was willing to admit; and though Castilian was not his native tongue, he had spoken it from an early age and in addition knew some Latin. Thus when confronted with Tuscan he already was trilingual. And one might recall the quip of Cervantes that only three grains of Italian were necessary to unravel the love concepts of León the Jew. It might be worthwhile to remember also that the native tongue of this Jew was not Tuscan but Portuguese, with which Garcilaso of course was familiar.

Yet this is not to minimize the difficulties of the task, difficulties which Garcilaso readily admitted. He spent many hours correcting errors made in bringing the text from its original mold, and he passed much more time in an effort to remold the feeling and the sense into Castilian without distorting the Tuscan forms. This was a more intricate task, since the subtleties and elegancies of León Hebreo, so appropriate in Italian, relied upon special word symbols and arrangements of word symbols to convey special overtones and undertones of meaning. Moreover, the philosopher had worked industriously to make a readily comprehensible philosophy obscure for those who were unwilling to read it assiduously. Aware of the author's purpose and technique, Garcilaso felt that to alter the subtleties and inventions of León Hebreo would be to divorce the context from the art and to deprive the author of the honor due his ability to enclose an elevated doctrine in a vulgate language; he also felt that to add superfluities would be equally disastrous since they would render sublime doctrines commonplace and rob an equally elevated rhetoric of its subtlety. Thus Garcilaso sought to keep the form of the Castilian version as close as possible to the original; and, conscious that Spanish readers might overlook linguistic and stylistic eccentricities, he later admonished them to be on guard for imperfect consonances and passages depending on relatives for their meaning and to keep in mind that the author had intended the book for those who read attentively and creatively and who could philosophize along with him. It was a sweet and comforting philosophy enhanced by the vulgate tongue, but it was not for the careless reader. To present it in Castilian required both courage and ingenuity.

It is not to be supposed, therefore, that this gentlemanly exercise involving a careful study of both the style and concepts as well as the language of a volume of profound philosophy was the labor of a few days or months. And while it was in progress, Garcilaso had not abandoned the task of recording the story of La Florida. In the fashion of the Italian novella, he already had drawn a picture of De Soto's great galleons as they sailed in splendor over the treacherous sand bars of San Lúcar de Barrameda, on to the Canaries, and across the great ocean to the ports of Cuba and the green Indian regions of La Florida. At this point it was a pageantry of majestic ships and pirate seas, of gallant cavaliers and timid, effete young courtiers, of horses and dogs and captive Christian slaves, of intrigue and seduction. In this first section more than in any other is to be found the tone of the courtly literature of Spain and Italy. And dashing in and out of the picture, always shining, is the figure of that sword-flashing, hard-riding Gonzalo Silvestre. For like a fleeting but garrulous ghost, the old raconteur still haunted the plains of Andalusia, passing from time to time in and out of the quiet retreat of his amanuensis. Here he always found a warm welcome as well as fuel for his capers and extravagances. Despite his tangible resources, Silvestre appears to have been ever in need of more than he possessed, and Garcilaso over the years had lent him funds, though always in exchange for proper legal receipts.

Silvestre's perennial shortage doubtlessly was due in part to a never-fading dream of heroic deeds in pursuit of arms. Even as an aging warrior he was seen journeying to Toledo to purchase twelve swords of well-tempered steel from the famed Sahagún the Elder. In general, life for him had been a gallant adventure, though some of it had been sordid and had left scars. Still seeking favors at Madrid, sometimes for a pension and sometimes for a permit to barter slaves, he may have regretted not having accepted the generosity of Cañete in exchange for nuptials with a woman of suspect chastity. But ironically, though Silvestre had never contracted marriage he had contracted the Gallic pox. An old acquaintance has described him on one occasion entering Montilla, not as the swift and intrepid horseman Garcilaso has pictured racing through the seemingly impenetrable jungles of La Florida, but as an obese and swollen old man, nursing his venereal curse and drawn in a cart by a lumbering ox. An aged crone, touched by the sight, came out to inquire as to the source of his misery, and on being informed, directed him to Las Posadas, where, in the spring of the year, one could find a blessed herb to palliate such afflictions. The search for this balm surely accounts for Silvestre's decision to abandon his native village of Herrera and settle in Las Posadas, where the mestizo Garcilaso was to draw from him much of the story of La Florida.[12]

The sight of his old friend gradually corroding brought to Garcilaso a realization that he must make haste if he were to complete Silvestre's story of Hernando de Soto. As yet he apparently had not brought the governor and conqueror of "the flowery land" through

---

[12] Archivo de Protocolos de Córdoba, Oficio 29, Protocolo 35, fols. 505–57; Vargas Ugarte, "Nota sobre Garcilaso," *Mercurio Peruano*, Vol. XX, Enero–Febrero, pp. 47–50.

the first stages of his expedition, and there was a long way to go before he could terminate the story with a picture of ragged remnants of a lost conquest trudging naked and starving into the City of Mexico. Moreover, he had not abandoned his dream of bringing to its true light the whole story of his native Peru, a story with which Silvestre could and would be of invaluable assistance. For even as they toiled over the saga of De Soto, Silvestre told of his own adventures in the land of the Incas and corroborated many of the events which the mestizo had witnessed. Together they analyzed the characters and the motivations of the loyal and the disloyal; and together they judged the truth and the falsity of what Garcilaso eventually was to quote from other historians. In the marginal notes to the aforementioned copy of López de Gómara's history, which undoubtedly both used, the hand of the old warrior can be detected in the comments on events wherein he played a signal role, passionate outbursts such as, "Here he lies," "Here he is false," and, in one instance, "The book as well as the one who wrote it deserves to be burned." And the marginal comments of the mestizo, though more modest, at times reveal an unwonted heat. Where López de Gómara told of the idolatries and superstitions of the Indians, the mestizo added, "May God give us his grace and some years of life in order that . . . we may correct the many errors that appear in this history, principally those pertaining to the customs of the natives and the lords of the land." And where López de Gómara stated that in the province of Esmeraldas, Pedro de Alvarado found Indians who practiced cruel idolatry, lived like sodomites, spoke like Moors, and looked like Jews, Garcilaso added, "Of course they are not Jews or Moors but gentiles, in spite of the author and the one who told him this."[13] The same scrutiny shared by the aging raconteur and his more youthful amanuensis in their perusal of López de Gómara undoubtedly was shared in their perusal of other historians. For they had found a compatibility of mind and spirit in their interpretation of the nobility of the Indians as well as the motives of conquerors who in some instances had left questionable marks along the trails of Spanish exploitation and conquest.

[13] Raúl Porras Barrenechea, *El Inca Garcilaso en Montilla*, pp. 219–235.

Thus Silvestre was to become a central or a strongly supporting figure in many of Garcilaso's most dramatic accounts.

And now the whole of Garcilaso's literary ambitions was to find nourishment and support in his project for translating the classic philosophy of León Hebreo. It would strengthen his confidence in his own talents and at the same time provide an incentive for democratizing the nobility of the two races which had given him being. Moreover, his admiration for the Jewish scholar may very well account for a decision to let all of his works appear under a name which left no doubt as to the author's racial identity. In this respect, there is a close parallel between his life and that of the man whose philosophy he was interpreting. For in 1492, when because of his medical skill the Catholic Kings had offered haven to Judah Abarbanal, he had chosen to cast his lot with his own people and, following them into exile, had made his intellectual outbursts in a language to which he was not native. Furthermore, he had affixed to his *Dialoghi di Amore* a pseudonym which left no doubt as to his abused and despised race —he was León the Hebrew. It appears more than coincidental, therefore, that Garcilaso should take similar steps at a time when he came so intimately into contact with the philosophy of this learned Jew. He had severed himself to some extent from his Indian past by exchanging his Peruvian name for that of his father; but there can be little doubt that over the years in Spain he had been referred to repeatedly and oftentimes disdainfully as the Indian Garcilaso. Never having succeeded in emerging into the Spaniard, he now was willing to accept his adversity and utilize it as much as possible to his honor and advantage. He was therefore resolved to declare "full-mouthed" that he was the Indian, Garcilaso Inga de la Vega. Thus once more he was to take upon himself a title which may have been the first by which he ever heard himself addressed—*el Inca*. This name, the most glorious symbol of his Indian heritage, represents a defiant assertion of his Indianism, and it was to appear in print first on the title page of his translation of the synthetic philosophy of a Portuguese Jew, a philosophy which he found sweet and soothing.

CHAPTER FOURTEEN

As Garcilaso in the pastoral serenity of Montilla was laboring with the Tuscan of León Hebreo, his attention would have been drawn to the turbulent affairs of Portugal, birthplace of the Jewish philosopher, and to the shifting fortunes of the house of Braganza, the noble family which in past years had offered protection to the Abarbanals. The youthful King Sebastián, who was ruling under a regency when Garcilaso passed through Lisbon, had developed into a strong-willed but weak-minded ascetic and celibate who entrusted the welfare of the empire to the Jesuits. In 1578 he foolishly and stubbornly set forth upon a crusade against the Moors of Africa, accompanied by, among others, Teodosio II, ten-year-old son of the sixth Duke of Braganza and his duchess, Catalina. Shortly after, in the valley of Al Kasr al Kebir, King Sebastián was slain and the boy Teodosio, who had defied orders to stay out of the combat, was wounded and captured. The Portuguese throne now fell to the late King's feeble and senile great-uncle, Cardinal Enrique, who, though he could anticipate but a few more years of life, resolved to seek a dispensation from his vows of celibacy and enrich the throne with an heir. Report spread that this bald, toothless, and palsied septuagenarian planned to carry out his resolution by marrying the thirteen-year-old daughter of the Duque de Braganza, and there also was a rumor that court politicians, fearing that the Cardinal might prove impotent, were scheming to provide him with a bride already impregnated. Thus there was initiated a mad sequence of intrigues among pretenders, chief and most obstinate of whom were the prior, Antonio of Crato, bastard son of a converted Jewess; the sixth Duque de Braganza, whose claim rested entirely upon the heritage of his duchess; and Philip II, whose claims were strongest and who now saw an opportunity to unite the Iberian peninsula into the most powerful empire the world had ever known. And deeply involved were two of Philip's intimates, Antonio Pérez and Ana de Mendoza, Princesa de Éboli. Indeed Pérez was so conversant with Philip's ambitions for annexing Portugal that he was known in Madrid as "el Portugués," and when he conveyed his secrets to the Princesa de Éboli, widow of the Portuguese Ruy Gómez, she began to nourish plans to marry one of her manifold brood to the boy Teodosio de Braganza, whose release from captivity Philip had secured in 1579.

In the ensuing intrigues Philip began attempts to bribe those with claims to the Portuguese throne. The lesser pretenders were no bother, but Antonio of Crato and the Braganzas were difficult. Among the temptations offered the latter was the empire of Brazil with a crown for the Duke, and though doña Catalina refused this offer, the Braganzas, after the death of Cardinal Enrique in 1580, did abandon their claim and pledge allegiance to the Spanish King in exchange for a collar of the Golden Fleece and under a system of autonomy which left them almost in the quality of sovereigns at Lisbon. A satisfactory agreement could not be reached with Antonio of Crato, and eventually Philip, utilizing the services of the aging Duque de Alba, enforced his claim on the Portuguese throne. Nevertheless, Antonio escaped and with the help of France and the sympathy of England carried on a campaign of resistance in the Azores, only one island of which had pledged allegiance to Spain. The most obstinate efforts occurred in Terceira, but in 1583, after being reduced to a reeking slaughterhouse, it too succumbed and all of the Azores were brought under the dominion of the Spanish Crown.

Garcilaso had never forgotten his indebtedness to the people of Terceira, Fayal, and Lisbon for the hospitality offered him when as a lonely alien he had arrived in the Old World, and he later was to admit that he had known a desire to serve both the Portuguese and the House of Braganza. Possibly, having fought the Moriscos of Spain, he had felt an urge to join the ill-fated Sebastián in his expedition against the Moors of Africa. One scion of the Marquisate of Priego had done so at the cost of his life; and it stands to reason that there were others from the region of Montilla who had rallied to the call of the youthful Portuguese sovereign, whose courage, as well as that of Teodosio de Braganza, had fired the imaginations of Hispanic-speaking people. Certainly in the recent intrigues and martial struggles Garcilaso's sympathies had extended to the Portuguese in their efforts to preserve an empire independent of Spain. And surely at some time during the process of his translation of the *Dialoghi* he would have visualized the appropriateness of dedicating this labor to the noble house which in past years had favored the family of Judah Abarbanal and whose present members had manifested signal interest in the Greek classics and astronomy, both of which constitute such an integral portion of the text of the *Dialoghi*. Moreover, it is difficult to conceive that he would not have been aware of the general interest of the Portuguese in the De Soto expedition and of the existence of the only printed account of that expedition, the "true relation" of the "Fidalgo of Elvas." For though this writer had kept himself anonymous in print, as one of the few Portuguese accompanying the expedition and as a survivor he would have been known to Gonzalo Silvestre, and he may already have made his appearance anonymously in the Garcilaso manuscripts as one of the noble cavaliers of Yelves whom the mestizo was to present and praise in his story.

Yet, though perhaps this early Garcilaso had entertained the idea of turning to the Braganzas for literary sanction, by 1586, when he had completed the task of transferring into Castilian the Tuscan rhetoric of the Hebrew-Portuguese humanist, shifting circumstances and a latent ambition would have demanded that he modulate his plans. Philip II was now sovereign of the whole of the Iberian world, and past disappointments and disillusionments had not succeeded in erasing from the mestizo's heart all hopes of renewing his pretensions at court. Doña Luisa Ponce de León obviously was approaching the end of her life, and the inheritance which he was assured of receiving at her death was sufficient to provide encouragement and support for such an undertaking. Moreover, by now Lope García de Castro had been dead for a decade and none served on the Council whom the mestizo had encountered in 1563. Surely old accusations had been forgotten and the ghost of a horse no longer haunted the chambers of the King's Council. But more important were Garcilaso's long-range aspirations. For though undoubtedly he yearned for a nod of favor which would reveal a recognition of his hidalguía and remove an old stigma, he primarily sought support for his translation and protection for his chronicles, all of which he by now had begun. Thus it was that when on January 19, 1586, he composed a dedication for his translation, he directed it to Philip II and proudly identified himself as "Garcilaso Inga de la Vega."[1]

This dedication, though appropriately humble, was more than a mere laudation and pledge of obeisance. It was a plea which carried the assertion of old and unrewarded claims. Herein Garcilaso once again told of the loyal services of his father and his uncles under two Spanish monarchs and of his own services with don Juan in the Alpujarras. And while wisely admitting that it was audacious for an Indian to address his sovereign, he begged that his translation be accepted as a first fruit of Peru and as an example of what might be expected of Peruvians. But more important still, he told of two chronicles now in preparation which, should he win the King's approval, he hoped to present as a token of his affection: the first, an account of the expedition of Hernando de Soto into La Florida, "an expedition too long buried in the shadows of oblivion"; the second, an account of the conquest of Peru in which he planned to enlarge upon its antiquities, since he, as a native, was better qualified than an alien to disclose them. These, he added in words reminiscent of the Toledan Garcilaso, were to be regarded as tokens that he served his sovereign with pen as well as sword.

The translation of the Dialoghi was now ready to run the gauntlet of inspection required before printing, a tedious process in the Spain of the Prudent King. It would necessitate powerful approval even before

---

[1] This dedication and a second communication to the King, as well as all of Garcilaso's correspondence with Maximiliano de Austria, are to be found in the prefatory material affixed to his Diálogos de amor.

coming to the hands of Philip II, and a humble Indian dared not make a direct approach. Then it would require the sanction of both the Holy Office and the Supreme Council. Where Garcilaso turned first for support has not been revealed. Possibly he passed the completed document to the hands of the learned theologians who in the beginning had encouraged him, or possibly he turned it over to the Marqués de Priego with a plea for protection. Be that as it may, it eventually came to the attention of Juan and Alonso de Herrera, sons of Luisa Ponce's cousin, Francisco de Aranda, who was serving as Alcalde in the village of Priego, and these men assumed the responsibility of placing it in more powerful hands.[2]

On Holy Friday, April 4, 1586, Luisa Ponce de León died at Córdoba and her resources, with the exception of what was due her husband's nephew and sister, fell to her universal heir, María Leonor de Angulo.[3] Consequently, though a portion of the Priego annuities now came into the hands of Garcilaso, those which had been retained to repay Luisa Ponce's dowry ironically were added to the tangible assets of this erratic niece, for whom the Marqués de Priego already had been given opportunity to form some distaste. Moreover, during the years since her departure from Montilla, additional reasons for enmity had been provided by her brother Luis. For in 1579, after three years at Salamanca, Luis de Góngora had returned to Córdoba, without degree but with some experience already in the gentlemanly art of poesy, and at some time during the next few years he had written certain barbed couplets which were interpreted as being aimed at the humiliation of the proud grandee of Priego. Furthermore, both brother and sister had incurred additional animosity by offending equally the Cordoban Inquisitor and Presbyter, Alonso Jiménez de Reynoso, the former with more barbed lines, and the latter by an act committed on a warm afternoon in a Cordovan grove where by chance both she and His Grace had retired for an hour of repose. While meditating beside a sylvan pond, doña María was proffered insolent remarks by one of the Inquisitor's effete pages, and when the upstart lad paid no heed to her sug-

---

[2] Garcilaso to Maximiliano de Austria, September 18, 1586.
[3] Document dated April 5, 1586, Archivo de Protocolos de Montilla, Escribano Gerónimo Pérez, Año de 1586, fol. 110. Luisa's will was opened on April 9, 1586.

gestion that he "go on his way with God," she seized him in all of his sartorial splendor and tossed him in the murky waters, where he remained in imminent peril of drowning. When Jiménez, accompanied by other splendidly vested lackeys, arrived on the scene and demanded an explanation for such unprecedented behavior, doña María made tart and speedy response, and then quipped that if anything more were said about the matter, others might find themselves in the same predicament. Recognizing their adversary as a women known throughout Córdoba as a female "Hector," the Inquisitor and his companions took hasty retreat, meanwhile offering thanks to God for having delivered them from her capable hands.[4]

Jiménez never forgave either this incident or the metrical needles of doña María's brother, and when in 1585 the latter made application for the prebendal stall of an uncle in the Holy Cathedral of Córdoba, both the Inquisitor and the Marqués de Priego conveniently recalled that there was a grandmother in the Góngora lineage whose blood was not clean; and they raised the same objection when in 1587 Luis's brother Juan applied to succeed to his father's office in the Holy Inquisition. Their opposition caused considerable and uncomfortable delay since the Marqués de Priego, so it is recorded, held such high standing in the Holy Office that his testimony sometimes was accepted even when it was false. Some poetic retribution might be seen, however, in the circumstances that after the marriage of doña María in 1587, some of the assets she had inherited from her Aunt Luisa fell to her lyrical brother, and in consequence the annuities based on a loan made by Alonso de Vargas thirty years previously to the present Marqués de Priego now came to be held jointly by the poet Luis de Góngora and the mestizo Garcilaso de la Vega.[5]

With the death of Luisa Ponce de León, Garcilaso, at the mature age of forty-seven, had succeeded to the bequest of his uncle with no encumberances other than the responsibility of his own household and the scant donations specified for his two aging aunts at Zafra. His Aunt

---

[4] Miguel Artigas, *Don Luis de Góngora y Argote*, pp. 103–104.

[5] Documents dated September 27 and October 1, 1586, respectively, Archivo de Protocolos de Córdoba, Oficio 30, Protocolo 73, fols. 1901–1908. See also marriage certificate dated May 24, 1587, Córdoba, Archivo de la Parroquia del Sagrario, Libro 3 de Matrimonios, fol. 24v.

Isabel, whose interests he had protected at Montilla, apparently was dead.[6] With his heritage cleared and his translation complete, he now could concentrate on his story of La Florida, and his eagerness to do so was increased by the diminishing strength of Gonzalo Silvestre. So whenever opportunity afforded, he collected his manuscripts, mounted his horse, and traveled to Las Posadas, a journey which under the circumstances must have required at least two days.

Meanwhile, Alonso de Herrera succeeded in bringing the mestizo's translation of the *Dialoghi* to the attention of Maximiliano de Austria, Chief Abbot of Alcalá la Real, a village which lay but a few leagues from Priego and thus not a great distance from Montilla. The Abbot in turn not only proffered his services but expressed a desire to know both the translation and the translator. This unanticipated response offered unlimited horizons for Garcilaso's ambitions, since he was fully conscious of the influence this noble man might offer in his behalf. A son of Leopoldo de Austria and thus a direct descendant of the great Emperor Maximiliano de Austria, the Abbot was a member of the King's Council and was much loved by the whole of the Imperial House. His ecclesiastical influence is attested to by the fact that he later became Bishop successively of Cádiz, of Jaén, and of Segovia, and afterward Archbishop of Santiago de Compostela. Moreover, as generally was true of the Austrian branch of the Hapsburgs, he was a man of many languages and great erudition. Hence he was capable of assimilating the refinements of the Hebrew philosopher and of receiving with sympathy what Garcilaso had to say about both La Florida and Peru.

Thus on September 18, 1586, Garcilaso addressed his royal benefactor in a lengthy letter which, after the customary rhetoric of flattery and obeisance, explained the origin of his ambition to translate and publish the dialogues of León Hebreo as well as the process followed and the care taken to preserve in his translation the tone and the cunning of the erudite Jew. Yet aware of the perils of these subtleties to the faith of the average reader, Garcilaso several times mentioned the boldness of his efforts as well as his inability to present them directly

---

[6] On July 16, 1586, Isabel's husband appeared as guardian of her children to authorize a collection from the property of Alonso de Vargas. Aurelio Miró Quesada y Sosa, *El Inca Garcilaso*, pp. 104–105.

to the King, and then with equal daring begged Maximiliano to serve as an intermediary and protector. But Garcilaso's ambition now had soared beyond the mere publication of the *Diálogos*, and he closed his letter with an expression of hope that under the same princely favor he might complete the weaving of his chronicle of La Florida and cast on the loom his story of Peru.

The response of Maximiliano de Austria had found Garcilaso with only a second draft of his *Diálogos* and in need of a third. Montilla afforded few scribes, and the best one available so mutilated the first section that the mestizo was forced to recopy it himself. In haste to take advantage of the Abbot's good will as well as to depart again for Las Posadas to continue work on his history of La Florida, now one-fourth completed, he left the remainder of the translation in the second draft and permitted Juan de Herrera to convey the whole to Maximiliano, along with a letter dated March 12, 1587. Herein he explained his delay and his desire to journey to Las Posadas and complete his story of La Florida while both he and the narrator were still living, since "one without the other will not be able to do anything." Again he mentioned both of his uncompleted histories and humbly acknowledged the boldness of his ambitions since he heretofore had not been concerned with books but with arquebuses and with the raising and breeding of horses. But, as he explained, it was better to record them poorly than to leave them unrecorded, and since they were histories he could afford a mediocrity of rhetoric not permitted in poetry. Yet a greater daring of Garcilaso might be read in the closing lines of his letter, when, in speaking of these histories, he declared: "I believe that the titles of the dedications are not against the royal ordinance, for though, as the same ordinance stipulates, there should be no understanding with the Royal House, the dedications were already made before the royal ordinance appeared." Could it be that Garcilaso now was about to reveal to Maximiliano that he already had dedicated his histories, as he eventually was to do, to the House of Braganza, recent rivals of the King for the throne of Portugal? Such a circumstance might account to some extent for the long delay in their publication.

Garcilaso's manuscript and letter reached the Abbott on June 17, 1587, and two days later the latter responded with hyperbolic grace mingled with caution. Though he thanked the chronicler for the favor of both words and works and suggested that Garcilaso's translation was superior to another he already had read, and though he agreed to receive all that came from Garcilaso's hands, he made no overt offer of protection for the mestizo's histories. Nevertheless, he did ask to keep the manuscript until the close of September, promising to return it at that time, and since there is no record of its return, he probably passed it on with his approval to the King and his Council.

And now as Garcilaso awaited the outcome of his translation and continued his account of La Florida, he was forced to turn his attention to the affairs of Montilla and contemplate some of the economic vexations of a nation again preparing for war. The annexation of Portugal had indeed placed the Catholic King at the head of a vast and far-flung empire, but it also had increased the jealousies and boldness of heretic and enemy nations. To sustain his multiple enterprises, Philip had continued to drain Peru of its lifeblood and its ore, but much of that precious metal was drawn off along the sea routes into the coffers of the taunting British Queen. In the early part of 1579 Sir Francis Drake, after raiding Callao in Peru, had craftily eluded the guardians of the Straits of Magellan, among them the chronicler Sarmiento de Gamboa, by sailing around the world, and on his return to England in 1580 with seven hundred and fifty thousand pounds of Spanish gold he had been knighted by a jubilant and grateful Queen. The insult was not lost on the Prudent King, and before long, mountainous vessels began to rise in the Bay of Cádiz. Then one day in 1586 the English "Dragon" slipped down from the Channel and, burning ten thousand tons of those proud ships, made a boast which was to become a shibboleth among English-speaking people—he had "singed the beard of the King of Spain."

Patiently Philip rebuilt his galleons. He would never forget the mushrooming flames at Cádiz, and he would never forgive the insults of a heretical queen and her royal privateer. He could not efface from his Catholic mind the divine legend that the gold and the heathens of the far reaches of the world were the heritage of the true spiritual heirs of Aaron and Jesse; and he could not admit to these messianic hosts the upstart Tudors. Worming through his mind were memories of a fateful day when he had saved from the scaffold a pale and fairhaired princess to whom, through the faithful Conde de Feria, he later had vainly offered his hand in marriage, and who now, as Queen of England, defied both the Pontiff at Rome and the most powerful King of all Christendom. This defiance was rendered even more intolerable when in February, 1587, Elizabeth permitted the head to be struck from Catholic Mary Stuart, in whom Philip had placed hopes. Meanwhile the Holy See had damned the English Queen and transferred her titles and rights and realms, just as it had transferred most of the realms of the Indies, to the King of Spain. It was time for another crusade, and to accomplish such, His Majesty could draw resources from the veins of Tahuantinsuyu, the golden vaults of the Midas Jews in the Low Countries, and a modicum, with stipulations, from the closely guarded treasury of Sixtus II. The bulk of the food, ships, horses, and men must be derived from Spain. Thus once more a plague of commissary officials was set to work and purveyors began to scour the land.

Over the years, taxes and donations for the King's defenses and crusades had proven exhausting for the cities and villages of Andalusia. Particularly offensive had been the system of demanding that caballeros contiosos be ready at all times to provide forces and keep them armed. Equally offensive were the levies made on grain, olive oil, and other commodities, for the Crown paid lower prices than customary, and often these payments were slow in coming, especially when there were delays in the arrival of gold from the Indies. Moreover, purveyors carried permits to search the domiciles of both lay and ecclesiastical residents, and frequently were prone to divert money into their own pockets, squeezing the ordinary people on the proverbial but realistic theory that "cries from the humble are not heard in Heaven."

As preparations for the Armada proceeded, quotas were sent to the Cabildo of Montilla, which, while awaiting the Commissioner, was to receive agitating reports from adjacent communities in the Priego demesne, among which was nearby Écija, where some of them held property and where an unprecedented scandal had arisen. For Miguel de Cervantes Saavedra, the King's purveyor at that village, far from being dishonest, had followed royal orders to the letter and seized stocks of bread and grain belonging to the parish of Santa Cruz as well as to the Dean and Cabildo of Seville. In consequence he was promptly excommunicated by the Archbishop's steward, and his little-respected name was posted by the Vicar of Écija on a bulletin outside the door of the village church. Moreover, this upstart purveyor had no sooner extricated himself from damnation by restoring the grain at Écija than he fell into similar difficulties at Castro del Río. For here, when the sacristan interferred, Cervantes committed the madness of placing the pious man under arrest. Immediately orders for excommunication came from Córdoba, and once more, as an immortal soul hung suspended over the flames of Hell, an immortal name was pilloried on a church door. The reckless purveyor promptly restored the confiscated grain and hastened to Seville to clear himself with the curate of souls. During the eight years that Cervantes served the King in the shabby office of purveyor he was embroiled constantly with the obstinate peasants and local officials, who, taking their cue from the prelates, sent out barrages of petitions and protests.[7]

Garcilaso had relatives and held annuities on property in Écija, and it was in Castro del Río that he had purchased Alonso, a slave whom he was to sell in the present year. He was well aware of the agitation in those villages, and in Montilla he had witnessed previous conscriptions of food, money, and men which had worked a particular hardship on the vassals of the lords of Priego. Furthermore, he was keenly remindful of the fact that he had received no reimbursement for his contribution in the suppression of the Moriscos; and whereas his participation in that war had represented the ardor of an alien youth, some of that ardor had vanished, and his recent inheritance undoubtedly had subjected him to the demands made upon caballeros contiosos. Thus when news reached Montilla that a Commissioner was en route to Córdoba to raise forces, Garcilaso on July 12, 1587, joined with the Cabildo in a bold petition asking that the commissioner be forbidden to enter Montilla and that the demands on caballeros contiosos be abolished. Then when the Cabildo chose Garcilaso,

---

[7] Sebastián Juan Arbó, *Cervantes*, pp. 151–158.

"because of his honesty, efficiency, and zeal for God," to represent them before the King in this delicate request, he agreed to do so without salary. Since the appeal required the sanction of the Marqueses de Priego, don Alonso and now his son Pedro, Garcilaso also was empowered to seek their approval; and he thereupon prepared himself, as he said, to carry on his mission "with zeal in the service of God and the Marqueses."[8] The immediate results can only be surmised, but the possibility is that the petition went no further than the lords of Priego, who would have been hesitant about contravening the zeal of their sovereign. But if the petition reached the King he ignored it; for only a short time later demands on the caballeros contiosos were increased and the village of Montilla was forced to contribute both men and food for a new crusade against heretics. But since the neighboring villages had been invited to join Montilla in its plea, it stands to reason that the purveyor Cervantes may have been discommoded with communications received by the people of Écija and Castro del Río from Captain Garcilaso de la Vega.

In July of 1588 a majestic half-moon of Spanish galleons, purged of prostitutes and blessed by the Pope's vicar, rode into the English Channel to begin a new crusade against a heretic nation. It was not a fleet of warships but a transport fleet carrying men who expected to fight on land; yet the battle was destined to be fought in the Channel —an encounter between great lumbering Spanish vessels and swift and easily maneuvered English craft, manned by men who knew not only the sea roads of England but also the channels of the world. And when at length the minions of Spain became aware of the hopelessness of their struggle, flight was impossible. For their massive galleons now became playthings of cruel and indifferent winds—first a gale from the south which was seized by the Furies and converted into a hurricane that bore Spanish vessels on to the north with such demoniac speed that the men of England abandoned the chase and returned to London. Soon the shores of Scotland and Ireland were strewn with bodies of shipwrecked cavaliers, and while eager natives stripped cadavers of clothing, the miserable remnants of Philip's Armada, un-

---

[8] Document dated July 19, 1587, Archivo Municipal de Montilla, Libro tercero de Actos Capitulares, 1562–1590, Legajo no. 431, fols. 307v–309v.

willing to risk fate again in the Channel, sailed around the heretic Isles and headed back sadly for the port of Santander. "God breathed and they were scattered," the jubilant English proclaimed on a medal struck for the occasion. Back in Seville, Cervantes wrote an apologetic apostrophe to the men of Spain and blamed the disaster on the implacable sea and the winds of heaven which sometimes "permit the enemy to raise its head a little." Any comments of Garcilaso on the fate of the Armada must be read into the suggestive maxims and proverbs which adorn his histories. But a passage which he soon was to insert in one of his chronicles suggests that he may have placed the source of the tragedy in the fact that the men of Spain had grown effete and in the circumstance that the bulk of the expense had been drained from the bleeding veins of Peru.[9] No speculations, however, were necessary for the Prudent but unwise King. When news of the humiliating fiasco reached Philip in the granite walls of the Escorial, he piously declared that for him to win was not God's will, concealed his grief, and, while his vassals clamored for revenge, turned to his customary duties, insisting still on supervising each detail of his government and each petition before his Councils.

In this dismal moment of defeat, two weeks before the Duke of Medina Sidonia led the crippled remnants of Philip's Armada back into Santander, there was brought to the attention of His Majesty the manuscript of "an Indian," a neo-Platonic treatise on universal love with a dedication that pledged loyalty to the Spanish sovereign and carried a plea for the men who had served Spain as well as for the natives of its richest possessions. Philip, it is hoped, read that dedication, though he may not have read the treatise itself since the document already carried the approval of his Council as well as that of the Holy Office.[10] The translation had been found to be "good, faithful, and true, and possessed of many qualities revealing great intellectual ability, scholarship and labor," and the worthy philosophy therein was not considered to be contrary to the faith. On September 7, 1588, at San Lorenzo, in a document addressed to "Captain Gar-

---

[9] Garcilaso, *Comentarios*, Pt. II, Bk. I, Chap. 7.
[10] All licenses and privileges are carried within the book.

cilaso Inga de la Vega," Philip licensed the printing and the sale for a period of ten years of a book entitled *La traducción del Indio de los tres diálogos de amor de León Hebreo*. With this act, the staunchest and most egoistic lay defender of the Roman Catholic faith approved circulation in the Spanish Kingdoms of a Peruvian Indian's translation of an exiled Jew's clever synthesis of Greek, Hebraic, Arabic, and Christian doctrines. The occasion was momentous.

More than a year was to elapse before the first printed sheets of Garcilaso's translation were checked, evaluated, and approved for distribution. It could be that the delay was occasioned by new inquisitorial objections, since Garcilaso apparently had not deleted the passages previously banned; but more than likely it was due to a financial uneasiness arising with the death of Alonso Fernández de Córdoba y Figueroa, Marqués de Priego, which occurred on March 10, 1589.[11] Apparently, however, there was no serious cause for delay, and the King's cedula, though it applied only to the translation, Garcilaso had taken as an indication that he could hope for the royal approval of his chronicles. Thus he made haste to complete his account of the De Soto story, and in late August or early September he once again set out for Las Posadas. It therefore would have been during these autumnal days and under the strict supervision of Gonzalo Silvestre that he brought to a close the first draft of the book he was to call *La Florida del Inca;* for on November 7, 1588, while still in this Andalusian village, he wrote the King that he was preparing for His Majesty a "clean" copy of this story and that he hoped his efforts would entice Philip's vassals to increase their honor and advantage and to serve their sovereign by conquering and populating the Kingdom of La Florida.

This second communication to the King was, in a sense, to become an appendage to Garcilaso's original dedication, but like the first its import soared beyond the limits of an obeisance or eulogy. It was a

---

[11] Document dated June 9, 1590, Archivo de Protocolos de Montilla, Escribano Andrés Capote, Año de 1590, sin foliar; Andrés de Morales y Padilla, *Historia de Córdoba*, Bk. III, Chap. 5, pp. 137v–146. Marcelino Menéndez y Pelayo, after comparing the three Spanish translations of the *Dialoghi*, declared that Garcilaso's was the most faithful to the thought of the author.

reiteration of his Indianism and of his yearning to serve with his pen the people of his native land. Not only did he aspire to set for them an example of what they themselves could do, but he wanted his efforts to be regarded by his sovereign as evidence of the capabilities of all the people of the New World. Thus he declared that as a mestizo he was offering his literary services in the name of both the Spaniards and Indians of Peru; and once more, in addition to mentioning his history of La Florida, he added that he was preparing for the Crown the most accurate account yet presented of the Incas in the days of their paganism.

For an Indian to make such claims and such a plea as Garcilaso made in his correspondence with both the King and Maximiliano was audacious, as the chronicler was quick to admit. Indeed, his communications reflect some past bitterness, not the least of which was his despair of historians who through ignorance or carelessness reported inaccurately. Yet they also reflect evidence of a lingering hope and a faith in the generosity and understanding of his sovereign, and within them is to be detected what now possibly was his supreme desire, a yearning for a royal nod which would make him a royal commentator, an official chronicler of the Indies. This was a privilege which less accurate and less qualified historians had enjoyed.

On December 22, 1589, Gonzalo de la Vega, Court scribe of the Royal Council, certified that each sheet of the printed translation had been evaluated and that the book could be sold; and in 1590, there came from the printing establishment of Pedro Madrigal at Madrid an edition bearing the title *La Traduzion del Indio de los Tres Dialogos de Amor de Leon Hebreo, hecha de Italiano en Español por Garcilasso Inga de la Vega, natural de la gran Ciudad del Cuzco, cabeza de los Reynos y Provincias del Piru.*[12] In addition to its dedication to *La Sacra Catolica Real Magestad del Rey don Felipe nuestro señor* it carried as prefatory material the supportive communications which Garcilaso had directed to and received from both Maximiliano and the King.

---

[12] "The translation of León Hebreo's three dialogues of love from Italian into Spanish by Garcilaso Inga de la Vega, a native of the great city of Cuzco, capital of the kingdoms and provinces of Peru."

Philip's immediate reaction to the mestizo's first publication, noted and reported by a friend at court, was described afterward by Garcilaso in a preface to his histories. When the little tome was placed in the hands of His Catholic Majesty, he summoned his "keeper of jewels" and gave an order: "Take care of this book for me," he said, "and when I come again to the Escorial, remind me that you have it. Make a memorandum of the fact and do not forget." And when Philip did pass again to his great palace, he summoned the Prior of the Royal Convent of San Gerónimo and gave a second command. "Examine this book, Padre," he said, "and consider it as something novel from Peru."[13]

Garcilaso's translation of León Hebreo could stand on its own merit, but since there had been other translations of the *Dialoghi* into Castilian, one can readily suspect that the genial reception of this one was due at least in part to the fact that it was a "first fruit" from Peru and the labor of an Indian. Many in Renaissance Spain would not be impressed so much by the quality of the accomplishment as by the fact that anything at all literary could be achieved by an Indian; and some surely would attribute the achievement to the presence of Castilian blood in the man's veins. Garcilaso's consciousness of this fact possibly accounts for his identification of himself as a mestizo, an Indian and an Inca. And it does not detract from the genius of the translator to believe that he had anticipated this circumstance when he determined to emphasize both his nationality and his race on the title page of his book and in the dedicatory letters which accompanied it. He knew how to turn adversity into advantage, and he was aware that a first fruit or a novelty always carried an especial appeal. Afterward, when his literary efforts had caught the attention of the humanist, Francisco Murillo, he responded to an invitation to visit the great maestro. Timidly entering the chambers of this learned antiquarian, who lay abed nursing the gout, the mestizo was saluted with a dyspeptic though not unsympathetic query. "An Antarctic Indian," Murillo exclaimed, "born in the New World underneath our own hemisphere and suckled in the general language of the Indians of Peru, what

[13] See Prólogo to Garcilaso's *Comentarios*, Pt. II.

business of his is it to serve as an interpreter between Italians and Spaniards? And since he has aspired to do so, why did he not select any book other than that which Italians esteem most and Spaniards understand least?"

Summoning his courage, Garcilaso gave a quixotic reply which appealed to the genial spirit of the old man. It was the temerity of a soldier, he declared, whose greatest deeds are accomplished in the same spirit; for such actions, if successful, are esteemed as valiant, whereas, if not, they are simply regarded as the work of a fool. [14]

On the surface Garcilaso may appear to have accepted his Indian stigma in good humor, but, if so, it was a wry humor with undertones of pride and defense. In his full-mouthed identification of himself he in general was careful to emphasize that he was not a mere Indian but a mestizo and an Inca; and when he referred to himself as an Indian, he did so with an ironic undertone of accusation against man's presumption in assigning intellect and genius to any particular race. And he continued to proclaim, as he already had proclaimed to Maximiliano and the King, that any talent he may have displayed in his translation of León Hebreo was to be regarded as representative of the potentialities of his Peruvian compatriots. Within a year after its publication, copies of his *Diálogos* were being conveyed to Peru, where its eventual translation into Quechua gave Garcilaso opportunity to boast further of the eagerness of Peruvians to learn.[15]

The whole of Garcilaso's *Diálogos* and at least a first draft of his account of the De Soto expedition were written during his residence at Montilla. But by now circumstances had arisen which impelled him to abandon Montilla for the more promising literary environment of Córdoba. Already in the latter city he would have encountered scholars and ecclesiastics who offered sympathy and encouragement for his projects; and much of the stimulation he had received at Montilla

[14] *Ibid.* The term "Antarctic" was commonly used in the sixteenth century to designate people who lived below the equitorial line and to distinguish between North and South American Indians.

[15] *Ibid.* Pt. II, Prólogo; Miró Quesada y Sosa, *El Inca Garcilaso*, p. 192. Six copies were recorded in the inventory of the vessel *San Gabriel* when it sailed from San Lúcar de Barrameda on December 24, 1591. No Quechuan translation has been found.

would have passed with the two Marquesas, both of whom now were dead. As early as 1587 the marquisate had fallen to Pedro Fernández de Córdoba y Figueroa, who, in that year, at the age of twenty-six, had married Juana de Zúñiga y de Ribera, proud daughter of the Duque de Alcalá and granddaughter of Hernán Cortés, conqueror of Mexico. Alonso Fernández de Córdoba, the former Marqués-Consort may already have passed to Madrid before his death in March of 1589. These men were proud Figueroas, and it is doubtful if their piety, like that of the Marquesas, was ever of sufficient strength to prevent their rankling over the fact that a debt incurred in a rash moment had left the farmlands of Montalbán encumbered with liens now held in part by a kinsman who was an Indian. Alonso de Vargas had proven wise in having that debt ratified by the honest old Marquesa-Condesa, for with the passing of years her heirs apparently regarded the obligation with diminishing respect. Such a shift in atmosphere perhaps inspired the mestizo's shift of residence to Córdoba, which occurred more than likely in 1590 and certainly by October 11, 1591, at which time he is known to have disposed of an interesting portion of his heritage, his uncle's house in the Calle del Capitán at Montilla. [16] But it would have been given even greater impetus by the brightening literary horizons which came with his first publication.

No records show that the King gave any encouragement to the mestizo's long-range ambitions other than the faint hope that came with approval of the translation, or that Garcilaso ever sent Philip the promised "clean" copy of *La Florida*. The latter intent, however, could have been delayed by Garcilaso's ever-present propensity to add and correct, a propensity which he would have felt especially in the case of *La Florida* since he was participating in a species of reporting that demanded much caution. He was reporting from hearsay. Even after he had brought the story to a close with an account of the survivors of the expedition, he had added a chapter which told of the religious who had perished in La Florida before 1568. Certainly at some time during the months immediately succeeding the comple-

[16] Archivo de Protocolos de Montilla, Escribano Gerónimo Pérez, Año de 1591, fols. 482–484. This document specifically states that Garcilaso had inherited the house from his uncle.

tion of his first draft and before he could despair of royal favor, there came to his hands two manuscripts which he felt should be collated with and at least partially incorporated into the story he had received from Silvestre.

The first of these documents, no more than ten pages of a very diffuse and legal style of handwriting, was forwarded to Garcilaso personally by Alonso de Carmona, a resident of Priego, who had survived the De Soto expedition to La Florida and afterward settled in Potosí, where he sired two mestizos. Returning to his native Priego about 1572, he had become a prosperous producer of wine and silk and at one time served as alcalde ordinario of the village. Since the town of Priego lay within the same marquisate as Montilla, Garcilaso may have encountered this man previously in Spain, if not in Peru; and though Carmona played no role in the story drawn from Silvestre, the latter would have known him well. Carmona had written his scanty account of the De Soto expedition, which he called *Peregrinación a la Florida y principales sucesos de su conquista,* solely to entertain his friends, and on hearing of the Garcilaso project, surely through the Herreras of Priego, he had determined to reveal to the mestizo what he himself had experienced. Just when Garcilaso received the Carmona manuscript is not known, though it definitely was in his hands by 1591, since by March of that year Carmona was dead. [17]

It appears fairly certain also that the Carmona document came to Garcilaso after he had left Montilla, for only two days after receiving it he encountered, while browsing in the shop of a Cordovan printer, a second manuscript of eight and a half compactly written pages, a moth- and rat-eaten document which told of the same magnificent expedition. This had been written by Juan Coles of Zafra, another eyewitness and survivor, at the request of Friar Pedro de Aguado, a Franciscan who, after collecting accounts of the first explorations in the Windward Islands, Vera Cruz, Tierra Firme, Darién, and other provinces of those regions, had abandoned his manuscripts and departed to perform other duties in the services of his order. [18]

---

[17] Garcilaso, *La Florida del Inca,* Proemio al Letor; José de la Torre y del Cerro, "Alonso de Carmona," *Adarve,* Octubre 31, 1954, p. 8.
[18] Garcilaso, *La Florida del Inca,* Proemio al Letor.

The fact that the names of neither Juan Coles nor Alonso de Carmona had appeared in Silvestre's account indicates that neither were men of particular distinction, but Silvestre could have vouched for their authenticity, and their very lack of distinction gives a new dimension, a less poetic perspective, to Garcilaso's story. Much to his surprise and delight, Garcilaso found that both accounts coincided with what he already had written; and he realized that by utilizing them he could claim the authority of at least three reliable eyewitnesses. And now, while occupied with the incorporation of this new material, he received much needed encouragement from the famed humanist and historian, Ambrosio de Morales.[19]

Morales long since was cognizant of the existence if not the literary ambitions of the Peruvian. The father of the humanist had served many years in the house of the Priegos, and he himself was well acquainted with both the parents and grandparents of Luisa Ponce de León. But it surely was to some extent the novelty of encountering such genius in a native of Peru that first brought Garcilaso to the personal attention of this great patriarch of Andalusian letters who, after having attained eminence at the University of Alcalá, was residing again at Córdoba. An ascetic who early had insured himself permanently against worldly temptations by self-castration, Morales long had devoted his pen to the preservation of antiquities. Interested in the Latin foundations of Castilian, he was none the less reluctant to glorify the Castilian vulgate and had declared that Castiglione's "courtier" discoursed no better in Italy where he was born than in Spain where Boscán had exhibited him so admirably well. The rendition of León Hebreo from Tuscan into Castilian by a man whose native tongue was Quechua could not have failed to capture the linguistic interests of Morales, but he would have been no less interested in the mestizo's knowledge of the antiquities as well as the contemporary events of the New World. Writing later of the success of a visit with Morales, Garcilaso remarked proudly: "I had the privilege of kissing his hands, and he honored me to the extent of adopting me as his son and accepting my work as his own."

[19] Eugenio Asensio, "Dos cartas desconocidas del Inca Garcilaso," *Nueva Revista de Filología Hispánica*, Año VII, Nos. 3–4, 1953, pp. 583–593.

Just how many of Garcilaso's manuscripts Morales saw is debatable, but it is certain that he was entrusted with a fourth of the manuscript of *La Florida*. He could have been of tremendous assistance in many respects to a novice chronicler, for since 1570 he had served as royal historiographer to the Crown of Castile. But whatever visions the mestizo may have harbored as a protégé of the famed antiquarian and historian were cut short, for by 1591 Ambrosio de Morales also was dead. "God carried him away," Garcilaso lamented the following year, "when I had most need of him." And in the same letter which carried this statement he spoke of the lack of gratitude on the part of a certain prince and a want of appreciation on the part of his sovereign.

Two years had sped by since the publication of Garcilaso's *Diálogos de amor* and seven since he first laid before the Crown plans for his chronicles of the Indies. The translation Philip apparently continued to regard as a first fruit and a novelty; the plea for recognition and further protection he apparently found it convenient to ignore. But Philip had grown cautious about the circulation of records concerning the activities of Spain in the New World, and his archives gradually were accumulating valuable reports and chronicles which were to remain in oblivion until long after his death. His conscience was as sick as had been that of his father, but the conscience of a king who ruled a troubled realm and needed gold often had to be left unattended. He was apprehensive of histories that inflamed conquerors or strengthened the pretentions of their progeny; and he feared histories that substantiated the claims of Indians. He had curbed the circulation of López de Gómara and Fernández; and somewhere, somehow, the manuscripts of Cieza dealing with the conquest as well as those of Gutiérrez de Santa Clara, Bernal Díaz, and Sarmiento de Gamboa had been allowed to remain in oblivion. And always there were the perils attending the spread of the "black legend," though the unpublished manuscripts of Las Casas no longer offered an immediate threat, since on his death in 1566 that zealous nonagenerian had ordered that they not be published for another forty years. These historians had received scant rewards for their labors and all now were dead except Sarmiento, who in 1590, in spite of his signal services in the establishment of outposts along the Straits of Magellan, was left by the Crown to pay his own ransom from Huguenot captors. Again, all of these men had been Spaniards and had written under some kind of official protection. What hope, then, could a native Peruvian and a mestizo entertain for royal favor? To Philip it had been worth the novelty for this Indian to do an exercise in translation, but it was a different matter for an Indian to comment on the progress of Spanish conquest, especially at a time when the light of the realm was fading. Philip had awakened to the dangers but not to the value of such a perspective, and he already may have been made aware that Garcilaso had a tendency to augment the pretensions not only of Indians but sometimes of the wrong Spaniards. Moreover, he surely could not have been unmindful of the fact that this mestizo's own pretensions had been denied at court on the basis of what other historians had said. Be that as it may, when in 1592 Philip named a new historiographer of the Indies, he chose a learned and experienced historian, Antonio de Herrera y Tordesillas, and provided him with every facility for pursuing his researches. Yet Herrera, like López de Gómara, had never set foot in the New World.

License to print and sell his rendition of León Hebreo for a period of ten years ostensibly was the sole gesture of recognition Garcilaso was ever to receive from the Prudent King. So as the days passed and he labored with his chronicles, his lingering illusions slowly faded. The pain he had experienced at Madrid in 1563 he could attribute to Lope García and the careless historians; and the social rebuffs he had received in Spain he could attribute to some of the Figueroas and a decadent code of nobility. But his long-festering disillusionment, which for some time had been fed by the polemics of past and contemporary humanists and especially by the soothing philosophy of the famed Jew, now encompassed "Heads of State." He had made his last appeal to Philip II as well as his first and last dedication to a Spanish sovereign; and as the fabric of his histories spread, they took on increasingly ironic subtleties when depicting the temporal overlords of Spain. He had painfully emerged from the cocoon of enchantment which in his earlier years had been woven so tightly about him from the varicolored silks of tradition, myth and fable.

CHAPTER FIFTEEN

THE LULL WHICH CAME with the defeat of the Armada had served to rid Andalusia temporarily of irksome commissioners; but at the same time it had left certain royal purveyors unemployed, among them Miguel de Cervantes Saavedra. Thus by 1589, while still attempting to resolve his affairs at Écija, Cervantes had determined to seek his fortune in the Indies, and in 1590 he drew up a petition detailing the past services of himself and kin, declaring that he had been among those recommended for favor by don Juan de Austria, and asking for a post at Cartagena, Guatemala, Nueva Granada, or La Paz. One month later this petition was examined by the Crown and filed with the scribbled note that the supplicant should seek some post in Spain. In consequence, Cervantes soon found himself reinstated in the tedious office of a purveyor and by December, 1591, he was foraging for the King at Montilla.[1]

To the disappointment of scholars, no records show any definite personal contact between Cervantes and Garcilaso, and so far as is known, neither has referred to the other in his works, unless Cervantes

---

[1] See documents dated December 2 and 3, 1591, Archivo de Protocolos de Montilla, Escribano Andrés Capote, Año de 1591, fols. 1551–1551v and 1553; also the Amazúa y Mayo edition of *El Casamiento engañoso y El coloquio de los perros,* pp. 171–177. Documents show Garcilaso listed as a resident of Montilla in 1591, 1592, and 1593, and since he still held property in Montilla he would have been subject to the demands of the commissary there.

had the Peruvian at least partially in mind when he quipped that but
three grains of Italian were necessary for an understanding of the
erotic disquisitions of León Hebreo. But it seems incredible that their
paths should not have crossed, either in Córdoba or in one of those
several towns of the Marquisate of Priego where Garcilaso held annuities that would subject him to the demands of the King's purveyor.
Already in *La Galatea* Cervantes had plagiarized some of the *Dialoghi*
for the complaints of a lovesick shepherd; so surely in 1591, when he
came to Montilla to negotiate with the Cabildo for wheat, barley, and
chickpeas, his attention would have been drawn to the phenomenon of
an Indian who was a relative of the ruling Marqués and who had successfully converted these Tuscan dialogues into Castilian. Certainly at
one point Cervantes was aware of the existence of Garcilaso, for in his
posthumously published *Persiles y Sigismunda* he ostensibly utilized a
description of the premarital sexual initiations found in Garcilaso's
history of the Incas; and but for the widespread and tenacious roots of
the scene upon which he focused his satire, one might be tempted to
believe that sometime and somewhere during the inception or composition of *Don Quixote* he caught glimpses of the unpublished manuscript of *La Florida*. Yet though the person of Garcilaso does not appear in the pages of Cervantes, both the people and the scene they each
had known at Montilla are to be observed in *El coloquio de los perros*,
narrative dialogues which constitute one of Cervantes' *Novelas ejemplares*. These were far from the Arcadian polemics of Lenio and Tirsi
in *La Galatea* or the neoclassic disquisitions of Filon and Sofia in the
Dialoghi; for in the tradition of the *perro sabio*, or wise dog, which
Garcilaso had treated with some credulity in *La Florida*, they represent
ironical sidelights thrown upon Spanish life and character by Cipión
and Berganza, two dogs endowed with the gift of both human insight
and speech. "In the course of our march, we came to Montilla, home of
that great and famous Christian, the Marqués de Priego, lord of the
houses of Aguilar and Montilla," Berganza remarked to Cipión, and
then this astute mongrel launched into a hilarious, erotic story of the
famed La Camacha, who in her abominations had not overlooked the
grandees of Priego; and in doing so, he unrolled a colorful vignette of

the little village which for thirty years had provided Garcilaso a comfortable haven.

Some question arises as to which of the Marqueses the articulate canine referred, first, because in this instance it is not easy to determine how much acid Cervantes was mixing with his ink, and again, because of the amount of time which elapsed between his unhappy experiences in the Priego demesne and the publication of his *Novelas ejemplares*. By 1613, when these stories first appeared in print, the lord of Priego was the sixth Marqués, a deaf-mute who was but an infant when Cervantes came to Montilla. In 1611 Garcilaso had praised this young Marqués in print for his devoutness and Christian virtues, and in a manuscript he never published he had paid the same tribute to this man's grandmother and her grandmother in turn, both marquesas de Priego. But pious endorsements often were awarded to those of the exalted who adhered with sufficient ostentation to the basic etiquette of the established faith, and some of the great, as Cervantes well knew, wore the tribute with an uneasy conscience. Thus, though all the lords of Priego dutifully gave outward signs of sanctimony, the master satirist no doubt had in mind the fifth Marqués, Pedro Fernández de Córdoba, since he held a high office in the Holy Inquisition at Córdoba and may have been responsible for burdening the immortal purveyor with a temporary excommunication.

Pedro Fernández de Córdoba provided a fair target for irony, and some significance is to be read in the fact that though Garcilaso at some time or other offered printed tributes to this man's grandmother, father, mother, and son, he paid no such honor to the proud Marqués himself. But of all the lords of Priego this fifth Marqués appears to have been the most reluctant to respond to the impositions on the farmlands of Montalbán, now held jointly by Garcilaso and Luis de Góngora. On assuming his title he had ignored payment of annuities, and by June of 1590 Garcilaso was contemplating a suit against the Priego estate. Yet when by the close of the following year all arrears had been paid, he was sufficiently encouraged to bargain with Góngora for his shares in the imposition. The purchase was made on December 31, 1591, at which time Garcilaso parted with six thousand six hundred reales of gold and silver escudos and doblones; but since this was considerably less than the amount demanded, Garcilaso was left exposed to future economic pressure from the proud and dyspeptic poet.[2]

Much can be written and much has been written about the economic struggle of Garcilaso from this time on until the close of his life. Yet ironically his struggle seems not to have been that of an impoverished mestizo seeking to gain property, but that of a man attempting to collect rents and tributes on what appears to be a somewhat vast, scattered, and assorted amount of property which he owed primarily to his good fortune. There is a plethora of documents revealing his issuing powers to collectors and instituting suits, all for the purpose of reaping profits from rent houses, shops, orchards, vineyards, and pasturelands in the vicinity of both Montilla and Córdoba.[3] To ignore these documents is to miss much of the background of the routine existence of a man of estate in Spain, as well as that aspect of the Inca's nature which enabled him to cope with the economic eccentricities and intricacies of what, but for his already lengthy residence, he might have considered an alien land. Moreover, in these documents one can see reflected many of the non-literary and non-ecclesiastic associations of the chronicler—men who ranged in caste from the lowliest tinker to lords of the land. It suffices to say, however, that because the Inca Garcilaso was now a man of considerable property, his life henceforth was to be entangled with those vexations which accompany ownership—vexations which were to rob him of some of the time and leisure and health requisite for literary pursuits. It is true that during the remainder of his life he complained often of the abuses of "Lady Fortune," but considering the extent of his assets one must regard his complaints as springing from sources more emotional than material.

Garcilaso was settled now, at least temporarily, in some rent houses in the narrow winding Calle de Las Cabezas in the district of Santa

---

[2] See three writs dated December 31, 1591, Archivo de Protocolos de Córdoba, Oficio 22, Protocolo 41, fols. 2487v–2489, 2493–2499; also document dated August 16, 1592, Archivo de Protocolos de Montilla, Escribano Juan Díaz, fols. 547v–549.

[3] For the vast majority of the published Garcilaso manuscripts, see José de la Torre y del Cerro, *El Inca Garcilaso de la Vega*, and Raúl Porras Barrenechea, *El Inca Garcilaso en Montilla*.

María.[4] There were occasional journeys back to Montilla and others down the dusty road to Las Posadas to recapture still what he could from the ailing Silvestre, whose days were ebbing fast. In 1592, after receiving an additional grant from the Crown and after demanding that his body when placed in the sepulcher be resplendently armed, the gallant old adventurer expired. To his nephew, Alonso Díaz de Belcázar, he left the bulk of his estate; to a convivial friend, Diego de Córdoba, he left his well-tempered sword of Sahagún the Elder; to the daughter of the crone at Montilla who had pitied his frailty and directed him to Las Posadas he left considerable gifts, including a dowry; and to the mestizo Garcilaso, who since 1552 had responded to his beguilements, he left a legacy of priceless data and an ever-enduring inspiration, but along with them notes of obligation to the extent of eight hundred ducats.[5] To the world, he left the most picturesque of all accounts of a courageous journey through the vast regions of La Florida. Woven through it is the old cavalier's most splendid eulogy. He himself had dictated it to his Peruvian amanuensis, who treated it with the warmth and sympathy it deserved.

Garcilaso had succeeded in drawing from Silvestre not only authentication for much of his proposed story of Peru but also reliable eyewitness accounts of De Soto's explorations north of Mexico. Yet in spite of efforts to place the latter story under the protection of the powerful, he had failed to find a suitable sponsor. Maximiliano de Austria apparently had ignored his plea, and the loss of Ambrosio de Morales had terminated hopes for assistance from this influential literary figure. It may be, however, that before death Morales helped to bring the Peruvian to the attention of Juan Fernández Franco, a highly respected antiquarian who is known to have dedicated at least two manuscripts to Pedro Fernández de Córdoba, Marqués de Priego, and who in 1593 wrote Garcilaso a letter praising his translation of León Hebreo. Seizing the opportunity, Garcilaso on December 31 dis-

---

[4] Writ dated May 12, 1592, Archivo de Protocolos de Córdoba, Oficio 22, Protocolo 42, fols. 1117v–1118.

[5] Archivo de Protocolos de Córdoba, Oficio 22, Protocolo 43, fols. 396v–397; Protocolo 46, fols. 1548v–1549; Protocolo 54, April 29, 1599, sin foliar; also Oficio 29, Protocolo 35, fols. 505–507.

patched a reply in which he bewailed his failure to receive favor at court, lamented the loss of the protection of Morales, begged Fernández now to assume that role, and promised to send him within the coming year a copy of the manuscript of *La Florida*, which he declared to be completed and only in need of a scribe to make it readable. Fernández may have read the manuscript of *La Florida*, since in a subsequent letter he spoke of his desire to travel to the Indies, but there is as yet no indication that he ever offered to serve as the mestizo's sponsor.[6]

Meanwhile, Garcilaso had been revising the annotations to his *Diálogos* with an eye to reprinting. The continued popularity of León Hebreo's work had been made manifest by a number of reissues in Italian and by translations into several languages; and by now Garcilaso, although he may not have seen them, would have been cognizant of the existence of the two Castilian versions which had preceded his own. Moreover, in 1593 news also must have reached him that the Montesa translation had been indexed at Zaragoza and that the *Dialoghi* had been forbidden to circulate there except in its expurgated Latin form.[7] Almost half the time allotted him for the printing and selling of his own translation had elapsed, and he was well aware of the perils it faced because of its subtle and heretical philosophy. On June 1, 1594, he for some reason transferred his license to print and sell to Francisco de Garay and Gerónimo de Bercedo, residents at court, at the same time giving them authority to pocket whatever might accrue from the new printing.[8] Since the translation now showed some revisions, it would have demanded new inspections; and since this edition was never to appear, it is conceivable that the Holy Inquisitors already were initiating plans to ban the Garcilaso translation, as they eventually did. Meanwhile, the mestizo had revived his old dream of presenting to Spain a cleansed and spiritualized version of the *Lecciones de Job* by recalling the long-expurgated

---

[6] Eugenio Asensio, "Dos cartas desconocidas del Inca Garcilaso," *Nueva Revista de Filología Hispánica*, Año VII, Nos. 3–4, 1953, pp. 583–593.

[7] *Index Librorum Prohibitorum Ac Expurgandorum Novissimus*, Vol. II, pp. 809–812.

[8] Archivo de Protocolos de Córdoba, Oficio 22, Protocolo 45, fols. 1109–1110.

passages for someone capable of the task. In 1593, he found just such a man at Córdoba, the Jesuit Juan de Pineda, a recognized authority on the Book of Job. A collaboration was arranged for the holidays of 1594, but before plans could be realized, Garcilaso was forced to leave the city to collect rents and annuities, and when he returned Pineda's services were no longer available.[9] Several years later Pineda published a commentary on the book of Job, but the profane imputations of Garcí Sánchez de Badajoz were never removed from the *Lecciones* and the bold Indian was left with his dream.

By continuing to tamper with supect books as well as with liberal concepts, Garcilaso revealed a certain defiance which was not always to go unnoticed. "Fortune bestows its favors on the daring, as they are the ones who merit it," he had written in his *La Florida*; and he had persistently colored this chronicle with comments which risked the censure of both Church and State. For instance, at some time during its composition he had inserted a potentially dangerous passage disclosing Inca concepts of corporeal resurrection and immortality and then added another which questioned laws that demanded the punishment of women taken in adultery while making no provision for men guilty of the same offense. "It must be that always and in all nations such laws are rigorous in regard to women and favorable in regard to men," he wrote concerning the latter subject, "for as a dowager of this bishopric whom I have known once said: 'Men and not women made these laws because they feared the offense; had women made them, they would have been ordained in a different manner.' " Neither this disclosure of an ancient concept of immortality nor this early appeal for a single sex standard was pleasing to some Jesuits, and in describing the passages Garcilaso later declared with indignation: "All of this account I wrote in my history of La Florida and then removed it from its appropriate place by order of the venerable Fathers of the Company of Jesus, Miguel Vázquez de Padilla, a native of Seville, and Gerónimo de Prado, a native of Ubeda, who demanded that I do so; and it was with reluctance and under pressure of certain tyrannical acts. I now am inserting it again in its proper place so that the edifice will not lack so

---

[9] Garcilaso, *La descendencia de Garcí Pérez de Vargas*.

important a stone."[10] Both passages eventually appeared in the published version of *La Florida*.

But the daring of the Indian is even more pronounced in the
maxims, proverbs, and ambiguous and even concrete allusions which,
apparently during the lifetime of Philip II, he continued to weave into
the context of *La Florida*. Such passages came dangerously near to
questioning the divine honor and justice of royal administrators. For
instance, he may have been pointing a scornful finger at the policy of
Philip in suppressing a revolt in Aragón when he spoke of those sovereigns who "violated the laws and statutes of their kingdoms and,
without regard for person or rank or for sworn and promised faith,
handed over those who had not offended them in exchange for those
who had, solely for the purpose of satisfying their anger." Again, he
could have been alluding to the despotism utilized in repressing an
insurrection in Flanders when he wrote that "princes, kings, and monarchs should take care not to permit the passage of laws so rigorous or
the election of judges so severe that vassals and subjects are forced to
lose respect for them, deny the obedience due them, and seek the government of other princes"; and he continued with a touch of irony,
"Through sacred and profane histories, both ancient and modern, our
experience has taught us that no kindom rebels against its sovereign
because of his good treatment, but because of his harshness, cruelty,
and tyranny as well as an excess of taxes and tributes."

More suggestive still is an annotation to his description of the generosity of an infidel cacique, Mucozo: "It suffices to represent the
magnanimity of an infidel so that princes of the Faith may make efforts
to imitate and if possible surpass him, not in infidelity, as some do who
are undeserving of the title of Christians, but in virtue and similar ex-
cellences; for being of more lofty estate, they are under greater obligations." But in another passage, which some have thought is an allusion
to Philip's despicable treatment of the Duque de Alba, after the annexation of Portugal, the Indian reached a summit which put him even
closer to those who were seriously questioning "reason of state."

[10] Garcilaso, *Los comentarios reales*, Pt. I, Bk. II, Chap. 7; *La Florida del Inca*,
Bk. III, Chap. 34.

When tyrannous princes and powerful men feel, with or without reason, that they have been offended, they are seldom or never wont to grant the favor of reconciliation and pardon that generous spirits deserve. On the contrary, it would seem that the more such a person insists on his virtues, the more he offends. Therefore, it appears to me in my poor judgment that he who sees himself in such a predicament should go, for the love of God, and beg his food wherever he may find it rather than persist in the service of this kind of master; for regardless of what miracles he may succeed in performing, they will not be sufficient to restore him to the grace of the one he has angered.

The danger of the quoted passages from *La Florida* as well as others equally censorious possibly lay in the fact that taken out of context they could be interpreted as a criticism of contemporary events in Spain; yet it was equally easy to interpret them as oblique references to events which had passed in Peru, an account of which Garcilaso concurrently was preparing. Because of the lapse of at least fifteen years between his announcement of the completed first draft of *La Florida* and its publication, it is hardly possible to determine when revisions and additions were made. Certainly to give autobiographical significance to provocative passages it is necessary to assume that they originated with the amanuensis and not with his sources. To accept literally Garcilaso's published statement that Silvestre saw and approved the whole of *La Florida* is to assume that such passages were present before the latter's death in 1592. Nevertheless, they do represent the mature mestizo after court disappointments and humanistic reasoning had completely cleared his eyes of illusions concerning the Spanish concept of nobility and had renewed his faith in the virtues of a New World social milieu as well as the nobility of the pagans of La Florida and Peru. And they surely were present when he was engaged in composing an account of his rich Spanish lineage, an account which asserted his own claims to hidalguía.

Today in the archives of Madrid there is preserved an exquisitely written little manuscript, a rare document from the hand of the Inca Garcilaso, which bears the title, inserted by another hand, of *La Descendencia de Garcí Pérez de Vargas*. Though internal evidence indicates that the document was in progress in 1594, it is dated "From Córdoba, from this poor rent house, the 5th of May of 1596." It is of interest not only because of what it discloses of the lineage of the Inca Garcilaso but also because it reveals that he now was seeking to place his *La Florida* under the protection of Garcí Pérez de Vargas, a direct descendant of the legendary Vargas ancestor and at present head of the Estremaduran branch of the Vargas family. But this document is of equal significance because of what it discloses of the mestizo's emotional development and his attitude concerning his position in the contemporary Spanish scene. Internal evidence supports without question that it was intended as a portion of a previously written preface for *La Florida*.[11]

There is little reason to believe that Garcilaso's earliest manuscript preface to *La Florida* was not essentially the same as that which in 1605 appeared in print. The content of the latter, with some exceptions, parallels what he already had communicated elsewhere to Philip II, and it contains nothing that could have gravely offended a sovereign. It gives details of origin, purpose, sources, and plan, lists those works accomplished and those in progress, and makes a plea for understanding and consideration. Moreover, it bears the complaint which always dominated his psyche, having been generated in his early years by vanquished Inca relatives. He is the man of pride and quality who has been denied recognition by what he euphemistically terms the vicissitudes of fortunes, and who consoles himself with platitudes which he could but faintly have accepted. Buffeted by fate, and saved from a worse evil by adversity, he has resigned himself to the triumph of a moral victory and now in a spirit of altruism hopes for no more than the success of his literary efforts.

But the fragment addressed in 1596 to Garcí Pérez de Vargas and planned as an intercalation, by its very nature adds depth to the picture of the mestizo's emotions. For while revealing still a resignation in despair and a spiritual humility, it discloses pride in defense and in no manner can it be regarded as an indication that Garcilaso had re-

---

[11] La Sala de Manuscritos de la Biblioteca Nacional de Madrid, No. 18–109. This fragmentary manuscript begins with a clause of a broken sentence, "que voy ya más en la mitad," and some of the sentences which follow are to be found in the printed pages of Garcilaso's *La Florida*.

linquished his yearning for status and favor or that he attributed his adverse experiences wholly to the mere whimsies of an impersonal Fortune. Its detailed catalogue of the noble descendants of an ancient knight famed in classic chronicles, though ostensibly designed to flatter a haughty relative and prospective patron, was designed also to proclaim the noble lineage of an aspiring mestizo. Furthermore, it carried an undertone of social indictment which at times linked his relatives to a decadent system.

For here, as elsewhere, the writer is the noble Indian lamenting the shabby treatment he has received and professing to find comfort in forgetfulness and indifference while actually luxuriating to some extent in self-pity. Over him still hangs the memory of the debasement at Madrid and he plays the familiar refrain of the inadequately recognized virtues of himself, his father, and his uncles in the service of the Crown. Within his heart rankle the social slights he has received as well as his failure to clarify his nobility even in the eyes of some of his kinsmen. In one instance, undoubtedly in reference to the lords of Feria and Priego, he declared point-blank that certain of his Figueroa relatives had refused to recognize him because he was an "Antarctic Indian." He was mentioning these kinsmen, he said, not because of a yearning to honor himself thereby, since such actions betrayed a want of taste in the humble, but merely because God had made them his kinsmen and he wished to acknowledge them as natural lords and to serve them, not as a mercenary, but as one born to their lineage. And though with customary humility he admitted that it was an impertinence for an Indian to inform such an exalted individual as Garcí Pérez of his lineage, he made it clear without hesitancy that he too was a blood descendant of a mutual ancestor who several centuries previously had earned the honor which the Vargas family enjoyed. Then he added with a touch of irony that since nobility does not exist where virtue and noble deeds are lacking, one should not boast of such descendancy unless willing to emulate the virtues of such an ancestor.

In cataloguing his Spanish family, Garcilaso gave ample praise to those whom he felt deserved it, but he remained silent about a number whom he might very well have mentioned. In most of his records he has revealed an Incaic propensity to consign to oblivion things which were distasteful to him, or which might defame, and not the least of the autobiographical dimensions of his *Descendencia* are to be detected in his omissions. For instance, the manuscript discloses that at one point he had included a passage which he later attempted to delete: "The vile and low men who have no regard for their relatives," he wrote, "who, because of their despicable baseness and infamous greed, have become unworthy of this succession and similar honors, not having respect for either the nobility of their fathers and grandfathers or the cleanness of their blood, it is pardonable to erase from the descendancy and condemn to perpetual oblivion as infamous and wicked creatures, lest they stain with their dishonor that which in itself is most resplendent, cleanness of blood and nobility."

This passage may have had reference to some of the Mendozas, who had not been careful about their racial purity, and its author may have felt it untimely to say much about them because of the comparatively recent scandals involving Ana de Mendoza and the King, and because of the current criticism of the present Marqués de Cañete, García Hurtado de Mendoza, who was just terminating his services as Viceroy to Peru. But Garcilaso may also have considered its implication too delicate to be raised by one who, though clean of Semitic taint, carried blood in his veins which some of his relatives regarded as equally undesirable. Be that as it may, though the passage does partially explain some of his omissions it leaves others open to conjecture, especially those concerning certain of his immediate family. He mentioned each of his father's brothers and sisters as well as the mates and progeny of those who had married. He frankly admitted that he himself had been gotten on the body of an Indian. But he stressed his mother's noble lineage and said nothing of her marriage, apparently preferring to picture her as a royal concubine rather than as the legitimate wife of Juan del Pedroche. About his father's other offspring he remained silent. Understandable is his reluctance to name the illegitimates, Francisca de la Vega and Leonor, for their mothers may not have been noble and their presence suggested a promiscuity out of keeping with the tenor of the document. But there is also no mention of Sebastián's legitimate daughters, Blanca de Sotomayor and Francisca de Mendoza; and there is not one word concerning the highborn Luisa Martel de los Ríos.[12] It would appear that the mestizo wished to represent an idyllic relation between his father and mother and to erase from the picture Sebastián's legal marriage. This circumstance, combined with the fact that the name of Luisa Martel never appears in any of Garcilaso's chronicles, strongly supports the theory that he regarded her with distaste and some embarrassment, though most surely he also would have been aware that his *Descendencia* was hardly the place to mention a stepmother whose second husband, an illegitimate of unclean blood, represented an offense to the Figueroas and possibly some of the Vargases. Moreover, to have described her adequately would have been to violate the chivalric code of the ancestor he was honoring, the guarded precaution of never defaming.

Yet even while Garcilaso so obviously was omitting his stepmother's name from the Vargas family tree, she was initiating actions in Tucumán which would record again the fact that she once had been the legitimate spouse of Sebastián Garcilaso de la Vega. After failing to obtain recompense for the murder of Cabrera, she had married one Juan Rodríguez de Villafuerte, a man apparently much younger than she, who before long gave evidence that he intended to rob her of her Peruvian revenues and abscond to Spain. But she had quickly thwarted his reckless ambitions with a court order and as the years passed never ceased to grasp at all assets to which she felt she could lay claim.[13] Thus on October 16, 1593, almost thirty years after the death of her first husband, she empowered a son-in-law to act for her at La Plata in an effort to regain the plantation of Guanipaya, which she claimed to have inherited as the widow of Garcilaso de la Vega on the death of her daughters, and to re-establish her claim to the four thousand pesos of annuity which had been promised her by the Conde de Nieva. Moreover, again declaring her previous status with the deceased Garcilaso, she empowered two of her sons to journey to Spain and attempt to

---

[12] Although Garcilaso in his *Comentarios* twice mentions the existence of a stepmother, the closest he comes to identifying her is in his identification of Antonio de Quiñones as his father's brother-in-law. Quiñones is known to have married Luisa Martel's sister, Beatriz de Mendoza. See Luis G. Martínez Villada, *Los Cabrera*, p. 118. Garcilaso, *Comentarios*, Pt. II, Bk. VII, Chap. 2.

[13] Martínez Villada, *Los Cabrera*, pp. 27, 123, 127, *et al.*

collect for her through the King and his Council not only the Garcilaso estate but her dowry, her inheritance from her deceased parents, and the amount due her from the goods of her second husband's mother, the infamous María de Toledo. This property she sought now for the offspring she had borne Cabrera. Her third husband, though he appears to have abandoned her, still lived, and documents show him one day in 1595 at Callao, bidding farewell to some of his father's friends who were embarking for Spain. Among them was the only surviving child of Francisca de la Vega, a daughter named Leonor del Castillo, who one day, with Rodríguez as a witness, was to file suit for claims on the basis of the services of her grandfather, Captain Garcilaso de la Vega.[14]

The descendancy of the famed Garcí Pérez eventually was deleted from the preface to *La Florida*, and the burden of patronage never fell to the proud shoulders of the contemporary patriarch of the house of Vargas. It has been suggested that the change was due to inordinate length and a shift in allegiance. Certainly a minute cataloguing of Spanish forefathers was incompatible with the spirit of a book whose title page declared full-mouthed that its author was an Inca and whose context, while glorifying the sons of Spain, did not ignore their weaknesses and carried an outspoken plea for the pagans they had vanquished. Moreover the democratic New World concept of nobility that echoed throughout must have given pause to the man it was designed to honor. It is not beyond reason to presume that Garcí Pérez de Vargas, like some of the Figueroas, was also reluctant to acknowledge publicly his blood ties with an Indian, and that he deemed it unwise for a number of reasons to give protection to the offspring of a man who, in spite of his laudatory accomplishments in the Indies, grave historians had declared seditious.

The cry of poverty which appears in Garcilaso's *Descendencia* was not altogether pretense, since he once more was unable to collect revenues from the Marqués de Priego and in consequence could not satisfy the demands of Luis de Góngora, which he received in May and again in December of 1596. But in August of the following year he man-

---

[14] Martínez Villada, *Los Cabrera*, pp. 130–131; Aurelio Miró Quesada y Sosa, *El Inca Garcilaso*, p. 256; Sarmiento Palacio expediente.

aged to fulfill this obligation and thus became complete owner of his uncle's imposition on the Priego lands. The document of receipt which this transaction produced not only marks the termination of his business dealings with the progenitor of Gongorism, but in it, for the first known time, Garcilaso's name appears with the title of "cleric."[15] It can be assumed, therefore, that though he long may have contemplated ecclesiastical ordination, it was not until 1596 or 1597 that Garcilaso actively joined the ranks of the religious. Since his status was to be that of a minor ecclesiastic, his duties would not rob him of the leisure necessary for his literary projects, and they would be compatible with his literary mission, which in both his *Diálogos* and his *La Florida* he had proclaimed to be altruistic and evangelic. And more intensely than ever there now burned within him a desire to utilize his efforts to bring inspiration and help to the natives of the Indies, and especially to give contemporary Spain a true account of the tragic history of Peru.

It appears rather evident, as has been noted, that Garcilaso's original dream as a historian had encompassed the whole story of his mother's people, their fortunes under Inca rulers, and their fate under the conquerors. Certainly by 1586, according to his message to the King, his plans for this story were definite; and by 1589, when he had completed his first draft of *La Florida*, the greater part of his record of preconquest Peru, according to the closing pages of *La Florida,* was "already in the loom." A statement in the fragmentary *Descendencia* discloses that by 1596 at least half of this record had been completed, and during the next few years, which were to witness the close of the reign of the Prudent King, Garcilaso would concentrate upon the task of completing the annals of ancient Tahuantinsuyu. He was now the new quipucamayu, chanting the glories of a lost and golden world, and in the classic atmosphere of Córdoba he was flooded with memories of faraway days when as a boy he listened, entranced, to the myths and legends of his mother and her relatives, and to the tales of those affectionate Indians who had borne him upon their shoulders across

---

[15] Archivo de Protocolos de Córdoba, Oficio 22, Protocolo 49, fols. 807v–808; Protocolo 51, fols. 296–297; Oficio 29, Protocolo 12, fols. 510–511. Garcilaso is again identified as a cleric in a document dated Oct. 22, 1607, Archivo de Protocolos de Córdoba, Oficio 34, Protocolo 16, fols. 1010v–1012.

swift-flowing rivers and over the narrow footpaths of the Andes. In this book he himself was to be the principal source, and yet there persisted within him such a strong desire to disclose the truth that in the composition he did not hesitate to give and even to quote the opinions and reports of others, always, however, placing his greatest confidence in those with a knowledge of Quechua. Over the years he had corresponded with his former mestizo companions as well as relatives who had continued to report to him of things past and present and to verify his facts or remind him of matters of importance which he may have forgotten. Moreover, he had continued to gather information from those who had passed to Spain, many of them exiles from their Indian world or hopefuls seeking redress from the sovereign who had never ceased to drain their land.

For, sixty years after Francisco Pizarro had introduced the light of a new and long-awaited culture to the Indians at Cajamarca and the natives of Tahuantinsuyu had yielded to an old prognostication of Huayna Cápac, there was little change to be seen in the pattern of Spanish domination. Toledo had contributed organization and stability to the colonial system, but his tax rates, which incoming viceroys had continued to utilize, had left the natives in virtually the same condition they had known in the days of the conquest. By the beginning of the last decade of the century the royal Incas had been permitted some nominal recognition, but there still were the "indios de servicio," and great numbers of those forced to labor under compulsion were perishing in the newly discovered mines. The mulattoes and the mestizos with their somewhat debatable claims and dubious allegiances still constituted one of the most vexing problems, and while governors with little or no claim on services rendered in the conquest continued to collect, in addition to their salaries, plate and jewelry to send to Spain, the Indians were paying tribute to encomenderos as well as other taxes which had been levied on harvests, imports, coca, and goods sold in the markets. Moreover, as Philip continued his struggles with European heretics and Spanish malcontents, Peru was forced to bear much of the financial burden. Cognizant of the inhuman drainage on the whole realm, Garcilaso may already by 1596 have begun an ironic comment which was to appear in the second part of his *Comentarios*:

"Only this I can affirm," he wrote with some caution, "since it is public knowledge and widely known, that because of the damage received by the armada sent to England, the Kingdom of Castile, in the year one thousand five hundred and eighty-nine, delivered to Philip II eight millions, which are eighty times one hundred thousand ducats."

Even while Garcilaso was weaving through his histories a plea for the natives of the Indies, the Peruvian mestizo, Melchor Carlos Inca, godson of the Viceroy Toledo and last legitimate heir to the Inca throne, had journeyed to Los Reyes to present a petition for aid and to beg that the descendants of those who once had possessed the land not be permitted to end their lives in poverty.[16] And yet this scion of Inca kings was forced to await the convenience of a monarch who was old and sick and harassed by the enemies of both himself and the faith he protected. England especially had continued to harbor and breed his worst enemies, and British corsairs had continued to harry the Spanish Main. On February 7, 1596, the dreaded Sir Francis Drake died after having contracted yellow fever in the Isthmus of Panama, and there was great rejoicing in Spain. But there were others to carry on the scourge, and one June morning of 1596 the residents of Cádiz awoke to behold a line of menacing sails spread across the horizon, a fleet of sixty ships under the command of Lord Howard and laden with English and Flemish soldiers. In the end Cádiz was plundered and burned, and the marauders sailed home with a cargo of treasure. Among those items which perished in the flames were certain documents and manuscripts belonging to the Peruvian Blas Valera, a mestizo who, after devoting thirty years to the study of the history and ancient customs of Peru, had arrived in Spain in 1594 with a manuscript account, written in Latin, of his discoveries. Valera himself had managed to escape from Cádiz to Málaga with a portion of his history, which eventually was to fall to the Inca Garcilaso.[17]

News of the holocaust at Cádiz reached Philip when he was thought to be dying; but the King rallied and by the middle of October ordered a new armada to sail. Again, however, the winds were obstinate, and

---

[16] Expediente dated April 30, 1600, Seville, Archivo General de Indias, Patronato, Ramo 20, Legajo 191, fols. 1–7v.

[17] Garcilaso, *Comentarios*, Pt. I, Bk. I, Chap. 6.

the great galleons had scarcely put to sea when they became victims of a southwester. One year later, still seeking vengeance on the minions of the hated British Queen, Philip assembled an armada equal to that of 1558. Yet once more tempestuous Furies turned against the Catholic King, and his fleet was wrecked before it could reach the Channel. Philip sighed, piously gave thanks for his frustration, and retired to his cell at San Lorenzo to pray that God might somehow see fit to turn magnificent failures into glorious triumphs. But Spain had reached its ascendency, and grave men had reason to shake their heads over memories of celestial warnings. In 1598, after days and weeks and months of indescribable agony, the Prudent King yielded his soul to his Catholic God, and the Spanish Crown passed to the hands of a Picture King.

Scarcely a year later, in the far-off Indies, a fiery young creole, scion of Spanish grandees, was tried and convicted of treason. For even while French and English heretics were harassing the Catholic King, this youth had plotted a scheme which would have placed him at the head of a vast kingdom uniting Peru, La Plata, and Tucumán, and drawing its nobility not from Spain but from England and France. It was a premature and ambitious vision of unification and separation from Spain, and one which very well may have been inspired by a daring and ambitious mother. For the youth with a vision was Gonzalo Martel de Cabrera, third son of Gerónimo Luis de Cabrera and Luisa Martel de los Ríos. On March 13, 1599, while muffled drums rolled in the plaza at La Plata, Gonzalo Martel de Cabrera was deprived of his head.[18]

Over the turbulent years, the mestizo Garcilaso's stepmother not only had persisted in her rights to the Garcilaso repartimientos, but had never erased from her memory the ugly events which had robbed her of claims in Tucumán. She had seen her progeny occupying positions of importance in both Tucumán and Peru, but whether or not she lived to witness the miserable fate of this third son is not known. Nevertheless, before her death she surely planted a seed of ambition in the mind of her grandson, Gerónimo Luis de Cabrera, who like his grandfather and namesake did become Governor of Tucumán. Moreover, he afterwards became Governor of Buenos Aires. Indeed, he

[18] Martínez Villada, *Los Cabrera*, pp. 46–47, and "Don Gonzalo Martel de Cabrera," *Revista de la Universidad de Córdoba*, Año 7, No. 5–6, 1920, Vol. 3, pp. 54–75.

waxed so eminent as to aspire to the habit of Santiago. But fortunes of others were thereby imperiled and some of the Figueroas in Spain were put on guard. He could prove his New World hidalguía, since he rode in a carriage, kept horses and arms, and consorted with gentlemen. But in his veins there flowed the blood of María de Toledo, and in Spain there persisted the old story that his grandfather was a bastard whose blood was not clean. Miguel Gerónimo de Cabrera had been stripped of the coveted habit of Santiago before being lowered into the tomb; his great-grandson, the Governor of Buenos Aires, was denied the privilege of ever wearing it.[19]

The career of Luisa Martel de los Ríos, bold and intrepid granddaughter of the treasurer who had maneuvered the execution of Balboa, has never been given adequate attention in the annals of a land where the honors of conquest have fallen almost entirely to men. She was not a mere mannish woman such as one finds in the notorious transvestite known as "La Monja";[20] she was a creole lady of courage and persistence who, in a wilderness world where even men were forced to struggle with intrepidity for their rights, faced political vicissitudes without flinching. And yet to her contemporaries she must have appeared as seditious as her first two husbands had been accused of being.[21] One can but regret that her mestizo stepson, who could have told so much of interest about her, condemned her, in a manner, with silence. But after all, the role that she had played in his life was not one to encourage him to write of her warmly, and what he might have disclosed, he no doubt felt was better left in oblivion.

With the death of Luisa Martel de los Ríos, which must have occurred before the turn of the century, any claim to a second life on the Garcilaso repartimientos could not be honored. But hopes persisted among Sebastián Garcilaso's descendants for claims on the basis of his services to Charles V and Philip II, though hovering over these hopes

[19] Martínez Villada, *Los Cabrera*, pp. 73–78.

[20] La Monja Alférez was the name given the famed seventeenth-century transvestite and adventurer, Catalina de Erauzo.

[21] In 1578, when two shameless priests were arrested and hanged for plotting to kill Abreu de Figueroa, Governor of Tucumán, and replace him with one of Luisa Martel's sons, it was generally accepted that Luisa had instigated the plot. See Martínez Villada, *Los Cabrera*, p. 122.

always was the old accusation of sedition. Those most likely to invoke this accusation were dead, and the sovereign most likely to be offended by the ghost of a horse lay moldering in the princely vaults of the Escorial. Yet there still were the records, printed and accepted, of López de Gómara, Zárate, and the Palentino, and there still was no printed history which denied what they had said of the conduct of Sebastián Garcilaso at Huarina.

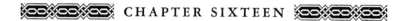

CHAPTER SIXTEEN

THE CENTURY JUST TERMINATED had witnessed the beginning of a golden tradition of literature which was to reach its apex in the reign of Philip III, appropriately known as "the Picture King." Significant among literary contributions had been the classic records of Spanish achievements in the Indies which had been given circulation during the reign of Philip II, and by 1599 the royal chronicler, Antonio de Herrera, had announced his history, the first section of which was to appear two years later. Each of these records had thrown light on both the conquerors and the conquered, but with few exceptions they had failed to treat the latter with the sympathy and understanding that Garcilaso felt they merited, and as yet nothing concerning Peru had reached the press from the hands of a native. Through the years Huaman Poma de Ayala was compiling a strange, pictorial account which as a rare source of Peruvian history cannot be disregarded, but several centuries were to elapse before it was rescued from oblivion by the Danes. Moreover, the Jusuit mestizo, Blas Valera, had assembled valuable information, possibly the most authoritative yet because of his knowledge of Quechua and his long labors among the Indians; but by 1597 Blas Valera was dead, and the fragments of his chronicle which had survived the holocaust of the previous year at Cádiz did not appear in print until quoted by Garcilaso himself, who had received them from a Jesuit at Córdoba. Furthermore, though sixty years had slipped by since Hernando de Soto first set foot in La Florida, still the only published account of his significant exploration was that of the anonymous Portuguese "Gentleman of Elvas."

Since 1589 the original draft of Garcilaso's account of the De Soto expedition had been completed, but as yet he had not been able to arrange for its printing and circulation, and on September 7, 1598, only a few months after the death of Philip II, his permission to print and sell the *Diálogos de amor* was due to expire. In this year the Yahia translation was reprinted at Venice, and possibly Garcilaso found some new hope now in the ascendency of Philip III, for on March 1, 1599, he empowered Juan de Morales, a gentleman usher in the King's chamber of the Council of the Indies, to request both an extension of the time limit on the *Diálogos* and permission to print his *La Florida.* Simultaneously, he agreed to underwrite the project himself and authorized Morales to arrange for the printing of both books. Morales' appeal apparently met with success, for on May 29, 1599, in a new power issued to his solicitor, Garcilaso stated that he had been granted license to print both *La traduzión del Indio de los tres diálogos de amor* and *La Florida del Inca.*[1] Yet for some reason, possibly an inability to collect annuities, Garcilaso now ceded his rights to Morales, and while specifying that the latter was to pay for the printing, agreed that he also should have all the proceeds from the sales.

Meanwhile, Garcilaso had pressed on with the compilation of his history of the Incas and while doing so had continued in contact with some of his Peruvian compatriots, among them his cousin Garcí Sánchez de Figueroa and his mother's brother, Francisco Huallpa. Diego de Alcobaza, working as a priest among the Indians, had supplied him with valuable information concerning the ruins of Tiahuanacu as well as news concerning recent events in Chile; and other of his classmates had verified some of the information he was giving concerning Peru. Both Pedro del Barco and Juan Arias Maldonado were dead, but Alonso Fernández de Mesa was living at Toledo, and in 1602 the mestizo Melchor Carlos Inca, who in 1599 had begun press-

---

[1] Archivo de Protocolos de Córdoba, Oficio 22, Protocolo 54, sin foliar; Oficio 29, Protocolo 15, fols. 695v–697.

ing his claims before the Audiencia at Los Reyes, brought his petition to Spain.

The example set by Melchor Carlos Inca of course encouraged other Indians to seek their fortunes with the new King, many of whom claimed falsely to be of the lineage of Manco Cápac. But on March 20, 1603, fourteen authentic Incas representing five hundred and seventy-one others, all descendants through the male line from eleven of the former rulers of Tahuantinsuyu, signed a document asking the King and his Council to exempt them from paying tributes as well as from performing services daily forced upon them, and to provide them with the income and allowances necessary for supporting themselves and their immediate families. To substantiate their request, they offered documentary evidence of their royal lineage, not the least interesting of which was a yard and a half of white Chinese silk on which had been painted portraits of all Inca rulers from Manco Cápac to Huayna Cápac. None being able to undertake the long journey to Madrid, the petitioners empowered as their representatives in Spain "Captain Garcilaso de la Vega Ynga, resident of the city of Badajoz [sic], don Melchor Carlos Ynga, resident of Cuzco, don Alonso Fernández de Mesa, citizen of the city of Toledo, and Alonso Márquez de Figueroa." These deputies, all mestizos, were empowered to act individually and collectively, and though only Garcilaso and Melchor Carlos were honored with the title of Inca, all apparently were charged equally with the responsibility of the petition. Since the first three of them are known to have been already in Spain, it is to be assumed that the petition was brought from Cuzco in person by Alonso Márquez de Figueroa, who, as the son of Luisa de Herrera and Pedro Márquez Galeote, was the Inca Garcilaso's nephew.

The petition was entrusted first to the Inca Garcilaso and was accompanied by a message written in a linguistic amalgamation of Quechua and Spanish that was replete with expressions of misery and sorrow as well as confidence that once Philip III had knowledge of the plight of the royal Incas he would offer redress. Though dated April 16, 1603, this communication was not put into Garcilaso's hands until the end of the year, many days after he had brought his first "royal commentaries" to a close with an account of Atahualpa's attempt to exterminate the Inca race, an atrocity which led to a state of degradation that seventy years later made it necessary for their descendants to beg sustenance from alien masters. The fact that Garcilaso was the first to receive their supplication is indicative that they recognized him as a trusted representative and as a royal descendant with the right to bear the title of Inca, and he was deeply touched by their confidence. But, as he later explained, other crucial matters intervened and he felt that he could serve these Incas best not by pleading their cause at court but by presenting to Spain his account of the glories and tribulations of their vanquished realm. Thus he now forwarded the petition to Melchor Carlos Inca with the request that he bring it before the proper court, and then in a display of pride and sincerity he added to his commentaries a brief chapter which told of the petition and of the growing number of descendants of worthy Incas who now were awaiting a show of justice and gratitude.[2]

In January 1604, surely almost simultaneously with his receipt of the petition of his Inca compatriots, a report was made before the Council on the plea of Melchor Carlos Inca, and before long this mestizo Inca was honored not only with membership in the highly coveted Order of Santiago but also with an enviable annuity as well as funds for bringing his wife to Spain. News of the success of this noble kinsman reached Garcilaso on the final day of March, and with it he brought to a close the first part of his *Comentarios reales,* rejoicing not merely over the triumph of an Inca scion but over the hope it offered for the petition of the renascent Incas as well as for a renewal of his own claims. Then with buoyed aspirations he issued a document empowering his newly arrived nephew to present these claims. Citing herein his own services to both Philip II and Juan de Austria as well as his father's contribution to the conquest, Garcilaso declared that he already had sought in vain for compensation and now was asking that these services be given the attention of the King and his Council; and he added that any emoluments he might receive

[2] Expediente dated April 30, 1600, Seville, Archivo General de Indias, Patronato, Ramo 20, Legajo 191, fols. 1–7v; also document dated March 20, 1603, Audiencia de Lima 472, fols. 1–1v; El Inca Garcilaso, *Los Comentarios reales,* Pt. I, Bk. IX, Chap. 40, and Pt. II, Bk. VIII, Chap. 21.

would be transferred to his young kinsman, whom in this instance
he referred to as "Alonso de Bargas Figueroa Inca," while specifically
identifying him as the son of his sister, Luisa de Herrera.[3]

For some reason the previous agreement with Juan de Morales for
the reprinting of *Los diálogos de amor* and the publication of *La
Florida* had not been realized, even though the royal licenses had
been granted. Undoubtedly the circulation of León Hebreo in the
vulgate had not been prohibited, for the banned translation of Carlos
Montesa was reprinted in 1602, and there is no evidence that the
circulation of Garcilaso's translation was forbidden before 1612. Still,
one cannot altogether allay the suspicion that Garcilaso in his revision had included passages which met the disapproval of Spanish
inquisitors. Certainly such was true in the case of the chronicle of
La Florida, for Garcilaso himself has stated, with some irony, that
because of the objection of certain Jesuits, in 1602 he had been forced
to delete some passages. Be that as it may, in the year 1604, Garcilaso,
with the story of De Soto's conquest and his history of Tahuantinsuyu
ready for publication, was racing with time and physical weariness
to complete his account of the conquest of Peru. And there still may
have remained the task of finding patronage for his histories and the
pecuniary means for converting them into the magic of print. The
expenses, he would realize by now, must be met with his own resources, which as usual remained uncertain because of the unrelia-
bility of the Priego annuities. In the closing months of 1602 he had
been able to obtain these rents only by bringing the matter to the attention of the Royal Audiencia at Granada, and now after a lapse of
two years he still was empowering attorneys to collect delayed payments.[4]

The question of literary protection was a matter of even more consequence. The response of Garcí Pérez to his plea, in the light of
subsequent events, appears to have been negative. To whom had he

---

[3] Archivo de Protocolos de Córdoba, Oficio 29, Protocolo 21, fols. 1265v–1267.
For the other two known children of Luisa de Herrera, see Aurelio Miró Quesada y
Sosa, *El Inca Garcilaso,* pp. 258–259.

[4] Archivo de Protocolos de Córdoba, Oficio 5, Protocolo 53, fols. 1122–1123; also
Oficio 29, Protocolo 18, fols. 1122v–1123.

turned in 1599 when given the King's permit to print and sell *La Florida?* Any suspected political allusions therein would have lost some of their offensiveness with the death of the Prudent King, but they would have given some let still for a dedication to the Picture King. It is reasonable to assume, therefore, that even this early, Garcilaso, in despair of restoring himself to the grace of Spanish princes, had resolved "for the love of God to go and beg his food wherever he might find it rather than persist in the services of such masters." Certainly by 1604, if not much sooner, he had turned to the increasingly powerful and ambitious Portuguese family that would have resented least any critical allusions to a Spanish sovereign. For the dedication of the first part of his *Comentarios reales,* his history of the Incaic civilization, was directed to Catalina of Portugal, granddaughter of King Emanuel, Duquessa de Braganza, and some years previously one of the chief rivals of Philip II in his struggle for the Portuguese Crown; and the dedication to his *La Florida,* which soon was to appear, was directed to Catalina's son Teodosio, legendary boy hero of King Sebastián's African campaign, and since the death of his father in 1583, the reigning Duque de Braganza y Barcelos.

Someday the archives of Spain and Portugal may yield information as to what contact Garcilaso had with the Braganzas or what may have been their interest in him. Surely his solicitation of their patronage followed the usual route of an intermediary, and his known negotiations later with Portuguese Jesuits opens the possibility of his having been assisted in this instance by that brotherhood, which long had exerted a powerful influence in Portugal. In his tribute to the Duquessa Catalina, aging widow of the sixth Duke, he first observed the customary flattery expected of the humble in addressing the exalted and then suggested that this splendid woman, while rightfully aware of the significance of her lineage, was even more aware of the truth that nobility should justify its position of fame and honor with virtue and good deeds. And in his dedication to her son, the seventh Duque de Braganza, he declared that he had been inspired not only by what he had heard and read of the accomplishments of both the Portuguese and the Braganzas throughout the known world, but also by the hospitality once bestowed upon him in the Azores and in Lisbon and by the deeds he had recorded in his account of native Portuguese hildalgos in the conquest of La Florida. And then he closed this dedication with a somewhat enigmatic passage.

I beseech Your Excellency, therefore, to deign to accept this small service with the affability and approbation consistent with your royal blood, and to look favorably upon the desire I always have had and still have of seeing my name among those of the subjects of Your Excellency's royal household. Should you grant me this favor, as I trust you will, I shall be more than humored in my fondness, and I shall at the same time be able to repay an obligation to the natives of this most Christian kingdom, for through Your Excellency's generosity I shall become as one of them. May our Lord preserve your Excellency for many happy years as a refuge and protection for the poor and needy. Amen.

This expression of a yearning to serve the Braganza household has lent itself to various interpretations, some accepting it as a literal declaration of a desire at one time or another to serve with the Portuguese legions and some as a common literary tribute customarily paid to a patron. But Garcilaso considered his intellectual efforts as services to his sovereign, and it is not unreasonable to suppose that since these services had been spurned by the kings of Spain he was, in a manner, shifting his literary allegiance and seeking from the ruling house of Portugal the honor of serving them as a royal chronicler. Certainly it was with the encouragement and approval of these renowned patrons of letters that he gave the title of *Comentarios reales* to his account of the Incas, and one strongly suspects that he received from them at the same time an indication of protection and patronage for his story of the Spanish conquest of Peru, which he always intended as a part of his entire history of Peru, and which he was to refer to as the second part of his *Comentarios reales*.

Be that as it may, it was under the sanction of the Braganzas that Garcilaso eventually submitted his *La Florida* as well as his history of the Incas for the approval of the Portuguese Inquisition.[5] On November 16, 1604, Friar Luys dos Anjos, examiner for the Supreme Council of the Holy Office at Lisbon, declared that the Inca Garcilaso's

---

[5] Privileges and licenses for printing and selling are to be found within the books themselves.

book which "treated of the discovery of La Florida" contained nothing contrary to the Holy Faith and merited reading. Ten days later
he gave his approval to the *Comentarios reais dos Incas,* saying that it
too was worthy of printing. On November 23, Marcos Teixeira and
Ruy Pirez da Veiga, representatives of the Portuguese Council, gave
license for the first impression of a book entitled *Discobrimento da
Florida* and made the usual demand that this impression before circulation be returned to the Council for comparison with the original.
And on December 4 these same men gave a similar license for a first
impression of "este primeiro livro intitulado *Comentarios reais dos
Incas.*"

Portuguese permits having been obtained, it apparently still was
necessary for the chronicler to appeal again to Philip III and to seek
a printer. On December 9, 1604, he empowered the licentiate Do-
mingo de Silva, presbyter and citizen of Córdoba, to appear before
the King and his Royal Council as well as other judicials for the purpose of obtaining a "licencia particular" permitting the printing and
selling of one book entitled *La Florida del Inca* and another entitled
Los comentarios reales, and at the same time he gave power to his
attorney, once the desired license was obtained, to arrange for the
printing of the first impression and to sell to whomever he might wish
the privilege of printing the entire issue in exchange for a set number
of maravedís or for books themselves or under an arrangement wherein
Garcilaso himself would pay half or all the expenses. In the event
of the latter, only half an issue of each book was to be printed, that
is, only seven hundred and fifty copies of each. [6] Apparently this
special license was obtained without delay, for on February 21, 1605,
Damião D'Aguiar and Sousa, having checked the printed pages with
the original, gave the "licenca do Paço" or "Palace license" for the
printing of a book entitled *Descobrimento da Florida,* and on March
15, D'Aguiar and Costa gave the same license for the printing of a
book entitled *Comentarios reais dos Incas.* Already on March 8 a document issued in Portuguese at Lisbon had carried the King's agreement to penalize any printer or bookseller who printed or sold *Des-*

---

[6] Archivo de Protocolos de Córdoba, Oficio 29, Protocolo 22, fols. 2563–2564.

cobrimento da Florida without permission of the author within a period of ten years, and since this issue bears the date of 1605, it is assumed that it appeared shortly after. It was published at Lisbon by the famed Flemish printer, Pedro Crasbeeck, and it appeared, not under the title with which it had received Portuguese licenses, but under that with which he had submitted it to the King: *La Florida Del Ynca. Historia del Adelantado Hernando de Soto, Gouernador y capitan general del Reyno de la Florida, y de otros heroicos caualleros Españoles e Indios; escrita por el Ynca Garcilasso de la Vega, capitan de su Magestad, natural de la gran ciudad del Cozco, cabeza de los Reynos y prouincias del Peru.*[7]

Sixty-three years had elapsed since a few naked and starved men had straggled into the City of Mexico and presented an account to the Viceroy, Antonio de Mendoza, of the marvels and miseries of La Florida. A manuscript of this account eventually had come to the hands of "a chronicler of His Catholic Majesty" who compared it with the manuscript of Garcilaso's story, which he somehow had managed to see. From him, the mestizo had received the following note of encouragement: "I have compared your history with an account in my possession, the one comprising the statements made to don Antonio de Mendoza in Mexico by survivors among the followers of that excellent Castilian who entered La Florida; and I find that your history is true and conforms to the said account."[8] In relating this incident, Garcilaso failed to name either the author of the manuscript or the royal chronicler who made the comparison. The former has been suspected of being De Soto's factor, Luis Hernández de Biedma, whose brief and semi-official record was presented to the Council of the Indies in 1544; but Biedma's account is more in the nature of a diary than a compilation of the information others had given to Mendoza. The royal chronicler of course could have been Ambrosio de Morales, who did see a portion of the manuscript of *La Florida;* but

---

[7] "The Florida of the Inca, a History of the Adelantado Hernando de Soto, Governor and Captain General of the Kingdom of La Florida, and of other heroic Spanish and Indian cavaliers, written by the Inca Garcilaso de la Vega, an officer of His Majesty and a native of the great city of Cuzco, capital of the Realms and provinces of Peru."

[8] Garcilaso, *La Florida del Inca,* Proemio al Letor.

he more than likely was Antonio de Herrera, who as the officially appointed historiographer of the Indies under both Philip II and Philip
III had access to multiple manuscripts of importance, and who eventually was to plagiarize great portions of Garcilaso's story. That Garcilaso ever submitted any of his manuscripts to Herrera is doubtful,
though the latter could have obtained them very easily from one of
several men such as Juan Fernández Franco who did see them, or, if
it were presented, from the draft of *La Florida* intended for the King.
In truth the mestizo chronicler in one instance expressed some trepidation lest his story be plagiarized before it came into print, [9] and
when in 1601 Herrera published the first four "decades" of his *Historia general*, he had revealed himself to be unscrupulous in his borrowings. Nevertheless, it was to be some years before Herrera
published his "decade" dealing with the conquest of La Florida, and
by 1605 the only other published account of this expedition which
had opened to Spain one of the richest regions of the New World was
still that of the Portuguese Fidalgo de Elvas. And now this second
published account, brought to print also in Portugal, was the work of
a mestizo Indian, whose services to Spain, ironically, were rendered
always at his own cost. Like his translation of León Hebreo, it too
was a first fruit from Peru, and as the earliest published chronicle of
Spanish conquest written by a native of the Indies, it was destined to
become an American classic.

In his published preface to *La Florida* Garcilaso openly acknowledged his sources. He told of his use of the manuscripts of Alonso de
Carmona and Juan Coles, and he cited other supporting sources in
addition to naming numerous men from the expedition whom as a boy
he had encountered in Cuzco. Moreover, he modestly confessed that
in the unfolding of the story his role had been primarily that of an
amanuensis. The true authority for his story, he declared, was "a
great and noble friend of mine who accompanied the expedition to
La Florida." But like his Portuguese predecessor of Elvas, he kept
the narrator anonymous, and it remained for twentieth-century schol-

---

[9] Garcilaso, *Comentarios*, Pt. I, Bk. I, Chap. 7. See also Miró Quesada y Sosa,
"El Inca Garcilaso y su concepción del arte histórico," *Mar del Sur*, Vol. VI, No. 18,
Julio–Agosto, 1951.

ars to probe the archives and establish his identity as Gonzalo Silvestre. [10]

Yet the reader does not advance far into the book without suspecting its primary source. For as the giant cavalcade of men, horses, dogs, and swine push on through the green wilderness of La Florida, the hero who too often takes second place only to the Adelantado De Soto in picturesqueness and boldness is Silvestre. From beginning to end there hovers the spirit of this man and the Amadisian culture of which he is such an apt symbol. It was a spirit that was fading in Spain and one that was to receive a lethal blow at the time La Florida was placed before the reading public. For even as the Spanish and Portuguese inquisitors were probing the pages of Garcilaso, they were scrutinizing the pages of Miguel de Cervantes Saavedra, and in the selfsame year in which the ebullient and cavalier knight-errant of the Indies appeared in the pages of La Florida, there loomed over the horizon the immortal knight of La Mancha. In truth, both knights may have squeezed through the crude presses of Pedro Crasbeeck almost simultaneously, for in that same magic month of March when Portuguese authorities gave this printer permission to print La Florida del Inca, they also licensed him to print an edition of El ingenio hidalgo, don Quixote de la Mancha. [11]

The Inca Garcilaso was cognizant of the changing attitude in Spain toward a worn and exaggerated chivalric spirit, and even in the first section of La Florida he, in a mood of defense, had inserted a

[10] In addition to giving Silvestre a prominent role in the story, Garcilaso has a number of times referred to him as a source in his Comentarios; the only other survivor of the La Florida expedition whom he mentioned as having known in both Peru and Spain was a Juan de Vega, "a native of Badajoz," who does not appear in the pages of the Comentarios; in Spain Silvestre is known to have lived at Las Posadas, and in 1587 Garcilaso wrote Maximiliano that in order to conclude his La Florida he was hastening to Las Posadas to write from the account of a cavalier who had taken a personal part in all the events of the De Soto expedition; and finally, Íñigo de Córdoba Ponce de León, who had known Garcilaso in Córdoba, wrote that the latter "went to Las Posadas and in the company of the said Gonzalo Silvestre wrote the Comentarios reales and the book of La Florida." See Garcilaso, La Florida del Inca, Proemio al Letor, also Bk. V, Pt. II, Chap. 6; letter to Maximiliano de Austria, March 12, 1587, in prefatory material of Los diálogos de amor; Rubén Vargas Ugarte, "Nota sobre Garcilaso," Mercurio Peruano, Vol. XX, Enero–Febrero, 1930.

[11] James Fitzmaurice-Kelly, The Life of Miguel de Cervantes Saavedra, p. 329.

denunciation of the books of chivalry, though continuing all the while to tint his passages with the rose and gold that Silvestre was spilling spontaneously upon the recording quill and with the colors, the rhythm, and the dramatic accents he himself had derived from romantic literature.[12] Such hues and overtones have made it easy for later critics to regard Garcilaso as little more than a poetic historian. Yet beneath this rhapsodic veneer which has provoked skeptics to question the veracity of the picture, there lies an authenticity of significant scope. The various cults of romanticism were very much alive when Hernando de Soto entered the "flowery land" and by utilizing their hues, the chronicler was able to fashion a more faithful picture of the Spaniard who rode that conquest than others which have come from men more accurate in their details of time and geography. Furthermore, his data, both historical and geographical, compare favorably with that of other chroniclers, and reputable geologists have declared that De Soto's route can be traced accurately by means of the Inca Garcilaso's description of both the land and the food it provided for men as well as horses. One cannot minimize the quickening role played by Gonzalo Silvestre in both the expedition and in Garcilaso's record of it. Nevertheless, it remained for the mestizo with his liquid pen and flowing prose, maturing and taking on dimensions and tones as he polished his Castilian, to give this fantastic story a precise beauty along with a sense of reality.

Over the years, as he continued to fill his pages with colorful history, Garcilaso's interest had not lain solely in the recorded fact. He was acutely aware always of rhetorical techniques which could be utilized to make his message more effective. Thus he had developed a flexible style. He had mastered the lofty, subtle style of León Hebreo; he had learned to subdue his pen to the exclusion of ornament; and he had perfected his talent for a histrionic and florid rhetoric which oftentimes was, and sometimes was not, appropriate and functional. That he had persuaded himself of his ability to direct and control his

---

[12] In attempting to judge Garcilaso's distaste for books of chivalry, one should keep in mind that by the time he expressed his opinion in print, there had been such an uninterrupted series of similar declarations that they had become something of a formula of style demanded of all who considered themselves worthy authors.

manner and tone of communication is to be seen in an unusually "floral" explanation of the technique employed in his second publication:

In truth, I wrote the chronicle of *La Florida,* indeed a land of flowers, not in my barren style, but with the flow of Spanish excellence, so that when replanted in the cold plateaus of uncultivated regions it might bear blessed fruit, uprooting by dint of merit the thick brambles of rank paganism and planting with the waters of Heaven the Tree of the Cross and the emblem of our Faith, the flowering rod of Aaron and Jesse.[13]

Where Garcilaso may have failed was in utilizing the same baroque hues and pigments to color two distinct racial cultures. In fact, in his title he has employed the paradoxical phrase "heroic Spanish and Indian cavaliers"; and often in both speech and conduct the latter assume such chivalric and utopian qualities that they have been accredited with inspiring the subsequent cult of "the noble savage." A reasonable criticism is that in presenting the Indians of La Florida, which he knew only through hearsay, the chronicler, in addition to endowing them with chivalric mores of which they were ignorant, gave to many of them his own understandably slanted concept of the character of the Incas. Thus his error to a great extent was anthropological. Yet one should keep in mind that *La Florida* to a degree represents the literary apprenticeship of the Inca and he was following the example of accepted models.

Self-consciously anticipating just such objections to both his style and substance, the chronicler in his earlier pages intruded defenses designed to allay skeptics. Bitter experience had taught him that in general many people, including most chroniclers, regarded the Indians as bestial and simple folk, too devoid of reason and understanding to do and say such lofty and memorable things as he had ascribed to them. Thus he was aware that since all of the regions of the New World were regarded as the Indies, such people would accuse him of having fictionalized and lavished praises on the Floridians in order to exalt the natives of Peru. In reply to the first objection, he merely re-

[13] Garcilaso, *Comentarios,* Pt. II, Prólogo.

ferred his readers to the *Historia natural y moral del nuevo orbe* of the venerable and respected Father José de Acosta. His reply to the second was to a degree an evasion of responsibility.

But in regard to what concerns our particular Indians and the truth of my history, as I said in the beginning, I have simply recorded the words of another who witnessed and supervised the writing personally. This man was so anxious to be accurate that he corrected each chapter as it was written, adding what was lacking or deleting what he himself had not said, for he would not consent to any word other than his own. I, therefore, as the author, contributed no more than the pen, and can truthfully declare that this account is not a fabric of my imagination.[14]

This last statement, though made in sincerity, is only partially acceptable. The facts and much of the coloring certainly can be ascribed easily to the cavalier source whom the chronicler never saw fit to name. But it is too difficult to accept that the rhetoric and the inserted comments did not originate with Garcilaso himself. To believe otherwise is to deny the book much of its purpose and genius. Moreover, it follows naturally that any book spanning the amount of time required by *La Florida* from the date of its inception until the day of its birth will reveal shifts in both tone and purpose. Not to be forgotten is that when Garcilaso began his story, he was a cavalier mestizo youth, seeking in a web of enchantment to merge with his Spanish family; when he finished his first draft, he was a disappointed man of fifty who already had resigned himself to his Indian heritage; and when eventually he saw his work going into the presses, Silvestre had been dead for almost fifteen years, the reign of the Prudent King had come to an end, the moral atmosphere of Spain had shifted, and he himself was an aging and disillusioned religious with a determination to bring before the world, not just the heroism of Spaniards, but a true picture of the worth of all Indians as well as their sad plight in the slough of both political and spiritual darkness and despondency. The plea which he made in his closing pages was for Spaniards to colonize the region of La Florida, a region without gold but rich in other resources, and to

[14] Garcilaso, *La Florida del Inca,* Bk. II, Pt. I, Chap. 27.

be more mindful than they had been of their divine appointment as messiahs among the heathen. And in his closing lines, after having catalogued the sacrifices of some of the Christian martyrs in the Indies, he revealed a further penetration into the baser nature of the Spanish character when he wrote:

And I do trust God that the blood of these men is not crying out and pleading for vengeance like that of Abel, but for mercy like that of Christ our Lord, so that these pagans may come into the knowledge of His Eternal Majesty under the obedience of Our Mother the Holy Roman Church. Thus we may believe that the land which has been watered so frequently with so much Christian blood may yield fruit in proportion to the irrigation of this Catholic blood that has been poured upon it.[15]

In writing *La Florida,* Garcilaso several times had inserted passages concerning Peru, some of which he removed and placed more appropriately in his history of the Incas. It would have been well, therefore, if this second chronicle could have appeared simultaneously, as he had hoped, with *La Florida,* but for some reason never yet explained, its publication was deterred. Though licensed in Portugal, it still, apparently, would have needed a final approval from Philip III and his Council, who, because of the plethora of pretensions from Peru, may have deemed it unwise at the moment to permit such a document to circulate. For not only did this book attest the nobility of the Incas, but in its closing pages it told of a new petition which might make unlimited demands upon the resources of the Crown. Thus Garcilaso merely by mentioning the petition may have retarded the progress of his chronicle. It is possible also that some conflict could have arisen over the title, which, if taken in one sense, suggests that the author was a "royal commentator" on Spanish affairs who had been designated as such by the rival house of Braganza.

But there of course remains the possibility of a lack of finances. For by August of 1605 Garcilaso had left his dwelling in the district of Santa María to take up residence in the Hospital of the Immaculate Conception of Our Lady of Córdoba in the district of San Nicolás

---

[15] Garcilaso, *La Florida del Inca,* Bk. VI, Chap. 22.

de la Villa. [16] Here he was to serve as majordomo, having been appointed to the position by the patrons, the Dean of the Cabildo, the Dean of the Cathedral, the supervisor of the Franciscan Monastery, and the Prior of San Gerónimo. Though as a religious he may have accepted the task as an assignment and a pious duty, the fact that he received a salary and commodities indicates that to some extent he was inspired either by frugality or by financial urgencies. Ironically, though many of his duties were merely those of an ecclesiastic, he was to spend several years dividing his time between the tedious collection of his own annuities and those of the hospital.

The Hospital of the Immaculate Conception, known also as the Antón Cabrera Hospital, had been founded in 1505 primarily for the treatment of males with venereal afflictions, and with the rapid increase of this scourge over the years, it had come to devote itself exclusively to such maladies. Though its original regulations had specified the admittance only of men of impoverished condition, it soon was flooded with pleas for admission from men of wealth and at times from children from seven to nine years of age. Soon the afflicted had exceeded the number of available beds, and those who were turned away continued to spread a disease which became one of the worst agents of destruction in Spain. In 1598 the priest Andrés de Morales left money to the hospital on condition that women be admitted, but ten years were to elapse before the institution was sexually integrated. Garcilaso of course had witnessed the ravages of the buboes, which included all forms of venereal diseases, in both the New and the Old Worlds, and he had had a close view of its wasting effects upon his old friend Gonzalo Silvestre. But here in the Cabrera hospital he was to witness a mass atonement. Salved and shrouded in blankets, all victims were put to bed to sweat for a period of the hottest Cordovan days, while a surgeon remained at hand to burn regional tumors whose infarct had begun to generate pus. Scarce wonder that they conjured

---

[16] Document dated August 26, 1605, Archivo de Protocolos de Córdoba, Oficio 22, Protocolo 65, sin foliar; also Oficio 29, Protocolo 23, fol. 1949. For a history of this hospital, see Germán Saldaña Sicilia, *Monografía histórico-médica de los hospitales de Córdoba*, pp. 141–150.

up the most contemptuous name they could for their affliction—the *mal francés*, or the Gallic pox, though many must have found the source of their misery in those utopian Indian realms beyond the Ocean Sea.

In this sordid environment, while commiserating with unfortunate and impoverished adventurers, many of whom had fought the battles of Spain without reward in both the Old and the New Worlds, Garcilaso now devoted whatever time he could to his story of the Spanish conquest of Peru, a story which he had been planning at least since 1586. Having completed his tapestry of the Inca realm with a sanguinary picture of a noble race gasping under the brutality of the tyrant Atahualpa, he continued to weave through his new commentaries the somber thread of the destiny of these people under men to whom they had vainly looked for the rescue and re-establishment of their ancient throne. And though ostensibly he was recording the story of the Conquest from the entry of Francisco Pizarro into Peru through the ensuing civil struggles and on to the stabilization of the government under the Viceroy Toledo, in a manner he was writing his own biography as well as that of his father, since their lives had been inextricably woven into the travail of early colonial Peru. Moreover, he was making a plea and an indictment which only after the passage of many years, Spain would fully realize carried a potential of danger. For even as he unrolled a picture of internal wars and rebellions, he continued to focus upon his picture the light of certain social and political truths—the truth that the perils of the conquest had been borne by men who too often went unrewarded while the fruits of their labors were reaped by those who took no risks; the truth that these conquerors had been forced to submit to the authority and judgment of court favorites whose lack of on-the-scene experience made them unfit to comprehend the psychology of the conqueror; the truth that much of the Crown's knowledge of what had happened in Peru had been obtained from biased and not always reliable sources; and the truth that Spain still was draining its gold from the veins of Tahuantinsuyu while the natives of that land cried out in misery and despair.

In several of the early chapters of this chronicle, chapters which internal evidence indicates he was rounding out in the early part of the new century, Garcilaso set a tone by describing the comparative penury of the Spanish Crown before the conquest and then attempting to evaluate the wealth that had been drawn from Peru since the steps taken by the first conquerors in 1525. Juan de Morales, he said, had written him in 1599 that the confusion of records was so great as to preclude such an estimate but that the revenue of the King was "a prodigious mass of wealth and treasure." But he had obtained more concrete details from a conversation with Father Paulo de Laguna, formerly President of the Council of His Majesty's Exchequer, afterward President of the Council of the Indies, and in 1603 the elected Bishop of Córdoba. By 1602, Laguna reported, two hundred million registered pieces of eight and at least one hundred million unregistered ones had been transported to Spain from one single mountain in Peru, and he continued that during his services to the Crown twenty-five millions in gold and silver had been brought to Spain by one single fleet. Then the Bishop, whose word could not be questioned, had climaxed his report by assuring his amazed listeners that all the kings of Spain joined together from King Pelayo to the present had never been masters of so much money as Philip II.

In exposing this picture of Spain's indebtedness to the Indies, Garcilaso was hurling an indictment of indifference and ingratitude, and he was prepared to carry his charge into even more dangerous shoals. It was not merely an injustice to Peruvians that he saw but the degradation which ill-gotten wealth had imposed on the whole of the Spanish world. In the opinion of men of keen perception, he declared, these riches had proven more harmful than beneficial, since they had given rise to vice rather than virtue, inclining men to pride, ambition, gluttony, and luxury. For, while enjoying an affluence of fortune, they had waxed so lazy and effeminate as to be unfit for governing in time of peace or for enduring the exigencies and toils of war. All of their time and thoughts now were employed in contriving new dishes to appease their appetites or new and fantastic fashions to flatter their vanities. And in this last passion they had attained such a climax of extravagance that they scarcely knew what to wear and had reached such a state of indecency in dress that their apparel was more like that of women than men. And sadder still was the fact that to support such lusts and conceits, the revenues of the exalted had been increased while the poor were being reduced to rags and starvation. Indeed, with the accumulation of wealth among the powerful, the needy had become even more destitute than previously because of the resultant rise in the cost of commodities and provisions. Thus the poor were being starved by the very abundance of the rich. For even though the latter were able to increase their alms, their gifts still were insufficient to meet the high cost of living which an excess of wealth had raised in the world. It was apparent, therefore, to men capable of understanding, that since the wealth derived from the New World had failed to provide materials necessary for support of human life but instead made them more dear, and since this wealth had rendered men more effeminate by enfeebling them in both body and understanding and by debauching them in their habits and manner of living, mankind as a whole had become more degenerate and less content. And in consequence, whereas in ancient times Spaniards had been so formidable as to be feared by the whole world, they now, thanks to the corruption of excess fortune, had become so weak as to be regarded with contempt. [17]

This lucid comment on hedonism and poverty and on the mutability and decadence of a once powerful empire, Garcilaso was cautious enough to record as the opinion of some of his contemporaries. For, he said, being biased by his affection for Peru, he dared not disclose his own thoughts lest he reveal excessive zeal for his mission. Yet he left no doubt as to either his opinion or his cause. He had made a plea for the poor and oppressed of both Spain and Peru, and he had obliquely expressed with unusual boldness his contempt for the social structure of the Spain of both Philip II and his prodigal son, the Picture King. Moreover, he had paved the way for an old theme which was reiterated often in the chronicle he now was writing: nobility and high position, even in Spain, should justify its recognition by deeds of honor and virtue, and the powerful who accumulated their strength and wealth by disregarding the human heart were guilty of a cardinal error which must lead inevitably to debasement and decay. It was a

[17] Garcilaso, *Comentarios,* Pt. II, Bk. I, Chap. 7.

theme which merely reflected a new contemporary humanism, but it was uttered with both perception and honesty and with a force which would continue to make it compatible with each new wind of democracy.

And even as the chronicler was contemplating this moral and social slough and devoting his own efforts to find alms and annuities for the destitute and stricken in the Hospital of the Immaculate Conception, he was forced to continue wrangling with the Priego estate for his rents. On August 24, 1606, Pedro Fernández de Córdoba y Figueroa had died and the marquisate had fallen to Alonso Fernández de Córdoba y Figueroa, now but eighteen years of age. Though reputed to be an idiot in addition to being a deaf-mute, this highborn youth, according to some reliable sources, not only learned to speak and write but developed into a man of uncommon culture who fomented and protected belles lettres and established a successful press in Montilla. Nevertheless, there were limits to his perspective, and ostensibly he had a tendency to treat his obligation to the Indian Garcilaso with the same indifference as had his father. Indeed, by 1608 Garcilaso, disgusted and worn by this vexatious matter, ceded, apparently in exchange for a loan, his Priego annuities to the Jesuits for the amount owed him, but when this astute brotherhood was unable to collect more than a fraction of the debt, the chronicler returned to them the difference and empowered another attorney to take up the cause in his own name. [18]

Meanwhile, the petition to the Council which Garcilaso had entrusted to his attorney-nephew had met with no success, and by now he must have learned of the pretenses of Leonor del Castillo, daughter of the illegitimate Francisca de la Vega and wife of Juan Sarmiento Palacio, who at present was serving as the King's Treasurer in Mexico. In 1608, doña Leonor instituted a suit for favors, basing her claims on the services of both her father, Pedro Sánchez del Castillo, and her grandfather, Captain Garcilaso de la Vega. As witnesses she presented a number of men whose relations with the Inca Garcilaso had been significant, among them Juan Rodríguez de Villafuerte, the aged Juan

[18] Writ dated October 14, 1608, Archivo de Protocolos de Córdoba, Oficio 30, Protocolo 153, fol. 1914.

de Alcobaza, and, oldest of them all, Juan Álvarez Maldonado, who was her godfather.[19] The outcome of her suit apparently was unsuccessful, as had been previous claims based on the services of Sebastián Garcilaso.

In the year 1608, at some time after May 13, the venerable Inca chronicler relinquished his duties as majordomo of the Hospital of the Immaculate Conception and returned to a residence in the Calle de los Deanes to devote the remainder of his life to other pious works and to the completion of his literary mission. Almost four years had elapsed since the licensing in Portugal of the first part of his commentaries on Peru, but in this year of 1608 he managed somehow to have a first impression of the manuscript run off at Lisbon. Any further obstacles must have been eased now by the evangelical interests of his Jesuit friends, who in 1609 were celebrating the anniversary of the beatification of St. Ignatius de Loyola. During the Córdoba festivals Garcilaso, at the request of the Jesuit Francisco de Castro, designed native Peruvian costumes for a splendid and singular quadrille of participating horsemen and prepared a report of the event for his powerful friend; and on June 19, 1609, after declaring that he held in possession at Lisbon the impression of a book entitled *Comentarios reales*, he empowered the Jesuit Gerónimo Ferraz, a resident of Lisbon, to pay the printer Lorenzo Lombardo and take charge of its publication, while observing all caution about obtaining receipts and letters of payments. [20] On September 2, 1609, the Portuguese Saravia, referring to the approval of the Holy Office in 1604, once more declared that the issue could be printed, and before the close of the year, the House of Pedro Crasbeeck at Lisbon brought it out under the following title: *Primera parte de los Comentarios Reales, que tratan del origen de los Yncas, Reyes que fueron del Peru, de su idolatria, leyes, y govierno en paz y en guerra: de sus vidas y conquistas, y de todo lo que fue aquel Imperio y su Republica, antes que los Espanoles passaran a el. Escritos por el Ynca Garcilasso de la Vega, natural del Cozco, y Capitan de su Magestad.*[21] As mentioned previously, the book was dedicated

[19] Sarmiento Palacio expediente.

[20] Garcilaso, *Comentarios*, Pt. I, colophon; Pt. II, Prólogo; also Archivo de Protocolos de Córdoba, Oficio 30, Protocolo 154, fol. 734.

[21] "First part of the Royal Commentaries, which treat of the origin of the

to *"la Serenissima Princesa Doña Catalina de Portugal, Duqueza de Barganza, etc."*

Thus, at the age of seventy, a Peruvian mestizo who as an impudent boy had chided an ancient uncle on the fact that the Incas had no written records of their past glories was able to place before the world the first printed record of their history from the hands of a native. In a foreward to the reader he modestly declared that his intention was not to contradict what Spaniards had said concerning the Incas, but merely to comment upon such statements and to serve by improving upon what had been said by men who, not knowing Quechua, had erred in their interpretation; and to emphasize the point he added a chapter on the native language of Peru. But Garcilaso's story of Tahuantinsuyu was more than a comment upon the records of Spanish historians. It was the story he had imbibed with his mother's milk and from the ancient amautas and quipucamayus; it was a proud effort to reveal to Spaniards a civilization which he proclaimed to believe was in many respects equal to their own; and in the light of the further record he was in the process of writing, its last somber picture of a gasping empire and a people capable of merging peacefully and progressively with the conquerors might be regarded as preparation for an indictment. And not to be ignored is what it reflects of Garcilaso's true character, which, like the strange architecture of his native Cuzco, represents a superstructure of Hispanicism resting upon an indestructible Inca foundation. Attached to this first edition of his history was his coat of arms. Here proudly displayed are heraldic Christian symbols as well as two significant phrases—"con la espada y la pluma" (with the sword and the pen) and "Ave Maria gratia plena"—which link him with some of the most noble and most renowned families of Spain; yet here also, conspicuously represented, are pagan symbols which link him with a race of Indians whose nobility he was seeking to make evident—the red llatu or fringe of Inca authority, entwined serpents, the great Inca Sun deity, and his sister-consort, the Moon.

Incas, who were the Rulers of Peru, of their idolatry, laws and government in peace and in war: of their lives and conquests, and of all those things pertaining to that Empire and its Dominion, before the Spaniards entered it. Written by the Inca Garcilaso de la Vega, native of Cuzco and Captain of His Majesty."

CHAPTER SEVENTEEN

IT WAS THE HOARY SAGES of Tahuantinsuyu who had kept alive the traditional glories of the Incas, and age surely had silvered the dark hair of the Inca Garcilaso when at last he saw preserved in print his own account of his Indian progenitors. A man of medium height, swarthy complexion, and kindly countenance, according to one of his contemporaries, he undoubtedly still retained many of the physical characteristics of the people with whom he had come to identify himself, both in his recently published chronicle and in his continual and open assertions that he was an Indian, a mestizo, and an Inca. But he was set apart in a number of respects from some of his compatriots who had come to Spain, not only by the richness of his lineage and his literary contributions but also by the ample contents of his purse. The extent of his assets was public knowledge in Córdoba, though he often was heard to declare that he took little pride in his substance since so much of the general wealth of Spain had been drawn from Peru.[1] Such a protest, even if sincere, carries a semblance of Renaissance moralizing, and whatever shame the Inca may have suffered in possession was safeguarded by precaution, for he was well aware of the traditional dishonor attached to any semblance of poverty in Spain, and he wisely cultivated an astuteness in handling the estate

[1] Rubén Vargas Ugarte, "Nota sobre Garcilaso," *Mercurio Peruano,* Vol. XX, Enero–Febrero, 1930, pp. 47–50.

bequeathed him by fortune. Though from time to time he disposed of assets in both Córdoba and Montilla, he was careful in most cases to reinvest his principle; and though he was renowned in Córdoba for his benevolence, he could never be accused of prodigality, and his pecuniary caution, in spite of its soundness, appears at times unduly frugal if not penurious to anyone unacquainted with the multifarious snares offered assets in Renaissance Spain.

Bound though he was to a clerical order, Garcilaso's affiliations had not discouraged physical comforts, and his vows, one must accept, still had not encompassed poverty. Thus the household which he maintained in the Calle de los Deanes was well attended. Assisting him still were his captive slave, Marina de Córdoba, and four servants, Francisco de Servillano, María de Prados and Diego Pabón, both children, and Beatriz de Vega; and with him also was his natural born son, Diego de Vargas, who aided him constantly as a scribe. The presence of this youth and his mother in the household of the cleric would not have been regarded as particularly unusual, and the paternity of Diego, who resembled his father in appearance, was no secret in Córdoba. But Garcilaso, while giving his son protection and some intellectual advantages, apparently denied him the open recognition and love he himself had received from his own father. Among the chronicler's known records it is only in his will that the name of this youth is mentioned, and even then he is not mentioned with affection or referred to as a son. Yet such seeming indifference cannot be credited solely to an absence of regard or a desire to veil an old guilt. For Diego, though identified in various documents as a holder of a bachelor's degree, as a licentiate, and as a cleric of minor orders, was in youth both arrogant and boastful and never revealed evidence of unusual ability; and though he could claim noble paternal lineage, he was born of a woman of such lowly origin that she remained always little more than a slave.

A minute inventory of Garcilaso's household goods made after his death reveals a comfortable establishment which to some might have been considered relatively sumptuous. In addition to such necessities as table silver, linens, and domestic furnishings common to a well-provided household, there is a record of articles that give a more intimate insight into the chronicler's personal tastes. There were five canary birds in their cages as well as two empty cages, two deer heads and weapons for hunting, and an enameled gold ring with a diamond. And to remind him of his brief sallies against Moslem heretics there were various accoutrements of war: molds and rollers for making ammunition, two wheel arquebuses, a crossbow for pellets and another for shafts with hooks, iron jars for powder, an arquebus powder flask with a cord of yellow and turquoise silk, an engraved helmet, a small cutlass, a warrior's axe, and spurs. Among the items of furniture were a great desk, stands for papers, a crucifix with a pedestal, and a large black cross. But more significant were the books which constituted his relatively extensive library and which today throw light upon his literary interests, his erudition, and his character—books on religion and philosophy, recreation and military science, extensive collections of Italian Renaissance writers, histories of the Roman epoch, and chronicles of the Indies. [2]

By now Garcilaso had gained some renown as a chronicler, and his years in Córdoba had brought him into personal contact with respected men of letters, among whom have been mentioned the humanists Francisco Murillo, Ambrosio de Morales, Juan Fernández Franco, Juan de Pineda, and Francisco de Castro. Tangible evidence of the admiration of other contemporary scholars is to be seen in the comments of Bernardo de Aldrete, Canon of the Cathedral of Córdoba, who had seen the first part of the *Comentarios reales* three years before it was published and who cites Garcilaso in his *Del origen y principio de la lengua castellana*;[3] and of Francisco Fernández de Córdoba, Abbot of Rute, who paid tribute to the mestizo chronicler in his *Didascalia multiplex*. [4] And when in this year of 1611 Francisco de Castro pub-

---

[2] Archivo de Protocolos de Córdoba, Oficio 29, Protocolo 35, fols. 501–504, 521–525. For an excellent identification and discussion of the books found in Garcilaso's library, see José Durand, "La Biblioteca del Inca," *Nueva Revista de Filología Hispánica,* Año II, No. 3, 1948, pp. 239–264.

[3] Durand, "Dos notas sobre el Inca Garcilaso: Aldrete y el Inca," *Nueva Revista de Filología Hispánica,* Año III, No. 3, 1949, pp. 278–290; also Aurelio Miró Quesada y Sosa, "Un amigo del Inca Garcilaso," *Mar del Sur,* Vol. I, No. 2, Noviembre–Diciembre, 1948, pp. 20–26.

[4] Eugenio Asensio, "Dos cartas desconosidas del Inca Garcilaso," *Nueva Revista de Filología Hispánica,* Año VII, Nos. 3–4, 1953, pp. 583–593.

lished his *De Arte Rhetorica,* he dedicated it to "Principi Viro D. Garcia Lasso de la Vega, Inca Peruano clarisisimo, Duciq. Regio"; and then in three full pages of Latin he paid floral tribute to his Peruvian friend. Comparing himself to Elias, who fled the wrath of Jezebel and found protection eventually under the shade of a juniper tree, famed for its ability to repel venemous serpents, this great Jesuit humanist declared that, harassed by the poisonous barbs of the ignorant, he had found refuge in the protecting shadow of the Inca Garcilaso.[5] Following this dedication is a sonnet by Luis de Góngora, the one great literary figure with whom Garcilaso must have been in frequent personal contact, in both ecclesiastical and lay activities, but with whom he appears to have formed no amicable relations. Yet Góngora was notably eccentric and caste-conscious, and his literary interests as well as his poetic techniques were alien to the tastes of the Inca Garcilaso. Moreover, as has been seen, the chronicler's business dealings with the prebendary poet had not been altogether smooth, and the latter, as the nephew of Luisa Ponce de León, may have been permanently chilled by the fact that this Indian had stood as a let to his own family fortunes.

Also among Garcilaso's literary associates were the so-called maestros of books, the booksellers and printers of Córdoba. It was while browsing in a Córdoba bookshop that he had found the moth-eaten manuscripts of Juan Coles, and he is known to have had some relations with Francisco de Zea Tesa, who in 1588 had established a printing dynasty that was to last into the eighteenth century. Furthermore, he was well received in the household of Andrés de Barrera, whose widow, Lucía de Leries, since her husband's death in 1603, had managed his printing establishment. Married to Barrera's daughter Ana was Francisco Romero, a bookseller and personal friend of Garcilaso, who eventually became a partner in the Barrera establishment. Though Zea Tesa and the widow of Barrera in general published only small items, both apparently had business transactions with the New World, for the Córdoba mansion of Zea Tesa was known as "La Casa del Indiano," and among those owing money to the widow

[5] Raúl Porras Barrenechea, *El Inca Garcilaso en Montilla,* pp. 260–263.

of Barrera at her death was Miguel Méndez, "maestro of books in the Indies." [6] It could be, therefore, that these bookdealers already were involved in the circulation of Garcilaso's books in the New World, though the greater possibility is that this circulation was begun by travelers, especially religious, who journeyed from Spain to the various outposts of the Indies. One such man was Friar Luis Gerónimo de Oré, a native Peruvian, whom Garcilaso encountered in Córdoba. Oré himself had published a volume on the subject of the martyrs of La Florida and certain outstanding religious who had flourished in the Indies, and Garcilaso now gave him three copies of his La Florida and four of his Comentarios to carry to La Florida, whence he was hastening along with others to preach the Christian gospel. "May his Divine Majesty prosper them in this undertaking," Garcilaso afterward wrote, "to the extent that they may draw those poor wretches out of the dark abyss of idolatry to the knowledge and service of the true God." [7]

The deep tones of evangelism carried within Garcilaso's La Florida continued to shade his pen, and always accompanying his plea for Christianization of the Indies was an insistence that the natives thereof were intellectually capable and worthy of the attention of Spain. Haunting his memory still were the words of his old preceptor, Juan de Cuéllar, who had longed to see his mestizo scholars in the academic cloisters of Salamanca. Feliciano Rodríguez de Villafuerte had indeed achieved that honor, distinguishing himself in sciences, and when in 1611 Garcilaso received from this classmate an exquisitely hand-worked reliquary and an ingeniously contrived sun and moon dial, he proudly exhibited these objects as proof of Peruvian acumen. [8] Yet though later-born mestizos already were receiving instruction in the Colegio de San Borja at Cuzco and the Universidad de San Marcos

---

[6] José María de Valdenebro y Cisneros, La Imprenta en Córdoba, pp. xviii–xix; also the will of Lucía de Leries, May 10, 1621, Archivo de Protocolos de Córdoba, Oficio 28, Protocolo 47, fols. 495–500.

[7] El Inca Garcilaso, Los comentarios reales, Pt. II, Bk. VII, Chap. 30. In addition to his Relación de los mártires de la Florida, Oré had published Descripción del nuevo orbe and a book of ritual, Rituale seu Manuale Peruanum, the latter of which had been translated into a number of Indian dialects.

[8] Garcilaso, Comentarios, Pt. II, Bk. VII, Chap. 22.

at Los Reyes, most of those who had aroused the optimism of Canon Cuéllar had been too involved in the turmoils of Peru for intellectual pursuits. At least two of them, however, both now dead, Garcilaso had seen rewarded by the King on the basis of their fathers' services, and the son of a third, now dying at Madrid, on the basis of his Inca lineage. But Garcilaso, whose claims were even more ample, as yet had received no such favor from his sovereign. So once again, on July 7, 1611, he empowered his nephew to represent him at Madrid before "the King, the lords of his Council of War and his Council of the Indies." In this instance, however, he asked only for the reward of his services against the heretic Moriscos and thereby left a suspicion that he had determined not to endanger this plea by inviting a revival of the old rum-rum about his father's conduct at Huarina. [9] Yet, though he may have been unaware of the fact, his father's name still held some magic in the courts of New Spain. For when during these same days Juan Sarmiento Palacio, who had been cast into a debtor's prison in the City of Mexico, asked for exemption from incarceration for civil offenses, he was permitted to go free, at least in part, because he had produced documents that gave evidence of the nobility of his wife, Leonor del Castillo, granddaughter of Sebastián Garcilaso and his Indian concubine, María Pilcocissa.[10]

A common species of publications in Renaissance Spain was the religious tract. Bibliographical sources show many such publications emanating from Córdoba printers, among them Francisco de Zea Tesa and the widow of Barrera, and for years such publications had provided a pious pastime for the lords of Priego. In line with this trend, Garcilaso now undertook the publication of a sermon which was printed by Francisco de Zea Tesa in 1612 under the following heading: *Sermón que predicó el Reverendo P. F. Alonso Bernardino, Predicador de la orden del Seráfico P. San Francisco, en la ciudad de Málaga, en la fiesta del bienaventurado San Ildefonso Arcobispo de Toledo, primado de las Españas. El cual Sermón se imprime a pedimento del Yndio Garcilaso de la Vega, para la gloria y honra de Dios*

[9] Archivo de Protocolos de Córdoba, Oficio 29, Protocolo 29, fol. 922.
[10] Sarmiento Palacio expediente.

nuestro Señor, y de la Virgen María Su Madre. En Córdoba. Por Francisco de Zea. Año de 1612.[11] This sermon was one of a collection which had been presented to Garcilaso by "a friend," who may have been his overseer, Cristóbal de Luque Bernardino, a relative of the predicator, or even the present Marqués de Priego, a man of famed piety to whom the Inca had dedicated it. This dedication, the only one he ever made to a Figueroa, and the fact that the published sermon bore the Priego arms, suggest that the deaf-mute Marqués may have financed the publication, and that Garcilaso even may have hoped to place under the protection of this powerful Figueroa kinsman his chronicle of the conquest, which in this same year would be brought to a close. But in his dedication, Garcilaso simply declared that he had been inspired by the devoutness of the Marqués, so the publication of the sermon possibly represents no more than a pious gesture compatible with the spirit of a man bathed, like San Ildefonso, in Mariolatry, and associated constantly with ecclesiastics of all ranks and degrees of holiness.

Such associations had increased as he became more involved in his clerical duties, which kept him in personal contact not only with sundry religious orders but with those who performed the rituals in various Córdoba shrines. His past experiences and his humility had drawn him to the Franciscans, but his intellectual and humanistic proclivities had drawn him to the Jesuits, especially in his later years. As a mere cleric, his ecclesiastical functions would have been limited, and strangely he has failed to define or even mention them in any of his records. But as chief steward of the Hospital of the Immaculate Conception he undoubtedly substituted for men of higher ecclesiastical rank in administering to the spiritual welfare of those atoning sin-

---

[11] "A sermon delivered by the Reverend Padre Friar Alonso Bernardino, preacher of the order of the Seraphic Padre San Francisco, in the city of Málaga during the festival of the blessed San Ildefonso, Archbishop of Toledo and Primate of Spain. This sermon was printed in Córdoba in the year 1612 by Francisco de Zea and at the request of the Indian Garcilaso de la Vega for the glory and honor of Our Lord God and his Mother the Virgin Mary." See Valdenebro y Cisneros, *La Imprenta en Córdoba*, pp. 52–53; Durand, "Un sermón editado por el Inca Garcilaso," *Nueva Revista de Filología Hispánica*, Año VII, Nos. 3–4, 1953, pp. 594–599; Miró Quesada y Sosa, "Una Dedicatoria del Inca Garcilaso," *Mar del Sur*, Vol. VII, No. 20, Marzo–Abril, 1952, pp. 63–64.

ners in his care; and his mention in his will of clerics who performed memorial masses for the dead indicates that he had not been denied this privilege. Certainly a cursory glance at the multiple masses demanded for those who had left adequate stipulations for such makes clear that some of these duties of necessity were relegated to minor religious; and Garcilaso's later caution concerning the choice of clerics who were to assist his own soul through Purgatory reveals an unusual awareness of the virtues and vices of those who served as deputies in the Holy Cathedral. Though records show him participating at various Córdoba shrines, it was with the Holy Cathedral that he formed his firmest ties, and it was within the walls of this famed edifice that he wanted his remains eventually to lie. But his ambitions soared beyond the status offered by a mere crypt, and on September 18, 1612, he arranged with Diego de Mardones, Bishop of Córdoba, for the purchase of an arch and a chapel within the Cathedral. On October 29 the deed of sale was ratified by the Dean and the Cabildo of the Cathedral and Garcilaso thereupon began arrangements for the construction of his tomb. [12]

But there was still much to do before he could die. The second part of his *Comentarios* must be brought to a close. He had recorded the annals of Peru through the civil rebellions to the government of the Viceroy Toledo; and he had now come to what he felt to be the most tragic episode of all, the execution of the Inca Túpac Amaru and the ruthless dispersion of the Incas and mestizos to alien regions of the world. This was a fitting scene with which to terminate his story since it represented the denouement of a dynasty as well as the fulfillment of a prognostication which had foretold the doom of an empire. And as his tired hand wrote, the timeliness and the pity of the scene were emphasized by news of the recent death of the last of the indirect heirs to the Inca throne through the male line, the infant son of Melchor Carlos Inca, who himself had died the previous year. Thus he wrote with exceptionable emotion; and then, when he had brought this lamentable story to an end, he added a pious benediction and laid down his pen. Collecting his manuscripts, he now at the close of the

[12] Archivo de Protocolos de Córdoba, Oficio 29, Protocolo 31, fols. 1801–1804, 2086–2087.

year 1612 submitted them as *La segunda parte de los comentarios reales* for the initial approval required. [13]

Yet, as in his earlier histories, Garcilaso could not resist adding a codicil, and even as his manuscript was being examined for errors and perils, he began writing two additional chapters. In the first he told of the rebuke which Francisco de Toledo had received from the Crown for the murder of Túpac Amaru, and of the award of Toledo's Peruvian marquisate to a granddaughter of the Inca Sayri Túpac, whose nobility of lineage had been substantiated by reference to the first part of the *Comentarios reales*. This award, he felt, was evidence not only that he had rendered service to this scion of an old Inca who once had treated him kindly in Cuzco but that in the future his works might render equal service to descendants of Incas. Closely related in thought was his last chapter, an exoneration which, with his chivalric attitude toward defamation, he must have pondered long before including. Only recently he had learned that the petition of the Incas entrusted to his care in 1603 had never reached the attention of the King and his Council because of the willful neglect of Melchor Carlos Inca, who had feared that this petition might weaken his own chances for reward. So now, lest his Peruvian compatriots attribute this circumstance to a lack of interest on his own part, Garcilaso exposed the self-interest of this mestizo kinsman. Then, near the beginning of 1613, Garcilaso, with a new and florid benediction, brought to a close the last chapter he was ever to write.[14]

The nature of Garcilaso's second volume on the history of Peru, a resounding symphony of multiple voices, gave the chronicler the opportunity to develop his own central theme of what he, through personal experience and from authentic sources, knew to be the truth; and his continual insistence that he aimed at verity tempts one at times to mistranslate his title as "true commentaries" rather than the less meaningful "royal commentaries." He generously bestowed praise

[13] Garcilaso, *Comentarios*, Pt. II, Bk. VIII, Chaps. 18, 19.
[14] *Ibid.*, Pt. II, Bk. VIII, Chaps. 20–21. In a document dated March 23, 1748, the archivist Manuel Santiago de Ayala reported to the King that there was not the slightest evidence that the petition of the eleven Incas had ever been presented to the Council of the Indies. Seville, Archivo General de Indias, Audiencia de Lima, 472.

where he thought praise was due, and he boldly gave the lie to careless reporters and a hypocritical social structure. He deplored men who based their accounts on bias and hearsay, focusing his bitterest attack on López de Gómara and the Palentino; and he rashly exalted men whose lineage was commonly regarded as base, as well as others, such as Gonzalo Pizarro and Francisco de Carvajal, whose attitudes had been condemned as seditious. And while aiming his interpretations at verity, he permitted his emotions to sweep him even further into political depths which held the possibility of overwhelming him. After recording what he sincerely believed to be the truth about his father's actions at Huarina, he at some time added a chapter which told of the false and unproven accounts that grave historians had given and of the fatal curse which those accounts had thrown upon his father's honor as well as upon his own pretenses. And when he had given the lie to these accounts, he declared, in a tone of proud and ironic disdain, that if people would not believe him, he, in emulation of covetous men who pursued fame at the cost of ignominy, would accept and utilize the false as a means of boasting that he was the offspring of a cavalier who was so valiant and so manly that he was willing to dismount, to give his horse to a friend, and thereby to aid him in winning such a significant battle as that one had been. There had been no nobler deed, he said, in the history of the world, and if people interpreted it as a disservice to the King, his reply was that such a deed, regardless of where perpetrated, deserved honor and fame for itself alone and without any other support. This was his answer to López de Gómara and the Palentino, and this was his final and best eulogy of a man whom he had never ceased to love as a father and whom he had never ceased to regard as an example of true nobility.[15]

Renaissance thinkers in their polemics over the rights of the individual no longer were willing to justify tyranny and abuse on the basis that it was for the common good; and Garcilaso long since had declared that reason of state was a philosophy which merely countenanced tricks invented and practiced by ministers of the Devil.[16] In defending his father, he, unlike some of his contemporaries, had not counten-

[15] Garcilaso, *Comentarios,* Pt. II, Bk. V, Chap. 23.
[16] *Ibid.,* Pt. II, Bk. V, Chap. 29.

anced violence for the sake of the common good, but had praised a
deed which, though noble, was contrary to the good of the state. Unbiased readers will recognize that his naive defense, as he himself
promptly admitted, was but the outburst of a long-pent passion engendered in the bitterest hour of his life, and that it was paradoxical since
it simply annotated a hypothetical story which he, possibly with some
misgivings, had insisted was false. But taken along with what he had
said elsewhere concerning loyalty to heedless authorities, it adds even
deeper colors to his Renaissance concepts of the rights of the individual.

The sources of Garcilaso's mature concepts ranged from personal
experience to humanist studies, not the least of which had been the philosophy of León Hebreo. Of some interest, therefore, is that even as
he was bringing his final manuscript to a close, he learned, undoubtedly
from the *Index* of 1612, that the Holy and General Inquisition of
Spain, in its last expurgation, had forbidden the circulation of this
subtle philosophy in any vulgate language.[17] But in truth the Inca
Garcilaso, in his intellectual and cultural development, had in some
ways completed a cycle. Having failed to realize the Hispanic ideals
which he as a hopeful mestizo had crossed the Ocean Sea to find, he
had turned in spirit toward his homeland, his lost people, and to the
ethical and juridical concepts he had derived from the Incas and from
his own experiences with men who were writing the annals of the New
World with brave deeds. And though this last chronicle may have been
initiated with the purpose of recording the glories of Spanish conquest,
it had evolved into a record of the tribulations of Peruvians, and it had
ended with a firm faith in the rights of brave men to pursue honorable
routes to hidalguía. Thus, when he had brought it to a close, he once
again declared that all of his literary efforts had been pursued with
the intention of advancing the cause of his compatriots, and at some
time, though possibly not before July of 1614, he affixed to it a Prologue addressed "to the Indians, the mestizos, and the creoles of the
dominions and provinces of the most glorious and most opulent empire
of Peru."

Ironically, it was this Prologue which, with the passage of years, was
to represent the most inflammatory portion of his last volume of his-

[17] *Ibid.*, Pt. II, Prólogo.

tory. For in it one finds an epitome of the tone which, though always present, had taken on depths. He paid tribute to Spain, mother of noble men and divine custodian of the world's heathens, and he asserted the indebtedness of the pagans of the New World to this nation for the light of Christian faith. Moreover, he emphasized the valor and courage of the sons of Spain who had sailed uncharted seas and forged their way through unmapped regions for the greater glory of God and the sovereigns of Spain. But he also reminded Spain that her evangelic mission was but partially accomplished, and that in the whole of the Indies and especially in La Florida and the frozen regions of Magellan the heathen still lay in the shadow of spiritual death and thirsted for the waters of salvation. "Indeed," he remarked offhandedly, "the Spanish nation, as true heirs of God, did inherit from the eternal Father, who says in a psalm of David: 'Ask of me and I shall give thee the heathen for thine inheritance and the uttermost parts of the earth for thy possession.' " And then he admonished: "Share generously of the celestial heritage of faith and truth with the Indians as with younger brothers to whom is extended the paternal blessings of God."

In such tributes and pleas, one finds a key to Garcilaso's purpose in his Prologue—a wedge through which he might enter to pay an equal if not greater tribute to the natives of Peru and thereby urge them to demand their rights as humans in a world of caste and racial bias. In a rhetorical style heavy with classical metaphors he extolled the past and present of the Indians, mestizos, and creoles of Peru. In both arms and ethics, he said, their ancestors had equalled the heroes and lawgivers of the ancient world, and their spiritual zeal, according to certain Jesuits, was closer to that of the early Christians than to that of contemporary Europe. Moreover, they had proven themselves equal to Spaniards in all arts, scientific, political, and intellectual, and must not be regarded, therefore, as barbarians. They lacked only refinement and were to contemporary Spain what she previously had been to ancient Rome. Herein lay one of the chronicler's persistent grievances against Spain, its worn superstition concerning the Indian as a race and its stubborn refusal to recognize the intellectual acumen of its Indian colonials. So even now, as he told of the recent manifesto forbidding the circulation of his *Diálogos* in the Indies as well as else-where, he declared that this great treatise had been translated into many languages, including Quechua, and that the very fact that Peruvians read it was evidence of their intellectual curiosity. Moreover, osten-sibly to emphasize royal approval of his *Diálogos,* he inserted the two dedications to Philip II which the book had borne, dedications which in their present context subtly disclosed how he had pled in vain for royal recognition of those chronicles he had hoped to present as a sym-bol of the mental ability of all of his Peruvian compatriots. And, surely in a desire to set an example, he re-emphasized his own boldness as a mestizo in attempting such projects.

These were forceful words, but there were others which were more so. For in this impassioned exhortation which eventually was to nettle the rulers of the land, he also admonished his compatriots "as brothers and friends, relatives and masters," to "arise and press forward in the pursuit of virtue, wisdom, and the art of warfare, defending them-selves and redeeming their good name to the end of making it famous on earth and eternal in Heaven." The pollen of a New World ideology which long ago had fallen upon the genius of a little mestizo in the Incaic capital of the Sun had generated a classic historian who went beyond the mere recording of facts and embraced ancient truths. It is these truths which blend the myriad voices of his symphony.

Whether the Portuguese house of Braganza had offered to extend its protection to both parts of Garcilaso's *Comentarios* is not known. Teodosio de Braganza still lived, as did his mother, though she was to die in 1614; but in the end, Garcilaso addressed his chronicle to a pro-tector whose power and compassion, he felt, transcended that of earthly potentates. In the early stages of his story of the conquest, he had disclosed a hallowed moment in Cuzco when a celestial Mother ap-peared in the Andean heavens to offer succor to valiant Spaniards and to salvage the Children of the Sun from spiritual death. The Indians had learned to pronounce her name in Latin, Spanish, and Quechua; and the limits of her mercy, he now boasted, had encompassed his lost Inca mother, augmenting her nobility by bringing her into the folds of Catholic Christendom. Moreover, he bore upon his escutcheon an "Ave Maria gratia plena," for he was descended from "a Spanish

Mars," who in the name of the holy Maria had destroyed a profane
Moorish giant on the vegas of old Spain. To her, he declared, all who
wore the proud name of Garcilaso de la Vega were peculiarly obligated,
and through her they could find intercession. Thus this mestizo who
had affixed to his borrowed name the proud title of those who always
had adored the Moon and the Sun, now dedicated his last chronicle to
a queen who traditionally was represented as shod and vested in the
moon and the sun, "the most glorious Virgin Mary, Our Lady, daughter, mother, and virginal wife of her Creator, supreme princess of all
creatures."

As has been stated, Garcilaso, with the exception of the two final
chapters, had completed his chronicle by the close of 1612, for on December 13 of that year he submitted it under the title *La segunda parte
de los comentarios reales* to the Bishop of Córdoba, Diego de Mardones, who examined it and passed it on for the inspection of the
Jesuit Francisco de Castro.[18] Only a little more than a month later, on
January 26, 1613, Castro, after praising its intellectual content, its
clarity and unimpassioned style, its zeal for presenting the unbiased
truth, its authoritative source, and its freedom from anything contrary
to the faith, recommended its printing, and it was thereupon placed
in the hands of the inquisitors of the Crown. On January 6, 1614, the
Royal Council of Castile proclaimed the manuscript worthy, and fifteen
days later, on January 21, Philip III issued his approval for the printing and selling of a book entitled *La segunda parte de los comentarios
reales* by the Inca Garcilaso de la Vega. In granting his sanction the
King made what possibly was a customary stipulation. While demanding that the first copy printed be checked by royal inspectors before
other copies were allowed to come from the press, he demanded that
none of the prefatory material, which included such things as licenses,
dedications, prologues, et cetera, be printed until the first printed copy
had been inspected and approved.

Since the final two appended chapters were not completed until the
beginning of the year 1613, they may not have been seen by either
Mardones or Castro when they made their inspection, yet these chapters

[18] As in Garcilaso's other books, all licenses and privileges are to be found within
the book itself.

362   EL INCA

surely would have been seen by the King and his Council before they gave the royal sanctions of 1614. But what is significant is the fact that though some prefatory material may have accompanied the approved manuscript, all that eventually was to appear with it did not; for in his eventual Prologue to the Indians, mestizos, and creoles, Garcilaso was to mention the death of the Archbishop of Santiago de Galicia, Maximiliano de Austria, who did not die until the closing days of July, 1614. Just when his complete Prologue was submitted is not known, but the text had royal sanction, and on October 23, 1614, Garcilaso signed a contract with Francisco Romero for the printing of fifteen hundred copies of a book which in this instance was called *Segunda parte de los comentarios del Pirú*.[19] Garcilaso was to supply paper for half of the printing, and the completed edition was to be divided equally between author and printer. The sale of the book was to be entrusted to Romero since he was a recognized book vendor; and since he was to print the book, it can be assumed that he already had become a business partner of his mother-in-law, the widow of Barrera. Printing was to begin one month hence, and the issue was to be ready by the end of ten months from the date of the contract. The first proceeds were to be divided at the termination of a year and a half, or on approximately April 23, 1616. The slight variation in title from that specified in the King's approval, "Commentaries of Peru" instead of "Royal Commentaries," suggests that already some question had arisen about the word "real" in the title.

Meanwhile, throughout the year 1614 Garcilaso was preoccupied with negotiations concerning the construction and embellishment of the chapel which was to serve as his sepulcher.[20] Apparently one of the autumnal gratifications of a Renaissance gentleman was a somewhat

[19] Archivo de Protocolos de Córdoba, Oficio 29, Protocolo 33, fols. 1669–1670. A record of the transaction is also to be found in the inventory of Garcilaso's goods.
[20] Various documents issued before Garcilaso's death and receipts for payments issued after his death reveal his plans for his chapel and crypt. See, for instance, documents dated March 5 and July 9, 1614, Archivo de Protocolos de Córdoba, Oficio 29, Protocolo 33, fols. 428v–430 and 1078v–1079. For discussions of the historian's sepulcher and those who eventually shared it, see José de la Torre y del Cerro, *Obras*, Vol. I, pp. 243–247; and especially Rafael Aguilar Priego, "Curiosidades sobre la capilla de Garcilaso en la Catedral de Córdoba," *Boletín de la Real Academia de Ciencias, Bellas Letras y Nobles Artes de Córdoba*, No. 61, 1949, pp. 77–83.

sensuous contemplation of his tomb, a combination of egoism and masochism which had reached a glorified pinnacle in the Escorial of Philip II. It was a last attempt to cling to the luxuries of mortality that could preserve a man's dignity and status even after his soul had departed and his body had been submitted to the indignities of the grave. Garcilaso's temporal dream of hidalguía long since had faded in the acid atmosphere of Spanish social mores, but deep within him there still lingered a persistent yearning planted by a cavalier father when he informed a small mestizo of his noble Hispanic heritage and placed in his hands a Latin grammar and a gentleman's bridle. At least in his magnificent tomb, as he slept alongside hallowed figures of Islam and Christendom, he could achieve some of this coveted status. Within the great mosque-cathedral his well-endowed chapel would face out upon many rows of Islamic palm branches, chiseled into crescents of crimson striped marble and supported by columns of porphyry and jasper that interlaced and multiplied into labyrinthian naves; and directly before it would lie the plateresque and filigreed sanctuary where priests and acolytes and singing boys would mumble and chant the sacred ritual of the Roman faith on down through the years. It would be necessary to pave an aisle between the high altar and his chapel and to enlarge the archway. And there must be a firmly forged and ornamental grill as well as an appreciable amount of precious jasper to conceal the repugnance of oozing and crumbling mortar. Over his own altar he would have a crucified Jesus carved from the finest of pine wood and set against a well-painted background of the New Jerusalem. Nor would he tenant this sacred place alone. For above ground there were to be two earthen sepulchers for his servants and their descendants, and within the crypt beneath where he himself would lie, space was to be provided for a number of men of high merit. But one other Renaissance luxury, though made evident today by no more than a few decayed fragments of cloth, he surely must have begged while indulging in pleasurable funereal contemplations: a pall which bore colors symbolic of noble blood and splendid accomplishments.

With this yearning for status in the grave, there persisted still a counterpart yearning for recompense and recognition at Madrid. Thus on November 13, 1614, some few days after contracting with Romero for the publication of his last chronicle, Garcilaso once again empowered his nephew to present to the King and his Council claims for services which the chronicler had rendered against the Moriscos, and once again, apparently, the efforts of Alonso Márquez came to nought.[21] But the proud Inca Garcilaso was not to be deterred. He still bore the smarting scar of that deep psychic wound received long ago when a royal inquisitor had permitted a battlefield rumor to outweigh a rich heritage of blood and noble deeds and thereby damned the aspirations of the son of Sebastián Garcilaso de la Vega. Ignoring the failure of his nephew's pleas, he now prepared another suit, which was presented on May 4, 1615. What a dramatic scene the presentation of this suit might have offered had this aged religious and intellect of noble mien carried it himself before the judges at Madrid or placed it in the perfumed hands of an effete Picture King! He had the wealth now for such an encounter and his clerical robes would have sufficed for the usual sartorial splendor demanded of a gentleman at Court. Yet for some reason—illness, age, political astuteness, or possibly an old vow—he relegated the task to an attorney and resident at Court, Cristóbal de Burgos y Arrellano.[22]

This was to be the Inca Garcilaso's final effort to obtain favor and recognition at Madrid, and in it one detects more defiance than hope, a final test, so to speak, of the verity of Spanish justice, and yet a persistent yearning to vindicate his father's honor. Moreover, it was an ultimate declaration, as he anticipated the tomb, of his identity with the New World rather than the Old. He was rich in lineage and clean of blood, and he had virtuously pursued, without recognition, three honorable routes to hidalguía, those of the sword, the pen, and the cross. There was little of the material that he needed and little to gain. But there was less to lose, and there was a profit to be found in the satisfaction of seeing justice prevail. His legal instructions indicate that he wished his attorney to omit nothing when he appeared before those august judges of the Council of the Indies; but rather, let him lay before them the complete picture of a mestizo from Peru and ask

---

[21] Archivo de Protocolos de Córdoba, Oficio 29, Protocolo 33, fols. 1725–1726.
[22] Archivo de Protocolos de Córdoba, Oficio 25, Protocolo 61, fols. 182–183.

that he be given what is due him through both lineage and service. Tell them that he is a scion of noble Inca sovereigns, and that he is the son of that Captain Garcilaso de la Vega who, as a first conqueror and a citizen encomendero of Cuzco, had "served His Majesty at his own cost and diminution as a loyal vassal on all occasions offered him." Tell them that he himself has served Philip II with both sword and pen, without recompense, in the rebellion of the Moriscos and in the writing of four books, the last of which is now licensed and in the press. And while asking favor for these services, proclaim his identity as the offspring of an Inca palla and a viracocha, and make a request for the stipulation which the King has ordered for the descendants of Inca kings. These things done, let his attorney make another appeal, this time before the Council of Castile, for permission to reprint and sell his translation of León Hebreo, which the Holy Inquisition within the past few years after some debate had forbidden to circulate.

The reception which Cristóbal de Burgos y Arrellano must have received in those velvet chambers, where more than a half century previously the mestizo Gómez Suárez de Figueroa had passed one of his gloomiest hours, is worth contemplating. Before a King and Council plagued with the pretensions of descendants of Incas and indoctrinated in the expediency of minimizing Incaic nobility, lay a plea from the mestizo, soldier, cleric, and chronicler who had done most to magnify this nobility and to convince Peruvians of their right to demand favor. It was a plea based in part on an old claim long since denied with a charge of sedition, and in part on a manuscript which, though already licensed and shielded with a dedication to the Virgin, carried subtleties that were to inspire a Spanish King more than a century later to declare that it should never have been allowed to circulate. And finally, it was accompanied by a second plea for permission to reissue in the vulgate a humanistic treatise which grave prelates had declared perilous to the masses, and which in its expurgation had aroused a controversy.

The outcome of this petition is unknown, but if it was given consideration, the final judgment was delayed until too late to bring satisfaction to the Inca Garcilaso. Since there is no extant evidence that the chronicler was ever favored in any of his five claims presented at Madrid, one can but fall back upon Garcilaso's own statement that once a man was pronounced seditious, both he and his descendants were doomed, and that the accusation hurled against Sebastián Garcilaso by Lope García de Castro in 1563 had closed the doors to the mestizo's pretensions forever. The damning version of Huarina surely persisted still in the chambers of the Picture King, for as yet no grave historian had denied it in print. An authentic denial lay in a manuscript now going through the presses at Córdoba, but though the complete issue of fifteen hundred copies had been promised by August 23, 1615, something had halted the publication.

And herein lies another enigma. Garcilaso's statement in his petition of May 4, 1615, that the second part of the *Comentarios* was being printed surely refers to the first copy which by royal order had to be compared with the rubricked manuscripts before licenses or prefaces or any additional copies could be printed. The fact that neither this final approval, with its correction of errors, nor the evaluation, with its statement of price, appeared before 1616, indicates that the delay may have been due to new objections which arose during the process of checking. The eventual approvals declared that the printed text corresponded with the original rubricked manuscript. If there were objections, one therefore must conclude that they were primarily to prefatory material, and especially to the Prologue addressing the Indians, mestizos, and creoles. Indeed the tenor of this Prologue suggests that Garcilaso may have added it after the failure of his last effort to gain his rights as both an Indian and a Spaniard, and to obtain permission to reprint and sell his translation of León Hebreo. On the other hand, as has been suggested, some question may have arisen concerning the title under which the printing of the book had been licensed. For Garcilaso was not a "royal" commentator, as his title at least slightly intimated; and in this same year of 1615, Antonio de Herrera, the officially designated "royal" historian of the New World, was publishing the last four "decades" of his *Historia general,* in which, incidentally, he made generous use of Garcilaso's *La Florida.*[23] Moreover,

[23] Theodore Irving in his preface to *The Conquest of Florida by Hernando de Soto* claims that Herrera's account of this expedition, which begins in the sixth "Década" of his *Historia general,* is an almost full-length incorporation of Garcilaso's *La Florida.* But Herrera, in his seventh "Década," Bk. I, Chap. 15 and Bk. VII, Chap. 12, declared that his material had been drawn from an account writ-

Garcilaso had persistently emphasized that the accounts of several other chroniclers who had written under royal approbation were careless and sometimes false, and that his intention was to give the "true" picture of what had transpired in the Indies. Such a declaration of intention would not have been offensive to the Crown so long as he treated the fate of the Inca under Incaic rulers, but it took on different colors when applied to the fate of the Incas under their Spanish conquerors and the fate of those same conquerors under the kings they had served "at their own cost and diminution." Not only would royal inquisitors have sensed the dangers latent in what Garcilaso had written, especially in his preface, but they would have questioned the wisdom of having such information appear under a title which suggested that the author wrote under a royal appointment.

The first printed copy of his last chronicle which had been prepared for inquisitors, the Inca Garcilaso may have seen; but if he did, that was all. Old, sick, and weary, he rapidly was approaching the end of his life, though he still persisted in expending energy on pious works. At some time during the ensuing days, he entered a hospital where he had volunteered to care for the poor. Here, as he awaited the outcome of his last plea at Madrid, the final license for his history, and the permit to reprint his translation, he succumbed to the affliction that was to terminate in his death.[24] Seventy-seven years previously he had opened his eyes in the umbilical center of a waning Inca realm, and he was closing them now in the heart of a decadent Spain. As he had traveled that long road from the pagan capital of the Sun to the capitals of Christendom, he had learned to look with compassion on all mankind. Thus now, while he awaited the end, there would flash across his memory the myriad faces of men and women he had encountered through the fleeting years—faces of friends he had esteemed as well

---

ten by one of De Soto's captains and presented later by a friar to Pablo de Laguna when he was President of the Council of the Indies. In Bk. II, Chap. 5 of the same "Década," Herrera told of having encountered Gonzalo Silvestre at Madrid in 1570.

[24] Vargas Ugarte, "Nota sobre Garcilaso," *Mercurio Peruano*, Vol. XX, Enero–Febrero, 1930, pp. 47–50. The nature of Garcilaso's last illness is not known. By August 20, 1615, because of "a trembling of the hand," he was unable to sign a letter of payment for Cristóbal de Luque, though in December of the same year he appeared as a godfather.

as of those he had held in contempt, of multiple godchildren to whom he had pledged spiritual paternity, of the humble and the lofty, the selfish and the lost, men with pale skins and men with dark pigments, humans sick with paganism and thirsting for salvation—and woven conspicuously into the fabric of that vision would be the countenances of the ecclesiastics and laymen who now attended him, the five servants who formed his household, and his dark son, who though lowborn carried in his veins the rich blood of Inca emperors. He had set out confidently to seek the solution to the enigmas of life in social caste and literary fame, and he had found it eventually in a social consciousness, a concern for the travail all men must endure both on earth and in the hereafter. And since his faith had embraced a concept in which earthly wealth could be utilized to alleviate or hasten the end of spiritual atonement, he now determined to name as universal heirs to his considerable assets all souls locked in Purgatory; and to assure his ghostly heirs of their mundane assets, he made arrangements for the establishment of a lucrative chaplaincy.

On April 18, 1616, the dying chronicler called for scribe, curates, and witnesses, and in their presence initiated a revision of his will.[25] "Let all who may see this testament," the scribe wrote, "know how I, Garzia Laso Ynga de la Bega, cleric, who formerly was called by another name, Gomez Juares de Figueroa, illegitimate son of Garzia Laso de la Bega, deceased native of Badajoz, citizen that I am of the city of Cordoba in the district of Santa Maria, being ill of body and sound of will, in my good senses, judgment, memory, and natural understanding . . ." Herein was to be his last magnanimous act before the awesome mutation of death and the grave, his confession of faith and plea for intercession, his disposal of worldly goods, and his contract for masses—more than five hundred in the days immediately following his interment and then as many *per diem ad infinitum* as the income from his estate would accommodate.

The major portion of Garcilaso's last testament was dedicated to matters concerning his chapel, which he named the Chapel of the

---

[25] For Garcilaso's will and its various codicils, see Archivo de Protocolos de Córdoba, Oficio 29, Protocolo 35, fols. 467–488, 505–507; Oficio 25, Protocolo 62, fols. 217v–218.

Blessed Souls of Purgatory, his chaplaincy, and the management of the estate which was to support such an institution. He expressed his desires concerning those who might be permitted to share his tomb, and he made further arrangements for the ornamentation of the chapel beneath which they were to lie, providing, among other things, fuel for a taper which must be kept burning eternally. And with all the astuteness of a successful man of affairs, he gave meticulous instructions as to how his estate should be managed and as to who should be responsible for that management—the patrons who would administer the whole, the administrator and accountant who would check the proceeds, the majordomo who would collect the income from rents, and the sacristan who would keep the chapel in order and supply the wine and host as well as the alms for the cleric priests saying the daily masses. For these tasks he designated men whom he felt to be trustworthy, and he demanded that the cleric priests who assisted be chosen from the poorest and most virtuous. But a long life in a grasping world had taught him that among ecclesiastics as well as laymen there always would be frail men who might be tempted to take advantage of departed souls. So he now emphasized that all masses from his income, even though ordered otherwise by the highest ecclesiastical dignitary, must be said in his chapel and for his soul and the souls of Purgatory. Moreover, he demanded that the cleric priests who received his silver be continually admonished not to omit the responses and always to sprinkle the sepulcher with Holy Water; and to avoid petty wrangling among hungry prelates, he specified that daily sacerdotal duties were to be given to those clerics who arrived first. And always, regardless of who was involved, there were to be inventories, books of account, and letters of receipt.

And yet in his concern with the material welfare of departed souls, Garcilaso did not forget those who had served him in life and would need sustenance after he was gone. To his old friend Cristóbal de Luque Bernardino he left an annuity; to three of his servants he left monetary gifts; and to his captive slave, Marina de Córdoba, he bequeathed freedom as well as an annual income of fifty ducats. And then there remained those two figures whose lives had touched him most intimately, Beatriz de Vega and their natural son. To each he now bequeathed an annuity of eighty ducats, requesting that in the event Beatriz died first, her income should be added to that of Diego de Vargas. All specified annuities were granted for life and one year after, but even in this phase of his generosity the chronicler revealed a typical Renaissance caution. Should any recipient be so frail or so foolish as to instigate a lawsuit, his or her income must cease at once.

The will was brought to a close and validated by witnesses. But the dying Inca still was unable to deliver his mind of the responsibilities detailed in his testament, and during the succeeding four days, with the aid of a scribe and witnesses, he added five separate codicils. Twice more he supplemented his gifts to Marina de Córdoba and Beatriz de Vega, leaving them but slightly more comfortable with additional household furnishings and food; he altered clauses concerning the patrons of his chaplaincy; he made further specifications concerning those who were invited to share the crypt of his chapel, one of whom was a female, who now must be excluded; and he asked that all dis-agreements over the administration of his chapel be referred to the Dean of the Cabildo of the Cathedral. His last codicil was made on April 22 and signed for him, as had been his will and all other codicils, by attendant officials, since he now was unable to pen so much as his own name. Yet as the hours passed he continued to fret about matters he had forgotten or overlooked in his testament; and in the absence of a scribe he asked the licentiate and prebendary Andrés Fernández de Bonilla to take a memorandum that could be affixed as a legal supple-ment. He wanted a change in plans for the succession of chaplains; the cancellation of a pecuniary obligation of the printer Francisco de Zea Tesa; and the provision of mourning apparel for his servants as well as for Juan Chamizo, tipstaff and musician. And in these final moments his thoughts turned once more to a beloved old knight-errant who had been interred with all the accoutrements of chivalry except a horse, and who for almost a half century had charmed a mestizo's fancies with magic words and a true heart. Since 1552, more or less, he now told Fernández de Bonilla, Gonzalo Silvestre had been his friend; yet con-tinually over those years he had lent ducats to this magnificent prodigal who had an unfortunate habit of spending more than his estate pro-vided. Furthermore, Silvestre had had an ingenious but charming manner of disregarding obligations, and at the time of his death had extended the debt to eight hundred ducats. Had Silvestre survived him, Garcilaso undoubtedly would have canceled the obligation out of affection; but he now wanted Fernández de Bonilla to collect the gold from Silvestre's nephew, Alonso Díaz de Belcázar, who had enjoyed the fruits of the loan and in 1599 had admitted that the debt was legal. This money, he surely felt, could be used to augment the sum he had specified for atoning souls in Purgatory, among whom he of course would visualize his old friend who had served as the source for *La Florida*. Fernández de Bonilla carefully recorded the memorandum and signed it in Garcilaso's name.

As the memory of the dying chronicler dwelled on the man who had provided so much of the information for his histories, it must have dwelled also upon the fate of his still unpublished account of the conquest. For it was approximately on this day, according to contract, that Francisco Romero was to have divided proceeds from the sale of the second part of the *Comentarios reales*. Indeed, Romero had witnessed a codicil signed two days previously, yet there is not one word in will, codicil, or memorandum concerning either Romero or the last volume from the pen of the Inca chronicler. But what could be said? The only printed copy undoubtedly still lay in the hands of inquisitors at Madrid, who through sloth, indifference, or caution were withholding the final license and an assessment of the price for which each book was to be sold. So during these terminal hours, when the mind of the chronicler agonized over the perils and perplexities of a lost world, and when his thoughts must have turned repeatedly to the tragedy of Tahuantinsuyu, he would have been sadly and poignantly aware that the world might never see in print his "true" interpretation of the conquest and his vindication of a father about whom the Fates had woven an inextricable web at Huarina. This grief the Inca Garcilaso would carry to the tomb; for by the late hours of April 22, or the early morning hours of April 23, he was dead.[26]

[26] Archivo de Protocolos de Córdoba, Oficio 29, Protocolo 35, fols. 501–504; Archivo de la Parroquia del Sagrario de Córdoba, Libro I de Defunciones, fol. 60. The inscribed marble slabs placed several years later in Garcilaso's chapel record that he died on April 22, 1616. The inventory of his property made on April 26, 1616, records that he died "three days ago," which would have been April 23. His official

On April 24, 1616, while the great iron bells of Córdoba tolled the dead, the body of the Inca Garcilaso was borne to his coveted sepulcher in the Chapel of the Blessed Souls of Purgatory. In death he wore neither shining armor nor silks and taffetas, but the sable robe of an humble religious; and in those hands which had earned the right to bear a sword even in the tomb, he clasped a simple cross. Yet as a customary indication that he, like his famed cavalier ancestors, had harried heretics in the service of his King, this renowned mestizo, according to dim but acceptable evidence, was laid to rest with legs crossed; and apparently, according to the same evidence, as a gesture to his rich lineage, his casket was sheathed in crimson velvet embossed with ribbons of silver silk and held taut by studs of hammered copper.[27] Among the little group assembled to mourn would have been three forlorn and obscure figures: Juan Chamizo, tipstaff; Beatriz de Vega, faithful concubine-servant; and Diego de Vargas, illegal and unacknowledged son. They had been given appropriate raiment for the occasion.

---

death notice records that he died (murió) on April 24, 1616, but the word "murió" sometimes referred to burial rather than death. It seems plausible that, though buried on April 24, he died on April 23, a surmise which is supported to some extent by the fact that subsequent documents show his legatees collecting their annuities on October 23 and April 23 respectively.

[27] Porras Barrenechea, El Inca Garcilaso en Montilla, pp. 256–259.

POSTLUDE

D IEGO DE VARGAS, only known offspring of the Inca Garcilaso de la Vega, apparently survived his father some thirty-five years, dying about 1652. On July 26, 1619, the Cabildo of the Holy Cathedral at Córdoba elected him sacristan of the Chapel of the Blessed Souls of Purgatory, an office which he was still holding as late as 1646. To him, therefore, fell the task of maintaining provisions for daily masses, doling out petty compensations to clerics who performed them, and providing oil for the taper which his father had ordered to burn forever. Documents show him frequently renting new houses and attending horticultural interests; and on the death of his mother in 1620, he, according to Garcilaso's stipulations, would have begun to receive the meager income she had inherited. But he often suffered necessity and was forced to beg for sustenance from the funds his father had provided for pious works. In 1647 he rented living quarters in the Calle de los Judíos near the gates of Almodóvar, and it was here, apparently, when he had passed his seventieth year, that he died. Íñigo de Córdoba Ponce de León, who had known him both as an arrogant youth and as a quiet and composed old man, wrote that don Diego many times boasted that he had transcribed the whole of the *Comentarios reales.* Thus, in this bastard son begotten on a serving woman, Garcilaso surely had found an untiring and reliable scribe.[1]

[1] Archivo de Protocolos de Córdoba, Oficio 25, Protocolo 96, fols. 377–377v; Oficio 29, Tomo 39, fols. 148–149; also documents published by Rafael Aguilar Priego, "El Hijo del Inca Garcilaso," *Boletín de la Real Academia de Ciencias, Bellas Letras y Nobles Artes de Córdoba,* Año XVI, No. 54, Julio–Diciembre, 1945, pp. 281–300; Rubén Vargas Ugarte, "Nota sobre Garcilaso," *Mercurio Peruano,* Vol. XX, Enero–Febrero, 1930, pp. 47–50.

And what was the fate of the inflammatory manuscript which on Garcilasco's death remained still in the hands of a cautious tribunal at Madrid? Though there is nothing in Garcilaso's will to indicate that he left plans for the publication of this chronicle posthumously, it is hardly conceivable that he would not have done so. Indeed, there is much to suggest that before death he instructed the guardians of his estate to consider the task as one of the conditions of his legacy and to use the proceeds from the sale of the book for the benefit of the souls in Purgatory. And now undoubtedly Francisco Romero and Lucía de Leries, his mother-in-law and business partner, still held the original plates and awaited only the final licenses for printing and circulating the entire issue. On October 29, 1616, the Cabildo of the Cathedral Church commissioned the Prebendary Andrés Fernández de Bonilla to go in person to Madrid to complete the writs necessary for "the printing of the books included in the pious endowment of Garcilaso de la Vega," and Fernández de Bonilla's efforts apparently met with immediate success.[2] Within two weeks, on November 12, 1616, the licentiate Murcia de la Llana, at Madrid, after listing various printer's errors and calling the book *Historia general del Pirú,* declared that it corresponded with its original. Five days later, on November 17, Gerónimo Núñez de León, royal scribe for the King and his Councilmen in residence, declared that His Majesty as well as the Council had seen and licensed for printing a book by the Inca Garcilaso de la Vega entitled *Segunda parte de los comentarios reales* and that the total price of each copy was to be eighteen reales and sixteen maravedís. Since the only printed approbations of the King and his Council appearing in the published copy are those made almost two years previously on January 6 and 21, 1614, which of course refer to the book by its original title, and not as the *Historia general del Pirú,* it is doubtful if Philip III and his Inquisitors took the time or had the patience to examine the printed book, or if they ever saw the "Prologue to the Indians, mestizos, and creoles," at least a part if not all of which had not been written at the time they had approved the manuscript. Shortly after all final licenses were received, and surely before the end of the year, there

---

[2] Archivo del Cabildo Eclesiástico de Córdoba, Actas Capitulares, Tomo 39. All licenses and privileges for this volume are included within the book itself.

was issued from the Córdoba press of doña Lucía de Leries, who signed her imprint as "the Widow of Andrés de Barrera," at least one copy, but possibly no more than one, of the *Segunda parte de los* page, and only the title page, reading: *Historia general del Perú. Trata comentarios reales,* but for some reason as yet unknown, with the title page, and only the title page, reading: *Historia general del Perú. Trata el descubrimiento del; y como lo ganaron los Españoles. Las guerras civiles que huvo entre Pizarros, y Almagros, sobre la partija de la tierra. Castigo y levantamiento de tiranos: y otros sucessos particulares que en la Historia se contienen. Escrita por el Ynca Garcilaso de la Vega, Capitán de su Magestad.*[3] The bulk of this first edition, however, was not published until 1617, when it appeared under an identical title with a somewhat modified format, which already had been altered at least once in the 1616 issue. For instance, in all copies of title pages the wording, with the exception of the imprint, remains the same, but there are differences in the design and arrangement of the type and especially in the etched Virgin symbols. These differences can be seen in at least three extant title pages of the 1616 issue, and very noticeable modifications appear in that of 1617. However, the prefatory material of both the 1616 and 1617 issues undoubtedly was printed from the same plates, and one can assume, without much doubt, that such is true of the text.

Garcilaso, of course, had intended this volume to be a continuation of his first commentaries on Peru, and he always had referred to it as such. Moreover, as has been seen, its various approvals and licenses make manifest that its proper title was *La segunda parte de los comentarios reales.* Of significance, therefore, is that within the context of this chronicle, each of its eight books is entitled *Libro . . . de la segunda parte de los comentarios reales,* and these same words are used as running heads throughout the entire volume. In 1621, when Diego de León, a Córdoba bookseller, bought from Juan Chamizo Garrido, now majordomo of Garcilaso's chapel, ninety-four reams of the Inca's

[3] "General history of Peru, which treats of its discovery and of how it was won by the Spaniards, of the civil wars that occurred between Pizarrists and Almagrists over the partition of the land, of the punishment and insurrection of the tyrants, and of other particular events contained within its history. Written by the Inca Garcilaso de la Vega, Captain of His Majesty." Some 1616 title pages have been discovered bound with the 1617 issue, and it has been said that no 1616 issue was ever cir-

chronicles, he called them the *Comentarios reales del Peru primera e segunda partes.*[4]

Possibly the most significant variance in the title pages of the 1616 and 1617 issues is to be found in the line identifying the publisher. For to the earlier imprint, "En Cordova, Por la Viuda de Andres de Barrera," the 1617 issue has added the significant words "a su costa," and it omits the "de" before "Barrera." In commissioning Andrés Fernández de Bonilla to complete the task of bringing Garcilaso's last chronicle to light, the Cabildo had ordered that money be advanced from his endowment but had added that if there were not sufficient funds in this source, they should be borrowed or sought out elsewhere. Thus by settling the bulk of his estate upon the souls of Purgatory and obligating its income to such a medley of pious works, Garcilaso had hazarded the birth of his great classic. Some credit, therefore, appears due the Córdoba widow who dipped into a lean purse and played midwife to the publication. When on May 10, 1621, this woman drew up her last will, she declared that she once had held in possession certain volumes by the Inca Garcilaso de la Vega, half of which belonged to the chaplaincy of the said Garcilaso and the other half equally to herself and her son-in-law, Francisco Romero. These volumes, she disclosed, she had permitted to be conveyed to the Indies by the Canon Pedro de Aranda. So to this astute and pious woman also can be given credit for being one of the first, if not the first, to make Garcilaso's inspiring commentaries available in Peru; and to the Canon Aranda, possibly a kinsman of Garcilaso's aunt, Luisa Ponce de León, must be given some credit for their early circulation among the people to whom they were addressed.[5]

The story of many of the books which were conveyed by Spanish galleons to the far reaches of the Indies has been told; but the devious routes followed by Garcilaso's chronicles as they were carried to his native Peru may never be traced. One might suspect that they appeared

---

culated. There is, however, a complete copy of this issue in the Bibliothèque Nationale at Paris.

[4] Archivo de Protocolos de Córdoba, Oficio 29, Protocolo 40, fol. 877.

[5] Archivo de Protocolos de Córdoba, Oficio 28, Protocolo 47, fols. 495–450 (*sic*). Doña Luisa had an uncle named Pedro de Aranda.

first at Los Reyes in the little book mart of Miguel Méndez, who is known to have done business with the widow who published some of them.[6] But again they may have been dispersed mainly among the religious who still guarded the intellectual as well as the spiritual development of the natives. But Garcilaso's chronicles were read in Peru, and as time moved swiftly down the dreary years of Indian suffering and despair, his exhortations kept a flame burning among men whose emotional fibers penetrated deeply into the subsoil of a once golden empire, feeding their hearts with a pride of heritage as well as with an angry ambition to rise above their miseries and demand their rights as members of the human race. At length, when a century and a half later the tide of Spanish abuses had reached flood, the enduring power of Garcilaso's words became evident in a prophetic insurrection led by José Gabriel Condorcanqui, heir-at-law of the Inca Túpac Amaru, whom Francisco de Toledo had so injudiciously executed.

José Condorcanqui was a man of dignity and sense who had distinguished himself as a scholar in the Colegio de San Borja at Cuzco. In his early dealings with the emissaries of Spain he had utilized diplomacy, and only when this method failed had he resorted to arms and intrigue. The circumstance which rendered him particularly menacing to Spain was that to the Indians and all those of Indian lineage, he represented a symbol of a lost empire and a hope for the eventual restoration of the Inca throne under the leadership of a true descendant of the Moon and the Sun. Because of an influx of creole blood, the Incaic strain in this man was weak; but in his veins did flow the blood of the great Inca Huayna Cápac, and he captured emotion by assuming the name of his martyred ancestor, becoming Túpac Amaru II.[7] His rebellion was menacing and bloody but short, and his subsequent execution on May 18, 1781, represents one of the most cruel spectacles in the annals of Cuzco. Not only was he forced to witness the mutilation, beating, and garroting of his beloved wife and other kinsmen, but he himself was deprived of his tongue, and then, after futile efforts were

[6] In her will the widow of Barrera declared that Miguel Méndez, a maestro of books "who is in the Indies," owed her a thousand reales. Irving A. Leonard in his *Books of the Brave*, pp. 273, 277, identified a Miguel Méndez as a merchant of Lima.

[7] For the ascendency of Condorcanqui, see Rómulo Cúneo-Vidal, *Historia de las guerras de los últimos Incas peruanos contra el poder español*, pp. 304–307.

made to pull his limbs from his body by four straining horses, his head was severed and placed on a pike for exposure and his body was sent to Machu Picchu for burning. Meanwhile, his ten-year-old son Fernando, whose shrieks had pierced the Andean air as he witnessed the terrible agony of his father, was sentenced for life to the dungeons of Cádiz, and within the next few years most of the patriot's kin were disposed of in some equally diabolical manner.

The terrible punishment wrought upon José Gabriel Condorcanqui, at least in part, represented another vain effort to subdue a long-burning spirit of veneration and to extinguish an ancient culture. For the order which condemned him also had forbidden the wearing of traditional Indian dress, the presentation of Quechuan dramas and spectacles, and even the use of the Quechuan language. Furthermore, it had demanded that all documents and pictures relating to this Inca and his lineage be seized and burned and that the reading of the histories of the Inca Garcilaso de la Vega be prohibited.[8]

Royal officials must long since have been aware of the latent perils in the substance of Garcilaso's chronicles and in the symbolism of the man himself. His story of the bleak consequences of his own search for favor and his bold innuendoes concerning the Spanish conquest had damned Spain's persistent indifference to the welfare of its colonies and to the rights of the men who had won them. By openly proclaiming himself a mestizo, an Indian, and an Inca, he had established himself as a leader among the survivors of the Incaic dynasty; and his magnificent account of the annals of Tahuantinsuyu rang with such truth that he quickly had won confidence as an authority on the Incaic lineage. The first part of his *Comentarios,* as has been mentioned, had been used before his death to bolster the claims of royal Incas; and even as late as 1747 the King, while investigating the pretenses of the mestizo Juan de Bustamente Carlos Inca, had sought the document which Garcilaso in 1603 had told of receiving from the Incas of Cuzco.[9] This document was never located; but the chronicles of Garcilaso still were

---

[8] Clements R. Markham, *A History of Peru,* p. 205; Aurelio Miró Quesada y Sosa, *El Inca Garcilaso,* p. 184.

[9] Documents bearing two dates, June 22, 1747, and February 18, 1748, Seville, Archivo General de Indias, Audiencia de Lima, Legajo 472, fols. 1–2v.

to be found in sundry parts of the Indian world. These histories, in addition to keeping alive the Inca tradition, could be utilized as a basis for pretenses; and through the years such pretenses had continued to vex the watchdogs of the Royal Hacienda, not merely because of the growing number of those with honest pretensions but because of the flux of false pretenders.

Yet it was the inspiring exhortations of a preface which after years of futile pleas and disappointments Garcilaso had affixed to his final chronicle, a plea for spiritual and intellectual enlightenment and a bold stand against tyranny, that Spain now regarded as most perilous to her colonial affairs. On May 1, 1781, thirteen days before he ordered the execution of José Condorcanqui, the Royal Inspector José Antonio de Areche, alarmed by false rumors that the British hoped to restore the Peruvian throne to this patriot, had written the court that the Indians should be forbidden to read the *Historia* of Garcilaso, and the dangers therein once more were brought to the attention of His Majesty when at the close of the year 1781 Areche was recalled to Spain to give an account of the uprising and the extermination of the rebellious Inca.[10] Thus on April 21, 1782, the Spanish King saw fit to address the following confidential order to his Viceroy at Lima:

The Indians of the Kingdom of Peru and of all the other provinces in general are possessed of many abuses that have given rise to a number of abominable practices, among which is their desire to preserve the memory of their ancient pagan customs. In the whole of their confusions and enthusiasms, there is to be noted most especially the lack of gravity and truthfulness with which they convince themselves that the fact of their relationship with or descent from the original pagan kings gives them the right of nobility or of calling themselves Incas. Their reports, one notes regrettably, have been approved many times by the government and at times implicitly and explicitly sanctioned by the Royal Audiencia, a practice which is abominable and the authority of which should be denied.

In view, therefore, of this long-standing and senseless abuse, the King, as his magistrates should have done for its correction and eradication, has resolved for the present that Your Lordship should make clear, though with

---

[10] José Toribio Medina, *Biblioteca hispano-americana*, Vol. VI, p. 32. One of Areche's suggestions was that Garcilaso's history be permitted to circulate in Latin.

caution, to the Royal Audiencia of Lima that it is not to admit for qualifica-
tion any reports of such descendancy, or any proofs or declarations of nobility
on the part of any Indians regardless of their class; for His Majesty desires
that this faculty be reserved for the Royal Chamber of the Supreme Council
of the Indies, to which for such judgments all processes and papers are to be
submitted in advance, without the necessity of His Majesty's resolution having to be declared before an opportune time, at which he will order Your
Excellency to execute it.

Likewise the King desires Your Excellency to seek with the same caution
to collect, sagaciously, the *Historia* of the Inca Garcilaso, from which those
natives have learned many prejudicial things, as well as other detractive papers of the tribunals and magistrates of the Kingdom, which were printed
at times when they were believed innocent, though the suppositious predic-
tion encompassed in the preface to the *Historia* should never have been permitted. For this purpose, I authorize Your Excellency, by order of His
Majesty, to take whatever normal means may be conducive, even though
it may be by having the copies of these works bought in all confidence and
secrecy by third parties and paid for from the substance of the Royal Hacienda, it being so important that the collection be carried out in order that
the natives be deprived of the additional incentive of such documents for
reviving their evil practices. Concerning this grave matter, Your Excellency
should bring his dispositions into agreement with don Jorge Escobedo, who
is to be advised of whatever is pertinent to its accomplishment. May God
protect Your Excellency for many years. Aranjuez, April 21, 1782. Gálvez—
Señor Viceroy of Peru.

Apparently the King's command reached all magistrates in the regions of the Andes, for a letter from Andrés Maestre, Governor of
Tucumán, to the Viceroy Vertiz at Buenos Aires reveals the precautions
being taken in that area concerning the chronicles of the Inca Garcilaso:

With the date of December 21 of the past year, Your Excellency confiden-
tially ordered me to seize the *Historia* of the Inca Garcilaso and any other
papers derogatory to the tribunals of the Kingdom and you advised of
measures to be taken to meet the difficulty in the case of persons who may
wish to sell them privately. With an ecclesiastic, who, I am informed, pos-
sesses them, I will take the necessary means of trying to buy them without
letting it be known why I am asking for them.

The Viceroy of Buenos Aires answered by return post:

Your reply to my confidential order of the twenty-first of December concerning the surreptitious collection of the books of the Inca Garcilaso and many others unfavorable to the tribunals of the Kingdom, makes manifest the obstacles presented by the question of people being willing to sell them, either his relatives or others who possess them, especially a pious ecclesiastic whom you know to have them. In which case I order that you take all precaution to obtain them, either by borrowing them or by getting possession of them by any other scheme that prudence and sagacity may dictate.[11]

Thirty years after these efforts to suppress Garcilaso's chronicles, the hosts of Napoleon swept across Spain and the masters of Peru themselves were made to feel the heel of the conqueror. Ironically, on entering Córdoba the invaders encountered the Hospital of the Immaculate Conception, over whose ancient portals still remained an invitation which to a Frenchman must have been an affront: "Enter here all ye who are afflicted with the Gallic pox." Seizing the therapeutic equipment of this venerable refuge which the Inca Garcilaso had once supervised, the marauders brought its services to a humiliating close. Meanwhile, other poachers, prowling the mosque-cathedral, paused at the Chapel of the Blessed Souls of Purgatory and from its altar purloined an exquisitely enameled chalice. But the little taper in Garcilaso's sanctuary was left to burn, and the Gallic invasion of Spain provided occasion for a renewed effort toward independence in the Spanish colonies.

Inflamed with the awakening spirit of liberty, José de San Martín, an aristocratic young creole long resident in Spain, returned to Buenos Aires to participate in a movement which eventually would deliver America from Spain. One of this patriot's first steps was to urge the Andean Indians to join in a rebellion aimed at restoring their patriarchal heritage; and when in 1816 Argentia on declaring its independ-

[11] For the King's order and the subsequent correspondence, see Medina, *Biblioteca hispano-americana*, Vol. VI, Prólogo, p. xxxii; Luis A. Arocena, *El Inca Garcilaso y el humanismo renacentista*, pp. 19–20, 68–69; Manuel de Mendiburu, *Diccionario histórico-biográfico del Perú*, Vol. XI Apéndice, pp. 413–414; Mariano Picón-Salas, *De la conquista a la independencia*, Chap. VII, pp. 168–169.

ence talked of forming a separate monarchy, this creole of pure Spanish descent encouraged a vain and fantastic scheme to place upon the throne a grandson of the Inca José Gabriel Condorcanqui Túpac Amaru. And at some time during his career, San Martín caused to be circulated once again the *Comentarios* of the Inca Garcilaso.[12] In 1821, command of the liberating forces was passed on to the great creole Simón Bolívar, who, as he moved south through the ancient realm of Tahuantinsuyu, had declared that he was marching to fulfill his promise to reunite the empire of the Incas to the empire of freedom. Four years later, at Cuzco, the famed Liberator in a moment of poetic ecstacy wrote to a friend of the unsurpassed wonders of the Imperial City and the civilization it symbolized. Its history, he declared, was a tapestry of cruelty to the Indians woven by Bartolomé de las Casas; its legend was to be found in the chronicles of the Inca Garcilaso de la Vega.[13]

Indians, mestizos, and creoles had heard the message of the Inca Garcilaso de la Vega, who once was known in the Indies as Gómez Suárez de Figueroa, and already he had become the fixed symbol that he remains today—the everlasting and lyric quipucamayu of the lost Inca realm of Tahuantinsuyu, and above all a persistent voice proclaiming the innate and cultural right of American Indians to demand a position of human dignity, respect, and sympathy.

[12] Miró Quesada y Sosa, *El Inca Garcilaso*, p. 184.
[13] Simón Bolívar to José Joaquín Olmedo, Cuzco, June 27, 1825, in *Cartas del Libertador,* Vol. V, p. 6–8.

GLOSSARY, BIBLIOGRAPHY, *and* INDEX

GLOSSARY OF SPANISH AND QUECHUAN WORDS

Adelantado (Sp.): Title given a man who was sent out to explore, conquer, and govern new lands.

Alcalde (Sp.): Justice of the Peace, Mayor of a city, or Chairman of the Council of the government of a town.

Alcalde Ordinario (Sp.): An Alcalde who takes cognizance of causes in the first instance.

Amauta (Q.): A philosopher, wise man, poet, or teacher of the Incas.

Auca (Q.): A tyrant, traitor, and liar.

Audiencia (Sp.): A supreme court presided over by a Viceroy or President; also the territory under the jurisdiction of this court.

Auqui (Q.): A title applied to the younger and unmarried sons of the ruling Inca and to those of his masculine relatives descended through male lineage. Thus, an unmarried prince.

Caballero contioso or cuantioso (Sp.): Literally, opulent cavalier. In Montilla, according to Porras Barrenechea, these men were not hidalgos but were of a new social class of villagers who had been enriched by commerce and trade.

Cabildo (Sp.): The governing body of a town or city and the building where it met.

Capitulación (Sp.): A stipulation or agreement.

Cédula (Sp.): An order, warrant, or decree.

Condado (Sp.): An earldom.

Corequenque (Q.): A bird sacred to the Incas.

Corregidor (Sp.): A Spanish magistrate in charge of a town, city, or dependent district, whose duty was to govern, correct, and punish.

Coya (Q): The empress or legitimate consort of the ruling Inca. Her daughters could use the title but only as an appendage to show their relation to the mother. Unless by special dispensation, the coya was always the Inca's sister.

Encomendero (Sp.): The holder of an encomienda.

Encomienda (Sp.): A tract of land which, along with the Indians living on

388   GLOSSARY

it, was granted by the Crown to favored individuals. In Garcilaso's time
the grants in Peru were made for two lives only.

Expediente (Sp.) : A collection of all the documents and papers relating to a
business matter or a lawsuit.

Factor (Sp.) : An agent or commissioner.

Hacienda (Sp.) : A landed estate.

Hidalguía (Sp.) : Hidalgoism; the status of an hidalgo, who, as a nobleman
of lesser rank, enjoyed certain rights and privileges.

Inca, Inga, Ynca (Q.) : The ruling emperor of Tahuantinsuyu or any member of its imperial caste.

Indios de servicio (Sp.) : The Indians forced to labor under the mita system.
See mita.

Llatu or llautu (Q.) : A colored fillet, band, or tassel worn around the head
of the ruling Inca as a symbol of his sovereignty.

Los Reyes or La Ciudad de los Reyes (Sp.) : The original name of the city
later called Lima. Lima is a Spanish corruption of the Quechuan Rímac,
the name of the river which runs through the city as well as of the surrounding valley.

Mama (Q.) : Mother. Also a title of respect borne by the married women of
the Imperial Inca caste.

Mar del Sur (Sp.) : Sea of the South, or the section known to the conquistadors of that body of water which Magellan was to call the Pacific Ocean.

Marrano or Maraño (Sp.) : A derisive or contemptuous word applied to
either a Moor or a Jew who had professed Christianity to escape persecution.

Mestizo (Sp.) : A man of mixed Indian and Spanish blood.

Mita (Sp. but first Q.) : A corvée or system of forced labor under which
Indians worked in turns and for a specified period of time.

Morisco (Sp.) : A Spanish Moor who ostensibly had accepted Christianity.

Ñusta (Q.) : A princess. Either the legitimate daughter of the ruling Inca
or of anyone of royal blood.

Oidor (Sp.) : A judge or justice of an audiencia.

Pachacámac (Q.) : The supreme god of the Incas; he who gave life to the
universe.

Palla (Q.) : A lady of royal blood. Although, according to his own definition, Garcilaso could have referred to his mother as a ñusta, he always
referred to her as a palla.

Pampa (Q.) : A plain.

Pancuncu (Q.) : A torch made of oiled straw.

Quechua (Q.) : The official language of the Inca Empire. Also any Indian
of those civilized tribes which formed the dominant element of that empire.

Quipu (Q.): A main cord from which hung colored and knotted string by which each succeeding generation of Incas kept accounts of their laws, their government, and the most important events of their times.

Quipucamayu (Q.): A man charged with guarding and recording the records or quipus of the Incas.

Repartimiento (Sp.): An allotment of Indians given as a reward to Spanish conquerors. Used interchangeably with encomienda.

Residencia (Sp.): An account demanded of Spanish authorities, usually when leaving their designated offices. A scrutiny of their official acts.

Santiago, San Iago, San Diego (Sp.): St. James the Greater, the Apostle who was commonly believed to have been the first to preach Christianity in Spain. Thus he became the patron saint of Spain and his name was on the lips of all Christian Spaniards as they entered battle. The first of the four great military orders in Spain was that of Santiago, and no person descended from Moor or Jew could claim admission to it.

Tahuantinsuyu (Q.): The four united sections which constituted the Inca Empire. The center or navel of the empire was Cuzco, and the regions to the north, east, south and west were called, respectively, Chinchasuyu, Antisuyu, Collasuyu and Cuntisuyu.

Tambo (Sp. corruption): A wayside stopping place or roadhouse which first had been built by Huayna Cápac to house himself and his army.

Villcapampa (Q.): The last remnant of the Inca Empire. It lay to the north of Cuzco.

Visita (Sp.): An official inspection of a jurisdiction.

Vega (Sp.): An open plain.

Viracocha (Q.): The name of the specter messenger sent by the Sun Deity to the Inca prince who adopted the name. Since the Indians believed the Spaniards were similar messengers and likewise sons of the Sun, they were called viracochas.

Vitcos (Q.): Capital of Villcapampa, last stronghold of the Incas.

Yáhuar (Q.): Blood.

Zúpay (Q.): The Devil.

A SELECTED BIBLIOGRAPHY

Archives and Libraries Consulted

Austin, U. S. A.: Latin American Collections of the University of Texas.
Badajoz, Spain: Archivo Histórico Provincial de Badajoz.
Córdoba, Spain: Archivo de Protocolos de Córdoba; Archivo del Cabildo Eclesiástico de Córdoba; Archivo de la Parroquia del Sagrario de Córdoba.
Cuzco, Peru: Archivo Histórico del Cuzco.
Lima, Peru: Biblioteca Central de la Universidad Nacional Mayor de San Marcos.
Madrid, Spain: Académica Biblioteca Perpetua de la Real Academia de la Historia; Biblioteca Nacional de España.
Mexico City, Mexico: Biblioteca Nacional de México.
Montilla, Spain: Archivo de Protocolos de Montilla; Archivo Municipal de Montilla; Archivo de la Parroquia de Santiago de Montilla.
Seville, Spain: Archivo General de Indias; Biblioteca Capitular Colombina.
Simancas, Spain: Archivo General de Simancas.

COLLECTIONS

La Audiencia de Charcas, ed. Roberto Levillier. 3 vols. Madrid: Imprenta de Juan Pueyo, 1918–1922. In *Colección de publicaciones de la Biblioteca del Congreso Argentino.*
La Audiencia de Lima, ed. Roberto Levillier. Madrid: Imprenta de Juan Pueyo, 1922. In *Colección de publicaciones de la Biblioteca del Congreso Argentino.*
Cartas de Indias. 2 vols. Madrid: Manuel G. Hernández, 1877.
Colección de documentos inéditos del Archivo de Indias. 45 vols. Madrid, 1865–1884.
Colección de documentos inéditos para la historia de España. 112 vols. Madrid, 1842–1895.
Colección de documentos inéditos relativos al descubrimiento, conquista y colonización de las posesiones españoles en América y Occeania [sic], *sacados, en su mayor parte, del Real Archivo de Indias.* 42 vols. Madrid, 1864–1884.

Colección de documentos literarios del Perú, ed. Manuel de Odriozola. 11 vols. Lima, 1863.

Colección de libros y documentos referentes a la historia de América. 19 vols. Madrid, 1904–1919.

Colección de libros y documentos referentes a la historia del Perú, Series II. 12 vols. Lima, 1916–1919.

Correspondencia entre la Nunciatura en España y la Santa Sede durante el reinado de Felipe III. José de Olarra Garmendia and María Luisa de Larramendi, Viuda de Olarra, comps. Rome: Iglesia Nacional Española (Publicaciones del Instituto Español de Historia Eclesiástica, Subsidia No. 7), 1965.

Gobernantes del Perú, ed. Roberto Levillier. 14 vols. Madrid: Sucesores de Rivadeneyra, 1921–1926. In *Colección de publicaciones de la Biblioteca del Congreso Argentino.*

Martel-Cabrera expediente. Collection of manuscript documents relating to the suit of Luisa Martel de los Ríos and her second husband, Gerónimo Luis de Cabrera, for the Garcilaso repartimientos. Archivo de Indias, Seville. Judicia, Legajo 433, fols. 1–243.

Nueva colección de documentos inéditos para la historia de España y sus Indias. 6 vols. Madrid, 1896.

Sarmiento Palacio expediente. Collection of manuscript documents relating to the suit of Leonor del Castillo and her husband, Juan Sarmiento Palacio, for remuneration for the services of Leonor's father, Pedro Sánchez del Castillo, who married the mestiza daughter of Sebastián Garcilaso de la Vega. Biblioteca Nacional de México. Ramo Inquisición, Vol. 496, fols. 264v–275v.

Silvestre expediente. Collection of manuscript documents relating to various petitions of Gonzalo Silvestre. Archivo de Indias, Seville. Patronato 101, R. 18, Peru.

BOOKS

Abarbanal, Judah. See León Hebreo.

Anonymous. *Relaçam verdadeira dos trabalhos q̃ ho governador dõ Fernãdo de souto e certos fidalgos portugueses passarom no descobrimẽto de provincia da Frolida. Agora novamẽte feita per hũ fidalgo Delvas.* Evora: Casa de Andrés de Burgos, 1557.

Arbó, Sebastián Juan. *Cervantes: The Man and His Time.* New York: The Vanguard Press, 1955.

Arocena, Luis A. *El Inca Garcilaso y el humanismo renacentista.* Buenos Aires: Artes Gráficas Bartolomé U. Chiesino, 1949.

Artigas, Miguel. *Don Luis de Góngora y Argote: Biografía y estudio crítico.* Madrid: Tipografía de la "Revista de Archivos," 1925.

Barrantes, D. Vicente. *Aparato bibliográfico para la historia de Extremadura.* Madrid: Pedro Núñez, 1875.

Bermúdez Plata, Cristóbal, ed. *Catálogo de pasajeros a Indias.* 3 vols. Seville: Imprenta Editorial de la Gavadia, 1942.

Birney, Hoffman. *Brothers of Doom: The Story of the Pizarros of Peru.* New York: G. P. Putnam's Sons, 1942.

Bolívar, Simón. *Cartas del Libertador,* ed. Vicente Lecuna. 10 vols. Caracas: El Comercio, 1929–1930.

Bolton, Herbert Eugene. *Coronado: Knight of Pueblos and Plains.* New York: Whittlesey House, and Albuquerque, New Mexico: The University of New Mexico Press [1949].

Cabrera, Pablo. *Córdoba de la Nueva Andalucía.* Córdoba de Argentina: Imprenta de la Penitenciaría, 1933.

Cabrera de Córdoba, Luis. *Relaciones de las cosas sucedidas en la Corte de España desde 1599 hasta 1614.* Madrid: Imprenta de J. Martín Algería, 1857.

Carbonero y Sol, León. *Índice de los libros prohibidos por el Santo Oficio de la Inquisición española.* Madrid: Imprenta de Pérez Dubrull, 1873.

Castro, Américo. *Structure of Spanish History,* trans. Edmund L. King. Princeton: Princeton University Press, 1954.

Cervantes Saavedra, Miguel de. *El casamiento engañoso y El coloquio de los perros,* ed. Agustín G. de Amazúa y Mayo. Madrid: Bailly-Bailliere, 1912.

———. *Don Quixote,* trans. Peter Motteux. 4 vols. Boston: Little, Brown and Company, 1865.

———. *La Galatea.* In *Obras completas de Miguel de Cervantes Saavedra,* eds. Rodolfo Schevill and Adolfo Bonilla. Madrid: Imprenta de Bernardo Rodríguez, 1914.

———. *Persiles y Sigismunda.* In *Obras completas de Miguel de Cervantes Saavedra,* eds. Rodolfo Schevill and Adolfo Bonilla. Madrid: Imprenta de Bernardo Rodríguez, 1914.

Cieza de León, Pedro de. *Parte primera de la crónica del Perú.* Seville: Martín de Montesdoca, 1553.

———. *La crónica del Perú.* Antwerp: Martín Nucio, 1554.

———. *Guerras civiles del Perú.* 2 vols. (Vol. I, *Guerra de las Salinas*; Vol. II, *Guerra de Chupas*). Madrid: Librería de la Viuda de Rico, n.d.

Clissold, Stephen. *Conquistador: The Life of Don Pedro Sarmiento de Gamboa.* London: Derek Verschoyle, 1954.

Cosio, José Gabriel. *El Cuzco, histórico y monumental.* Lima: Editorial Incazteca, 1924.

Cúneo-Vidal, Rómulo. *Historia de las guerras de los últimos Incas peruanos contra el poder español*. Barcelona: Casa Editorial Naucci [1925].

Cunninghame-Graham, R. B. *Hernando de Soto*. London: William Heinemann, 1912.

Fernández de Palencia, Diego (El Palentino). *Primera y segunda parte de la historia del Perú*. Seville: Hernando Díaz, 1571.

————. *Primera y segunda parte de la historia del Perú*. Vols. 8 and 9 of *Colección de documentos literarios del Perú*, ed. Manuel de Odriozola. Lima: Imprenta del Estado, 1876.

————. *Primera parte de la historia del Perú*. Edición prólogo y apéndices por Lucas de la Torre. 2 vols. Madrid: Biblioteca Hispania, 1913–1914.

Fernández de Oviedo y Valdés, Gonzalo. *Historia general y natural de las Indias, Islas y Tierra Firme del Mar Océano*. Edited by José Amador de los Ríos. 4 vols. Madrid: Imprenta Real Academia de Historia, 1851–1855.

Fitzmaurice-Kelly, James. *A History of Spanish Literature*. New York and London: D. Appleton and Co., 1925.

————. *The Life of Miguel de Cervantes Saavedra*. London: Chapman and Hall, Ltd., 1892.

Fitzmaurice-Kelly, Julia. *El Inca Garcilaso de la Vega*. Oxford: Oxford University Press, 1921.

García Carraffa, Alberto y Arturo. *Enciclopedia heráldica y genealógica hispano-americana*. 88 vols. Madrid: Imprenta de Antonio Marzo, 1919.

Garcilaso de la Vega, el Inca. *Antología de los comentarios reales*. Introduction by José de la Riva-Agüero. Madrid: M. Aguilar, 1929.

————. *Primera parte de los comentarios reales*. Lisboa: Pedro Crasbeeck, 1609.

————. *Comentarios reales de los Incas* (Parts I and II. Part II is entitled *Historia general del Perú*.) Ed. Angel Rosenblat. Prologue by Ricardo Rojas. 5 vols. Buenos Aires: Emecé Editores, S. A., 1945.

————. *La Florida del Inca*. Lisboa: Pedro Crasbeeck. 1605.

————. *La Florida del Inca*. Edición y notas de Emma Susana Speratti Piñero, prólogo de Aurelio Miró Quesada y Sosa, y estudio bibliográfico de José Durand. Mexico-Buenos Aires: Fondo de Cultura Económica, 1956.

————. *Historia general del Perú*. Córdoba: Viuda de Andrés de Barrera, 1616.

————. *Historia general del Perú*. Córdoba: Viuda de Andrés Barrera, 1617.

————. *Relación de la descendencia de Garcí Pérez de Vargas*. Reproducción facsimilar del manuscrito original con un prólogo por Raúl Porras Barrenechea. Lima: Ediciones del Instituto de Historia, 1951.

————. *La traduzión del Indio de los tres diálogos de amor de León Hebreo.* See León Hebreo.

Gutiérrez de Santa Clara, Pedro. *Historia de las guerras civiles del Perú.* Books II, III, IV, and X of *Colección de libros y documentos referentes a la historia de América.* See under COLLECTIONS.

Handbook of South American Indians, 7 vols. New York: Cooper Square Publishers, Inc., 1963.

Hanke, Lewis. *Bartolomé de las Casas.* Philadelphia: University of Pennsylvania Press, 1952.

Herrera y Tordesillas, Antonio de. *Historia general de los Castellanos en las Islas y Tierra Firme del Mar Océano.* 4 vols. Madrid: Juan Flamenco and Juan de la Cuesta, 1601–1615.

Index Librorum Prohibitorum Ac Expurgandorum Novissimus. Matriti: Emmanuelis Fernández, 1747.

Irving, Theodore. *The Conquest of Florida by Hernando de Soto.* New York: George P. Putnam and Son, 1869.

Irving, Washington. *Conquest of Granada,* in *Washington Irving's Works.* New York: John W. Lovell Co., n.d.

————. *Moorish Chronicles,* in *Washington Irving's Works.* New York: John W. Lovell Co., n.d.

Kelly, John Eoghan. *Pedro de Alvarado, Conquistador.* Princeton: Princeton University Press, 1932.

Keniston, Hayward. *Garcilaso de la Vega: A Critical Study of His Life and Works.* New York: Hispanic Society of America, 1922.

Lea, Henry Charles. *A History of the Inquisition of Spain.* 4 vols. New York: The Macmillan Co., 1906.

————. *The Inquisition in the Spanish Dependencies.* New York: The Macmillan Co., 1922.

León Hebreo (Abarbanal, Judah). *Dialoghi di Amore; Hebraeische Gedichte, Herausgegeben, mit einer Darstellung des Lebens und des Werkes Leones, Bibliographie, Register zu den Dialoghi, Uebertragung der Hebraeischen Texte, Regesten, Urkunden und Anmerkungen* von Carl Gebhardt. (Text is a facsimile of 1st edition, Rome, 1535.) Heidelberg: Carl Winters; London: Oxford University Press, etc., 1929.

————. *Diálogos de amor.* Traducidos por Garcilaso Inga de la Vega. Edición según la de Madrid de 1590, con observaciones preliminares de Eduardo Juliá Martínez. Madrid: Librería General Victoriano Suárez, 1949.

————. *The Philosophy of Love.* Translated into English by F. Friedeberg-Seeley and Jean H. Barnes with an introduction by Cecil Roth. London: The Socino Press, 1937.

————. *La traduzión del Indio de los tres diálogos de amor de León Hebreo.*

Hecha de Italiano en Español por Garcilaso Inga de la Vega. Madrid: En Casa de Pedro Madrigal, 1590.

León Pinelo, Antonio. *Tablas cronológicas de los Reales Consejos*. Madrid: Tipografía de Manuel Ginés Hernández, 1892.

Leonard, Irving A. *Books of the Brave*. Cambridge, Massachusetts: Harvard University Press, 1949.

Levillier, Roberto. *Don Francisco de Toledo: Supemo Organizador del Perú*. Madrid: Imprenta de Juan Pueyo, 1935.

López de Gómara, Francisco. *La historia de las Indias*. Zaragosa: Agustín Millán, 1552.

——. *Historia general de las Indias*. 2 vols. Madrid: Espasa-Calpe, 1941.

López de Haro, Alonso. *Nobiliario genealógico de los reyes y títulos de España*. Madrid: Luis Sánchez, Impresor Real, 1622.

Marcoy, Paul (pseud. of Laurent Saint-Cricq). *Travels in South America*. 2 vols. New York: Scribner, Armstrong and Co., 1875.

Mariana, Juan de. *Historia general de España*. 9 vols. Madrid: Imprenta de los hijos de doña Catalina Pineda, 1828.

Markham, Clements R. *A History of Peru*. Chicago: Charles H. Sergel & Co., 1892.

——. *The Incas of Peru*. New York: E. P. Dutton and Co., 1910.

Martínez Villada, Luis G. *Los Cabrera*. Córdoba de Argentina: Imprenta de la Universidad de Córdoba, 1938.

Means, Philip Ainsworth. *Fall of the Inca Empire and the Spanish Rule in Peru, 1530–1780*. New York: Charles Scribner's Sons, 1932.

Medina, José Toribio. *Biblioteca hispano-americana*. 7 vols. Santiago de Chile: Fondo Histórico y Bibliográfico José Toribio Medina, 1958.

Mendiburu, Manuel de. *Diccionario histórico-biográfico del Perú*. Formado y redactado por Manuel Mendiburu. Segunda edición con adiciones y notas bibliográficas, publicada por Evaristo San Cristóval. 11 vols. Lima: Imprenta "Enrique Palacios," 1931–34.

Merriman, Roger Bigelow. *The Rise of the Spanish Empire*. 4 vols. New York: The Macmillan Co., 1925.

Miró Quesada y Sosa, Aurelio. *El Inca Garcilaso*. Madrid: Instituto de Cultura Hispánica, 1948.

Mitre, Bartolomé. *Historia de Belgrano y de la independencia argentina*. Buenos Aires: Imprenta y Librería de Mayo, de Carlos Casavalle, 1876.

Morales y Pedilla, Andrés de. "Historia de Córdoba." Unpublished manuscript in the private archives of the Real Academia de Ciencias, Bellas Letras y Nobles Artes de Córdoba.

Netanyahu, B. *Don Isaac Abravanel, Statesman and Philosopher*. Philadelphia: The Jewish Publication Society of America, 1953.

Nuevos estudios sobre el Inca Garcilaso de la Vega: Actas del symposium realizado en Lima del 17 al 28 de Junio de 1955. Lima: Centro de Estudios Histórico-Militares del Perú, 1955.

Núñez de Castro, Alonso. *Vida de S. Fernando el III*. Madrid: Pantaleón Aznar, 1787.

Pérez de Barradas, José. *Los mestizos de América*. Madrid: Cultura Clásica y Moderna, 1948.

Picón-Salas, Mariano. *De la conquista a la independencia*. Mexico: Fondo de Cultura Económica, 1944.

Pires de Lima, Durval. *Os Primeiros Livros e Livreiros de Lisboa*. Lisboa: Publicações Culturais da Câmara Municipal de Lisboa, 1942.

Pizarro, Pedro. *Relación del descubrimiento y conquista de los reinos del Perú*. Prólogo de Ernesto Morales. Buenos Aires: Editorial Futuro, 1944.

Porras Barrenechea, Raúl. *El Inca Garcilaso en Montilla*. Lima: Editorial San Marcos, 1955.

Prescott, William Hickling. *History of the Conquest of Peru*. 2 vols. New York: Harper and Brothers, 1847.

————. *History of the Reign of Charles V*. 3 vols. Philadelphia: J. B. Lippincott & Co., 1860.

————. *History of the Reign of Philip the Second*. 3 vols. Boston: Phillips, Sampson, and Co., 1855.

Radicati Di Primeglio, Carlo. *L'Inca Garcilaso*. Lima: Imprenta "La Voce D'Italia," 1939.

Robertson, William. *The History of America*. 2 vols. Edinburgh: W. Strahan and J. Balfour, 1777.

————. *The History of the Reign of the Emperor Charles the Fifth*. With an account of the Emperor's life after his abdication by William H. Prescott. Boston: Phillips, Sampson, and Co., 1857.

Rojas, Ricardo. *San Martín: Knight of the Andes*. Herschel Brickell and Carlos Videla, translators. Garden City, New York: Doubleday, Doran and Company, Inc., 1945.

Romoli, Kathleen. *Balboa of Darién: Discoverer of the Pacific*. Garden City, N.Y.: Doubleday & Co., Inc., 1953.

Royer, Fanchón. *St. Francis Solanus: Apostle to America*. Patterson, New Jersey: St. Anthony Guild Press, 1955.

Sachar, Abram Leon. *A History of the Jews*. New York: Alfred A. Knopf, 1953.

Saldaña Sicilia, Germán. *Monografía histórico-médica de los hospitales de Córdoba*. Córdoba: Academia de Ciencias, Bellas Letras y Nobles Artes de Córdoba, 1935.

San Cristóbal, Evaristo, comp. *Apéndice al Diccionario histórico-biográfico del Perú* de Manuel Mendiburu. 4 vols. Lima: Librería e Imprenta Gil, S.A., 1915–1938.

Sánchez, Luis Alberto. *Garcilaso de la Vega, primer criollo.* Santiago de Chile: Ediciones Ercilla, 1939.

Santillán, Fernando de. *Relación del origen, descendencia, política y gobierno de los Incas.* In *Tres Relaciones de Antigüedades Peruanas,* ed. Marcos Jiménez de la Espada. Madrid: Imprenta y Fundación de M. Tello, 1879.

Sarmiento de Gamboa, Pedro. *Historia de los Incas.* Buenos Aires: Emecé Editores [1952].

Schafer, Ernesto. *El Consejo Real y Supremo de las Indias.* 2 vols. Seville: M. Carmona, 1935–1947.

———. *Indice de la colección de documentos inéditos de Indias.* Madrid: Consejo Superior de Investigaciones Científicas Instituto "Gonzalo Fernández de Oviedo," 1946 (Vol. I), 1947 (Vol. II).

Squier, Ephraim George. *Peru: Incidents of Travel and Exploration in the Land of the Incas.* New York: Harper and Brothers, 1877.

Stirling-Maxwell, William. *Don Juan of Austria.* 2 vols. London: Longmans, Green and Co., 1883.

Ticknor, George. *History of Spanish Literature.* 3 vols. Cambridge, Massachusetts: Houghton Mifflin Co. and The Riverside Press, 1863.

Torre y del Cerro, José de la. *El Inca Garcilaso de la Vega.* Madrid, Imprenta de José Murillo, 1935.

———. *Obras de don José de la Torre y del Cerro.* Vol. I. Córdoba: Imprenta Provincial, 1955.

Valcárcel, Luis Eduardo. *Garcilaso el Inca.* Lima: Imprenta del Museo Nacional, 1939.

Valcárcel Esparza, Carlos Daniel. *GarcilaZo-InKa.* Lima: Compañía de Impresiones y Publicidad E. Bustamente y Ballivián, Sucesores, 1939.

Valdenebro y Cisneros, José María de. *La Imprenta en Córdoba.* Madrid: Sucesores de Rivadeneyra, 1900.

Valle, Rafael Heliodoro. *Santiago en América.* Mexico: Editorial Santiago, 1946.

Vélez Picasso, José. *La Villa de Valverde del Valle de Ica.* Ica: Imprenta "Fray Ramón," 1931.

Walsh, William Thomas. *Isabella of Spain: The Last Crusader.* New York: Robert M. McBride & Co., 1930.

———. *Philip II.* London and New York: Sheed and Ward, 1937.

Yonge, Charlotte M. *The Story of the Christians and Moors of Spain.* London: The Macmillan Co., 1878.

Zárate, Agustín de. *Historia del descubrimiento y conquista del Perú.* Antwerp: Martin Nucio, 1555.

———. *Historia del descubrimiento y conquista del Perú.* Edición revisada con anotaciones y concordancias por Jan M. Kermenic y con prólogo de Raúl Porras Barrenechea. Lima: Librería e Imprenta D. Miranda, 1944.

Zimmerman, Arthur Franklin. *Francisco de Toledo.* Caldwell, Idaho: Caxton Printers, Ltd., 1938.

PERIODICALS

Aguilar Priego, Rafael. "Curiosidades sobre la capilla de Garcilaso en la catedral de Córdoba," *Boletín de la Real Academia de Ciencias, Bellas Letras y Nobles Artes de Córdoba,* No. 61, 1949, pp. 77–83.

———. "El Hijo del Inca Garcilaso," *Boletín de la Real Academia de Ciencias, Bellas Letras y Nobles Artes de Córdoba,* Año XVI, No. 54, Julio-Diciembre, 1945, pp. 281–300.

Asensio, Eugenio. "Dos cartas desconocidas del Inca Garcilaso," *Nueva Revista de Filología Hispánica,* Año VII, Nos. 3–4, 1953, pp. 583–593.

Barroso, Gustavo. "Garcilaso de la Vega, el Inca," *O Cruzeiro* (Edición Internacional), 1 de Maio, 1957, pp. 44–45.

"Documentos sobre el Inca Garcilaso de la Vega," *Revista del Archivo Histórico del Cuzco,* Año II, No. 2, 1951, pp. 11–23.

Durand, José. "La Biblioteca del Inca," *Nueva Revista de Filología Hispánica,* Año II, No. 3, Julio-Septiembre, 1948, pp. 239–264.

———. "Dos notas sobre el Inca Garcilaso: Aldrete y el Inca (sobre el nombre Perú)," *Nueva Revista de Filología Hispánica,* Año III, No. 3, Julio-Septiembre, 1949, pp. 278–290.

———. "La Idea de la honra en el Inca Garcilaso," *Cuadernos Americanos,* Noviembre–Diciembre, 1951, pp. 194–213.

———. "El Inca Garcilaso, historiador apasionado," *Cuadernos Americanos,* Julio–Agosto, 1950, pp. 153–168.

———. "La Redacción de 'La Florida del Inca': Cronología," *Revista Histórica de la Universidad Nacional del Cuzco,* Vol. 21, 1954, pp. 288–302.

———. "Un sermón editado por el Inca Garcilaso," *Nueva Revista de Filología Hispánica,* Año VII, Nos. 3–4, Julio–Diciembre, 1953, pp. 594–599.

Lohmann Villena, Guillermo. "La ascendencia española del Inca Garcilaso de la Vega," *Hidalguía,* No. 29, Julio–Agosto, 1958, pp. 369–384, 681–698.

Martínez Villada, Luis G. "Don Gonzalo Martel de Cabrera," *Revista de la Universidad de Córdoba,* Año 7, No. 5–6, 1920, Vol. III, pp. 54–75.

Miró Quesada y Sosa, Aurelio. "Un Amigo del Inca Garcilaso," *Mar del Sur,* Vol. I, No. 2, Noviembre–Diciembre, 1948, pp. 20–26.

————. "Una Dedicatoria del Inca Garcilaso," *Mar del Sur,* Vol. VII, No. 20, Marzo–Abril, 1952, pp. 63–64.

————. "El Inca Garcilaso y su concepcion del arte histórico," *Mar del Sur,* Vol. VI, No. 18, Julio–Agosto, 1951, pp. 55–71.

————. "Italia y el Inca Garcilaso," *Mar del Sur,* Vol. V, No. 28, Julio–Agosto, 1953, pp. 1–25.

Polo, José Toribio. "El Inca Garcilaso," *Revista Histórica,* Vol. I, Trimestre II, 1906, pp. 232–253.

Riva-Agüero, José de la. "Elogio del Inca Garcilaso de la Vega," published in "Páginas Escogidas del Inca Garcilaso," of the *Biblioteca de Cultura Peruana,* No. 3, Ser. 1., Paris: Desclée de Brouwer, 1938.

————. "Examen de la Primera Parte de los *Comentarios Reales* de Garcilaso Inca de la Vega," *Revista Histórica,* Vol. II, 1907.

Saltillo, Marqués de (Miguel Laso de la Vega). "El Inca Garcí Lasso y los Garcí Lasso en la historia," *Revista de Historia y de Genealogía Española,* Segunda Epoca, Año III, No. 16, Julio–Agosto, 1929, pp. 289–310.

Santisteban Ochoa, Julián. "El Oro de América y el Inca Garcilaso de la Vega," *Revista Universitaria* (de la Universidad Nacional del Cuzco), No. 76 Octubre, 1939, pp. 108–116.

Torre y del Cerro, José de la. "Alonso de Carmona," *Adarve,* 31 de Octubre, 1954, p. 8.

————, ed. "Documentos Gongorinos," *Boletín de la Real Academia de Ciencias, Bellas Letras y Nobles Artes de Córdoba,* Año VI, No. 18, Enero–Junio, 1927.

Valcárcel, Carlos Daniel. " 'Genealogía de Garcí Pérez de Vargas' por Garcilaso de la Vega," *Letras* (de la Universidad Nacional Mayor de San Marcos), Segundo Cuatrimestre, 1941, pp. 212–229.

Vargas Ugarte, Rubén, S. J. "Nota sobre Garcilaso," *Mercurio Peruano,* Vol. XX, Enero–Febrero, 1930, pp. 47–50.

INDEX

410

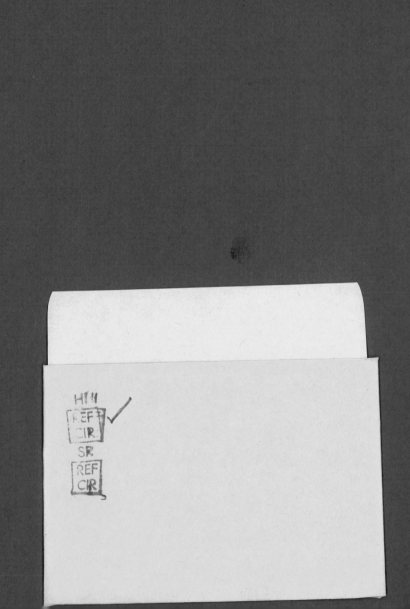